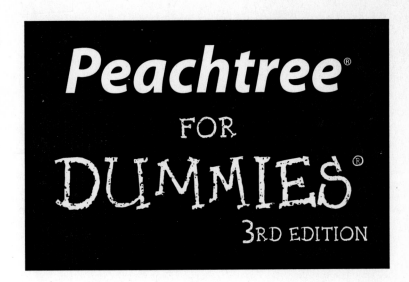

Peachtree®
FOR
DUMMIES®
3RD EDITION

by Elaine Marmel and Diane Koers

BICENTENNIAL
1807
WILEY
2007
BICENTENNIAL

Wiley Publishing, Inc.

Peachtree® For Dummies,® 3rd Edition

Published by
Wiley Publishing, Inc.
111 River Street
Hoboken, NJ 07030-5774

www.wiley.com

About the Authors

Elaine Marmel is president of Marmel Enterprises, LLC, an organization that specializes in technical writing and software training. Elaine has an MBA from Cornell University and has worked on projects to build financial management systems for New York City and Washington, D.C. This prior experience provided the foundation for Marmel Enterprises, LLC, to help small businesses implement computerized accounting systems.

Elaine spends most of her time writing; she has authored and coauthored more than 50 books about software products, including Quicken for Windows, Quicken for DOS, Peachtree, QuickBooks, Microsoft Excel, Microsoft Project, Microsoft Word for Windows, Microsoft Word for the Mac, 1-2-3 for Windows, and Lotus Notes. For 12 years, she was a contributing editor to monthly magazines that described ways to use Peachtree and QuickBooks.

Elaine left her native Chicago for the warmer climes of Arizona (by way of Cincinnati, Ohio; Jerusalem, Israel; Ithaca, New York; Washington, D.C.; and Tampa, Florida), where she cherishes her small piece of the desert with her human family (brother Jim and sister-in-law Mariann) and her animal family (Josh the dog and Cato, Watson, and Buddy, the cats) and sings barbershop harmony with the International Champion Scottsdale Chorus.

Diane Koers owns and operates All Business Service, a software training and consulting business formed in 1988 that services the central Indiana area. Her area of expertise has long been in the word processing, spreadsheet, and graphics area of computing as well as in providing training and support for Peachtree Accounting Software. Diane's authoring experience includes more than 30 books on topics such as PC security, Microsoft Windows, Microsoft Office, Microsoft Works, WordPerfect, Paint Shop Pro, Lotus SmartSuite, Quicken, Microsoft Money, and Peachtree Accounting. Many of her books have been translated into other languages such as Dutch, Bulgarian, Spanish, and Greek. She has also developed and written numerous training manuals for her clients.

Diane and her husband enjoy spending their free time traveling and playing with her grandsons and her Yorkshire terriers.

Dedication

Elaine's dedication: To my brother and sister-in-law: It's good to be sharing a city with you again.

Diane's dedication: To Tresee and Trina: my daughters.

Authors' Acknowledgments

We are deeply indebted to the many people who worked on this book. Thank you for all the time, effort, and support you gave and for your assistance.

Oh, where to start? First, thank you to Bob Woerner for your confidence in us and your support in pushing to get this book published, and for listening to us whine throughout the process.

Thank you to all our many editors and production staff, especially Blair Pottenger for your patience, guidance, and assistance, Teresa Artman and Jessica Parker for your assistance in making this book grammatically correct, and David Ringstrom for your assistance in making sure that we weren't fibbing about the product.

Lastly, thanks to our families for continuing their support of our stress tantrums and our late-night hours and for keeping us supplied with chocolate.

Publisher's Acknowledgments

We're proud of this book; please send us your comments through our online registration form located at www.dummies.com/register/.

Some of the people who helped bring this book to market include the following:

Acquisitions, Editorial, and Media Development

Project Editor: Blair J. Pottenger

Senior Acquisitions Editor: Bob Woerner

Senior Copy Editor: Teresa Artman

Copy Editor: Jessica Parker

Technical Editor: David Ringstrom

Editorial Manager: Kevin Kirschner

Media Project Supervisor: Laura Moss-Hollister

Media Development Specialist: Angela Denny

Editorial Assistant: Amanda Foxworth

Sr. Editorial Assistant: Cherie Case

Cartoons: Rich Tennant (www.the5thwave.com)

Composition Services

Project Coordinator: Erin Smith

Layout and Graphics: Carl Byers, Stephanie D. Jumper, Alicia B. South, Ronald Terry, Christine Williams

Proofreaders: Debbye Butler, Susan Moritz

Indexer: Potomac Indexing, LLC

Anniversary Logo Design: Richard Pacifico

Publishing and Editorial for Technology Dummies

Richard Swadley, Vice President and Executive Group Publisher

Andy Cummings, Vice President and Publisher

Mary Bednarek, Executive Acquisitions Director

Mary C. Corder, Editorial Director

Publishing for Consumer Dummies

Diane Graves Steele, Vice President and Publisher

Joyce Pepple, Acquisitions Director

Composition Services

Gerry Fahey, Vice President of Production Services

Debbie Stailey, Director of Composition Services

Table of Contents

Introduction

ou're not a dummy, even if you think you are. But accounting by itself can be a challenge — and then, when you add the computer part to it . . . well, the whole thing can seem so overwhelming that you avoid it. (What? Never crossed your mind?)

Okay, now that you're looking at this book, you probably decided that you've avoided it long enough, and now you're going to do it — bite the bullet and computerize your accounting with Peachtree. We want to help you get the job done as quickly as possible with the least amount of pain. You've got other things to do, after all.

About This Book

Accounting isn't exactly a fun subject — unless, of course, you're an accountant . . . and even then it might not really be all that much fun. Some people think that going to the dentist is more fun than playing with accounting software. We're here to help you get past the ugly part so that you can start enjoying the benefits quickly.

What benefits? Well, computerizing your accounting can save you time and effort — and can actually be easier than doing it by hand and cheaper than paying somebody else to do it. Oh, we don't mean that you don't need your accountant, because you do. But you can save money by doing daily stuff for yourself — and spend money paying your accountant for advice on making your business more profitable.

Peachtree For Dummies, 3rd Edition, shows you how to set up your company in Peachtree and then use Peachtree to pay bills, invoice customers, pay employees, produce reports about your financial picture, and more. But it's also a real-life-situation kind of book. We show you how to work in Peachtree by using everyday, real-life situations as examples. You know, the stuff you run into in the so-called real world that you need to figure out how to handle.

What You Can Safely Ignore

Throughout the book, we include Accounting Stuff tips — you can probably ignore those unless you're interested in that kind of stuff.

Oh, and the gray boxes that you see throughout the book? Those are side-bars, and they contain extra information that you really don't *have* to know but that we thought you might find useful and interesting. So feel free to skip the sidebars as well.

Foolish Assumptions

We'll be honest — we had to assume some things about you to write this book. So, here's what we assume about you:

- ✔ You already know a little something about the day-to-day stuff that you need to do financially to run your business — you know, write checks, bill customers, pay employees, and so on. We *don't* assume that you know how to do all that on a computer.

- ✔ You have a personal computer (that you know how to turn on) with Microsoft Windows 2000, Windows XP, or Windows Vista. We wrote this book by using Windows Vista.

- ✔ You bought Peachtree and installed it on your computer.

A free trial of Peachtree is available from www.peachtree.com/trial.

The Flavors of Peachtree

Peachtree comes in five versions, listed here from basic to advanced:

- ✔ Peachtree First Accounting
- ✔ Peachtree Pro Accounting
- ✔ Peachtree Complete Accounting
- ✔ Peachtree Premium Accounting
- ✔ Peachtree Quantum Accounting

In addition, Peachtree Premium is available in manufacturing, distribution, construction, non-profit, and accounting industry-specific versions. In this book, we cover Peachtree Premium Accounting.

Peachtree Quantum has all the features you find in all other versions of the software; it uses a slightly more advanced database and allows for larger file sizes. In addition, in a network environment, ten users can use Peachtree Quantum simultaneously, whereas Peachtree Premium and Peachtree Complete allow for five simultaneous users. You can't use other versions of Peachtree in a network environment.

Here are some of the other differences between the five flavors:

- ✔ Peachtree Premium contains all the features in Peachtree First Accounting, Peachtree Pro Accounting, and Peachtree Complete Accounting, plus a few additional features, such as the capability to store unlimited budget information instead of the two years available in the other products.

- ✔ Peachtree Premium and Peachtree Complete include a Time & Billing feature that you don't find in Peachtree First Accounting or Peachtree Pro Accounting.

- ✔ Peachtree Premium Accounting, Peachtree Complete Accounting, and Peachtree Pro Accounting allow you to customize reports and forms and prepare payroll, but Peachtree First Accounting does not.

- ✔ Peachtree Quantum, Peachtree Premium, and Peachtree Complete contain a job-costing feature, but you find only a job-*tracking* feature in Peachtree First Accounting and Peachtree Pro Accounting. (If you don't know the difference between job costing and job tracking, you probably don't need either one.)

Peachtree Quantum and two of the industry-specific versions of Peachtree Premium — Peachtree Premium for Construction and Peachtree Premium for Distribution — contain more extensive job-costing features than Peachtree Premium, such as tracking Bill of Material revisions. Because we cover Peachtree Premium, we don't cover those extensive features in Chapter 12 where we discuss job costing, but we want you to know that they exist.

Throughout the book, when we refer to the product as *Peachtree,* we mean Peachtree Premium. If we talk about one of the other flavors, we give you the full product name.

How This Book Is Organized

Every great book needs a plan. We divided this book into four parts, each made up of two to eight chapters so that you can easily find the information that you need.

Part I: Getting Started

If you're new to Peachtree, you probably want to read this part. We explain how to get around in Peachtree, how to create a company in Peachtree, how to build an effective chart of accounts, and how to set up default information that saves you lots of time later.

Part II: The Daily Drudge

In this section, we cover the stuff that you do on a regular basis:

- ✔ Buy and pay for goods to sell to your customers. (Yep, we cover inventory.)
- ✔ Bill the customers and collect your money (or you won't be able to pay the employees and the vendors).
- ✔ Pay the employees (or they won't work!).

Stuff like that. We also cover paying for services that keep your business running, and we cover a couple of more esoteric topics, such as billing customers for time that you spend working and tracking project costs.

Part III: The Fancy Stuff

In this section, we cover a variety of topics that you typically don't do every day. First, we show you how to customize forms and produce and modify reports. After all, you put information *into* Peachtree, so you should be able to get it out and see the effects of your business habits. Then we cover reconciling the bank statement and the stuff that you do monthly, quarterly, or annually. We also show you how to easily keep your accounting information safe — a *very* important chapter. Why? Because you spend so much time putting stuff into Peachtree that it would be criminal to lose it just because your hard drive crashes or your office is robbed. And Chapter 19 presents ways to handle real-life situations in Peachtree, such as handling customer prepayments and paying for purchase orders using a credit card.

Part IV: The Part of Tens

If you've ever read a *For Dummies* book, you've seen the Part of Tens. This part contains a collection of ten-something lists. Our Part of Tens comprises the following:

- ✔ Ten common error messages that you might see — and what they mean
- ✔ Ten things that you can get from the Web — not just Peachtree stuff like support and additional information, but fun stuff, too, just in case you've had a bad day and need a laugh

The Peachtree For Dummies Web Site

This book's Web site, www.dummies.com/go/peachtreefd, features useful information that's not necessarily mainstream knowledge. You can find the following Bonus Chapters:

- ✔ Bonus Chapter 1, in which you find out how to tailor Peachtree to support how you work.
- ✔ Bonus Chapter 2, in which we discuss how to use the Peachtree money management tools to analyze your business and help you manage cash, receivables, and payables.
- ✔ Bonus Chapter 3, in which we describe how to set up Peachtree to work in a network environment.
- ✔ Bonus Chapter 4, in which we list as many companion products for Peachtree as we can find. These products can enhance how you work in Peachtree.
- ✔ Bonus Chapter 5, in which we discuss who's to blame for the whole debit/credit thing and also how debits and credits work.

Icons Used in This Book

Throughout the book are symbols in the margin. These symbols, or *icons,* mark important points.

This bull's-eye appears next to shortcuts and tips that make your work easier.

When you see this icon, something could go wrong, so make sure that you read the paragraph. This icon warns you of common mistakes and ways to avoid them.

This icon marks any point that you want to be sure to remember. You might want to reread paragraphs that are marked with this icon.

This icon identifies information related to accounting in general — not just Peachtree. You can skip this stuff if you don't care about accounting.

This icon relates to geeky computer stuff that might interest you, but really has little impact on your use of Peachtree. You can safely skip them.

Where to Go from Here

Just getting started with Peachtree? Turn the page. Do you have a specific topic of interest? Use the index or the Table of Contents to find the topic and turn to that page.

Part I
Getting Started

In this part . . .

*E*very project has a beginning point. If you are just
getting acquainted with Peachtree, this part is the
place to start. In this part, you find out how to navigate
through the Peachtree screens and how to set up your
existing company records in Peachtree. If you've been
using Peachtree for a while, you might want to review
Chapters 3 and 4 in this part because they talk about
designing the Chart of Accounts and setting up defaults
to make using Peachtree easier.

Chapter 1

Mastering Peachtree Basics

゜゜゜

In This Chapter

▶ Starting Peachtree

▶ Opening an existing Peachtree company

▶ Navigating the Peachtree screen

゜゜゜

*I*f you've been keeping your financial records by using manual methods, you know how time-consuming it can be. Keeping books manually also provides too many opportunities for human error. Using Peachtree saves you both time and money; in addition, you can know at any moment in time your complete financial status. We know you're eager to get started. Operating a business is a non stop process, but to computerize your accounting, you have to put first things first.

To work effectively, take some time to get comfortable with some of the features unique to Peachtree. In this chapter, you find out how to navigate in the software as well as open and close companies as needed. If you're ready, it's time to dig in.

Starting the Program

You have a choice: You can start Peachtree the easy way or the hard way. We prefer the easy way. When you installed Peachtree, it placed a Peachtree icon (with your permission) on your Windows desktop. Assuming (we know, we're not supposed to assume) that you haven't thrown that icon into the Recycle Bin, you can simply double-click the Peachtree icon (the one with the peachy little peach on it), and the program starts.

To make sure that Peachtree always starts in a full-sized (maximized) window, right-click the Peachtree icon and choose Properties. In the resulting dialog box, on the Shortcut tab, click the drop-down arrow in the Run box, choose Maximized, and then click OK to accept the changes.

If you did throw the icon away or you have so many icons on your desktop that you can't find it, okay, you can start Peachtree the hard way. Choose Start⇨All Programs and locate your Peachtree Accounting folder.

Choosing opening options

After you start Peachtree, what do you do with it? The Peachtree Start Screen appears as seen in Figure 1-1, beckoning you to do one of several things. You can select any of the following options:

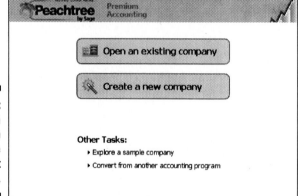

Figure 1-1:
Make a
selection
from the
Start
Screen.

- ✔ **Open an Existing Company:** Use this option to open a company already existing in Peachtree.

- ✔ **Create a New Company:** Select this option to set up your business with the New Company Setup Wizard. (Chapter 2 covers this wizard.)

- ✔ **Explore a Sample Company:** Use this option to explore one of several fictitious companies. One company, Bellwether Garden Supply, is a retail and service company that uses most of the features of Peachtree, including inventory and job costing. Depending on the Peachtree edition that you're using, you might have additional sample companies to investigate. You explore Bellwether Garden Supply in the steps in the following section.

- ✔ **Convert from Another Accounting Program:** If you've finally come to your senses and want to transfer to Peachtree from *that other software* (meaning QuickBooks or DacEasy), click this choice. Peachtree makes the conversion pretty painless.

Exploring a sample company

You can best explore Peachtree's features by opening the Bellwether Garden Supply sample company and finding out how to move around in Peachtree. To open a sample company, follow these steps:

1. **Click Explore a Sample Company.**

   If you're using Peachtree First Accounting or Peachtree Pro Accounting, Bellwether Garden Supply immediately opens.

   If you're using Peachtree Complete Accounting or above, the Explore a Sample Company dialog box opens.

2. **Select the radio button next to the sample company that you want to explore.**

   For this example, select Bellwether Garden Supply.

3. **Click OK.**

   The name of the currently open company appears at the top of the window in the Peachtree title bar.

Getting around town

When you first open a company, it might appear a little bit intimidating. On the left side, Peachtree displays the Navigation Bar. You click a Navigation Bar topic as one method to get into the seven various Peachtree Navigation Centers such as the Business Status Center shown in Figure 1-2 or the Employees and Payroll Center. The Navigation Centers show the work flow of the selected center and quickly take you to a window where you can perform relevant tasks. Each Navigation Center also displays key information relative to the selected center. For example, in the Employees and Payroll Center you can see a list of employees and 1099 vendors as well as quick links to recently used employee reports while in the Customers and Sales Center, you can see a list of customers.

Under the Navigation Bar is the Shortcuts section. The Shortcuts section contains links you can click to quickly jump into Peachtree windows that you use in your business on a day-to-day basis. See Bonus Chapter 1 on this book's Web site, www.dummies.com/go/peachtreefd, for instructions on customizing the Shortcuts so they include the features you use most often.

The large section on the right is where Peachtree displays the various Peachtree centers. By default, when you open your company, you see the Business Status Center. You can find out how to customize the Business Status Center in Bonus Chapter 2 on this book's Web site.

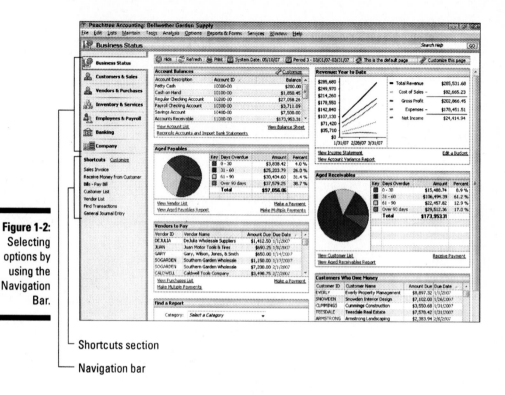

Figure 1-2:
Selecting
options by
using the
Navigation
Bar.

Shortcuts section

Navigation bar

At the top of the open center you see the Button Control Bar that displays, among other things, the current system date and the current accounting period. (See Figure 1-3.)

Figure 1-3:
The current
accounting
period
appears
on the
Navigation
Bar toolbar.

Like many applications today, Peachtree provides a variety of ways to use the software. You can perform your Peachtree duties by using the Button Control Bar, the Shortcuts section, or — a more traditional method — menu commands.

Choosing menu commands

The pull-down menus should be a familiar sight from your other Windows programs. Even though all the menu choices are important, you're likely to spend the majority of your time in Peachtree using the following four main menu choices:

✔ **Maintain:** Using the choices on this menu, you can set up and edit the information records that form the foundation for transactions in your Peachtree company. For example, you can store vendor, customer, inventory, and employee information, including names, addresses, and phone numbers.

A *record* is all the information about one person, product, event, and so on. Every record in a database contains the same fields. A *field* is one item of information in a record, such as an ID, a name, or a transaction number. To explore the kinds of information that you store in Peachtree, see the "Exploring fields and records" section, later in this chapter.

✔ **Lists:** This menu displays lists of . . . well, just about everything stored in Peachtree — customers, vendors, checks, journal entries, and so on. Any list can be sorted and customized (see Bonus Chapter 1 on this book's Web site) to better help you locate desired information. Figure 1-4 illustrates a list of Inventory Adjustments made during a specified period.

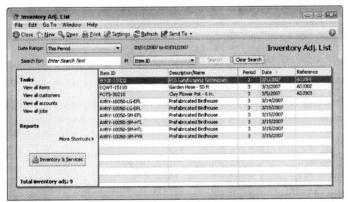

Figure 1-4:
Displaying
a list of
transactions.

✔ **Tasks:** Use this menu to do your normal day-to-day work. You can bill your customers, buy materials, and pay your workers by using the Tasks menu.

✔ **Reports and Forms:** This menu is where it all comes together and you can see the results of all your hard work.

Opening a Company

Maybe you need to keep numbers for more than one business. Peachtree enables you to account for the financial information of more than one company. Although you can open only one company at a time, you can switch back and forth between companies very easily.

The steps to open a company differ, depending on whether you're opening a company while already in a Peachtree company or whether you're opening a company from the Peachtree Start Screen.

Opening a Peachtree company from within Peachtree

If you're already in a Peachtree company and want to open a different one, follow these steps:

1. **Choose File➪Open Company (or press Ctrl+O).**

   You get an annoying little message telling you that you're closing the current company. Peachtree allows only one open company at a time.

   Select the Do Not Display This Message Again check box to permanently disable the message box.

2. **Click OK to acknowledge the message.**

   The Open dialog box appears.

3. **From the Open dialog box, click the company name and then click OK.**

   The newly opened company name appears at the top of the screen. No matter which company you open, the menu choices remain the same.

Opening a recently used Peachtree company

If you find yourself frequently switching back and forth between several companies, Peachtree provides an easier method, the Open Previous Company option. This option lists up to ten previously opened Peachtree company names from which you can select.

Choose File➪Open Previous Company. From the list of previously opened companies that appears, choose the one you want to open. If the annoying little message appears, click OK, and Peachtree opens the company you selected.

Opening a company from the Peachtree Start Screen

If you're opening a company from the Peachtree Start Screen, a different dialog box appears. To open a company from the Peachtree Start Screen, follow these steps:

1. **Click Open an Existing Company to display the Open an Existing Company dialog box.**

   This dialog box lists the companies that you recently opened in Peachtree. If the company name that you want to open doesn't appear, click the Browse button and make your selection from the Open Company dialog box.

2. **Click the company name that you want to open and then click OK.**

   The selected company opens.

Exploring Peachtree's Windows

Most windows in Peachtree are similar. They have places for you to fill in information and buttons that you use to take actions in that particular window. The Maintain Customers/Prospects window is typical of many other windows that you use in Peachtree. For an example, open Bellwether Garden Supply and choose Maintain⇨Customers/Prospects. Take a stroll around this window.

Managing window sizes and placement

Depending on your screen size and resolution, you might not see enough of a window to suit your needs. Some windows, such as the Sales/Invoice window, display more lines when made larger. If you resize the window manually, Peachtree remembers that setting and uses it each time. You can also click the Windows Maximize button (as shown here in the margin), and Peachtree remembers that you like the window maximized.

To manually resize a window, place your mouse pointer around the border of any window until the pointer appears as a double-headed arrow. Click and drag the border until the window is the appropriate size.

Exploring fields and records

The main part of a Peachtree window consists of fields. Stop for a moment and ponder these components. When we refer to fields, we're not talking about the places where corn grows. *Fields* are pieces of information that fit into a *record,* which is a type of electronic 3 x 5 index card. A record is all the information about one customer, vendor, employee, or inventory part, but a field is one piece of the record such as the ID, name, or phone number. In Figure 1-5, the record is all the information about Archer Scapes and Ponds, and Nancy Archer is in the Contact field.

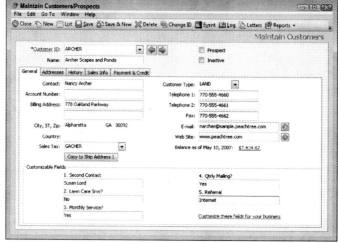

Figure 1-5:
Each record
has many
different
fields.

Looking up information

Some fields, such as Customer ID, have either a magnifying glass or an arrow for a drop-down list next to them. These fields contain *lookup lists* that display a list of your customers (or vendors, accounts, employees, inventory items, and so on). You can choose a record from a lookup list. Depending on the global options that you set, a lookup list might automatically appear as you type any character in the field, or you can click the lookup list button (the magnifying glass or down arrow, as shown in the margin here) to display the list that's relevant to the current field. (See Figure 1-6.) See Bonus Chapter 1 at www.dummies.com/go/peachtreefd for more information on setting global options.

Optionally, on most lookup list fields you can display the list by either clicking the right mouse button in the lookup list field or pressing the Shift key along with the question mark (?).

Figure 1-6:
Display
available
choices in a
lookup list.

You can do any of the following while in a lookup list:

- ✔ **Select a customer (vendor, item, and so on) and then click OK.** Peachtree displays the highlighted record and closes the lookup list.

- ✔ **Click Cancel to close the lookup list without selecting a record.**

- ✔ **Use the Find feature to search for a string of characters.** The search covers any text that you can see in the displayed list. The Find feature is not case sensitive. Press Enter after you type the lookup text in the entry box. Peachtree highlights the first item that matches your request.

- ✔ **Click Next to find the next instance of the previously entered Find text.** If no next instance exists, the Find feature skips to the first instance in the lookup list. If no instance exists, the Next feature does nothing.

- ✔ **Click Sort to sort the displayed list alphabetically by either the ID or the name.** Numbers come before letters.

- ✔ **Use the Help option.**

- ✔ **Use the New button.** This is available only in the Task lookup windows, to add customers, vendors, employees, or inventory items on the fly, which means Peachtree adds the record right in the middle of entering a transaction.

Just browsing

 Similar to buttons that you use with a Web browser, Peachtree includes Browse buttons (like the ones here) to quickly scan the next record or the previous record. If you're in a maintenance window such as Maintain Customers/Prospects or Maintain Inventory Items, the Browse buttons move between the records in the order of customer ID or inventory item ID.

If you're in a Task window, the Browse buttons move between the previous transaction and the next transaction.

Making a date

Many Peachtree windows have date fields where you need to enter information based on the calendar. If you're a keyboard-type person, you can simply type the date. Dates need to be typed as numbers. If you want, you can type the date by using the / (slash) key, but the slash isn't necessary. For example, to enter September 16, 2007, type **091607** or **09/16/07**. Be aware that Peachtree doesn't allow you to use a hyphen (-) in a date.

In most Peachtree date fields, you can get away with entering just the first four digits of a date. Peachtree then enters the year. The year is based on the system date displayed on the Button Control Bar.

Now if you're like us, we need a calendar in front of us to select dates. Fortunately, Peachtree fields that require you to select a date also include a calendar, as shown in Figure 1-7, so you can click that to select a date. To select a date from the calendar, follow these steps:

Figure 1-7:
Click a date
to insert
it into a
Peachtree
date field.

1. **Click the calendar icon next to a date field to display the current month.**

2. **Click the left-pointing arrow next to the month name to display a previous month or click the right-pointing arrow to display a future month.**

3. **Click the date that you want for the date field.**

    The small calendar closes, and the date appears in the field.

Using the window toolbar

Most Peachtree windows include a toolbar located across the top of the window. You use the Peachtree toolbar across the top of the window to complete the various tasks involved with the selected window.

The exact buttons vary slightly from window to window, but most of them have a Close button, as shown here. To get out of a Peachtree window, you can use the Close button or the Windows Close button (X).

If you position the mouse pointer over any button on the toolbar, a small yellow box — a *Tool Tip* — appears to explain the use of the button. Tool Tips are great for those CRS moments when you look at a button and cannot remember its function. CRS (Can't Remember Stuff) is a widespread disease that affects people of all ages, races, religions, genders, and hair colors.

You also use the Save button frequently. The Save button, as shown here, appears on the toolbar if you're modifying data records, such as customers, from the Maintenance menu or if you're using a transaction entry window under the Tasks menu, such as Payroll Entry or Inventory Adjustments. You click the Save button to save the displayed transaction — and if you're using the *real-time* posting method, Peachtree also posts the transaction to the General Ledger (GL). (See Chapter 2 for an explanation of posting methods.)

Post is one of those words with many different meanings. It can be a noun, such as the place you tie your horse, or it can be a verb and mean *to send.* Of course, the latter is how the word *post* is used in accounting, and it means *to save and send.* In Peachtree, you're sending transactions to the GL; then, when you want to find out whether you've made any money this month, Peachtree is able to show you.

Multitasking

Mothers have long been known for their multitasking skills. You've seen them — balancing the baby on a hip, stirring the soup, and answering the telephone all at the same time. You can multitask in Peachtree also.

In almost all Peachtree windows, you can stop and open another window without having to close the first one and then return to the first window whenever you're ready. For example, suppose that you're in the middle of entering a new customer invoice and your boss needs to quickly know how much you paid for the green widgets you ordered last month. You can just open another window such as a List window. Besides a button for the Main Peachtree screen, each open window appears in the Windows Taskbar. Take a look at Figure 1-8 where you can see four different Peachtree window buttons open. Click any button to display the selected Peachtree window.

Figure 1-8: Work on many different Peachtree tasks at the same time.

REMEMBER

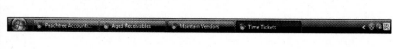

Don't forget to visit this book's Web site (`www.dummies.com/go/peachtreefd`) for more information on Peachtree.

Chapter 2

Setting Up Your Company

* *

In This Chapter

▶ Supplying your company information

▶ Specifying an accounting method

▶ Identifying accounting periods

* *

*P*eachtree tracks all kinds of information, including the names and addresses of your customers, vendors, or employees, as well as any business transactions that you've made with them. But before Peachtree can do any of that, you have to tell the software about your company. You need to tell it the usual stuff such as your name and address. (That's so you don't forget who you are. . . .) You also need to tell it when you want to pay Uncle Sam taxes on the money that you earn and spend. (Sorry, but *never* is not an option.)

Keep this important fact in mind: Two of the options that you determine when setting up a Peachtree company are written in stone — no going backward:

✔ Whether you run your business on a cash or an accrual basis

✔ The time frame of your accounting year

We talk about these issues in the accounting method and accounting period sections of this chapter.

Starting the New Company Setup Wizard

When you want to create a new company, or convert Peachtree Complete Accounting for DOS or Quicken data, the New Company Setup Wizard simplifies the task for you. It asks you the basic questions in the order that Peachtree needs to set up your business. (If you're not setting up a new company but are simply changing settings, see Chapter 4.)

You start the New Company Setup Wizard when you click Create a New Company from the Peachtree Start Screen. Like most wizards, the New Company Setup Wizard guides you through the process. You've probably used wizards dozens of times (not to mention when you've installed most applications, such as Peachtree), so we'll keep things short and sweet.

If you want to convert from QuickBooks or DacEasy, do not use the New Company Setup Wizard. Instead, choose the Convert from Another Accounting Program option that appears on the Start Screen. If you're already in Peachtree and want to create a new company, choose File⇨New Company to start the New Company Setup Wizard.

After you're done checking out the opening screen, click Next to move to the next screen.

The following sections walk you through each step of the New Company Setup Wizard.

Introducing Your Business to Peachtree

The left half of the New Company Setup Wizard screen is pretty self-explanatory. Fill in your business name, address, city, two-letter state abbreviation, and (optionally) country. Notice that we say *country,* with an *r* — not *county!* Many people misread this line. You see country fields in other places in Peachtree. Use the Tab or Enter key to move through the fields.

The first item on the right side of the screen asks for your business type. To fill in this side of the screen, follow these steps:

1. **Click the drop-down list to display and choose a Business Type.**

   Options are Corporation, S Corporation, Partnership, Sole Proprietorship, or Limited Liability Company. Selecting a type of business tells Peachtree how to set up equity accounts.

   Equity is what's left after you subtract the company's liabilities from the assets. The equity is the value of a company to its owners. In a corporation, the equity is divided among the stockholders. If the business is a sole proprietorship or partnership, though, the equity belongs to the individual owner or owners, respectively. If you're not sure what type of business you have, talk with your accountant.

2. **Enter your information in the Federal Employer, State Employer, and State Unemployment IDs fields.**

   If your state doesn't use employer IDs or unemployment IDs, leave these fields blank.

3. **Click Next to move to the screen where you select an option for how you want to build your Chart of Accounts.**

4. **Select an option (see Figure 2-1) and then click Next.**

   If you're not sure which option to select, read the section "Selecting a Chart of Accounts," later in this chapter.

   The last option shown here appears only if you're using Peachtree Premium or a higher version.

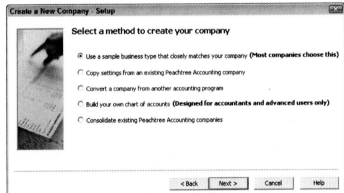

Figure 2-1:
Choose how
you want to
create your
Chart of
Accounts.

What you see next depends on the option that you select. For example, if you choose to set up a new company based on one of the several sample companies, a list of business descriptions appears. Don't worry if the accounts that you select don't match yours completely; you can edit them after you're done with the New Company Setup Wizard. (Chapter 3 shows you how to customize the Chart of Accounts.)

If you choose to copy settings from an existing Peachtree company, a list of existing Peachtree companies appears. Peachtree asks whether you want to copy default information from these other companies. Usually, you do want to copy default information.

5. **Select the sample Chart of Accounts that most closely matches your business or click the company from which you want to copy a Chart of Accounts; then click Next.**

   The Accounting Method screen appears.

6. **Select an accounting method and then click Next.**

   For important information on choosing an accounting method, see the "Selecting an Accounting Method" section later in this chapter.

   The accounting method is one of the two items that you can't change after you finish creating your Peachtree company. Be sure you select the correct method before proceeding.

7. **Select a posting method and then click Next.**

   To understand posting methods, see the "Selecting a Posting Method" section later in this chapter.

   The Accounting Periods screen appears.

8. **Select an accounting period structure option and then click Next.**

   See the "Selecting Accounting Periods" section, later in this chapter, if you're not sure which option to select.

   The accounting period is the second of the two items that you can't change after you finish creating your Peachtree company. Be sure of your accounting periods before proceeding.

9. **Select the month that begins your fiscal year, along with the year that you want to start using Peachtree.**

10. **Click Next.**

    The final setup screen appears.

    Congratulations! You're almost finished with the New Company Setup Wizard.

    We recommend using the Back button to double-check that the accounting method and accounting periods are correct before you click Finish. After you click Finish, you can't change them.

11. **Click Finish.**

    Peachtree creates a set of data files for your company and displays the Peachtree Setup Guide that's designed to walk you through the remainder of the setup process.

12. **Click Close (as shown in the margin here).**

    Peachtree closes the Setup Guide.

    Select the Don't Show This Screen at Startup check box if you do not want to use the Setup Guide.

Selecting a Chart of Accounts

The New Company Setup Wizard also asks you to choose how you want to set up your Chart of Accounts. If you're a new business, you might want to choose one of the samples provided by Peachtree, or you might already have a Chart of Accounts supplied by your accountant.

The Chart of Accounts lists the names that you use to classify transaction information and also categorizes the accounts so that they appear in appropriate places on financial statements. If you're not sure which Chart of

Accounts to select, you can choose one of the sample Charts of Accounts that are supplied by Peachtree. Peachtree lists dozens of business types (80 to be exact), and each one includes accounts typical to the selected business type. For example, the accounts that a shoe store uses are different from those that a drugstore, dentist, or taxicab company uses.

Accounts are the systematic arrangement of numbers and descriptions to organize the records of the business that your company transacts. Each time you buy or sell something, you record the transaction and assign it to one or more accounts. Accounts help you organize information by grouping similar transactions together.

Peachtree has several Chart of Accounts options (refer to Figure 2-1):

- ✔ **Use A Sample Business Type That Closely Matches Your Company (Most Companies Choose This):** This option allows you to select from one of the predefined Charts of Accounts that comes with Peachtree, many of which are industry-specific such as florist, auto repair, beauty shop, or video rental businesses.

- ✔ **Copy Settings from an Existing Peachtree Accounting Company:** This option copies the Chart of Accounts from a Peachtree company that's already set up. Use this option if you're starting your Peachtree company books over or starting another company with a similar Chart of Accounts.

- ✔ **Convert a Company from Another Accounting Program:** Select this option if you're switching from Peachtree Complete Accounting for DOS or from Quicken.

  If you want to convert from QuickBooks or DacEasy, choose the Convert from Another Accounting Program option that appears on the Start screen.

- ✔ **Build Your Own Company:** Use this choice if your accountant has supplied you with an account list or you're starting Peachtree after having used a manual system that uses account numbers.

- ✔ **Consolidate Existing Peachtree Accounting Companies:** If you're using Peachtree Premium or a higher version, you can select this option to combine the Charts of Accounts of other existing Peachtree companies to create a new consolidated Chart of Accounts.

Selecting an Accounting Method

At the beginning of this chapter, we mention that you enter two pieces of permanent information in the New Company Setup Wizard. Selecting your accounting method is one of those two pieces of info. Your business can be accrual-based or cash-based.

Accrual or cash: What's the difference?

An *accrual*-based business recognizes income in the month an invoice was issued to a customer, regardless of when that customer decides to pay. Also, accrual-based businesses recognize a purchase as an expense in the month that you make the purchase and receive the bill, not whenever you write the check to your supplier.

A *cash*-based business declares income in the month that you receive the payment from your customer and expenses in the month that you actually write the check to your supplier. Dates of customer invoices and vendor bills play no role in a cash-based business.

Say, for example, that you sell a $20,000 service to Smith and Sons on December 13, 2007. You invoice them right away, but they don't pay you until April 2 of the next year. Do you declare that $20,000 as part of your sales for December? If the answer is yes, you're running an accrual-based business. If that $20,000 doesn't show up on your income statement until April 2008, you're running a cash-based business.

Because you must report your accounting method to the IRS, don't just arbitrarily pick one. If you're not sure, ask your accountant. Doing so might just keep you out of jail.

Selecting a Posting Method

The *posting* method determines how Peachtree processes or transfers the transactions that you enter from the individual journals to the General Ledger (GL). You have two options: real-time or batch posting. You can switch posting methods at any time.

Journals are electronic or paper records of accounting transactions. Peachtree has many different types of journals. For example, the Cash Receipts journal stores transactions of money that you receive, and the Cash Disbursements journal stores transactions of the money that you spend. Through posting, the journals ultimately go into the GL, where Peachtree sorts the information and reports it to you on financial statements.

If you choose real-time posting, Peachtree posts the transactions to both the individual journals (such as Cash Receipts) and to the GL as you enter and save transactions. This posting method immediately updates the company's financial information. For example, if an accrual-based business using real-time posting enters an invoice to a customer and then prints an income statement, that invoice is included in the income totals.

Real-time posting can save you a lot of time and extra steps. We recommend that you use the real-time posting method.

If you choose batch posting, Peachtree saves the transactions and then posts them in a group when you initiate the posting process. When you use batch posting, you can print registers and check the batch of transactions before posting them to the journals.

While using batch posting, Peachtree prompts you to post journals when necessary. For example, before you enter a customer receipt, you need to have all the invoices posted.

Selecting Accounting Periods

According to a calendar in our office (the one with the Yorkshire terriers all over it), a new year starts on January 1. Some businesses, however, start their business years — or *fiscal* years — at other times. Maybe you can't watch Dick Clark as the new fiscal year rolls in, but we guess if you want, you could have champagne and throw confetti. (For details on closing a fiscal year, see Chapter 17.)

Setting up the fiscal periods correctly in Peachtree is very important because it's the second of the two permanent items you set in the New Company Setup Wizard. After you create fiscal periods, you can't change them.

You can choose from two options on this screen:

> ✔ **Twelve Monthly Accounting Periods:** Each accounting period's starting and ending dates match those of the 12 calendar months. On the next screen, you can choose the month to start your fiscal year.
>
> ✔ **Accounting Periods That Do Not Match the Calendar Month:** Select this option if you want to set up a custom fiscal year structure. For example, you might want four accounting periods per year or possibly 13 four-week accounting periods per year.

On the next screen, Peachtree prompts you to choose the year and month that you want to begin entering data. If you choose to set your own fiscal calendar month, Peachtree also asks you to enter the number of accounting periods that you want to use. Most businesses use 12 accounting periods, based on the calendar months.

Don't forget to visit www.dummies.com/go/peachtreefd for more information on Peachtree.

Chapter 3

Designing the Chart of Accounts

*W*e know you're eager to start using the software. But before you dive in, we need to tell you a little about the Chart of Accounts, which serves as the foundation for all your reports. To make sure that you get the reports you want, you might find that a little planning at this stage is wise. Some of the material in this chapter might seem a little dry because it deals with accounting principles and information that you need for your big picture financial tracking, but understanding this information helps you set up the Chart of Accounts that produces the business reports that you want.

Understanding the Chart of Accounts

You use accounts to keep records of the business that your company transacts. Each time when you buy or sell something, you assign the transaction to appropriate accounts. Accounts help you organize information by keeping similar transactions together. In today's world, for example, you probably get several different telephone bills for your regular phone, your fax phone, your cellular phone, your pager, and so on. But when you think of the big picture, all the bills are related to *telephone* expenses. So when you pay these bills, you record all the transactions in the Telephone Expense account.

The *Chart of Accounts* is nothing more than the list of all your accounts. The Chart of Accounts doesn't show any amounts — just titles and numbers that you assign to each account. Like any list, though, you can — and *should* — organize the Chart of Accounts to make the best use of it. So where do you get a list of your accounts and their balances? Use the General Ledger Trial Balance report. See Chapter 15 for details.

Understanding account types

Good accountants and bookkeepers are typically very organized people. They would hate what they do (and probably wouldn't do it for long) if they weren't. So, it should come as no big surprise that they've invented a method to help them organize things further.

To organize the Chart of Accounts, Peachtree uses *account types.* Usually, accounts are broken down into five general categories of account types:

- **Assets:** Things that you own. Money in checking and savings accounts, computers, trucks, and money that others owe you are all examples of assets.

- **Liabilities:** Debts that you owe to others. Bills from your vendors and bank loans are examples of liabilities.

- **Equity:** Also known as *net worth,* equity represents the amount that owners have invested in the company. Some people prefer to think of equity as the owner's claim against the assets of the company (as opposed to liabilities, which are outsiders' claims against the business). Basically, if you used your assets to pay off your liabilities, what you'd have left is equity.

- **Income:** The sales that you make to your customers. *Income* and *revenue* are interchangeable terms.

- **Expenses:** The cost of staying in business to do business. The wages that you pay your employees and the money that you spend advertising are expenses.

You can break down these account types even further to organize them. In Table 3-1, you see the account types that are available in Peachtree, their general categories, and what they represent. The sidebar "Accounting terms for account types" gives the accounting details on these types.

Table 3-1	Account Types and What They Represent	
Peachtree Account Type	**General Category**	**Represents**
Cash	Asset	Money in the bank that's available for transacting business.
Accounts Receivable	Asset	Money that customers owe but haven't yet paid. This asset account is required for accrual-based businesses.

Peachtree Account Type	General Category	Represents
Inventory	Asset	The value of the goods that you have on hand and available for sale.
Fixed Assets	Asset	The value of things (property and equipment) that you own for long-term use in your business rather than for resale. Fixed assets generally have an estimated life of longer than one year.
Accumulated Depreciation	Contra asset	The value by which fixed assets are reduced to indicate their decline in value, usually due to age. A truck doesn't last forever, no matter how hard you try to keep it in good running condition.
Other Current Assets	Asset	The value of nonworking capital that has a short life (usually less than a year). Employee advances and prepaid expenses, such as deposits made to utility companies, are examples of other current assets.
Other Assets	Asset	The value of nonworking capital that has a long life (usually longer than one year).
Accounts Payable	Liability	The value of the bills you owe to vendors, usually due in 30 or 60 days (a short time frame). This liability account is required for accrual-based businesses.
Other Current Liabilities	Liability	The value of debts that you must pay in less than one year. Short-term loans are other current liabilities.
Long-Term Liabilities	Liability	The value of debts that you must pay but you have longer than one year to pay them. A three-year bank loan to buy a truck is a long-term liability.

Reserves

(continued)

Table 3-1 *(continued)*

Peachtree Account Type	General Category	Represents
Equity–Doesn't Close	Equity	The value of things, such as common stock, that carries forward from year to year. Typically, you use this account type for a corporation that issues stock.
Equity–Gets Closed	Equity	The value of equity accounts that don't carry forward from year to year but instead become part of retained earnings. Use this account type for dividends that you pay to owners or shareholders.
Equity–Retained Earnings	Equity	The accumulated value of net profits or losses. Peachtree automatically updates this account for you when you close your year.
Income	Income	The value of sales that you make to your customers.
Cost of Sales	Expense	The known cost to your business of selling goods or services to customers. Typically, the price that you pay for purchased goods for resale or to use in manufacturing goods for resale is the cost of sales.
Expenses	Expense	The costs that your business incurs to operate, such as wages, rent, and electricity.

Accrual-based businesses must use an Accounts Receivable account and an Accounts Payable account, but many cash-based businesses also want to use these accounts to produce an aging report of customers' outstanding balances or of bills that are due to vendors. See Chapter 2 for more on accounting methods.

Accounting terms for account types

Nonworking capital is something that you own and don't sell to customers, but you could sell it to turn it into cash. Certificates of deposit (CDs) are an example of nonworking capital. The length of time before the CD matures determines whether it's an *other current asset* or an *other asset.* If your company owns CDs or bonds that don't mature for at least one year, you have *other assets.*

Income and *revenue* are interchangeable terms.

Some people call cost of sales, *cost of goods sold* — same thing.

Keep a couple of notes in mind about the account types and equity accounts in your Chart of Accounts: The account type that you choose for an account determines the financial report on which the account appears and the placement on the financial report. Consider the three main financial reports: the Income Statement, the Balance Sheet, and the Trial Balance. Income and Expense accounts appear on the Income Statement, but not on the Balance Sheet. The Balance Sheet shows all Asset, Liability, and Equity accounts, but no Income or Expense accounts. The Trial Balance shows *all* account types, in the following order: Assets, Liabilities, Equity, Income, and Expenses.

The account type also determines how Peachtree handles the account when you close your year. For example, Peachtree zeros-out Income and Expense accounts but doesn't zero-out Asset or Liability accounts. Keep in mind the following points about equity accounts:

✓ You can have only one Equity–Retained Earnings account.

✓ You should show the initial investment in the business as either Paid-In Capital, if your business type is a corporation, or Owner's Contributions, if your business type is a proprietorship (sole or partnership) or an LLC (Limited Liability Company). These are Equity–Doesn't Close account types.

✓ You should track withdrawals from the initial investment by using a Dividends Paid (corporation) or Owner's Draw (proprietorship) account; these accounts are Equity–Gets Closed account types.

The sum of the Equity–Retained Earnings account and any Equity–Doesn't Close accounts (you can have more than one Equity–Doesn't Close account types) equals the net worth of the company prior to the current year.

Numbering accounts

As we describe in the preceding section, account types help you organize the appearance of accounts on financial statements. The account numbers that you use can also affect the information that you can present on financial reports.

Peachtree places very few restrictions on the numbering scheme that you use. Be aware of the following points when you develop your account numbering scheme:

- ✔ Peachtree sorts Account IDs alphabetically. That means numbers first, and you need to use leading zeros to get numbers to sort in numerical order. (We know that sounds stupid, but it's true.) For example, to get the numbers 1, 27, 100, and 1000 to sort in the order just listed, you'd need to enter them as 0001, 0027, 0100, and 1000.

- ✔ Account IDs can contain any printable character except an asterisk (*), a plus sign (+), or a question mark (?).

- ✔ Account IDs can't contain leading or trailing blanks, but you can use blanks in the middle.

Most people use numbers — not letters — for Account IDs, and they use letters for the account's description. The description appears on all reports; the Account ID appears on only some reports.

Because Peachtree places so few restrictions on the Account ID, you can use any scheme you want, but we strongly suggest that you keep it logical. For example, many companies number all asset accounts in the 10000 range, liability accounts in the 20000 range, equity accounts in the 30000 range, income accounts in the 40000 range, cost of sales accounts in the 50000 range, and expense accounts in the 60000 range or higher.

Handling departments or locations

Suppose that your business has multiple geographic locations, and each location generates income and expenses. Or suppose that you don't have geographic locations but you do have multiple departments, and each department generates income and expenses that you want to track. Of course, you want to produce a company-wide income statement, but how do you want it to look?

Perhaps you want a detailed Income Statement that's broken down by department, like the one in Figure 3-1. Or maybe you want an Income Statement that summarizes the information for all departments, like the one in Figure 3-2. Or maybe you want to be able to produce Income Statements for individual departments, like the one shown in Figure 3-3.

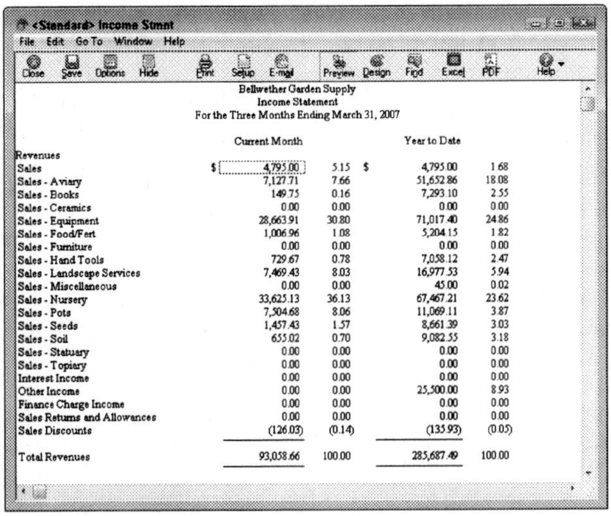

Bellwether Garden Supply
Income Statement
For the Three Months Ending March 31, 2007

	Current Month		Year to Date	
Revenues				
Sales	$ 4,795.00	5.15	$ 4,795.00	1.68
Sales - Aviary	7,127.71	7.66	51,652.86	18.08
Sales - Books	149.75	0.16	7,293.10	2.55
Sales - Ceramics	0.00	0.00	0.00	0.00
Sales - Equipment	28,663.91	30.80	71,017.40	24.86
Sales - Food/Fert	1,006.96	1.08	5,204.15	1.82
Sales - Furniture	0.00	0.00	0.00	0.00
Sales - Hand Tools	729.67	0.78	7,058.12	2.47
Sales - Landscape Services	7,469.43	8.03	16,977.53	5.94
Sales - Miscellaneous	0.00	0.00	45.00	0.02
Sales - Nursery	33,625.13	36.13	67,467.21	23.62
Sales - Pots	7,504.68	8.06	11,069.11	3.87
Sales - Seeds	1,457.43	1.57	8,661.39	3.03
Sales - Soil	655.02	0.70	9,082.55	3.18
Sales - Statuary	0.00	0.00	0.00	0.00
Sales - Topiary	0.00	0.00	0.00	0.00
Interest Income	0.00	0.00	0.00	0.00
Other Income	0.00	0.00	25,500.00	8.93
Finance Charge Income	0.00	0.00	0.00	0.00
Sales Returns and Allowances	0.00	0.00	0.00	0.00
Sales Discounts	(126.03)	(0.14)	(135.93)	(0.05)
Total Revenues	93,058.66	100.00	285,687.49	100.00

Figure 3-1: An Income Statement that shows all departments.

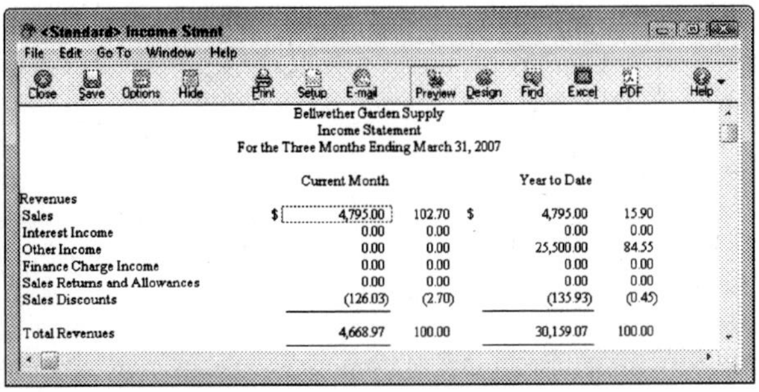

Bellwether Garden Supply
Income Statement
For the Three Months Ending March 31, 2007

	Current Month		Year to Date	
Revenues				
Sales	$ 4,795.00	102.70	$ 4,795.00	15.90
Interest Income	0.00	0.00	0.00	0.00
Other Income	0.00	0.00	25,500.00	84.55
Finance Charge Income	0.00	0.00	0.00	0.00
Sales Returns and Allowances	0.00	0.00	0.00	0.00
Sales Discounts	(126.03)	(2.70)	(135.93)	(0.45)
Total Revenues	4,668.97	100.00	30,159.07	100.00

Figure 3-2: An Income Statement that rolls up all department al numbers.

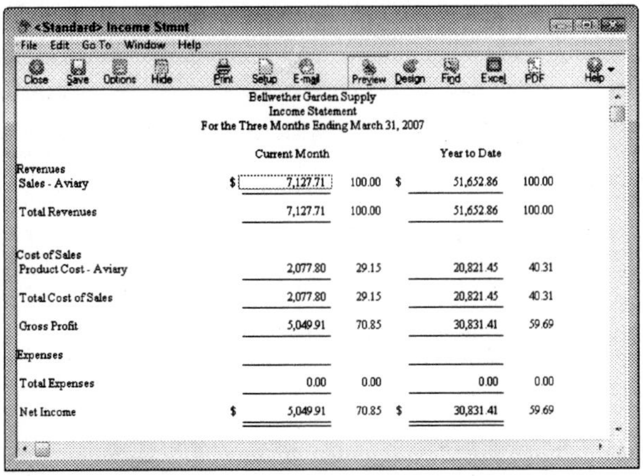

Bellwether Garden Supply
Income Statement
For the Three Months Ending March 31, 2007

	Current Month		Year to Date	
Revenues				
Sales - Aviary	$ 7,127.71	100.00	$ 51,652.86	100.00
Total Revenues	7,127.71	100.00	51,652.86	100.00
Cost of Sales				
Product Cost - Aviary	2,077.80	29.15	20,821.45	40.31
Total Cost of Sales	2,077.80	29.15	20,821.45	40.31
Gross Profit	5,049.91	70.85	30,831.41	59.69
Expenses				
Total Expenses	0.00	0.00	0.00	0.00
Net Income	$ 5,049.91	70.85	$ 30,831.41	59.69

Figure 3-3: An Income Statement for a single department.

Because we show you all three formats, it's safe to assume that Peachtree enables you to produce any of these reports. But to do so, you must correctly set up the numbering of your Chart of Accounts.

Setting up departmental account numbers

To produce these reports, Peachtree uses a concept called *masking* that enables you, through the use of account numbers, to easily limit the information that appears on reports. To use masking, you divide your account number into segments; assign the account number — say, 40000 — to the first segment, and then assign a digit or two to the second segment of the number to represent the department or location. That is, 40000-01 might be income for Department 1, and 40000-02 could be income for Department 2.

The implication here is that the first segment of the account (40000) appears several different times in your Chart of Accounts, but the second segment contains a different department number. You also set up a 00 level for the account (that is, 40000-00) that Peachtree uses to display the sum of all the departments and represent the company as a whole. You record sales and purchases or payments by using the account number that represents the department responsible for the sale, purchase, or payment. You would never record a transaction in the 00 level account. Your expense accounts work the same way if you want to track costs separately for each department.

If your situation is more complex, and you want to track expenses for multiple locations *and* for multiple departments at each location, your account number should include both a location segment and a department segment. To track sales for Location 1, Department 1, your Sales account number might be 40000-01-01, where the first 01 tracks the Location and the second 01 tracks the Department. Table 3-2 shows the various possible combinations for Sales accounts that you would find in your Chart of Accounts if you had three locations and three departments:

Table 3-2	Sample Combinations for Accounts Using Locations and Departments
Account Description	**Account Number**
Sales for Location 1, Department 1	40000-01-01
Sales for Location 2, Department 1	40000-02-01
Sales for Location 3, Department 1	40000-03-01
Sales for Location 1, Department 2	40000-01-02
Sales for Location 1, Department 3	40000-01-03

Account Description	Account Number
Sales for Location 2, Department 2	40000-02-02
Sales for Location 2, Department 3	40000-02-03
Sales for Location 3, Department 2	40000-03-02
Sales for Location 3, Department 3	40000-03-03

Don't forget to allow the maximum number of characters that you need for your departments and locations and keep future growth in mind. For example, if you have ten or more departments, you need two digits for your department number. Don't forget to use a leading zero for department numbers less than ten (for example, 01, 02, 03, and so on).

You can create up to five account segments, but the total number of characters you can use for an account number is 15, including the segment separators.

If you're using any version of Peachtree *other than* Peachtree Premium or higher and you want to use masking, do so when creating your Chart of Accounts by simply setting up the appropriate account numbers. If you're using Peachtree Premium or higher, you can add masking to your existing Chart of Accounts by setting up account segments. Follow these steps to identify your account segment structure in Peachtree.

1. **Choose Maintain⇨Default Information⇨General Ledger.**

   Peachtree displays the General Ledger Defaults dialog box, as shown in Figure 3-4.

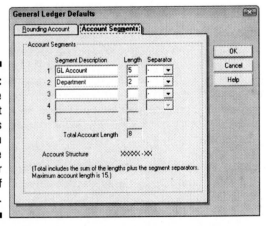

Figure 3-4: Set up the account segments that you want to use in your Chart of Accounts.

2. **Click the Account Segments tab.**

3. **Click in the Segment Description field and type a description of the portion of the account number that you want to define.**

4. **Click in the Length field and type the value that represents the number of digits you want to assign to this segment of the account number.**

5. **Click the Separator drop-down list arrow and select a character to separate portions of the account number.**

6. **Repeat Steps 3–5 for each segment that you want to define.**

7. **Click OK.**

If you're identifying segments for an existing Chart of Accounts, Peachtree displays a message that tells you how many accounts you currently have that don't match the segment structure that you defined when you clicked OK. Simply click OK when you see the message and edit your Chart of Accounts to provide the new segment numbers as appropriate by using the information in the next section. Remember, you don't need to assign numbers for any segment other than the first segment of your account number — the other segments are optional. Many people use them only for Income and Expense accounts.

Consolidating departmental figures

With Peachtree Premium or higher, you can extend the department/location scenario from the preceding section one step further. Suppose that you find yourself in the situation where you have two or three geographic locations that each need to use Peachtree — and you're not networked. You *can* set up separate companies in Peachtree, but at the end of an accounting period, you won't have a consolidated financial statement to show the true financial picture of your company. Then, you can consolidate the companies to produce reports.

In Peachtree Premium or higher, you can consolidate companies by creating a new company that contains — or consolidates — companies that you select. The New Company Wizard gives you the option to create a company that consolidates other companies, and then lets you select the companies to consolidate. The companies that you consolidate must have the same fiscal year and accounting method. See Chapter 2 for details on creating a new company.

If you segment the Chart of Accounts in each company in the same way, consolidating is quick and painless and lets you produce departmental as well as company-wide financial statements.

Modifying the Chart of Accounts

After you understand account types, numbering, and so on, you can dive in and make additions, changes, or deletions to the Chart of Accounts. To make *any* changes to the Chart of Accounts, use the Maintain Chart of Accounts window, as shown in Figure 3-5.

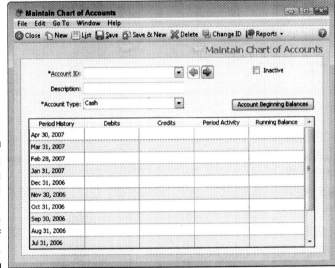

Figure 3-5:
Use this window to make changes to the Chart of Accounts.

Adding new accounts

To add an account, follow these steps:

1. **Choose Maintain➪Chart of Accounts.**

2. **In the Maintain Chart of Accounts window, type a number for the new account in the Account ID field.**

Peachtree opens the account list and shows you the number of the account that most closely matches the number you typed. Make sure that you type a new number — one that doesn't already exist. You can print a copy of your existing Chart of Accounts by clicking the Reports button, as shown here in the margin, and choosing Chart of Accounts.

3. **In the Description field, type a name for the account as you want it to appear on reports.**

4. **Open the Account Type drop-down list and select the correct account type for the account that you're adding.**

5. **Click Save.**

If you create an account number that doesn't match the segmenting scheme, you see a message. You can click OK and create the account despite the message.

Editing accounts

You can edit an account's Account ID, description, or account type by following these steps:

1. **Choose Maintain⇨Chart of Accounts.**

   Peachtree displays the Maintain Chart of Accounts window (refer to Figure 3-5).

2. **Click the drop-down list arrow beside the Account ID field or type the first few characters of the Account ID.**

   Peachtree displays the account list.

3. **Highlight the account and click OK.**

4. **Retype the description or change the account type.**

5. **To change the Account ID, click the Change ID button on the toolbar, as shown here in the margin.**

   Peachtree displays the Change Account ID dialog box, as shown in Figure 3-6.

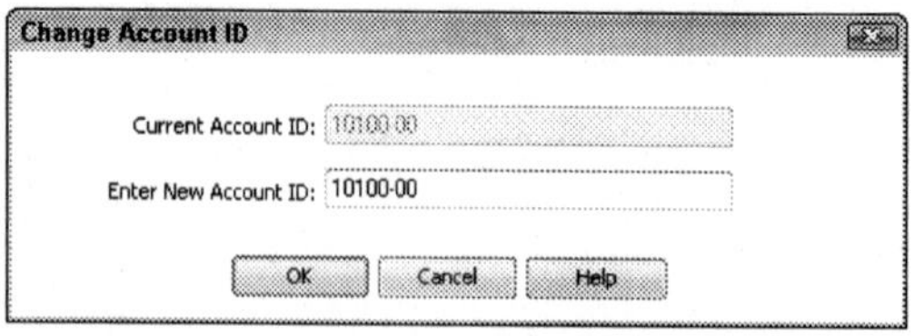

Figure 3-6:
Change an account number in this box.

Change Account ID	
Current Account ID:	10100-00
Enter New Account ID:	10100-00
OK Cancel Help	

6. **Type a new Account ID and click OK.**

7. **Click Save.**

Deleting accounts

You can delete accounts that have no activity — that is, you haven't used them in any transactions. Choose Maintain⇨Chart of Accounts to display the Maintain Chart of Accounts window. Select the account by using the drop-down list arrow or by typing the account number; then click the Delete button on the toolbar, as shown here in the margin.

If you try to delete an account that you've used in transactions, Peachtree tells you that it can't delete the account. You can, however, set the status of the account to Inactive and then set Peachtree options to hide inactive accounts. If you choose to hide inactive accounts, they don't appear in the list of any transaction window. In addition, hidden accounts don't appear on any report except the Chart of Accounts report. Only people who know the account's number are able to use it. To make an account inactive, display it in the Maintain Chart of Accounts window, select the Inactive check box, and click the Save button. You find out how to hide inactive accounts in Bonus Chapter 1 on this book's Web site, www.dummies.com/go/peachtreefd.

When you make an account inactive, you make it eligible for deletion when you purge. See Chapter 17 for information on purging.

Identifying the rounding account

Peachtree can round numbers on financial statements to either whole dollars or whole thousands of dollars. So, occasionally, when you prepare financial statements, Peachtree needs to round numbers. Also, Peachtree needs a place to store the difference caused by rounding. Although the account you select can be any account, Peachtree recommends that you use the Retained Earnings account.

To make sure that Peachtree uses the Retained Earnings account for rounding, follow these steps:

1. **Choose Maintain⇨Default Information⇨General Ledger.**

   Peachtree displays the General Ledger Defaults dialog box (refer to Figure 3-4).

2. **Click the Rounding Account tab.**

3. **Confirm that Peachtree has selected the single account that you've designated as Equity–Retained Earnings.**

   If necessary, click the magnifying glass next to the account number to display the list. In the unlikely event that Peachtree chooses the wrong account, change it to Equity–Retained Earnings.

4. **Click OK.**

Opening balances

The odds are good . . . very good . . . excellent, in fact, that you've been in business for some time now and that you're starting to use Peachtree after you've done some business. In cases such as these, you need to enter beginning balances into Peachtree to represent the business that you conducted before setting up your Peachtree company.

Timing the start of using Peachtree

And now is a good time to talk about timing. How do you know when you should go live with Peachtree? Well, ideally, start using a new accounting package on the first day of your accounting year — January 1 (if your business operates on a calendar year) or the first day of your fiscal year. If you can't wait that long, then start using Peachtree on the first day of a quarter. And if you can't start using Peachtree on the first day of a quarter, then start on the first day of a month.

Why these target dates? Well, you have the least amount of setup work to do. For example, if your business operates on a calendar year and you start using Peachtree on January 1, you don't need to enter any beginning balances for payroll or any of your income or expense accounts because the balances of these accounts start at zero on January 1. If you start at the beginning of a quarter and you're willing to forego monthly reports preceding that quarter, you can enter summarized information for preceding quarters. And, if you start on the first day of a month, you don't need to play catch-up by entering all transactions for the month — which you'd need to do if you'd started mid-month.

Where do you get the numbers?

If you've been using some other accounting package, you can print an Income Statement, Balance Sheet, and a Trial Balance as of the last month that you intend to use that accounting package. You can use a combination of the Balance Sheet and the Income Statement, or you can use the Trial Balance: The numbers on these reports in your old software represent the beginning balance numbers of your new Peachtree company.

If you've never used any other accounting package, contact your accountant. Provide the date that you want to start your company and ask for a Trial Balance, a Balance Sheet, and an Income Statement as of that date. Your accountant probably can't provide the information instantly, especially if you want to start on January 1, and you ask for the information in December of the prior year. Your accountant needs to prepare these reports *after* December 31 so that the reports include all the prior year's transactions.

But don't worry; you can start working in Peachtree without beginning balance numbers; in fact, you might as well start working in Peachtree without beginning balance numbers. You just need to remember that year-to-date reports aren't accurate because they don't show the entire picture until you enter beginning balances.

Entering beginning balances

After you get the numbers, entering them into Peachtree isn't difficult. If you're going to start using Peachtree at any time other than the beginning of your business year, we suggest you use the alternative method described in the next section. If you're going to start using Peachtree at the beginning of your business year (calendar or fiscal), we suggest that you use the Chart of Accounts Beginning Balances or Prior Year Adjustments window to enter beginning balances.

The two windows look and operate identically except for the name that appears in the title bar. You see the Chart of Accounts Beginning Balances window if you haven't posted any transactions in your Peachtree company. If you *have* posted transactions, Peachtree displays the Prior Year Adjustments window.

Follow these steps:

1. **Choose Maintain⇨Chart of Accounts.**

   Peachtree displays the Maintain Chart of Accounts window (refer to Figure 3-5).

2. **Click the Account Beginning Balances button.**

   Peachtree displays the Select Period dialog box.

3. **Select the period from the list.**

   Until you enter transactions, you can enter beginning balances in Peachtree by month for the year preceding your first open year, for your first open year, or for your second open year. If Period 1 for the company is January 2008, Peachtree makes available each month in 2007, 2008, and 2009; all balances prior to January 1, 2007, are lumped together into Before 1/1/07.

4. **Click OK.**

   Peachtree displays the Chart of Accounts Beginning Balances window or Prior Year Adjustments window (see Figure 3-7).

5. **Using the numbers that you've gotten either from your old accounting system's Trial Balance or from your accountant, enter the balances for each account.**

   If you have an unusual balance in an account (for example, your cash balance is a negative instead of a positive balance), enter a negative number for the account balance.

   After you finish, the Net Income number at the bottom of the window represents your Net Income for the period. Look for the Net Income at the bottom of your Income Statement.

6. **Click OK to store your beginning balances.**

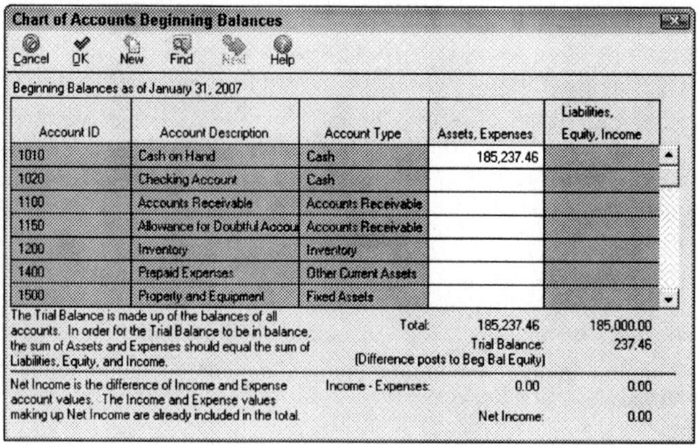

Figure 3-7:
Use this
window to
enter
account
balances
generated
before you
started
using
Peachtree.

You can find out more about posting transactions in Chapters 5–9.

An alternative method for entering beginning balances

If you start using Peachtree at any time other than the beginning of the business year, we suggest that you enter one (or more) journal entries to represent your beginning balances instead of using the Chart of Accounts Beginning Balances or Chart of Accounts Prior Year Adjustments window. We find that using journal entries for midyear starts seems to be less confusing. You'd enter the journal entries to provide balances as of the first day of the first open month.

Because we're trying to avoid using the *d* word and the *c* word this early in the book (debits and credits), we save the discussion of journal entries for Chapter 17 and Bonus Chapter 5.

The B word — Budgeting

Nobody likes to live on a budget, but for most of us, budgets are a fact of life. In the business world, budgets can help you compare how your business is actually doing to how you *thought* it would do.

You can create budgets for each account in Peachtree; you can then print Budget vs. Actual reports to see how well you're doing. Although we'd love to walk you through the details on budgeting, the wicked editors refused to give us enough space in this book. We know you're a pretty smart reader, so here's a synopsis.

If you're out of balance . . .

You know that you're out of balance if the Trial Balance number in Figure 3-7 is *not* zero. In this case, Peachtree wants to post the difference to an Equity–Doesn't Close account called Beg. Bal. Equity. This account doesn't appear in the Beginning Balances window, but it does appear on financial statements, General Ledger reports, and in the Chart of Accounts list. The chances are good that you're out of balance because of a typing mistake; double-check the numbers that you've entered and make sure you've entered *all* the numbers.

If you still can't find the mistake, you can click through Peachtree's warning and let it create the Beg. Bal. Equity account. Your company is

then in balance, and you can safely proceed to enter transactions. If you have to use this workaround, you need to live with the Beg. Bal. Equity account until you find the source of the problem. You can then correct it by clicking the Beginning Balances button in the Maintain Chart of Accounts window. Peachtree displays the Beginning Balances window if you haven't posted any transactions. If you *have* posted transactions, Peachtree displays the Prior Year Adjustment window, which looks and operates just like the Beginning Balances window. When the Beg. Bal. Equity account has a zero balance, you can delete the account.

 Choose Maintain➪Budgets. In the Maintain Budgets window that appears, select an Account ID for which you want to establish budget numbers. Then fill in budget amounts for each month in the available fiscal years. You can use the Autofill button, as shown here in the margin, to fill in the budget with actual data from Peachtree or to copy amounts from another budget and save yourself some typing. You can also start with a blank budget and import information stored in a CSV file. In the Budget Name box, type a name for the budget and, in the Description box, you can describe the budget in a way that's meaningful to you. Click Save, select the next account, and repeat the process.

yearly?

 If you don't know what a CSV file is, you probably don't have one to use to import budget information. However, many programs can create *comma-separated value* files (.csv) and, if you have budget information stored in such a program, you can use that program's features to create a CSV file that you can then import into a Peachtree budget.

 In Peachtree Premium or higher, you can create an unlimited number of budgets for a four-year period.

 Visit this book's Web site, www.dummies.com/go/peachtreefd, for more information on Peachtree.

Chapter 4

Setting Up Background Information

In This Chapter

▶ Setting purchasing preferences

▶ Determining sales preferences

▶ Setting up payroll preferences

▶ Choosing inventory preferences

*I*f you set up preferences in Peachtree before you dive into the day-to-day stuff of managing your company's books, you save time because Peachtree uses the default information as a model for the tasks you do daily. You know, stuff like creating vendors, customers, employees, and inventory items, and entering transactions (purchase orders, purchases, invoices, payroll checks, and so on). You can alter this global information when a particular person or item requires something other than the default.

Terminology alert: Peachtree switches back and forth between two terms when referring to bills that vendors send you: a *purchase* and an *invoice*. For the sake of clarity, we call a vendor bill a purchase; invoices are the things you send to customers so that *you* can get paid.

Setting Purchasing Preferences

"What kind of information do I need to supply for vendors?" you ask. Well, you set up standard terms. *Terms* describe how long the vendor gives you to hold a bill before you need to pay it and how you want Peachtree to respond if vendors offer you a discount for paying early. You also identify the default account to assign to most vendor bills and vendor discounts. And you specify how you want Peachtree to *age* bills that you enter. Lastly, you can set up custom fields for vendors so you can track information that you specify about the people from whom you buy goods or services.

Aging refers to how long you hold an invoice from the date it was issued.

Peachtree applies these preferences to all vendors you create and all purchases you enter. If a vendor or a transaction is unusual in some way, you make a change to the specific vendor or transaction. Using standardized information in this way saves you time because you need to change the standard information only for exceptions to the rule. And face it — we *all* like to save time. See Chapter 5 for information on setting up vendors.

Establishing default payment terms and accounts

Efficient bill paying is an art. You don't want to pay your bills too early or too late. For example, if your bank account earns interest, you don't want to pay a vendor's bill too soon, because you lose interest from the bank. On the other hand, if your vendor assesses late fees or finance charges for bills that you don't pay on time, you don't want to pay a bill too late.

Using the Peachtree Vendor Defaults dialog box, you can establish a typical set of terms to use for most vendors. Chapter 5 shows you how to create vendors and how Peachtree automatically assigns these default terms to each vendor. You need to change terms for only those vendors who *don't* use the typical terms.

To set default payment terms and accounts that most vendors use, follow these steps:

1. **Choose Maintain⇨Default Information⇨Vendors.**

   Peachtree displays the Vendor Defaults dialog box (see Figure 4-1).

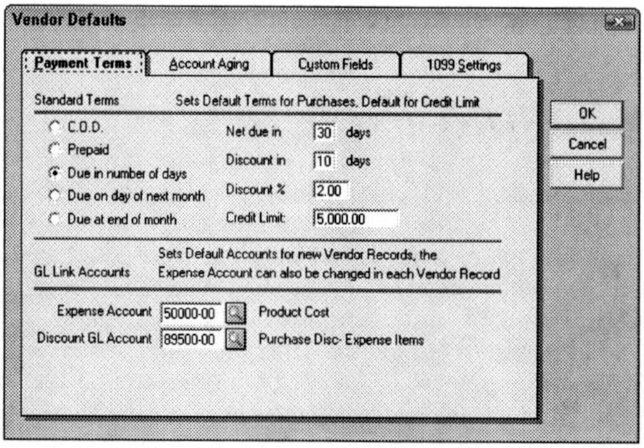

Figure 4-1:
Use the
Vendor
Defaults
dialog box
to define
typical
settings for
vendors.

Vendor Defaults
Payment Terms	Account Aging	Custom Fields	1099 Settings

Standard Terms — Sets Default Terms for Purchases, Default for Credit Limit

- C.O.D.
- Prepaid
- Due in number of days
- Due on day of next month
- Due at end of month

Net due in   [30] days
Discount in [10] days
Discount %   [2.00]
Credit Limit [5,000.00]

OK
Cancel
Help

GL Link Accounts — Sets Default Accounts for new Vendor Records, the Expense Account can also be changed in each Vendor Record

Expense Account [50000-00]   Product Cost
Discount GL Account [89500-00]   Purchase Disc- Expense Items

You can also choose Options⇨Default Information⇨Vendors to reach the same screen and set the same options.

2. **From among the Standard Terms option buttons, select the option that best describes the terms most of your vendors offer you.**

   The terms shown in Figure 4-1 are 2% 10 Net 30, which means you can discount the bill by 2 percent if you pay it within 10 days; otherwise, the entire amount of the bill is due in 30 days.

3. **Fill in the appropriate fields to the right of the terms you select in Step 2.**

   As you select an option button on the left, the fields on the right change. For example, if you select C.O.D. (cash on delivery) or Prepaid, only the Credit Limit field on the right remains available, because none of the other fields apply.

4. **At the bottom of the Payment Terms tab, click the magnifying glass to select the account that you use most often when you post purchases from vendors.**

   If you don't select an account, Peachtree prompts you for an account each time you create a new vendor. If you do select an account, Peachtree fills it in automatically when you create a new vendor.

5. **In the Discount GL Account field, select the account to which you want Peachtree to post discounts that vendors give you for paying in the specified time.**

   To select the account, type its account number or click the lookup list button (the magnifying glass) to the right of the account number to display a list. In the list, highlight the account number and then click OK.

6. **Click OK to close the dialog box or leave it open to review additional defaults in the sections that follow.**

Keep two points in mind: First, you may never receive discounts from your vendors, but Peachtree expects you to set up the account anyhow. Second, you may want to increase the credit limit while you're setting other vendor defaults. If you exceed the credit limit when buying from a vendor, you can still buy from the vendor, but you see an annoying message telling you that you've exceeded the credit limit.

Aging vendor bills

When you age a bill, you hold onto it for a specified period of time before you pay it. You can age purchases (that is, you can tell Peachtree to count the number of days you hold the bill) from either the billing date or the due date.

To set account aging defaults, choose Maintain⇨Default Information⇨Vendors. On the Account Aging tab, select a method to age bills: Invoice Date or Due Date. Optionally, you can change the number of days in each of the four columns on the Aged Payables report.

You may find the difference between the two aging methods easier to understand if you take a look at two Aged Payables reports, each prepared by using one of the aging methods. In Figure 4-2, we set the Aging option to Due Date and then prepared a customized Accounts Payable Aging report for only one vendor, Akerson Distribution, as of March 31, 2007. In Figure 4-3, we switched the Aging Option to Invoice Date and printed the same report for the same vendor and time frame. (Note that *invoice* here refers to bills your vendors send you — what we call *purchases.*)

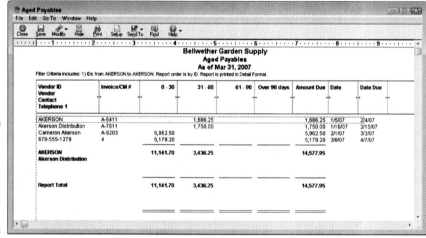

Figure 4-2:
An Aging report showing bills aged by due date.

Both reports show four outstanding bills for Akerson Distribution. Each bill, along with its date and due date, is listed on a separate line.

Notice the third bill — the one for $5,962.50. It was posted as of February 1, 2007, with terms of Net 30; that is, the bill is due 30 days from the bill date of February 1 — on March 3. On the first report, the bill appears to be somewhere between 0 and 30 days old, whereas on the second report, it appears to be somewhere between 31 and 60 days old. In actuality, according to the first report, on March 31, 2007, the bill is somewhere between 0 and 30 days past the *due date* of the bill. According to the second report, on March 31, 2007, the bill is somewhere between 31 and 60 days past the *invoice date* of the bill.

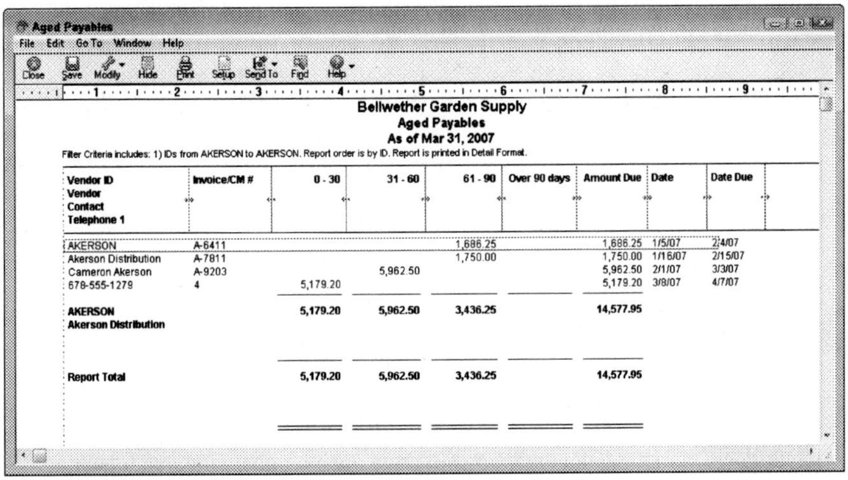

Figure 4-3: An Aging report showing bills aged by invoice date.

Bellwether Garden Supply
Aged Payables
As of Mar 31, 2007

Filter Criteria includes: 1) IDs from AKERSON to AKERSON. Report order is by ID. Report is printed in Detail Format.

Vendor ID Vendor Contact Telephone 1	Invoice/CM #	0 - 30	31 - 60	61 - 90	Over 90 days	Amount Due	Date	Date Due
AKERSON Akerson Distribution Cameron Akerson 678-555-1279	A-6411 A-7811 A-9203 4	5,179.20	5,962.50	1,886.25 1,750.00		1,886.25 1,750.00 5,962.50 5,179.20	1/5/07 1/16/07 2/1/07 3/8/07	2/4/07 2/15/07 3/3/07 4/7/07
AKERSON **Akerson Distribution**		**5,179.20**	**5,962.50**	**3,436.25**		**14,577.95**		
Report Total		**5,179.20**	**5,962.50**	**3,436.25**		**14,577.95**		

This report is *not* showing you what is overdue; it's showing you the bill's age based on the number of days *past* either the due date or the invoice date.

Many people choose to age vendor bills by due date because the bills look "less overdue" on the aging report.

Creating custom fields for vendors

Custom fields are a great way to store information about your vendors that doesn't fit elsewhere in Peachtree, such as details specific to your business or industry. For example, many businesses track a workers' compensation certificate number for subcontractors to justify not covering the subcontractor on the company's workers' compensation insurance. On the Custom Fields tab of the Vendor Defaults dialog box, you can create up to five fields for each vendor. In the Enabled column, select the check box next to each custom field that you want to use and then type the name of the custom field in the Field Labels text box.

When you set up vendors in Chapter 5, you can fill in this information for each vendor. On some reports in Peachtree, you can print this information.

1099 Settings

On the 1099 Settings tab of the Vendor Defaults dialog box, you can (if necessary) change the way that Peachtree calculates 1099 payments. For each account on the Chart of Accounts, you can identify whether and how Peachtree should calculate 1099 income. By default, Peachtree assumes that you will establish the correct 1099 type for each vendor when you create the vendor, so each account is set up to look at the vendor's record. You can, however, specify that a particular account should be used to calculate 1099 miscellaneous income or 1099 interest income, or you can specify that the account should not be used when calculating 1099 income. In most cases, you don't need to change the default settings.

Setting Sales Preferences

"What kind of information do I supply for customers?" you ask. Well, you set up standard terms for customers like you do for vendors. This time, though, you're the one establishing when payment is due and whether you offer customers a discount for paying early. Customer terms also tell Peachtree how to respond if customers pay early. You also identify the default sales account and discount account where you want Peachtree to assign most customer invoices. You specify how you want Peachtree to age invoices that you prepare. Like with vendors, you can set up custom fields for customers to track specific information that may help you increase sales or offer perks. You also can decide whether to apply finance charges to overdue invoices, and you can set customers' Pay Methods — cash, check, or credit card.

The concept of aging applies also to invoices you send to your customers. In this instance, aging refers to the specified period of time the customer waits before paying your invoice. You set payment terms that tell your customers how long you expect them to wait before paying an invoice — and potentially charge the customer finance charges for late payment.

Like with vendors, Peachtree applies these preferences to all customers you create and all invoices you enter. If a customer or a transaction is unusual in some way, you can make a change to the specific customer or transaction.

Establishing default payment terms and accounts

When customers don't pay you in a timely fashion, you may experience *cash flow* problems. That is, you have money going out of your business for expenses but not enough money coming in to cover those expenses. To encourage your customers to pay on time, you establish payment terms similar to the ones your vendors set for you.

From the Peachtree Customer Defaults dialog box, you can establish a typical set of terms to use for most customers. Peachtree automatically assigns these terms when you create customers (see Chapter 7). When you create customers, you can change preferences for those customers who don't use the typical terms.

To set default payment terms and accounts for most customers, follow these steps:

1. **Choose Maintain⇨Default Information⇨Customers.**

   Peachtree displays the Customer Defaults dialog box (see Figure 4-4).

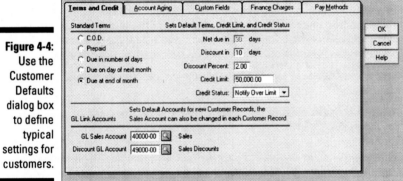

Figure 4-4:
Use the
Customer
Defaults
dialog box
to define
typical
settings for
customers.

2. **From among the Standard Terms option buttons, select the option that best describes the terms that you offer most of your customers.**

   The terms shown in Figure 4-4 are 2% 10 Net EOM, which means your customers can discount the invoice by 2 percent if they pay it within ten days; otherwise, the entire amount of the invoice is due at the end of the month. (EOM stands for *end of month*.) These terms are appropriate if you typically invoice at the beginning of each month.

3. **Fill in the appropriate fields to the right of the terms you selected in Step 2.**

   The options for customer terms work like the options for vendor terms. As you select an option button on the left, the fields on the right change. For example, if you select C.O.D. or Prepaid, only the Credit Limit field on the right remains available because none of the other fields apply.

You can use the Credit Status list to control Peachtree's behavior in relation to the customer's credit limit when you enter an invoice. The list contains five choices. On one end of the spectrum, you can record invoices without seeing any messages, regardless of the relationship between the customer's balance and credit limit. On the other end of the spectrum, Peachtree will not allow you to enter an invoice for a customer regardless of the relationship between the customer's balance and credit limit. In between these choices, you can have Peachtree display a warning or an error message when a transaction will cause a customer's balance to exceed the credit limit. And you can have Peachtree display a warning whenever you record a transaction even if the customer's balance doesn't exceed his or her credit limit.

4. **Select the GL Sales Account that you use most often when you sell goods or services to customers.**

   To select the account, type the account number or click the lookup list identifier (the magnifying glass) to the right of the account number to display and select from a lookup list. If you don't select an account, Peachtree prompts you for an account each time you create a new customer.

5. **Select the Discount GL Account you use to track discounts taken by customers.**

6. **After you finish setting payment preferences, click OK to save those preferences.**

Even if you never offer discounts to your customers, Peachtree expects you to set up the account anyhow. (If you haven't set up a Discount General Ledger account, see Chapter 3 for information on creating accounts.)

Aging customer invoices

We talk about aging a lot in our society, and now you're getting a whole new picture of wrinkled bills and invoices. Just as you can control the aging process for vendor bills, you can age customer invoices from either the invoice date or the due date. Unfortunately, you can't control the wrinkles from the other kind of aging. . . .

Accounts receivable aging works the same as accounts payable aging — that is, you can choose to age by due date or by invoice date. Suppose that you post an invoice as of February 20, 2007, with terms of 2% 10 Net 30.

If you set up accounts receivable aging to age by due date, the invoice is due 30 days from the invoice date of February 20, which is March 22. On the Accounts Receivable Aging report, the invoice appears to be somewhere between 0 and 30 days old — that is, on March 31, 2007, the invoice is somewhere between 0 and 30 days *past the due date* of the invoice.

Alternatively, if you set up accounts receivable aging to age by invoice date, the same invoice appears on the Accounts Receivable Aging report to be somewhere between 31 and 60 days old. That is, on March 31, 2007, the invoice is somewhere between 31 and 60 days *past the invoice date* of the invoice.

This report shows you all invoices, including those not yet due as well as those that are overdue. Although most people use this report to identify overdue invoices, the report's actual purpose is to show you the age of invoices based on the number of days *past* either the due date or the invoice date.

Many people choose to age customer invoices by invoice date because the aging report then reflects how old the invoice is. Others prefer to age invoices by due date so that they can see how many days the invoice is overdue.

Creating custom fields for customers

On the Custom Fields tab of the Customer Defaults dialog box, you can enter labels for up to five fields for each customer. Use these fields to store extra information about customers, such as noting new customers who found your business on the Web. In the Enabled column, select the check box next to each custom field that you want to use and then type the name of the custom field in the Field Labels text box. When you set up customers, you can fill in this information for each customer. On some reports in Peachtree, you can print this information.

Suppose that you've established a label and filled in information for customers. If you reopen the Customer Defaults dialog box and change the label, you *won't* affect the information you stored for each customer; you must edit each customer's record and make a change to match the new label you've established. If you simply don't want to show the information you've already entered, you can hide the stored information by deselecting the Enabled check box in the Customer Defaults dialog box. However, the information reappears if you enable the custom field once again.

Setting up finance charges

Finance charges are fees that you charge customers who pay late. Many businesses don't charge finance charges; others believe that finance charges encourage customers to pay on time and therefore improve cash flow. Still others believe that charging these fees is necessary if customers continuously ignore payment terms.

If you want to be able to charge finance charges, follow these steps:

1. **Choose Maintain⇨Default Information⇨Customers and click the Finance Charges tab of the Customer Defaults dialog box.**

2. **Select the Charge Finance Charges check box.**

3. **Complete the remaining information to tell Peachtree how to calculate finance charges.**

   Peachtree charges an interest rate that you specify on invoices that are overdue by the number of days you indicate. You can charge a higher rate on balances that exceed an amount you stipulate, or you can specify a minimum finance charge amount.

4. **(Optional) Select the Charge Interest on Finance Charges check box.**

   Selecting the Charge Interest on Finance Charges check box tells Peachtree to calculate interest on any unpaid balance as well as unpaid finance charges. Check with your accountant before you select this check box; in some states, it is illegal to charge interest on interest.

5. **Use the lookup list button to select a GL account for finance charges.**

6. **From the Appears on Invoices and Statements As list, select the description for the finance charge (either Late Charge or Finance Charge).**

7. **(Optional) Provide a warning message that Peachtree can print on invoices.**

   The Finance Charge Warning message at the bottom of the Finance Charges tab is printed on the bottom of invoices you send to customers. If you're not charging finance charges, you may want to change the message to something like *Happy Holidays* or *See our exhibit at the Business Expo March 16–19.*

8. **Click OK.**

   This information becomes part of your standard terms.

Enabling finance charges does *not* make Peachtree automatically assess finance charges. And you don't need to assign finance charges to *all* your customers. See Chapter 8 for information on assessing finance charges.

Establishing payment methods

Payment methods are exactly what they sound like — the various methods of payment that your company accepts. You establish these default settings on the Pay Methods tab of the Customer Defaults dialog box. Choose Maintain⇨Default Information⇨Customers and click the Pay Methods tab. Then, in the fields provided, type the names of the payment methods your company accepts.

These payment methods are available when you record payments you receive from customers. You can include the Payment Method field on reports. For example, you can add this field to the Cash Receipts journal and filter the journal to see transactions of only one particular payment method.

Adding a new payment method after you already recorded transactions in Peachtree doesn't affect previously recorded transactions. The new payment method is simply available for new transactions.

On the Pay Methods tab, you also can tell Peachtree to automatically assign deposit ticket IDs in either the Receipts window or the Select for Deposit window. Deposit ticket IDs help you group payments you receive from customers. To help you reconcile your bank statement, you typically use the same deposit ticket ID for all customer payments that you plan to deposit in the bank at the same time. See Chapter 8 for more information on recording receipts and using deposit ticket IDs.

Setting Payroll Preferences

You have three ways to handle payroll preparation in Peachtree. For a fee, you can use the Peachtree Payroll Service and let Peachtree do everything for you, or you can do your payroll in-house. If you choose to do payroll in-house, you can (again, for a fee) subscribe to the Peachtree Payroll Tax Update Service (which we recommend) or you can manually update payroll tax tables yourself.

Peachtree does *not* come with tax tables that calculate federal taxes. To subscribe to the Peachtree Payroll Tax Update Service, visit the Peachtree Web site at www.peachtree.com. Because the service sends you updates whenever laws change that affect payroll taxes, we suggest that you subscribe to this service to ensure that you're always using the most up-to-date tax tables. In addition, if you subscribe to the service, you'll be able to use the Print & Sign payroll tax forms to prepare 941 Quarterly Reports and W-2s. You can read more about these forms in Chapter 17.

For an additional fee, you can let Peachtree file federal and state payroll tax returns, make payroll tax deposits, and produce and mail W-2s for you. Also, with any in-house payroll solution, you can subscribe to Peachtree's Direct Deposit service.

If you decide to use the Peachtree Payroll Service and let Peachtree do payroll for you, you can skip this entire section. If you decide to use Peachtree features to prepare payroll, you need to identify some basic information, such as the state where your company operates. Understanding payroll is difficult even when you aren't worried about setting up payroll in an accounting program. On the Good News front, though, Peachtree uses a wizard to walk you through establishing the defaults for preparing payroll checks and tax-related forms (W-2s, Federal Form 940, and Federal Form 941).

You can use the Payroll Setup Wizard to help you set up payroll when you first create a company or later, after you've been using Peachtree for a while. No problem — take your choice. We suggest that you use the Payroll Setup Wizard after you subscribe to the Payroll Tax Update Service. In the paragraphs that follow, we show you how to use the wizard to set up basic payroll information.

Using the Payroll Setup Wizard

The Payroll Setup Wizard helps you set up basic information about payroll, including payroll fields that Peachtree then uses to calculate payroll checks. *Payroll fields* are things such as gross wages and federal income tax (FIT) — one of those many mysterious abbreviations that appear on your payroll check stub. Chapter 19 describes how to set up a payroll field for some common payroll deductions (or additions, for those lucky enough to get a bonus) that you want to include on a paycheck.

The Payroll Setup Wizard can be useful after you've set up payroll as well. For example, suppose that your company didn't have a 401(k) plan when you originally set up payroll but later decided to add one. The Payroll Setup Wizard makes implementing this change easy. Similarly, you can set up payroll and then decide to track vacation and sick leave. See Chapter 19 for information on setting up a 401(k) plan; you use the same basic technique to set up vacation and sick leave that you use to establish a 401(k) plan.

The Payroll Setup Wizard asks you for the General Ledger account numbers that you intend to use for payroll. If you base your Chart of Accounts on one of the standard companies when you create your company, the Payroll Setup Wizard suggests payroll accounts. If you haven't defined payroll accounts when the wizard asks for them, you can define them on the fly. Refer to Chapter 3 for details on setting up accounts.

Some people create separate payroll liability accounts for each payroll tax liability. To make your life easier when using Peachtree, we recommend that you create payroll liability accounts that correspond to the taxing authorities you pay. For example, you pay FIT, FICA, and Medicare to the same taxing authority, so set up only one payroll liability account for all three taxes. If you pay state and local taxes to the same taxing authority, set up only one liability account for state and local taxes. Check with your accountant if you're unsure. We recommend this approach because it makes writing your payroll tax liability checks easier.

To start the Payroll Setup Wizard, follow these steps:

1. **Choose Maintain➪Default Information➪Payroll Setup Wizard.**

   The Peachtree Payroll Solutions window appears, listing the options available to process payroll in Peachtree.

2. **Click the Payroll Setup Wizard link on the left side of the screen.**

   The first screen of the Payroll Setup Wizard appears, on which you select an in-house solution. You can select

   • *Peachtree Payroll Tax Update (to subscribe to the service)*

   If you have already subscribed to the Payroll Tax Update service, select the Check This Box If You Have Already Ordered the Tax Service check box.

   • *Payroll Tax Information Will Be Manually Maintained*

3. **Select an option and then click Next.**

   The Initial Payroll Setup screen appears (see Figure 4-5).

4. **Fill in the necessary information in the Initial Payroll Setup screen.**

   a. *Select the state in which you pay most of your employees.*

   Depending on the state you select, Peachtree may ask you for a locality and locality rate.

b. Provide your unemployment compensation rate as a percentage.

When you enter rates into Peachtree, you must express them as percentages, but many state forms express rates in decimals. For example, suppose the state form shows that your unemployment rate is 0.008. That's a decimal. To express it as a percentage (0.8%), you'd type **0.8** into Peachtree. Yeah, entering these numbers requires that high school math stuff, where you have to multiply a decimal by 100 to get the percentage equivalent. Yeah, yeah, yeah. . . .

c. Indicate whether you record employee meals and tips.

If you choose to record meals and tips, Peachtree tracks the amounts for reporting and tax calculation, but it won't post any entries to the General Ledger. For more information on recording meals and tips, refer to IRS Publication 15, Circular E, Employer's Tax Guide. You can download a copy of Circular E at the Web site of the IRS:

```
http://www.irs.gov/formspubs
```

d. Identify default General Ledger accounts.

5. **Click Next.**

   The 401(k) Setup screen appears. We'll assume that you don't have a 401(k) plan in place; if you do, see Chapter 19 for details on setting up Peachtree to support your plan.

6. **Select the Not Offered option and click Next.**

   The Vacation and Sick Time Tracking Setup screen appears. We'll assume that you don't want to track vacation and sick leave.

7. **Select the Vacation Time Not Tracked option and the Sick Time Not Tracked option and click Next.**

   The final screen of the wizard appears.

8. **Click Finish.**

   The Payroll Setup Wizard creates general employee defaults for you.

Establishing general employee defaults

After you run the Payroll Setup Wizard, you can change the payroll settings from the Employee Defaults dialog box (choose Maintain⇨Default Information⇨Employees). You can use the General tab to change your state or set a locality if necessary and to establish custom fields for storing miscellaneous information about each employee. To make a custom field available, select the Enabled check box next to the field. You also can decide whether you want to display employees' names First Name First or Last Name First.

Peachtree automatically assigns payroll fields to the various boxes on the W-2 form, employee-paid taxes, or employer-paid taxes. You can, however, edit the assignments by clicking the appropriate button in the Assign Payroll Fields For section.

Setting pay levels

Pay levels are names you set for various types of hourly and salary pay. Choose Maintain⊅Default Information⊅Employees and click the Pay Levels tab. By default, Peachtree automatically establishes the pay levels that appear on the tab. Hourly wage pay levels appear on the left, and salary pay levels appear on the right.

You can create up to 20 hourly pay levels and 20 salary pay levels, and you can assign different pay levels to different General Ledger accounts. Just type the name for the pay level in the Field Name list and assign the pay level to a GL account.

You can override these defaults as necessary when you set up your employees. For example, suppose that you need to keep track of wages by department. You can set the default GL account to the department with the largest number of employees and then, on an individual employee record, change it to the GL account of the department for that employee.

To make your General Ledger and income statement more meaningful, your accountant may want you to use a different set of pay levels, pointing some or all pay levels to different General Ledger accounts. For example, you can use pay levels based on your workers' compensation categories as one method of letting Peachtree help you determine your workers' compensation liability.

Employee fields and employer fields

Peachtree categorizes the payroll fields created by the Payroll Setup Wizard into employee-related fields or employer-related fields. On the EmployEE Fields tab (see Figure 4-6), you see payroll fields belonging to employees. These include FIT and the employee's share of Social Security (FICA) and Medicare. On the EmployER Fields tab, you can view payroll fields paid by the company, including Federal Unemployment Tax (FUTA), state unemployment taxes, and the employer's share of FICA and Medicare. You can see the General Ledger account and payroll tax table Peachtree associated with each of the fields.

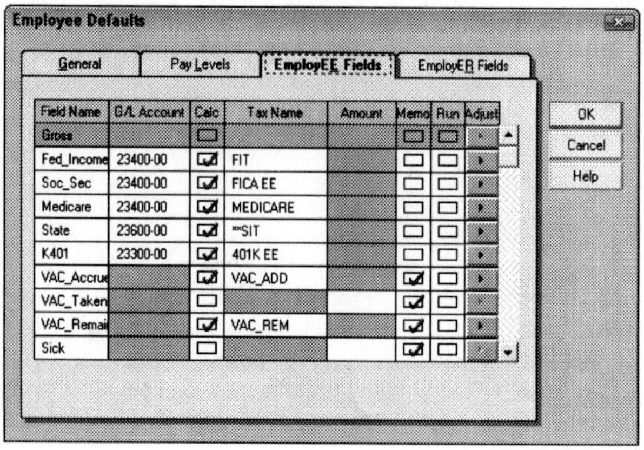

Figure 4-6:
On the
EmployEE
tab, you see
payroll
fields
belonging to
employees.

On the EmployEE Fields tab, you can do the following:

- ✔ Change the GL account for a payroll field.

- ✔ Change the tax table Peachtree uses to calculate a particular payroll field. Click in the Tax Name column to display a lookup list button that enables you to choose from a list of available tax tables.

- ✔ In the Memo column, select a check box next to a field, such as Tips, to tell Peachtree to calculate that field without updating your General Ledger or including the amounts in employees' pay. Note that Peachtree can use fields marked as memos to calculate taxes.

- ✔ Place a check in the Run column next to a field to tell Peachtree *not* to set the balance for this field to zero at the end of the payroll year. For example, if you allow your employees to retain unused vacation from year to year, set up your Vacation field by selecting the Run check box.

- ✔ For fields that Peachtree calculates, you can click the Adjust button beside the field to display the Calculate Adjusted Gross dialog box and check the fields you want Peachtree to add when calculating Adjusted Gross Wages. For example, you may want Adjusted Gross Wages to include gross wages, FICA, and Medicare, but *not* FIT when calculating an auto expense deduction.

- ✔ For fields that Peachtree doesn't calculate using a tax table, you can supply a default amount. For example, if most employees pay the same amount for medical insurance, you can type that amount in the Amount column, and on the individual employee's records, supply the appropriate amount for employees who don't pay the standard amount.

  If you're entering an amount you want deducted, enter it as a negative amount.

Although you're allowed to edit the names of payroll fields, *don't* change the name of a payroll field and *don't* change the order of the payroll fields after you enter payroll transactions. You'll get inaccurate information on the payroll earnings reports and W-2 forms. We recommend that you retain the names of payroll fields Peachtree creates for you because they are often used in payroll tax tables.

On the EmployER Fields tab, you can set these preferences:

✔ Change the General Ledger Liability and Expense accounts for a payroll field.

✔ Change the tax table that Peachtree uses to calculate a particular payroll field. Click in the Tax Name column to display the lookup list button and then select from a list of available tax tables.

✔ For fields that Peachtree calculates, you can click the Adjust button beside the field to display the Calculate Adjusted Gross dialog box and check the fields you want Peachtree to include when calculating Adjusted Gross Wages.

The same warning applies to EmployER field names that applies to EmployEE field names. *Don't* change the name of a payroll field and *don't* change the order of the payroll fields after you enter payroll transactions. These alterations create inaccurate information on the payroll earnings reports and W-2 forms. And the names of payroll fields are often used in payroll tax tables.

Setting Inventory Preferences

Before you start filling your virtual shelves in Peachtree, you need to set up the preferences that help track all those wonderful items as they come and go. *Inventory items,* in Peachtree terms, are typically things that you buy from vendors or sell to customers. It's important to understand that Peachtree inventory items don't necessarily have to be things that you keep on hand or that add value to the balance sheet. The item class of the inventory item determines whether it adds value to your balance sheet. In the "Inventory items and General Ledger accounts" section later in this chapter, you can read about item classes.

You can set preferences for inventory items by using the Inventory Item Defaults dialog box, which you open by choosing Maintain⇨Default Information⇨Inventory Items. The dialog box contains six tabs. On the General tab, you can specify whether to permit duplicate values in the UPC/SKU field and in the Part Number field of inventory items. Read on to find out about the other defaults you can set.

Inventory items and ordering defaults

The Ordering tab of the Inventory Item Defaults dialog box, as shown in Figure 4-7, helps you control issues related to, well, ordering inventory items. For example, you can choose to have Peachtree include items on purchase orders when it calculates the quantity available.

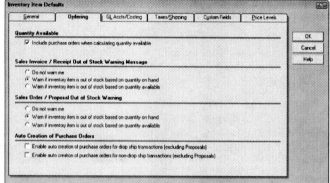

Figure 4-7:
Use the
Ordering tab
to set
ordering
defaults.

You can have Peachtree display an Out of Stock warning when you're entering a sales order, an invoice, or a receipt for an inventory item that is out of stock based on either the quantity on hand or the quantity available.

In the last section of the Ordering tab, you can enable the auto-creation of purchase orders for drop-ship transactions and non–drop-ship transactions. If you enable real-time posting and assign a preferred vendor to each inventory item, Peachtree automatically creates purchase orders for you when you convert a drop-ship quote to a sales order or to an invoice. Peachtree also creates purchase orders when you enter a drop-ship sales order or a drop-ship invoice containing inventory items.

If your transactions are not drop-ship transactions, you can have Peachtree automatically create purchase orders for you when the quantity of an item you specify causes the quantity available as of the transaction date to fall below the minimum stock levels you set for the item. Again, for this feature to work, you must enable real-time posting and assign a preferred vendor to each inventory item.

See Chapter 5 for details on automatically creating purchase orders and Chapter 7 for details on drop shipments.

Inventory items and General Ledger accounts

Peachtree uses *item classes* to organize inventory items. You assign each inventory item to a class when you create the item. You can choose the various accounts affected by inventory items in each of these item classes. For stock, master stock, and assembly items, you can also choose an inventory method. Chapter 11 includes information on how to create inventory items.

For the purpose of setting defaults, an item's class determines how Peachtree records the cost of the item.

All 11 of the item classes available in Peachtree Premium and higher appear in the following list. Peachtree Complete supports nine of these item classes, Peachtree Pro supports six of these item classes, and Peachtree First supports four of these item classes.

- ✔ **Stock:** For inventory items that you track for quantities, average costs, vendors, low stock points, and so on.

    In many cases an item class cannot be changed, so choose carefully. For example, when you assign an item to the Stock item class, you can't change the item's class. To change the item class, you must mark the item inactive and then create a new item with the proper item class.

- ✔ **Master Stock:** For items that consist of information shared by a number of substock items. For example, you might sell blue jeans, which consist of a number of attributes, such as size and style (straight leg, relaxed fit, classic fit, and so on). After you create a master stock item and define its attributes, Peachtree automatically generates substock items based on the attributes of the master stock item.

- ✔ **Serialized Stock:** Available only in Peachtree Premium or higher. Use this item class when the inventory items have serial numbers that you plan to track.

- ✔ **Non-stock:** For items that you sell but do not put into your inventory, such as service contracts. Peachtree prints quantities, descriptions, and unit prices on invoices but doesn't track quantities on hand. You must assign a Cost of Sales GL account, but it's not affected by a costing method.

- ✔ **Description Only:** When you track nothing but the description. For example, you can add comments to sales or purchase transactions by using description-only items.

- ✔ **Service:** For services you can apply to your GL salary and wages account to bill a customer for services provided by your employees.

✔ **Labor:** For third-party labor costs that you pass on to a customer. You can apply these costs to your GL salary and wages account and set the GL Cost Sales account to a Cost of Sales account for third-party labor.

✔ **Assembly:** For items that consist of components that must be built or dismantled.

✔ **Serialized Assembly:** Available only in Peachtree Premium or higher. Use this item class for assembly items that also have serial numbers.

✔ **Activity:** Available only in Peachtree Complete or higher. When using the Time & Billing feature, this item records how time is spent when performing services for a customer or job.

✔ **Charge:** Available only in Peachtree Complete or higher. When using the Time & Billing feature, this item records the expenses of an employee or vendor when working for a customer or job.

See Chapter 10 for more information on the Time & Billing feature.

Follow these steps to set or review the account assignments for the inventory item classes:

1. **Choose Maintain⇨Default Information⇨Inventory Items.**

   Peachtree displays the Inventory Item Defaults dialog box.

2. **Click the GL Accts/Costing tab.**

3. **Move the mouse pointer over any white box to see the lookup list mouse pointer (as shown in the margin), and then click to display the lookup list button, as shown in Figure 4-8.**

Lookup List button

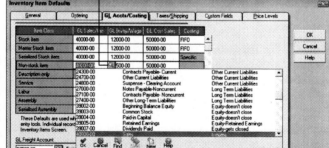

Figure 4-8: Set the default accounts for your inventory items.

Peachtree displays a list of your available accounts.

4. **Click the account you want to use.**

5. **Repeat Steps 3 and 4 as necessary in any white box in this dialog box to change an Item Class GL account assignment.**

6. **In the Costing column, choose FIFO, LIFO, or Average as your costing method.**

   Check with your accountant to help choose the correct method for your business. Just so you know what we're talking about, turn to the sidebar in Chapter 11.

7. **If necessary, change the GL Freight Account using Steps 3 and 4.**

   You use the GL Freight Account to assign freight charges to an invoice.

8. **When you're finished, click OK or click another tab and read the related information in the next section.**

Taxes and shipping

Ah, taxes. The government needs to get its cut when you sell something — and so, when appropriate, you must collect sales tax and pass it on to your state's taxing agency. Like you would expect with anything connected with the government, sales taxes are not straightforward. The government requires that you charge tax on some things but not other things. To take that concept a step further, some organizations (notably governmental and charitable agencies) don't pay taxes. And, of course, it's up to you — the seller — to keep straight who pays tax and for what.

If necessary, choose Maintain⇨Default Information⇨Inventory Items to display the Inventory Item Defaults dialog box. Click the Taxes/Shipping tab. On the left side of the Taxes/Shipping tab, you can define up to 25 item tax types. (You have our sympathy if you need all of them.) You use item tax types to organize the sales taxes that you remit and report to your state sales tax agency. Typically, you want to set up item tax types that match the categories that you must report on your state's sales tax return.

After you establish item tax types, you assign an item tax type to each inventory item you create — see Chapter 11 for more information. When you sell the item, Peachtree notes the item tax type. When you pay your sales tax, you use a report that segregates your sales by item tax type. So that's why you want to set up item tax types that match the categories you report on your state sales tax return. See Chapter 7 for information on setting up sales taxes and Chapter 6 for information on paying sales taxes.

You also can use the right side of the Taxes/Shipping tab to create up to ten shipping methods. Remember that shipping methods don't have anything to do with inventory items; you assign shipping methods to customers and vendors. The shipping methods you assign appear on quotes, sales orders, invoices, purchases, and purchase orders. Find out more about setting up vendors in Chapter 5 and setting up customers in Chapter 7.

Custom fields

Although you don't assign shipping methods to inventory items, you may assign custom fields to inventory items — for example, you may want to store alternate vendors in custom fields. Choose Maintain⇨Default Information⇨Inventory and click the Custom Fields tab. In the Enabled column, select the check box next to each custom field that you want to use and then type the name of the custom field in the Field Labels text box.

Price levels

Peachtree Complete and higher support multiple prices — price levels, so to speak — that can be calculated for inventory items. You can set up to ten price levels for each inventory item, assigning an easy-to-remember level name such as Retail, Wholesale, and Discount5 (for Discounted 5%), and then use the various price levels to establish pricing schemes. For example, you might establish Price Level 1 as your full retail price, Price Level 2 as a 5% discount off the retail price, and Price Level 3 as a 10% discount off the retail price. You start by identifying which of the ten price levels you want to use on the Price Levels tab of the Inventory Item Defaults dialog box, as shown in Figure 4-9. To use a price level, select the check box in the Enabled column next to the price level.

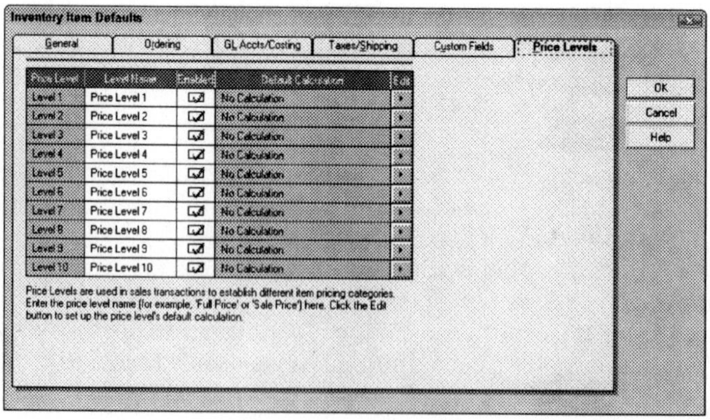

Figure 4-9: Identify the price levels you want to use by selecting the check boxes in the Enabled column.

Inventory Item Defaults					
General	Ordering	GL Accts/Costing	Taxes/Shipping	Custom Fields	Price Levels

Price Level	Level Name	Enabled	Default Calculation	Edit	
Level 1	Price Level 1	☑	No Calculation	▸	
Level 2	Price Level 2	☑	No Calculation	▸	
Level 3	Price Level 3	☑	No Calculation	▸	
Level 4	Price Level 4	☑	No Calculation	▸	
Level 5	Price Level 5	☑	No Calculation	▸	
Level 6	Price Level 6	☑	No Calculation	▸	
Level 7	Price Level 7	☑	No Calculation	▸	
Level 8	Price Level 8	☑	No Calculation	▸	
Level 9	Price Level 9	☑	No Calculation	▸	
Level 10	Price Level 10	☑	No Calculation	▸	

Price Levels are used in sales transactions to establish different item pricing categories. Enter the price level name (for example, 'Full Price' or 'Sale Price') here. Click the Edit button to set up the price level's default calculation.

OK

Cancel

Help

You also can set default price calculations for each price level. The calculation can be based on the last cost of an item or on Price Level 1. After selecting the basis for the calculation, you can increase or decrease the price by either a percentage or an amount. You set default price calculations by clicking the button in the Edit column next to the appropriate price level. Peachtree displays the Default Price Level Calculation dialog box (see Figure 4-10).

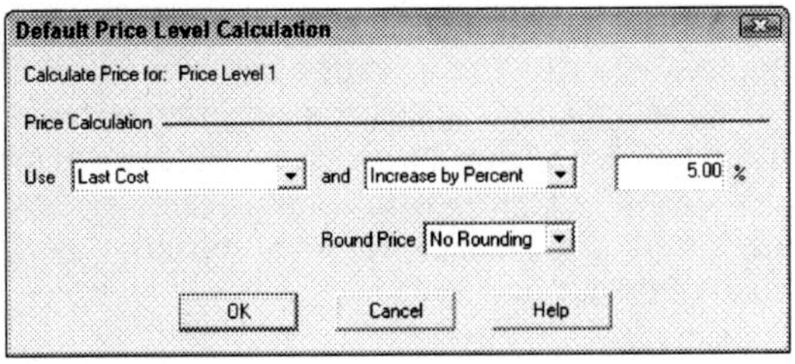

Figure 4-10:
Use this
dialog box
to establish
a calculation
for a price
level.

The calculations you establish in the Inventory Item Defaults dialog box are the defaults for all items. You also can establish a selling price for each individual item by using the Maintain Inventory Items window. Any prices you establish for an individual item override prices you set in the Inventory Item Defaults dialog box. See Chapter 11 for details.

The price level feature is powerful. Even after you establish defaults and then override them by setting price levels for individual items, you can override individual item price levels on invoices as you create them. See Chapter 7 for more information.

Peachtree also enables you to assign price levels directly to customers; suppose, for example, that you always discount all merchandise for a particular customer to Price Level 3. In the Maintain Customers/Prospects window, you can assign a customer to Price Level 3 so that all items on all invoices for the customer default to Price Level 3. Again, see Chapter 7 for more information.

You're probably wondering about how to change prices. After all, nothing stays the same price forever (unfortunately). Yes, you can easily raise (or lower, if you are so inclined) prices without editing individual items. See Chapter 11 for more information.

Setting Preferences for Printing Statements and Invoices

You can control the information printed on statements and invoices; you set these preferences by choosing Maintain⇨Default Information⇨Statement/Invoices.

Suppose, for example, that you don't use preprinted invoices or statements but you do want your company's name, address, and phone numbers to appear on the top of the invoice or statement. In the Statement/Invoices Defaults dialog box, as shown in Figure 4-11, simply select the last check box to print your company's name, address, and phone numbers as they appear in the Maintain Company Information window.

Figure 4-11: Use this dialog box to control the information that prints on invoices and statements.

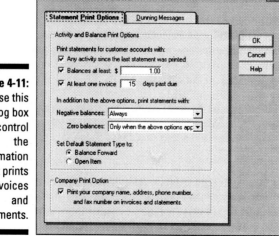

Use the rest of the fields on the Statement Print Options tab to control which customers are selected when Peachtree prints statements:

✔ **If you select the Any Activity Since the Last Statement Was Printed check box,** Peachtree prints a statement for any customer who has purchased something from you since the last time you printed statements.

✔ **If you select the Balances At Least check box** and supply a minimum balance number, Peachtree prints statements for customers with balances equal to or greater than the minimum balance.

✔ **If you select the At Least One Invoice X Days Past Due check box** and then type a number of days overdue, Peachtree prints statements for any customers who have an invoice overdue by at least the number of days you entered.

✔ **Use the Negative Balances list** to specify whether Peachtree should print statements for customers with credit balances — the people to whom you owe money. You can choose Always, Never, or Only When the Above Options Apply.

✔ **Use the Zero Balances list** to specify whether Peachtree should print statements for customers whose balance is $0. You can choose Always, Never, or Only When the Above Options Apply.

Strangely enough, these check boxes are yes-or-no questions, but the check boxes in this section of the dialog box work together. If a customer meets *any* condition that you have selected, Peachtree prints a statement. For example, suppose that you select the Any Activity Since the Last Statement Was Printed check box and also the Balances At Least check box, and you supply $1.00 as the minimum balance. Peachtree prints statements for all customers who have bought something from you *and* all customers whose balance is greater than $1.00. So, even if you do not want customers with $0 balances, Peachtree prints statements for those customers if they bought something and paid for it. Be sure to examine the logic of all the check boxes you choose to select.

Peachtree can print *balance forward* statements, similar to the way information appears on a MasterCard or Visa credit card bill, where an invoice appears only once on a statement, and its balance subsequently becomes part of the Previous Balance line. Or Peachtree can print open item statements, where all outstanding invoices — the ones that aren't paid in full — appear on the statement.

Using the Dunning Messages tab, you can specify four gentle or not-so-gentle reminders to appear on statements that an account may be overdue. You enter each message and then determine the invoices on which it will appear by entering a number of days overdue. The message that appears on a customer statement depends on the length of time a customer's account is overdue; Peachtree displays the message associated with the customer's oldest overdue invoice.

Don't forget to visit www.dummies.com/go/peachtreefd for more information on Peachtree.

Part II
The Daily Drudge

"Well, shoot! This eggplant chart is just as confusing as the butternut squash chart and the gourd chart. Can't you just make a pie chart like everyone else?"

In this part . . .

Data entry. It's a dirty job, but somebody has to do it. Whether you handle the day-to-day accounting responsibilities associated with your business or have someone in your office do them for you, you'll find this part valuable.

In this part, we show you how to keep up with tasks such as billing your customers and collecting money from them, purchasing and paying for goods and services used in your business, and paying employees. We also cover job costing and time and billing tasks.

Chapter 5

Buying Goods

● ◆ ●

In This Chapter

▶ Setting up vendors

▶ Tracking goods with purchase orders

▶ Entering a vendor bill

▶ Receiving inventory

▶ Getting credit for returns

● ◆ ●

*B*uying things is part of doing business. Some businesses buy goods from vendors and keep them in inventory to resell to customers. Some businesses buy goods to use in the manufacturing of a product to sell to customers. And all businesses buy the goods and services that they use to stay in business, such as office supplies and utilities.

So, no matter how you look at it, you can expect to receive bills in the mail. Paying bills isn't fun, of course, but at least Peachtree can make the process easier and save you time — time you can spend earning more money.

This chapter describes the typical actions you take to record and track vendors' bills.

Terminology alert: Peachtree tends to switch back and forth between two terms when referring to bills that vendors send you: a *purchase* and an *invoice.* For the sake of clarity, we call it a purchase unless the window on-screen calls it an invoice. For our purposes, invoices are things you send to customers so that *you* can get paid.

Working with Vendors

If you buy goods or services from a particular vendor on a regular basis, you can save time in the long run if you set up that vendor in Peachtree. In fact, if you *don't* set up the vendor, you'll find it difficult to track how much you spend with that vendor. There — you have two good reasons to set up vendors with whom you do business on a regular basis.

Adding vendors

When you set up a vendor, you supply name and address information, a Purchase account to use each time you record a purchase from the vendor, and custom field information. You also can view historical information about your purchases from the vendor for the previous 12 months.

To add a new vendor, follow these steps:

1. **Choose Maintain⇨Vendors.**

   Peachtree displays the Maintain Vendors window (see Figure 5-1).

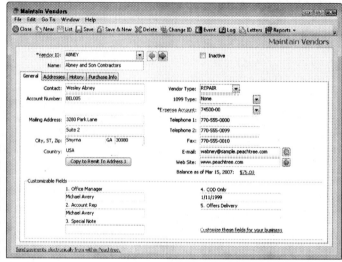

Figure 5-1:
Use this window to add, edit, or delete vendors.

2. **Fill in the Vendor ID and the Name field.**

   The ID is the number you use to select the vendor when you want to record a purchase or payment, so try to make it meaningful. The ID can be up to 20 characters and numbers long and is *not* case sensitive. By default, Peachtree sorts the vendor list and reports by the vendor ID, and numbers sort before letters. To get Peachtree to sort the vendor list in alphabetical order by default, use characters from the vendor's name as the ID.

3. **On the General tab, fill in contact information — your account number with the vendor and the vendor's address and phone numbers.**

   The account number you supply appears by default on checks you print from the Payment window. Find out more about the Payment window in Chapter 6.

4. **If you mail your payments to the address you supplied in Step 3, click the Copy to Remit To Address 1 button.**

   If you don't mail your payments to the address Peachtree displays by default, see the next step.

5. **If you need to store more than one address for the vendor, click the Addresses tab and enter the addresses, one per line.**

   You can store up to 20 Remit To addresses and you can select the default address for payments, purchase orders, and shipments.

6. **Use the Vendor Type field to group similar vendors together.**

   For example, you may want to distinguish between vendors who supply you with inventory and vendors who provide overhead services such as telephone. The text you enter in the Vendor Type field can be up to eight characters long; note that this field *is* case sensitive. Entering a vendor type is useful because you can limit some reports to specific vendor types.

7. **If appropriate, identify the vendor's 1099 type by selecting an option from the 1099 Type drop-down list.**

   According to IRS rules, you must issue a 1099 to a vendor who is an independent contractor if the contractor is not incorporated and you pay $600 or more per year to that vendor. Peachtree can print 1099s at the end of the year for vendors that you designate as 1099 vendors. Sales representatives might be considered 1099 vendors, based on the IRS definition of employees and independent contractors. If you have Peachtree Complete or higher, you can filter several Peachtree reports by 1099 Type; see Chapter 14 for more information on printing and filtering reports. See Chapter 9 for more on paying sales representatives who are also employees.

8. **In the Expense Account list, select the account.**

   Select the account that you'll typically assign to purchases from this vendor. You can override this account as needed when you enter purchases.

9. **If appropriate, supply an e-mail and a Web address for the vendor.**

   Both e-mail and Web addresses are interactive — if you supply an e-mail address and then click the icon next to the E-mail field, Peachtree opens your e-mail program and starts a message to the vendor. Similarly, clicking the button next to the Web Site field launches your browser and directs it to the vendor's Web site.

   To generate e-mail messages from within Peachtree, you must have a MAPI-compliant, default e-mail application installed on your computer. If your default e-mail system is AOL, you won't be able to send e-mail alerts from Peachtree because AOL is not a fully MAPI-compliant e-mail application.

MAPI is one of those techno acronyms and refers to a method by which programs like Peachtree can initiate e-mail messages. If you're not sure if your e-mail program is MAPI compliant, just click the e-mail icon. You'll either see a gobbledygook message about MAPI, or you'll have a blank e-mail cued up for you.

10. **In the Customizable Fields section, fill in the information you established in the Vendor Default dialog box.**

11. **Click the History tab, which shows you (after you begin to record transactions for the vendor) your total payments and purchases involving that vendor for each period.**

    You review information here instead of entering it.

12. **Click the Beginning Balances button.**

    Peachtree displays the Vendor Beginning Balances window, where you can enter, one per line, unpaid bills you received from vendors before you started using Peachtree. Click the Add button; then, for each bill, supply the vendor's invoice number, the date you received it, any purchase order number associated with it, and the amount. If you use the accrual method for your company, select an Accounts Payable (A/P) account.

    The total of the beginning balances you enter for all vendors must equal the total amount you entered for all Accounts Payable accounts when you set up your General Ledger beginning balances.

13. **Click the Purchase Info tab (see Figure 5-2).**

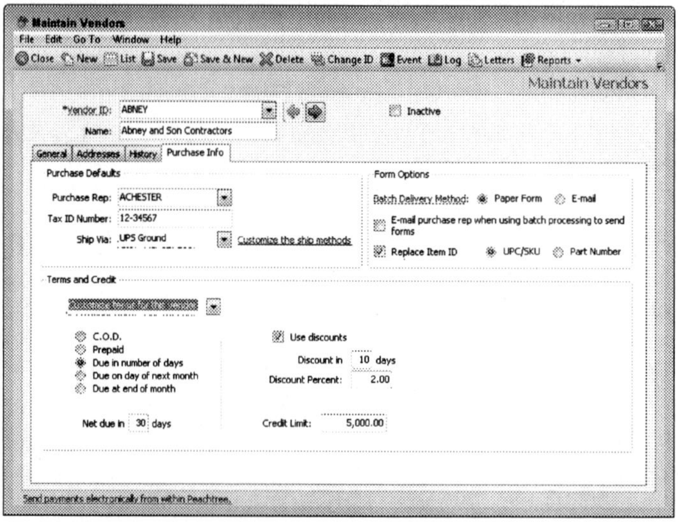

Figure 5-2:
This figure shows the fields that become available after you choose to customize a vendor's terms.

a. *Select a default purchase representative.*

An employee can serve as a purchase representative.

b. *If the vendor is a 1099 vendor, supply the vendor's tax ID number.*

The tax ID number eventually appears on the 1099.

c. *Select a shipment method and terms.*

You need to select a default Ship Via method and terms only if — for the vendor you're creating — they differ from the defaults you established in the Vendor Defaults dialog box. (See Chapter 4 for details on global default purchase settings.) To change the default terms, open the drop-down list under Terms and Credit and choose Customize Terms for This Vendor. Peachtree displays the various terms methods and the options for each.

d. *Select form options for the vendor.*

In the Form Options area, you can choose to e-mail forms (such as purchase orders) to vendors or print them and mail them. Regardless of the form delivery method you select, you can e-mail a copy of the form to the purchase representative whenever you e-mail the form to the vendor or whenever you prepare forms in batches. To prepare forms in batches, select the form from the Select a Report or Form window. Also regardless of the form delivery method you select, you can choose to replace, on purchase orders, the item ID number you assign in Peachtree with the item's UPC/SKU number or part number.

14. **Click the Save button (as shown in the margin) to save the vendor information or the Save & New button (also shown in the margin) to save the information and create another new vendor.**

Changing vendor information

You can change any information you enter about a vendor, including the vendor ID. If you need to make a change to a vendor's information, follow these steps:

1. **Choose Maintain⇨Vendors.**

2. **Type a few letters of the vendor ID or click the arrow next to the drop-down list to display a list of vendors.**

3. **Highlight the vendor you want to change and then click OK.**

The information you saved previously for the vendor appears.

4. **Click the tab containing the information that you want to change.**

5. **Make the change(s).**

6. **If you need to change the vendor ID, click the Change ID toolbar button, as shown in the margin.**

   Peachtree displays the Change Vendor ID dialog box. Type a new ID in the New Vendor ID field and then click OK. Peachtree changes the vendor ID.

7. **Click the Save button.**

Viewing vendor history

After you record purchases and payments for vendors, Peachtree tracks these transactions by month. Choose Maintain⇨Vendors to open the Maintain Vendors window. Type the vendor ID or select your choice from the drop-down list and then click the History tab to view a history of your activity with the vendor.

"De-activating" a vendor

If a vendor has gone out of business or you decide that you just don't want to do business with a particular vendor, you can change the vendor's status to inactive. After you make a vendor record inactive, Peachtree displays a warning if you try to buy something from the vendor.

Although you see a Delete button in the Maintain Vendor window, you can't delete a vendor unless no transactions exist for the vendor. You know, you put somebody in and then realize you don't want them after all — and you haven't recorded any transactions. *Then* you can display that vendor on-screen and click Delete. Otherwise, to get rid of a vendor, you must first make the vendor inactive. After closing a fiscal year, you can purge inactive vendors so that they don't appear in lists. See Chapter 17 for information on closing a fiscal year and purging.

To make a vendor inactive, choose Maintain⇨Vendors to open the Maintain Vendors window. In the Vendor ID field, select the vendor you want to make inactive. After the vendor appears on-screen, select the Inactive check box beside the Vendor ID field and then click the Save button. The vendor is now inactive. If you need to reactivate the vendor, deselect the Inactive check box.

An inactive vendor doesn't appear in lists if you decide to hide inactive records when you set the global options. You can find out how to hide inactive records in Bonus Chapter 1 on this book's Web site, www.dummies.com/go/peachtreefd.

Working with Purchase Orders

A *purchase order* is a document you use to request merchandise from a vendor. When you enter a purchase order, Peachtree doesn't actually affect any of your accounts. That doesn't happen until you receive the merchandise — or, if you're using cash-based accounting, when you pay the vendor.

Peachtree takes note of the transactions. That is, you can print reports that show you the accounts that the purchase orders *will* affect when they are filled. However, the purchase orders don't actually update the accounts when you save the purchase orders.

Entering purchase orders

"If a purchase order doesn't affect any of my accounts, why use it?" you ask. Well, you don't *need* to use purchase orders; Peachtree operates correctly if you don't use them. Most people use purchase orders as reminders, particularly when ordering inventory, because the purchase order shows the items that you've ordered but not yet received. Others use purchase orders for non-inventory items, such as office supplies or contract labor, to help track expected expenses.

Purchase orders provide you with a great way of remaining organized so that nothing slips through the cracks. You can use the Purchase Order report to help you stay on top of things. And we're great fans of being organized!

You can't enter purchase orders in Peachtree unless you've set up a vendor, but you can set up a vendor while working in the Purchase Orders window.

To enter a purchase order, follow these steps:

1. **Choose Tasks⇨Purchase Orders.**

   Peachtree displays the Purchase Orders window (see Figure 5-3).

   You can customize the appearance of the Purchase Orders window to better suit your needs; if you change these settings, your window won't look exactly the same as the window you see in Figure 5-3. See Bonus Chapter 1 on this book's Web site, www.dummies.com/go/peachtreefd, for more information.

2. **Type the vendor ID in the Vendor ID field or click the lookup list button, as shown here in the margin, beside the Vendor ID field to select the vendor from your list of vendors.**

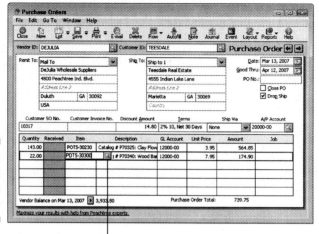

Figure 5-3:
A typical
purchase
order.

Lookup List button

If you need to add a vendor, click the lookup list button and then click the New button in the lookup list window. Peachtree displays the Maintain Vendors window. Refer to the earlier section in this chapter, "Adding vendors." Close the Maintain Vendors window after you save the vendor to return to the Purchase Orders window.

Peachtree fills in the vendor's name and the Remit To address. Your company's name also appears in the Ship To address field. At the bottom of the window, you see the vendor's current balance as of the system date, and you can click the button next to the balance to display a Vendor Ledger report of the purchases and payments that comprise the balance.

Click the Reports button, as shown here in the margin, on the window's toolbar to print any of the following reports for the selected vendor: Buyer report, Inventory Stock Status report, Items Purchased from Vendors report, Job Ledger report, or Vendor Ledgers report.

3. **If necessary, change the date of the purchase order. If you don't supply a date, Peachtree uses your computer's date.**

4. **Enter a date in the Good Thru field — the date after which the purchase order should not be filled.**

5. **In the PO No. field, type a number for the purchase order if you don't intend to print it but just want to save it.**

   If you intend to print the purchase order, leave the PO No. field blank, and Peachtree supplies a sequential purchase order number when you print the purchase order.

You can't use the same purchase order number more than once for a particular vendor. You can reuse a purchase order number as long as you assign it to a different vendor.

6. **If you intend to ship the goods directly to a customer, select the Drop Ship check box and select the correct customer and ship to address.**

   These fields appear only if you select the Drop Ship check box.

   Although you can change the A/P account, typically you shouldn't. Peachtree doesn't affect any of your accounts when you save the purchase order; however, when you later receive merchandise against the purchase order, Peachtree uses the account information on the purchase order to update your company's books.

7. **In the Quantity field, type the quantity you want to order.**

   For a whole number (such as three), type **3.0**. If you set global options to Automatic Decimal Entry and you type simply **3**, Peachtree assumes you want .03. See Bonus Chapter 1 on this book's Web site, www.dummies.com/go/peachtreefd, for details on setting global options.

8. **Click in the Item field.**

   The lookup list button appears. Click it to select the item you want to order from existing inventory items. Peachtree fills in the item description, the General Ledger account associated with the item, the item's unit price, and the amount (unit price times quantity).

   Read about setting up inventory items in Chapter 11. If you want to order something that you haven't set up as an inventory item, skip the Item field and fill in the Description, GL Account, and Unit Price fields. Peachtree calculates the amount. The Peachtree spell checker flags any spelling mistakes as they happen. See Bonus Chapter 1 at www.dummies.com/go/peachtreefd for more information on spell-checking options.

9. **If appropriate, click in the Job field to display the lookup list button and choose a job from the list.**

   If you're purchasing a stock item or an assembly item, you cannot assign it to a job. If you're purchasing any other type of item, however, you can assign it to a job. You also can assign the line to a job if you don't select any item from the Item list. Chapter 12 covers setting up and assigning job types.

10. **Repeat Steps 7–9 for each item you want to order from this vendor.**

11. **Click either the Save button or the Print button, as shown here in the margin.**

   If you want to continue entering purchase orders and then print them later in a group (or skip printing them altogether), click the Save button. Otherwise, click the Print button. To print your purchase orders in a group, read about printing forms in Chapter 13.

You can preview the purchase order before you print it by clicking the drop-down arrow on the Print button and selecting Preview.

But there's an easier way . . .

This feature is available only in Peachtree Complete and above.

In Chapter 4, where we discuss setting up inventory options, you can enable auto-creation of purchase orders for drop-ship and non–drop-ship transactions. If you enable these options and real-time posting, you can let Peachtree generate purchase orders for you, based on the information you supply when you define your inventory items. (See Chapter 11 for details on inventory items.)

To make this feature work, you need to assign a preferred vendor to each inventory item. To make the feature work well, you also need to supply a minimum stock quantity and a reorder quantity for each inventory item.

If you've already done these things, choose Tasks➪Select for Purchase Orders. The Select for Purchase Orders dialog box appears, as shown in Figure 5-4.

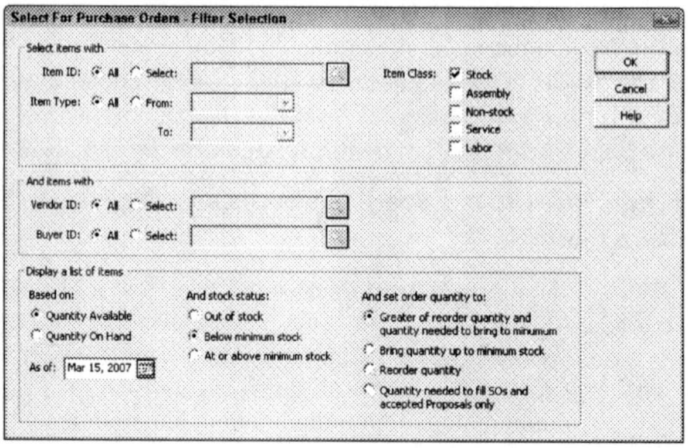

Figure 5-4:
Use the Select for Purchase Orders dialog box to identify the purchase orders that you want Peachtree to create for you.

In the Select for Purchase Orders dialog box, you set up the selection criteria that you want Peachtree to use to display a list of potential purchase orders to create:

✔ *In the Select Items With section of the dialog box*, you can choose which items to include by using the Item ID, Item Type, and Item Class options. For example, in the sample company we're using, you can select the All option for the Item ID, the Supply option for the Item Type, and the Stock option for the Item Class.

✔ *In the And Items With section*, you can narrow the selection by choosing only certain vendors or buyers. (Buyers are employees, and you identify buyers as well as vendors when you create inventory items; see Chapter 11 for details.)

✔ *In the Display a List of Items section*, you can indicate that you want Peachtree to select items to order based on the how many items are available or are on hand by selecting the Quantity Available or the Quantity On Hand options as of a particular date. You can also order based on the item's stock status. In the And Set Order Quantity To section, you can identify the quantity you want Peachtree to place on the purchase order(s) it suggests.

After you click OK, Peachtree displays the Select for Purchase Orders window shown in Figure 5-5, where you can review the proposed purchase orders and, if necessary, exclude any you don't want Peachtree to create by deselecting the check box in the Order column of the proposed purchase order.

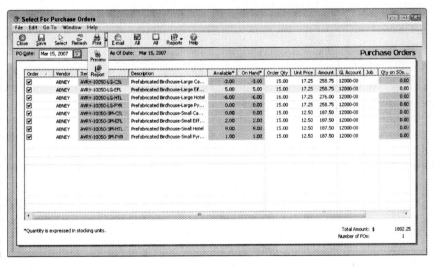

Figure 5-5: Use this window to select purchase orders that you want Peachtree to create for you.

You can make changes to the white columns of the purchase orders before Peachtree creates them. Click in the appropriate column and make your change. For example, you can select a different vendor or change the Order Qty or GL Account.

After you identify the purchases you want to create, you can preview them as they will appear to the vendor by clicking the drop-down arrow on the Print button (see Figure 5-5) and selecting Preview. If you want a hard copy of the Select for Purchase Orders window, click the drop-down arrow on the Print button and select Report.

To create purchase orders, click the Save button; if you prefer, you can click the Print button or the E-mail button. If you click the Print button, Peachtree prompts you to confirm the first purchase order number, prints the purchase orders and asks you to confirm that they printed properly. If you click Yes, Peachtree saves the purchase orders. If you click the E-mail button (shown in the margin), Peachtree displays a dialog box where you can assign a purchase order number (see Figure 5-6); after you click OK, your e-mail program displays the e-mail messages it will send to the vendors, including the purchase order in PDF format. After you send the messages, Peachtree displays a dialog box that asks you to confirm that the purchase orders e-mailed properly. If you click Yes, Peachtree saves the purchase orders.

Figure 5-6:
When you e-mail a purchase order, Peachtree prompts you to assign a purchase order number and select a purchase order form.

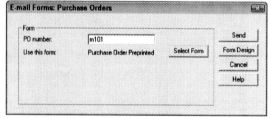

After you produce purchase orders from the Select for Purchase Orders window, you can click the Refresh button on the toolbar. Peachtree updates the information in the Quantity on POs column.

Editing and erasing purchase orders

You can change purchase orders, close purchase orders, and delete purchase orders. Good accounting practices say you shouldn't ever delete anything, but because a purchase order doesn't affect your accounts, the offense doesn't seem quite so serious. However, if you want to maintain an audit trail for canceled orders, simply close the purchase order. You close a purchase order by displaying it on-screen and selecting the Close PO check box.

You can change or remove items from purchase orders if you haven't yet received the items. If you know you'll never receive the items, you can close the purchase order. If the purchase order was simply a mistake and you haven't received any items listed on it, why not just erase it? To edit or delete a purchase order, choose Lists➪Vendors & Purchases➪Purchase Orders to display the Purchase Order List window (see Figure 5-7).

  You also can display this window while viewing the Purchase Orders window. Just click the List button (as shown here in the margin) on the toolbar.

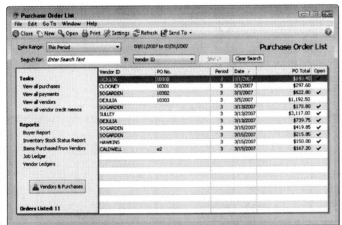

Figure 5-7:
Select a
purchase
order to
view.

You can edit any purchase order, whether it's open or closed. Look for the check mark in the Open column of the Purchase Order List window. If the Open column is blank, the purchase order is closed, meaning all the goods have been received and entered, or you got tired of waiting and canceled it.

  Select a purchase order to view and then click the Open button to display the purchase order in the Purchase Orders window. You can make any of the following modifications to the purchase order; after you finish, save the purchase order and then click the Close button on the toolbar, and Peachtree redisplays the Purchase Order List window:

✔ **Change the date entered in the Date or the Good Thru fields.**

✔ **Select a different shipping method from the Ship Via drop-down list.**

✔ **Enter a new amount in the Discount Amount field.**

✔ **Change displayed terms in the Terms field.**

✔ **Change the account number in the A/P Account field.**

✔ **Adjust the quantity you ordered on any line of the purchase order — even a line you've already received.**

Find out how to receive items that you order in the "Receiving goods against a purchase order" section, later in this chapter.

Remove

✔ **Remove any line if you have not received those items.**

Click anywhere in the line you want to delete and then click the Remove button, as shown here in the margin.

✔ **Close the purchase order.**

Select the Close PO check box that appears immediately below the PO No. field.

You cannot delete a purchase order if you have received any of the items listed on the purchase order; the Delete button appears grayed out (unavailable). If you know you'll *never* receive items remaining on a purchase order, close the purchase order.

Searching for transactions

The Purchase Order List window, like the other List windows in Peachtree, initially shows transactions for the current period. Using the Date Range drop-down list, you can select a different date range or period. If you change the date range, Peachtree displays information for the new date range next time you open the window.

If you prefer, you can search your company data for the transaction by using criteria that changes from List window to List window. In the Purchase Order List window, you can search for purchase orders by using vendor ID numbers; period; or purchase order dates, numbers, or totals. After you select a search criterion, type some information about the transaction into the

Search For box that matches the criterion you selected. The vendor ID number and purchase order dates, numbers, and totals are self-explanatory. If you choose period as your search criterion, set the Date Range box to All Transactions and enter the period number in the Search For box.

Finally, you can still search for transactions by using the Find Transactions window; see Bonus Chapter 1 on this book's Web site, www. dummies.com/go/peachtreefd, for details. In the same chapter, you also find information on customizing any List window to display the columns of information you prefer to see.

Entering Bills

Scenario: A vendor with whom you do business on a regular basis sends you a bill. (As we state earlier, remember that Peachtree uses the terms *purchase* and *invoice* interchangeably to represent a vendor bill.) You don't want to pay the bill immediately, but you *do* want to pay the bill in a timely manner. Enter the bill into Peachtree as a purchase, and Peachtree tracks the bill's age so that you pay it

✔ When it's still eligible for a discount

   or

✔ Before the vendor charges you a late fee.

Do you receive a bill on a regular basis from a vendor? Chapter 6 shows you how to create a recurring purchase or payment for things such as monthly utility bills or lease payments.

Purchasing without using a purchase order

Unlike purchase orders, purchases update your company's accounts. Whenever any transaction updates your company's books, at least two accounts are affected because of the double-entry bookkeeping concept that you can read about in Bonus Chapter 5.

Every purchase you enter automatically updates Accounts Payable. The other account Peachtree updates depends on whether you record a bill for an inventory item. If you select inventory items in the Purchases/Receive Inventory window, you tell Peachtree to update inventory for the other side of the transaction. If you don't select an inventory item, then you probably select an Expense account, such as your Telephone Expense account. In that case, Peachtree updates Accounts Payable and the Expense account.

Peachtree assumes that you wouldn't enter a bill from a vendor for merchandise without having first received the merchandise — and entering a bill for merchandise does update quantities on hand, so don't enter a bill until you receive the goods. You might, however, receive the goods without yet receiving the bill. In this second case, you enter a purchase and make sure that you select the Waiting on Bill check box.

If you're curious about the accounts Peachtree is updating (yes, *debiting* and *crediting*), read Chapter 17 to discover a neat way to find out what Peachtree is doing.

Peachtree assumes that you wouldn't bother to enter a bill from a vendor you use only occasionally; instead, you'd just pay that bill. Therefore, you can't enter purchases in Peachtree unless you've set up a vendor. For one-time or occasional purchases from vendors you don't expect to use often, use the Payments window to pay the bill directly. See Chapter 6 for more information on paying bills.

To enter a purchase (a vendor's bill) that doesn't reference a purchase order, follow these steps:

1. **Choose Tasks⇨Purchases/Receive Inventory.**

   Peachtree displays the Purchases/Receive Inventory window (see Figure 5-8).

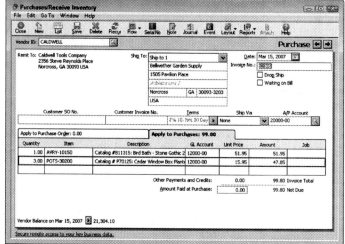

Figure 5-8: Use this window to record a bill from a vendor.

You can customize the appearance of the Purchases/Receive Inventory window to better suit your needs; if you do, the window won't look the same as the window you see in Figure 5-8. See Bonus Chapter 1 on this book's Web site, www.dummies.com/go/peachtreefd, for more information.

2. **Enter the vendor ID in the Vendor ID field or click the lookup list button and select a vendor from the list.**

   After you select a vendor, Peachtree fills in the vendor's name and Remit To address. Your company's name also appears in the Ship To address field. At the bottom of the window, you see the vendor's current balance as of the system date. You can click the button next to the balance to display a Vendor Ledger report of the purchases and payment that make up the balance.

   If you've previously entered purchase orders for this vendor, Peachtree displays the Apply to Purchase Order tab. If you want to receive goods against one of these POs, skip to the next section.

3. **In the Invoice No. field, type a number for the vendor's bill.**

   If you have vendors who don't provide you with an invoice number, your company might have a standard solution for this problem, such as entering a combination of the vendor ID plus the date or the primary PO number. This usually helps avoid duplications (but not always).

   You can't use an invoice number more than once for a particular vendor. You can reuse an invoice number as long as you assign it to a different vendor.

4. **If necessary, change the date of the purchase.**

   Yes, you can change the A/P account, but typically you shouldn't. Doing so can cause your accounts to get out of whack.

5. **In the Quantity field, type the quantity for which you're being billed.**

   For a whole number such as three, type **3.0**. If you set global options to Automatic Decimal Entry and you type simply **3**, Peachtree assumes that you want .03.

6. **You have two options for entering items that appear on the bill:**

   • If you're recording a bill for an item that you haven't and don't intend to set up as an inventory item, skip the Item field and just fill in the Description, GL Account, and Unit Price fields. By default, Peachtree flags any spelling mistakes as they happen. For more information on the Peachtree spell-checking options, see Bonus Chapter 1 on www.dummies.com/go/peachtreefd.

   • If you're recording a bill for an inventory item, select the item in the Item list. Peachtree fills in the Description, GL Account, the Unit Price, and the Amount (unit price times quantity) fields.

7. **If you're purchasing a serialized item, click the Serial No. button, as shown here in the margin.**

You can record serial numbers for inventory items if you're using Peachtree Premium or higher.

Peachtree displays the Serial Number Entry dialog box, as shown in Figure 5-9, where you can add the serial numbers of the items you're purchasing. Type the serial number for the first item and then click Add. Repeat the process for each serialized item you're purchasing. If the serial numbers are consecutive, select the Add Consecutive Serial Numbers check box and specify the number of items you're purchasing. After you finish, click OK.

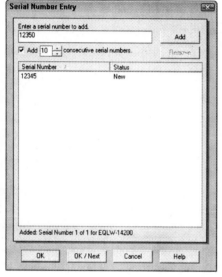

Figure 5-9:
Use this window to record serial numbers when you purchase serialized inventory items.

8. **Click in the Job field to display the lookup list button and choose a job from the list.**

   If you're purchasing a stock item or an assembly item (serialized or unserialized), you cannot assign it to a job. If you're purchasing any other type of item, however, you can assign it to a job. You can also assign the line to a job if you don't select an item from the Item list. You can read about setting up jobs in Chapter 12.

   If you assign a line to a job, Peachtree allows you to include it on a customer's bill as a reimbursable expense. Chapter 12 covers information about including reimbursable expenses on customer invoices.

9. **Repeat Steps 5–8 for each item you want to order or that appears on the bill you're recording.**

10. **Click the Save button to save the transaction.**

If you have a document on your computer related to the purchase you just created, you can attach the document to the purchase. Redisplay the purchase in the Purchases/Receive Inventory window and then click the Attach button. In the window that appears, click Add and then navigate to the document you want to attach. Click OK to close the Attachments window. From the Attachments window, you can print or rename the attachment. Renaming the attachment affects only the name shown in Peachtree, not the file name on your computer.

Receiving goods against a purchase order

Scenario: You order merchandise by using a purchase order, and the merchandise arrives. *Maybe* the bill comes with the merchandise, and *maybe* it doesn't. Either way, you need to update your company's accounts to reflect the receipt of the merchandise so that you know they're available to sell.

You use the Purchases/Receive Inventory window to receive goods against a purchase order. You can, simultaneously, indicate whether you received the bill. Follow these steps:

1. **Choose Tasks⇨Purchases/Receive Inventory.**

   Peachtree displays the Purchases/Receive Inventory window.

2. **Type the vendor ID in the Vendor ID field or click that handy magnifying glass to display the list of vendors.**

   After you select a vendor, Peachtree fills in the vendor's name and Remit To address. Your company's name also appears in the Ship To address field. At the bottom of the window, you see the vendor's current balance as of the system date. You can click the button next to the balance to display a Vendor Ledger report of the purchases and payment that make up the balance.

   You can print a variety of reports related to vendors and inventory by clicking the Reports button on the Purchases/Receive Inventory window toolbar.

   If you've previously entered purchase orders for this vendor, Peachtree displays the Apply to Purchase Order tab.

3. **On the Apply to Purchase Order No. tab, click the Apply to Purchase Order No. drop-down list and then select the PO number that lists the goods you ordered (see Figure 5-10).**

   Peachtree fills in the lines that appear on the purchase order.

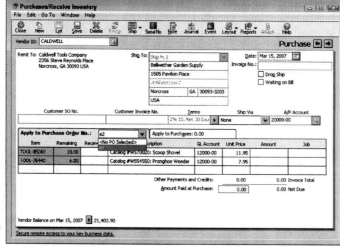

Figure 5-10:
The
Purchases/
Receive
Inventory
window
after you
enter POs
for the
vendor.

4. In the Invoice No. field at the top of the window, type a number for the vendor's bill.

You can't use an invoice number more than once for a particular vendor, so if you get stopped by this, be sure you aren't trying to enter an old invoice.

If you have vendors who don't provide you with an invoice number, your company might have a standard solution for this problem, such as entering a combination of the vendor ID plus the date or the primary PO number. This usually helps avoid duplications (but not always).

5. If necessary, change the date of the purchase.

6. If only the merchandise arrived but you haven't yet received a bill from the vendor, select the Waiting on Bill check box.

If you received both goods and a bill, leave the check box deselected.

Like with other transactions, you can change the A/P account, but typically you shouldn't.

7. On each line of the Apply to Purchase Order tab, in the Received field, type the quantity you received.

Remember that you have to put the decimal-zero after the whole number, or Peachtree adds the leading decimal: To get six, type **6.0**. Peachtree fills in the Amount field by multiplying the unit price by the quantity.

If you're purchasing a serialized item, click the Serial No. button, as shown here in the margin, to add the serial numbers of the items you're purchasing. In the Serial Number Entry field that appears, type the serial number for the first item and then click Add. Repeat the process for each serialized item you're purchasing. If the serial numbers are consecutive, select the Add Consecutive Serial Numbers check box and specify the number of items you're purchasing. After you finish, click OK.

8. **Click the Save button to save your work.**

When the bill arrives . . . finally

If you entered vendor receipts against a purchase order but didn't have a bill at the time you entered the vendor receipts, you should have selected the Waiting on Bill check box in the Purchases/Receive Inventory window. When the waiting is over and you have the vendor's bill, follow these steps to tie up the loose ends:

1. **Choose Lists⇨Vendors & Purchases⇨Purchases.**

   Peachtree opens the Purchase List window.

2. **Find the vendor's name in the Vendor Name column, and then look for a Y in the Waiting on Bill column.**

   Use the Invoice No. column to further help you identify the correct purchase.

3. **Select the correct purchase and then click Open.**

   Peachtree displays the purchase in the Purchases/Receive Inventory window.

4. **Deselect the Waiting on Bill check box.**

5. **Click the Save button.**

By making this status change, you indicate to Peachtree that you consider the bill eligible for payment. See Chapter 6 for information on paying bills.

Shipping Directly to Customers

Suppose that you need to buy something — maybe a special order for a customer — and you want to ship it directly to the customer. No problem. You can specify a customer's address in the Ship To field on either a purchase order or a purchase. Choose Tasks⇨Purchase Orders to display the Purchase Orders window or Tasks⇨Purchases/Receive Inventory to make a purchase. In either window, follow these steps:

1. **Type the vendor ID in the Vendor ID field or click the lookup list button to display the list of vendors.**

2. **Select the Drop Ship check box.**

   Peachtree displays a Customer ID field next to the Vendor ID field.

3. **Select the customer from the Customer ID list.**

   Peachtree supplies the customer's address and enables you to select a different shipping address if you click the Ship To drop-down list arrow.

   You can type the recipient's name and address if you haven't set up the recipient in the Customer List.

4. **If you've already entered an invoice to the customer into Peachtree, you can enter the invoice number in the Customer Invoice No. field. If you've entered a sales order but not an invoice, enter the sales order number in the Customer SO No. field.**

   Both of these fields are informational only; they don't tie to invoice or sales order transactions. You'll find them most useful, however, if you enter numbers that represent real transactions because they can help you track drop shipments on reports.

   You don't need to create the customer invoice before you set up the drop shipment, but don't forget to bill your customer. For more information about creating invoices for customers, see Chapter 7.

5. **Click the Save button.**

To help you track drop shipments, you can add the Drop Shipment, Customer ID, Customer SO No., and Customer Invoice No. fields to the Purchase Journal, the Purchase Order Journal, and the Purchase Order report. You also can filter the Purchase Order report so that it displays only drop shipments created in the Purchase Orders window.

Entering Credits

Suppose that you have a purchase transaction that you no longer need. Should you just erase it? If you want to practice good accounting, the answer is a definite *no.* Deleting purchases removes the *audit trail* — that thing accountants mean when they talk about the list of transactions you enter because your business does business. When accountants can trace transactions from beginning to end, they're really happy campers.

Having said that, you need to understand that Peachtree allows you to delete any *unpaid* purchase, even though your accountant won't like it. Display the purchase in the Purchases/Receive Inventory window and then click the Delete button.

However, Peachtree won't allow you to delete a purchase if you've applied any transactions to it. Suppose, for example, that you accidentally paid a purchase that you later determined you should not have paid. If you try to delete the purchase, the Delete button in the Purchase window is unavailable. In this case, you need to void the check you wrote that paid the purchase, and then you need to enter a vendor credit memo in Peachtree to cancel the effects of the purchase. (See Chapter 6 to find out how to void a check.) After you void the check, follow the steps in this section to finish canceling the purchase.

Besides fixing errors in purchases, don't forget about the times when a vendor issues a credit memo to you for merchandise you return. To reduce the balance you owe the vendor, you need to enter the vendor credit memo into Peachtree and match it to the original purchase. Although you can enter a vendor credit memo without having previously entered a purchase, typically you enter vendor credit memos for existing purchases.

In the following steps, we assume that you're returning any merchandise for which you receive a credit:

1. **Choose Tasks⇨Vendor Credit Memos.**

   Peachtree displays the Vendor Credit Memos window.

2. **Enter the vendor ID in the Vendor ID field. You can use the lookup list button to select the vendor from your list of vendors.**

   After you select a vendor, Peachtree fills in the vendor's name and Remit To address. You can see the vendor's current balance as of the system date, and you can click the button next to the balance to display a Vendor Ledger report of the purchases and payment that make up the balance.

3. **Enter a date in the Date field and then enter a credit number in the Credit No. field.**

   For the Credit No. field, we suggest that you enter the original invoice number followed by CM to indicate credit memo. This numbering scheme helps you tie the credit memo to a particular purchase.

4. **On the Apply to Invoice No. tab, click the Apply to Invoice No. drop-down list and select the invoice number of the purchase for which you're recording a credit memo.**

   Peachtree fills in the lines that appear on the purchase (see Figure 5-11).

5. **On each line of the Apply to Invoice No. tab, in the Returned field, type the quantity you want to return.**

Return

   If you plan to return everything, you can click the drop-down list arrow on the Return button, as shown here in the margin, and select All to have Peachtree fill in all the amounts for you.

   If you're using Automatic Decimal Entry, remember that you have to put the decimal-zero after the whole number, or Peachtree adds the leading decimal: To get nine, type **9.0**. Peachtree fills in the amount (unit price times quantity).

   If you're returning a serialized item, click the Serial No. button to display the Serial Number Selection dialog box and identify the serial numbers of the items you're returning. Select the check box next to the number(s) you're returning and then click OK.

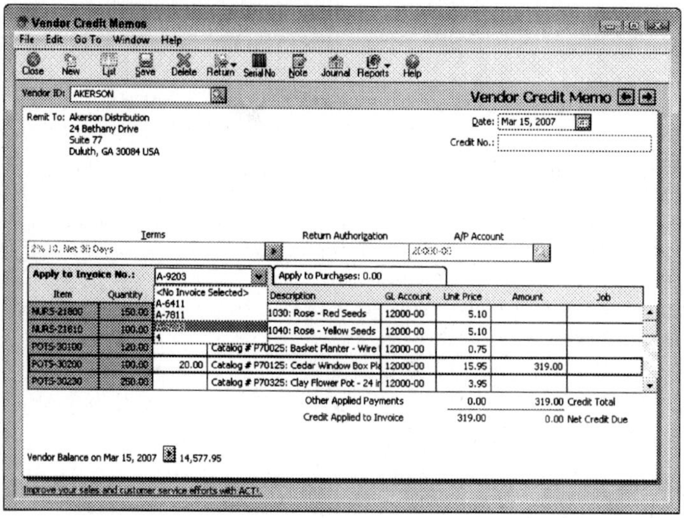

Figure 5-11:
Applying a
vendor
credit memo
to a
purchase.

6. Click the Save button to save the transaction.

Peachtree records the transaction; if you print your Aged Payables report, you see that the purchase no longer appears on the report.

You may become be aware of a vendor credit *before* you receive the vendor's credit or the vendor's bill. You can enter the credit by using the Apply to Purchases tab of the Vendor Credit Memos window and making sure that the credit memo affects the same things (vendor, General Ledger accounts, and inventory items) that the purchase affects. If you receive a credit for an existing purchase that doesn't involve returning items — for example, the items were damaged, and the vendor tells you not to return them — record the credit on the Apply to Purchases tab and don't select inventory items so that you avoid affecting inventory. You also can apply a credit for freight or tax by using the Apply to Purchases tab.

Reporting on Purchasing

To keep things short and sweet, Table 5-1 provides you with a description of the reports that pertain to buying goods. Chapter 14 covers the details on how to print reports.

Table 5-1	Reports Related to Buying Goods
Report Name	*What It Does*
Vendor List	For each vendor, lists the ID, name, contact name, telephone number, and tax ID.
Vendor Master File List	Similar to the Vendor List report, but also includes address information and terms.
1099 Vendor List	Lists all vendors set up as 1099 vendors and the amounts paid to them during the year. You use this report when you take care of year-end tasks; see Chapter 17.
Vendor Ledgers	Shows all transactions and a running balance for each vendor.
Purchase Order	Lists the details of all purchase orders by purchase order number.
Purchase Order Register	Lists purchase order numbers, dates, vendor IDs, and amounts. Optionally, you can use the PO State on the Filter tab to display only open purchase orders.
Purchase Order Journal	Lists only purchase orders. This report closely resembles the Purchase Journal.
Aged Payables	Lists outstanding invoices by vendor and the age of each outstanding invoice.
Purchase Journal	Shows the accounts Peachtree updated for each purchase in the period.
Items Purchased from Vendors	Lists, by vendor, the item ID, description, quantity, and amount of each item purchased from each vendor. If you sort the report by vendor name or ID, you can drill down to view the transactions in the transaction window.
Vendor Transaction History	Lists transaction details for vendor purchases and credit memos.
Vendor Management Detail	Lists, by vendor, the vendor's terms, the bills for the current period, the due dates, the amount you owe, and how long you aged a bill before paying it.

Visit www.dummies.com/go/peachtreefd for more information on Peachtree.

Chapter 6

Paying Bills

· ·

In This Chapter

▶ Paying a group of bills

▶ Generating checks and reports

▶ Paying one bill at a time

▶ Creating recurring transactions

▶ Tracking payments and voided checks

▶ Remitting sales tax

· ·

*A*lthough we wish things were different, the facts are simple: You can't hold those bills indefinitely — eventually, you have to pay them. If you prefer to let the bills pile up awhile, you can enter them gradually and pay all bills due by a certain date on your bill-paying day. Occasionally, you might need to pay only one or two bills or write a check to cover an unexpected expense — you know, the UPS person is standing there waiting for a check to cover the COD package being delivered.

Peachtree helps you pay groups of bills all at once or pay individual bills on the spur of the moment. You can make repetitive payments easily. And when you have to void checks or pay sales tax on all those goods you sell, Peachtree helps you keep all the amounts in the right accounts.

Terminology alert: Peachtree tends to switch back and forth between two different terms when referring to bills that vendors send you: a *purchase* and an *invoice*. For the sake of clarity, we use the term purchase (or bill) unless the window on-screen uses the term invoice. For our purposes, invoices are things you send to customers so that *you* can get paid.

Paying a Group of Bills

For a fee, you can subscribe to the Peachtree Online Bill Pay service and pay bills electronically. You don't have to enter information twice — once at the financial institution's Web site and once in Peachtree — and you use the same procedures we describe in this chapter. See Bonus Chapter 4 on this book's Web site, www.dummies.com/go/peachtreefd, for a few more details about this service.

Most people sit down on a regular basis — say, every two weeks — and pay all bills due by a certain date. They hold the bills that are due later until the next bill-paying day. In Peachtree, you can select all bills due by a certain date, or you can select bills that are past due by a number of days you specify (and you can specify the balance due on those bills). You can also select bills for certain vendors. Then you can simply tell Peachtree to write the checks and you can bid your bundle of bills bye-bye (nice alliteration, huh?).

Before you start paying your bills, you might want to print the Aged Payables report and the Cash Requirements report to get a handle on the outstanding purchases you entered into Peachtree. (See Chapter 14 for information on printing reports.) By reviewing these reports, you can determine whether you need to pay a group of bills or just a few bills. To pay a group of bills, you use the Select for Payment window. (To pay just a few bills or to pay a bill from an occasional vendor that you don't want to set up in Peachtree, see "Paying One Bill at a Time," later in this chapter.)

Using the Select for Payment window, Peachtree looks for purchases you entered that are eligible for payment based on the criteria you provide. You can use this window *only* to pay bills you entered as purchases. (See Chapter 5 for help entering bills.) To pay a group of bills, follow these steps:

1. **Choose Tasks⇨Select for Payment⇨Paper Checks.**

   You also can display this dialog box from the Vendors & Purchases Center in the Navigation Bar. Click the Pay Bills button and then choose Pay Multiple Bills.

   The Select for Payment – Filter Selection dialog box appears, as shown in Figure 6-1.

2. **Set the Check Date.**

   Most people use today's date.

   You can enter just the month and the day; Peachtree automatically uses the current year established by your computer's clock. If you enter only the day, Peachtree automatically uses the month and year established by your computer's clock.

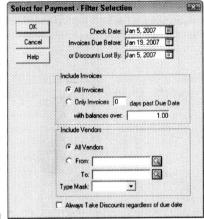

Figure 6-1:
Select bills
to pay in the
Select for
Payment –
Filter
Selection
dialog box.

Bills due

3. **Use the Invoices Due Before field to set a cutoff date for purchases that you want to pay.**

   Peachtree does not select any purchases due after the date you enter in this field.

   Peachtree calculates the due date when you enter the bill by using the terms you establish for the vendor. So the due date typically is *not* the same as the date you enter the bill and usually is 30 days later. We suggest that you set the Invoices Due Before date equal to a date that falls just before your next bill-paying day. That way, you won't be late paying bills.

4. **Set a date for the Or Discounts Lost By field if any of your vendors offer you discounts for paying by a specified date.**

   If your vendors don't offer vendor discounts, this date doesn't matter.

5. **In the Include Invoices section, select the range of invoices to include.**

   If you set dates in the preceding steps, you typically select the All Invoices option. However, you can select the Only Invoices X Days Past Due Date option and specify a number of days. In the With Balances Over field, you can also limit the invoices to only those more than a specified amount.

6. **In the Include Vendors section, make your choices regarding payees.**

   You might want to simply include All Vendors, but you can choose to include only a range of vendors. You can enter the vendor ID in the From and To fields or you can choose the vendor type from the Type Mask drop-down list. You can also use both the ID and type.

7. **If you always take discounts offered by vendors — even if you're paying later than the discount date — select the Always Take Discounts Regardless of Due Date check box.**

8. **Click OK.**

Peachtree displays the Select for Payment window shown in Figure 6-2, displaying purchases that meet the criteria you just specified.

Sort By
list box

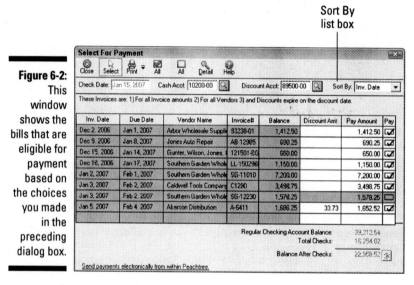

Figure 6-2: This window shows the bills that are eligible for payment based on the choices you made in the preceding dialog box.

 Peachtree initially displays the bills in Invoice Date order, but you can change to Due Date order or Vendor Name order by using the Sort By list box. Peachtree also selects a Cash account to use to pay the bills and a Discount account to use for any discounts you take, but you can select different accounts by using the lookup list button (the magnifying glass shown here in the margin) next to the appropriate fields.

 When the entire line for a bill appears gray, that entry is a purchase for which you haven't yet received a bill. (The Waiting on Bill check box remains selected on the purchase.) Peachtree won't let you pay for these purchases. If you think the entry should be eligible for payment, close the Select for Payment window and edit the purchase to deselect the Waiting on Bill check box. See Chapter 5 for more information on editing purchases.

Peachtree assumes that you want to pay all the bills it displays, but you can choose not to pay any bill by deselecting the check box in the Pay column.

You also can change the amount you pay by clicking in the Pay Amount column and typing a different number. If you allow Peachtree to calculate balances automatically, it updates the numbers that appear at the lower-right corner of the window.

 If you don't allow Peachtree to recalculate balances automatically, you see Uncalculated in the lower-right corner of the window. In this case, you can recalculate balances in this window by clicking the Recalc button (as shown here in the margin). For more information on setting recalculation options, see Bonus Chapter 1 on this book's Web site, www.dummies.com/go/ peachtreefd.

On the toolbar at the top of the window, you can click the arrow on the Print button and select Report from the drop-down list to print a report of the bills you selected to pay. The report sorts the bills by vendor. You also can preview the checks as they will look when they print by clicking the arrow on the Print button and choosing Preview from the drop-down list.

Detail

Select
If you click any line in the window and double-click or click the Detail button, as shown here in the margin, you can see but not edit the details for that line. Click the Select button, also shown in the margin, to change the filter options you set using the dialog box shown in Figure 6-1.

Printing Checks

As you might expect, Peachtree supports printing checks on your computer's printer. You must order check stock with the correct bank information on it. You can order checks from Peachtree; look for the check ordering information inside the box with your Peachtree software. You can also order checks from Deluxe Forms (www.deluxeforms.com — see Chapter 21 for more information), or you can ask your local forms supplier whether they have purchase check forms that work with Peachtree and your printer.

 Whoever supplies your checks can also supply window envelopes, or you can buy them at any office supply store. Using these envelopes saves you lots of time when paying bills because you don't need to use labels or address envelopes.

After you click the Print button in the Select for Payment window (see the preceding section for details on displaying this window), Peachtree displays the Print Forms: Disbursement Checks window (see Figure 6-3).

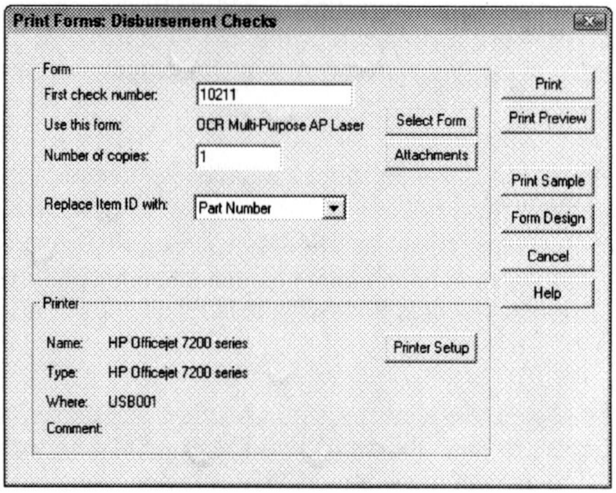

Figure 6-3:
Use this
window to
select a
check form
and the
starting
check
number.

Follow these steps to print checks:

1. **Confirm the starting check number.**

   Peachtree suggests a starting check number that you can change if
   Peachtree suggests an incorrect starting number. Peachtree assigns the
   starting number to the first check you print and subsequent numbers to
   subsequent checks when Peachtree saves your checks. If you had numbers preprinted on your check stock, make sure that both the check(s)
   you print and the check(s) that Peachtree saves use the same check
   numbers.

2. **If necessary, click the Select Form button to choose a check form.**

   Peachtree remembers the form you last used, so you may not need to
   change forms.

   Peachtree displays a list of available check forms; select one and then
   click OK to redisplay the dialog box shown in Figure 6-3. The form you
   select should match the type of check form you purchased. You can customize Peachtree forms; see Chapter 14.

   On the check stub, most of the Peachtree check forms print purchase
   information, such as the invoice number, date, and amount, but you can
   instead print the details of the items you bought (each line item that
   appears on the purchase, including item description, quantity, ID, and
   amount). To print details, choose the OCR Multi-Purp AP 1 Detail Cont or
   OCR Multi-Purp AP Detail Laser form, depending on the type of paper
   your printer uses. Use the first form with continuous-feed printers and
   the second form with laser or inkjet printers. You also can replace the
   Item ID with either the part number or the UPC/SKU number. Be aware
   that using this check form can cause Peachtree to void checks because
   it might need extra check stubs to print all the information.

3. **Specify the number of copies you want to print.**

4. **If necessary, select the correct printer by clicking the Printer Setup button.**

5. **Place check stock in the printer tray.**

6. **Click Print.**

   You can click the Print Sample button to print a practice check. Peachtree prints a check filled with Xs and 9s that you can use to determine whether the form alignment is correct.

   Peachtree prints the checks and a message appears on-screen asking whether the checks printed correctly. If you click Yes, Peachtree assigns the check numbers, saves the checks, and closes the Select for Payment window. If you click No, Peachtree doesn't assign the check numbers or save the checks, and leaves the Select for Payment window open so that you can print them again.

If you're following these steps to print a "one-at-a-time" check (as described in the next section), Peachtree doesn't ask you whether the check printed correctly; it simply assumes the check printed correctly. If the check didn't print correctly, read the "Voiding Checks" section later in this chapter.

Paying One Bill at a Time

Occasionally, you need to write only one or two checks. You know, you went to the office supply store and bought a box of copy paper, and you paid for it with a check. Now you need to record the check. You certainly don't want to enter a purchase and then pay the purchase by using the Select for Payment window. To print or record a single check, use the Payments window. Essentially, you use the Payments window in three situations:

✔ You don't need to print a check — you just need to record that it was written.

✔ You don't have many checks to write.

✔ You need to write a miscellaneous check, such as a refund check to a customer or a loan check to an employee.

From the Payments window, you can print checks that pay bills, print checks without first recording bills, or simply record checks you wrote manually. For example, suppose that it's bill-paying day, and you have only two bills to pay. Use the Payments window to print checks to pay the bills. Or suppose that the UPS guy is waiting for a check for a COD purchase. You can print the check from the Payments window without first recording a purchase. Or suppose that you enter the telephone bill in the Purchases/Receive Inventory window, intending to pay it on bill-paying day. Then you change your mind because you're going to be at the phone store anyhow, and you want to bring a check to pay the bill. Use the Payments window to print the check you want to take to the phone store.

You can use the Write Checks window to produce a single check, but *do not* use this window to write a check that pays a bill. If you enter a bill for a vendor, pay the bill by using either the Select for Payment window or the Payments window. We're not overly fond of the Write Checks window, because you won't see any warning if you select a vendor for whom a purchase exists. If you go ahead and write the check, you'll pay a bill without applying the check to the bill. For this reason, we strongly recommend that you use either the Select for Payment window to pay a group of bills or the Payments window to pay a few bills or write miscellaneous checks, and just ignore the existence of the Write Checks window. Really. We mean it. You'll avoid a lot of trouble.

From the Payments window, you can pay vendors that you set up, or you can write a check to someone you haven't set up in Peachtree. You also can use this window to issue an employee loan or (heaven forbid) write a refund check to a customer. Follow these steps:

1. **Choose Tasks⇨Payments.**

   Peachtree displays the Payments window.

2. **Select a vendor by using the lookup list button or type a name in the Pay to the Order Of field.**

   If the vendor doesn't have any unpaid purchases, or if you don't select a vendor but instead type a name in the Pay to the Order Of field, Peachtree displays the Apply to Expenses tab shown in Figure 6-4. If appropriate, fill in the quantity and select an item. If you don't select an item, you should fill in the description, supply the GL account, and, if appropriate, type a unit price. Peachtree calculates the amount. Finally, if appropriate, assign the line to a job.

   You can include payments that you assign to jobs as reimbursable expenses on customers' bills. See Chapter 7 for more information.

   If you select a vendor and the vendor has outstanding purchases, Peachtree displays the Apply to Invoices tab, listing all unpaid purchases for the vendor (see Figure 6-5). Select the check boxes in the Pay column next to all purchases you want to pay. Peachtree displays the dollar amount of the check on the check face.

   You can partially pay the purchase by typing an amount in the Amount Paid column on the line of the purchase you want to pay.

   You can display the purchase shown on any line. Double-click the purchase in any gray column, and Peachtree displays it in the Purchases/Receive Inventory window where you can edit it.

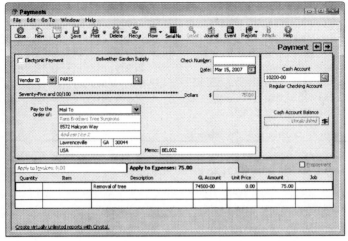

Figure 6-4:
Use the
Payments
window to
post (and
optionally
print) a
single
check.

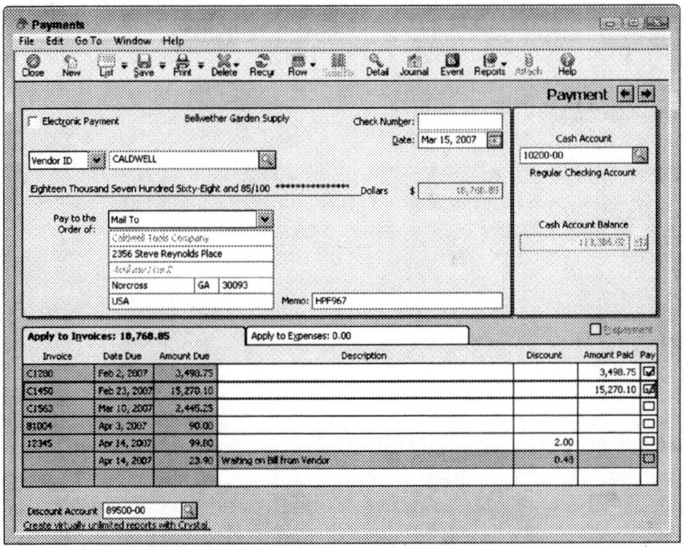

Figure 6-5:
If the
vendor has
outstanding
bills, check
the ones
you want
to pay.

3. If you *don't* intend to print the check, type the check number in the Check Number field at the top of the screen.

For example, if you're recording that check you wrote at the office supply store for the box of copy paper, you have no reason to print the check, but you must enter it. In this situation, enter the check number.

By default, Peachtree supplies a check number for any check you *print*. If you enter a check number in the Payments window for a check you intend to print, Peachtree prints the word *Duplicate* on the check face — and you don't want that to happen. Therefore, leave the check number blank if you intend to print the check. If you're a Type A personality who insists on completing all empty fields on a screen, you can suppress the printing of the word *Duplicate* by customizing the check form. See Chapter 13 for details.

4. **Supply a date for the check.**

5. **In the upper-right portion of the window, select the Cash account from which you want to write the check.**

6. **Depending on whether you enter a check number in Step 3, continue by clicking Save or Print.**

If you enter a number in the Check Number field, click the Save button (as shown here in the margin) to save the check.

If you don't enter a number in the Check Number field, click the Print button (as shown here in the margin) to print the check immediately. Peachtree displays the Print Forms dialog box, which we describe in the "Printing Checks" section earlier in this chapter. Select Print; after you finish printing checks, Peachtree assigns the check numbers and saves the checks.

If you prefer to keep working and print a batch of checks later, click the Save button to post your checks without assigning check numbers to them. See Chapter 13 for details on printing checks in batches.

Editing Payments

From an accounting perspective, there's little reason to edit a payment. In the real world, however, you'll come up with a reason. For example, when you entered that check for office supplies, you typed the wrong amount, which you notice when you are about to file the receipt. In this case, the amount of the check you actually wrote doesn't match the amount you recorded in Peachtree — and the actual check is, of course, right.

You edit payments the same way as you edit purchase orders and purchases, which we describe in Chapter 5. Choose Lists➪Vendors & Purchases➪Payments to display the Payment List window, which lists all payments you recorded. Click the check you want to edit and then click the Open button, as shown in the margin, to display the check in the Payments window, where you can make changes and then save the check. You also can delete checks. We talk more about that in the section on voiding checks later in this chapter.

Handling Repeat Bills and Payments

Suppose that you pay a bill — such as your rent or your health insurance — every month for the same amount. Peachtree lets you set up recurring purchases or payments. You enter the purchase or payment once and tell Peachtree how often to record the transaction. Recurring transactions save you data-entry time.

You set up recurring purchases and recurring payments in the same way; the only difference is the window you use. To set up a recurring payment, start in the Payments window.

Recurring transactions affect the General Ledger. In accrual-basis companies, both recurring purchases and recurring payments affect the General Ledger. In cash-basis companies, only recurring payments affect the General Ledger. Therefore, if you enter a recurring transaction, Peachtree updates the General Ledger in the appropriate period. If you print future period reports, you see the effects of the transactions in those future period reports. As you would expect, though, Peachtree displays each period's balances accurately for that period.

Use recurring purchases when you expect to print a check to pay a bill. If you *don't* expect to print a check — perhaps your health insurance company automatically deducts its payment from your checking account — use recurring payments.

To set up a recurring purchase, follow these steps:

1. **Choose Tasks⇨Purchases/Receive Inventory.**

   Peachtree displays the Purchases/Receive Inventory window.

2. **Set up the purchase (select the vendor and so on, as described in Chapter 5), but don't assign an invoice number.**

   You might want to select the Waiting on Bill check box so that you don't accidentally pay a future bill before it becomes due.

3. **Click the Recur button on the toolbar.**

   Peachtree displays the Create Recurring Purchases dialog box (see Figure 6-6).

4. **From the How Often Do You Want to Recur This Transaction list, select the frequency you want.**

5. **In the First Transaction Date field, enter or select the date for the first transaction.**

   You can click the small calendar beside the field to select the date from an on-screen calendar.

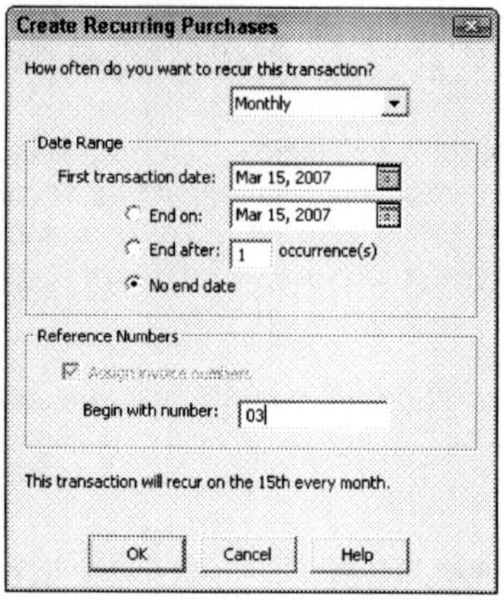

Figure 6-6:
Use this
dialog box
to set up
transactions
that happen
on a
recurring
basis.

6. **Select a date for the last transaction.**

   You can select the End On option and enter an ending date, or you can select the End After option and specify the number of times you want the transaction to recur. You can also select the No End Date option and Peachtree creates recurring transactions indefinitely.

7. **In the Begin With Number field, assign a starting reference number for the recurring purchase.**

   Peachtree assigns the number you supply to the first recurring purchase and increments subsequent transactions by one.

8. **Click OK.**

   You might hear some activity on your hard drive while Peachtree creates the transactions. Then Peachtree redisplays the Purchases/Receive Inventory window, ready for you to enter your next purchase.

If you open a recurring purchase, take a minute to notice a few interesting things:

✔ You can see multiple entries for the recurring transaction in the Purchase List window. For example, if on April 1 you set up the payment to recur weekly for seven weeks, look for at least four or possibly five entries in April. If you set up the purchase to recur monthly, you need to use the Date Range list in the Purchase List window to display All Transactions or a future period. To make viewing the transaction easier, limit the transactions you display to just the vendor for whom you set up the recurring transaction.

✔ When you display the recurring purchase in the Purchases/Receive Inventory window, look at the bottom of the window for an entry telling you how many more entries exist.

✔ After you edit and then save a recurring transaction, Peachtree prompts you to save the change for only the current transaction or the current transaction and all remaining transactions.

✔ In the Payments window, after you select a vendor for whom you set up a recurring purchase, you see lines for all recurring purchases, regardless of the period. Remember: You can double-click the gray portion of any line and view or edit the purchase in the Purchases/Receive Inventory window.

✔ When you click the List button in the Payments window to display the Payment List window, you see that recurring payments don't have check numbers. Peachtree leaves the number blank so that you can print a check for the payment. If you write the check by hand, edit the payment and assign a check number.

Voiding Checks

If you write a check and then discover a problem with the check, you can void it. After you void a check, Peachtree creates a negative check for the same amount as the check you void, but the value of the voided check *increases* your Cash account. Remember that the original check reduced your Cash account. In other words, if you add the two transactions, you get 0 (that's what accountants mean when they say the transactions "net to 0"), and a $0 transaction causes no change in your cash balance. The voided check transaction that Peachtree creates has the same number as the original check, but Peachtree appends a *V* to the number; that is, if you void check 101, Peachtree creates check 101V. You can view and edit the voided check in the Payments window the same way you can view and edit any other payment.

To void a check, follow these steps:

1. **Choose Tasks⇨Void Checks.**

   Peachtree displays the Void Existing Checks window, as shown in Figure 6-7.

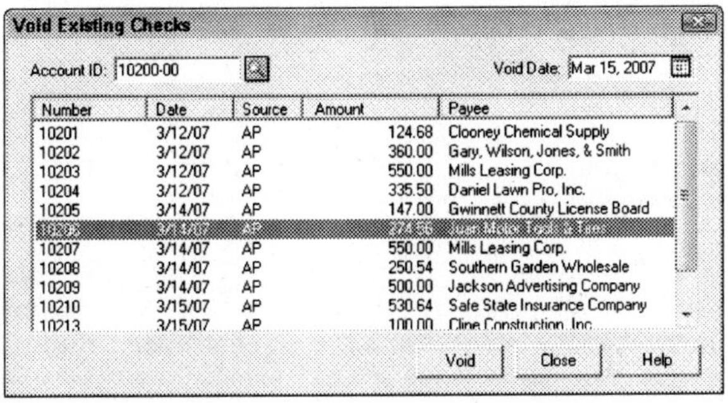

Figure 6-7:
Use this window to identify the check you want to void.

2. **If necessary, click the lookup list button to select the Cash account from which you wrote the check that you now want to void.**

3. **Enter the Void Date for the check.**

   Be sure this date falls in the period that you want the Cash account increased, which is not necessarily the same period that the check was written.

4. **Click the check you want to void.**

   You can sort the checks in the Void Existing Checks window in different ways to help you find the check you want to void. Click any of the column headings in the window (Number, Date, Amount, and so on) to sort checks by that column heading.

5. **Click the Void button.**

   Peachtree displays a message asking whether you're sure you want to void the check.

6. **Click OK.**

   Peachtree creates a voided check transaction.

After you void a check, you can see both the original check and the voided check transaction in the Account Reconciliation window when you balance your checkbook. Peachtree has already marked them both as cleared. For more information on balancing your checkbook, see Chapter 16.

After you void a check that paid a vendor bill, Peachtree changes the status of the bill from Paid to Unpaid. That is, Peachtree assumes you still want to pay the bill. If you do want to pay the bill, simply use the Payments window or the Select for Payment window to write a check. If, however, you don't want to pay the bill, enter a vendor credit memo for the bill. Chapter 5 has more information on creating vendor credit memos.

If you accidentally void the wrong check, open the Payment List window (choose Lists⇨Vendors & Purchases⇨Payments) and select the check. You can find the voided check in the window — the check number ends with a *V* for *Void*. Click that transaction and then click the Open button to display it in the Payments window. Then delete it by clicking the Delete button, also shown in the margin.

Paying Sales Tax

Most states expect customers to pay a sales tax on goods they purchase. In some states, customers also pay sales tax on services. In addition, the county or local government might also assess a tax on customers' purchases. If your business sells taxable goods, you collect the sales tax for at least one taxing authority. Then, of course, you're expected to remit the sales tax to the taxing authority, along with a sales tax return (so that they can make sure that you're not cheating them out of any of the sales taxes you collect).

Paying sales tax in Peachtree is no different than paying any other bill; you can enter a purchase to remind yourself that you owe the money or you can simply write the check. The tricky part? Finding out *how much* to pay, because not all sales are taxable in every state. And when the sales are taxable, local taxes might apply as well. To complicate the issue further, if you operate your business close to a border between jurisdictions, your business might be collecting taxes for more than one jurisdiction — and at different rates.

If you set up your sales taxes correctly (see Chapter 7 for more information), you can use the Taxable/Exempt Sales report (see Figure 6-8) to help you prepare the sales tax return and remit your sales taxes. Choose Reports & Forms⇨Accounts Receivable to display the Select a Report window; then print the Taxable/Exempt Sales report, which breaks down the taxes you owe by taxing authority.

For detailed instructions on printing reports, see Chapter 14.

If you set up multiple exempt categories (as described in the section describing Inventory Preferences in Chapter 4), you can customize this report to add a column for the Taxable Type, as we did in Figure 6-8, so that the report lists and identifies the totals for each exempt category that you need for the sales tax return. See Chapter 14 for help customizing reports.

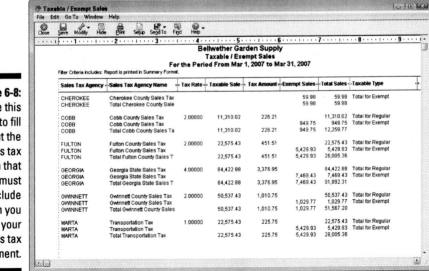

Figure 6-8: Use this report to fill out the sales tax return that you must include when you make your sales tax payment.

Using Reports to Track Money You Paid

When you need to track the outflow of money, Peachtree offers some reports that help you. Table 6-1 provides you with a description of the reports that pertain to paying bills. See Chapter 14 to find out how to print reports.

Table 6-1	Reports Related to Paying Bills
Report Name	*What It Does*
Check Register	Lists each check with the check number, payee, the amount, and the Cash account from which the check was written.
Cash Requirements	Lists all unpaid purchases and their due dates for the date range you specify.
Cash Disbursements Journal	Shows the accounts that Peachtree updated for each check you wrote in the period. You can filter this report for 1099 vendors.
Electronic Payment Register	Lists all payments you made electronically, including transmission information.

Visit this book's Web site, www.dummies.com/go/peachtreefd, for more information on Peachtree.

Chapter 7

Selling Products and Services

In This Chapter

▶ Setting up sales tax

▶ Creating customer defaults

▶ Entering quotes, sales orders, and invoices

▶ Shipping your packages

▶ Managing sales transactions and invoices

*W*hat incredible assets we have in our customers! Well, most of them anyway. After all, we wouldn't be in business without them, would we?

Peachtree operates under the assumption that you might generate a quote to a customer, convert that quote into a sales order, and then turn that sales order into an invoice after you produce the goods or service. You do not, however, have to use quotes or sales orders to use the Peachtree invoicing feature.

Even if you don't use quotes or sales orders, we suggest that you read this entire chapter. The steps for creating and editing quotes, sales orders, and invoices are almost identical. Therefore, to eliminate redundancy, we explain most of the details in one place (the "Bidding with Quotes" section). We show you the differences between entering quotes, sales orders, and invoices in the individual sections of this chapter.

In addition to talking about the forms you use to sell things to your customers, we start by talking about another important selling issue — sales taxes.

Working with Sales Taxes

Everyone hates to pay sales tax; taxes make us feel like we're paying more for our purchase than we should. Like it or not, though, most states expect customers to pay sales tax — usually on goods, but occasionally on services or freight as well. If you run your business in a locality that charges sales taxes, you, as the seller, are obligated to collect the sales tax from your customer.

Yielding to the agencies

If your business sells taxable goods or services, you collect the sales tax for the taxing *agency.* That's the term Peachtree uses to identify which government entity has the right to tell you to collect sales tax from your customers. That agency could be only your state government, but frequently other local agencies are involved as well.

For example, suppose that your state, along with several counties in your state, charges a sales tax. In this case, you need to set up sales tax agencies for your state and for each county as well.

Most states base the tax amount on the total invoice amount, but some states base their sales tax on the individual line item amount. Peachtree provides the ability to calculate sales taxes by using a variety of methods. Table 7-1 illustrates the different scenarios in which your state might calculate sales tax. (Of course, if your state doesn't have sales taxes, feel free to avoid this table completely.)

Table 7-1	Sales Tax Scenarios
Scenario	*What It Does*
Single tax rate	Applies the standard tax rate on all sales regardless of amount.
Maximum dollar sales	Applies the standard tax rate up to a ceiling amount. After that, no more tax is calculated. For example, if the tax is 3% on the first $4,000 of a sale and the sale is $5,000, only $4,000 is taxed at the 3% amount. The remaining $1,000 is untaxed.
Minimum dollar sales	Applies the standard tax rate only when sales reach a specified amount. For example, if the minimum taxable sale amount is $500, a sale of $450 is not taxed.
Maximum dollar tax	Applies the standard tax rate until the tax reaches a maximum amount, and then no more tax is calculated on that sale. For example, if the tax rate is 2%, with a maximum dollar tax of $20, sales up to $1,000 are taxed at the 2% rate, but sales of $1,000 and more are taxed a flat $20.

Scenario	What It Does
Maximum percent sales amount	Applies the standard tax rate to a specific maximum percentage, less than 100%. For example, the tax rate might be 3%, but it applies to only 75% of the sales price.
Each taxable line item	Calculates the tax rate on each line item instead of applying the previous tax rates to the grand total of the order.

Suppose that your business is located in the state of Georgia and that the state charges 6 percent sales tax. You pay the tax to the Georgia Department of Revenue. If you have a branch of your business located in Brown County, Georgia (which has its own local tax), you have to charge those customers the additional local tax — say, 1 percent — which, in turn, you pay to the Brown County Treasurer's office. In this situation, you have two taxing agencies: the State of Georgia and Brown County.

Before you set up a sales tax agency, you must set up a vendor to whom you remit the sales tax. You can find out how to set up a vendor in Chapter 5. To follow this exercise, you must have a vendor set up; we use Georgia Department of Revenue as the vendor name in this example.

To set up sales taxes, Peachtree provides a helpful wizard to guide you through the process. The steps you see depend on the method your state uses to calculate sales taxes. We take a look at two of them.

Single rate sales tax

If your state charges a 6% tax and your local county charges a 1% tax, for a total of 7%, you're using a single rate sales tax. Just follow these steps:

1. **Choose Maintain⇨Sales Taxes.**

   The Set Up Sales Taxes Wizard appears. You begin with this screen to create a new sales tax as well as modify an existing sales tax.

2. **Select the Set Up a New Sales Tax option and then click Next.**

   The Set Up New Sales Tax screen in Figure 7-1 is asking you for the *total* tax percentage for the sales tax you're creating. For our example, we enter **7** as the total tax percentage.

If one or more of your agencies charge tax based on a calculation instead of a flat rate, see the next section.

3. **Choose how many individual rates make up the total rate.**

In our example, the answer is two.

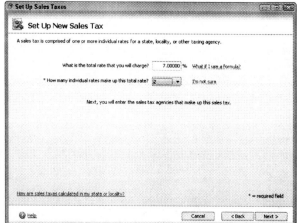

Figure 7-1:
Setting up
sales tax.

4. **Click Next.**

The Add Sales Tax Agency screen appears. Here is where you begin setting up your agencies. See Figure 7-2.

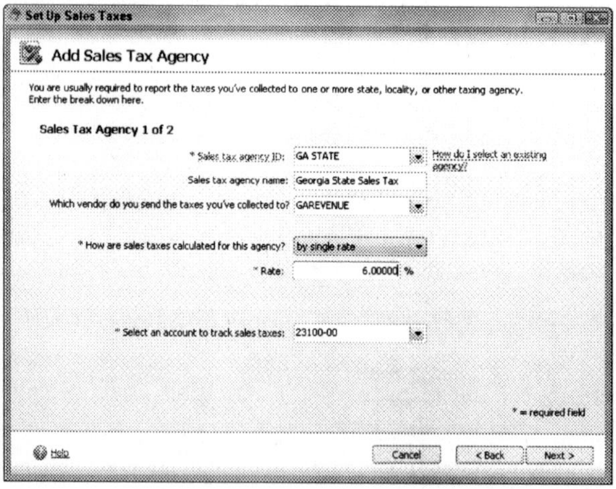

Figure 7-2:
Identify the
agencies
that make
up your
sales tax.

5. **Create an agency ID, or if you previously created the agency ID, select it from the drop-down list.**

   You can use up to eight letters or numbers (alphanumeric characters). Our example uses GA STATE.

6. **Type a descriptive name for the agency.**

   You can type up to 30 characters. We use Georgia State Sales Tax for our example.

7. **In the Which Vendor Do You Send the Taxes You've Collected To? field, type or select the vendor ID to which you remit this sales tax.**

   For our example, we chose the Georgia Department of Revenue.

8. **Click in the Rate field and enter the percentage this agency charges.**

   We enter **6** here.

9. **Select or enter the GL Liability account to which you want to post the sales tax you collect.**

10. **Click Next and repeat Steps 5–9 for each additional agency for this tax.**

    In our example, we need to set up an additional agency for Brown County.

    Peachtree displays at the top of the screen how many total agencies you specify in Step 3.

11. **Click Next.**

    After you set up the agencies, you're ready to finalize setting up the sales tax.

12. **Create an ID and a name for the sales tax.**

    Use a maximum of eight alphanumeric characters for the ID and 30 for the name. We suggest you use some type of description that indicates the reason for the sales tax. For our example in Figure 7-3, we use GABrown as an ID with the description Georgia, Brown County.

13. **Select whether your state charges sales taxes on freight.**

14. **Click Finish.**

    Peachtree saves your sales tax setup and the Set Up Sales Tax Wizard redisplays its opening screen.

15. **Set up another sales tax if needed or click Cancel to close the Sales Tax Wizard.**

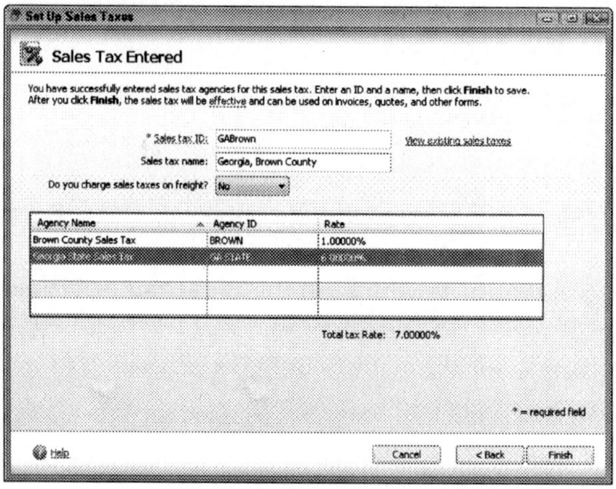

Figure 7-3:
Name the
sales tax.

Sales tax formulas

If your state uses a sales tax method other than a flat single rate, Peachtree can manage the calculation for you. For example, say your business is in Green County. In addition to the Georgia 6% state sales tax, Green County also charges 2% on the first $500 of your purchase, and then charges 1% on $500 and higher.

1. **Follow Steps 1–7 in the previous section** *except* **that in Step 2, leave the percentage field at zero. Refer to Figure 7-1.**

2. **Click the How Are Sales Taxes Calculated for This Agency? drop-down list and then choose By Formula, as shown here in the margin.**

   The screen changes to the one shown in Figure 7-4.

3. **In the Which Amount Should Be Used to Calculate Sales Taxes? drop-down list, select whether the tax should be calculated on total taxable sales or on each line item.**

4. **Create the formula for your state's calculation.**

   In our example, we stipulate that the county charges 2% tax on the first $500 of our purchase and then charges 1% on the remainder.

5. **Click Next and continue setting up agencies and sales taxes as described in the previous section.**

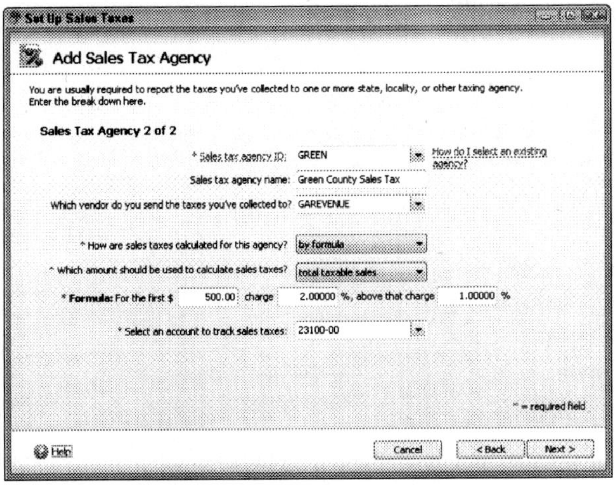

Set Up Sales Taxes

Add Sales Tax Agency

You are usually required to report the taxes you've collected to one or more state, locality, or other taxing agency.
Enter the break down here.

Sales Tax Agency 2 of 2

* Sales tax agency ID: GREEN   How do I select an existing agency?

Sales tax agency name: Green County Sales Tax

Which vendor do you send the taxes you've collected to? GAREVENUE

* How are sales taxes calculated for this agency? by formula

* Which amount should be used to calculate sales taxes? total taxable sales

* Formula: For the first $ 500.00 charge   2.00000 %, above that charge   1.00000 %

* Select an account to track sales taxes: 23100-00

* = required field

Help   Cancel   < Back   Next >

Figure 7-4:
Use this
screen to
create a
sales tax
formula.

Working with Customers

Before you can generate quotes, sales orders, or invoices, you need to set up
your customer defaults and enter the individual customers. In Chapter 4, we
show you how to create the defaults you use here. Peachtree identifies each
customer by a unique ID that allows Peachtree to track any transactions
related to the customer.

Adding customers

When you set up a customer, you supply the customer's name and address, a
Sales account to use each time you post a sale to the customer, credit information, and any custom field information you set up in your defaults. You
also can view historical data about your sales to and receipts from your customers over the previous 12 months.

To add or modify customer information, choose Maintain⇨Customers/
Prospects. Peachtree displays the Maintain Customers/Prospects window,
as shown in Figure 7-5. The following sections examine what you can do with
each tab in this dialog box.

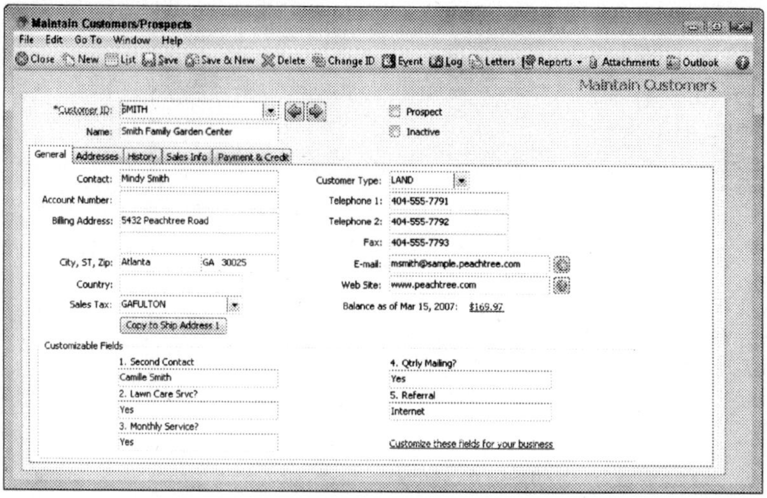

Figure 7-5:
Use this
window to
add, edit,
or delete
customers.

The General tab

On the General tab, supply basic customer identification information, such as ID, name, address, and phone numbers. You use the ID as the identification to select the customer when you create a customer transaction. Try to make it meaningful and easy to remember; in fact, we suggest you use part of the customer name as the ID.

You can enter up to 20 alphanumeric characters (except the characters *, ?, and +) for a customer ID. Peachtree sorts most customer reports by customer ID, and numbers sort before letters.

Customer IDs are not case sensitive.

From the Maintain Customers/Prospects window, fill in the General tab by following these steps:

1. **Type a customer ID and the customer's name.**

   You may enter up to 30 alphanumeric characters for the customer's name.

2. **If you do *not* want this customer ID included on any customer reports, select the Prospect check box.**

   A *prospect* is a potential customer: one who has not actually bought any goods or services from you. If you generate an invoice for the prospect or deselect this check box, the prospect becomes a regular customer, and Peachtree includes the ID on customer reports.

3. **Fill in the customer name and contact information, billing address, phone numbers, and (if applicable), e-mail and Web site addresses.**

If you enter an e-mail address and then click the icon next to it (as shown here), Peachtree opens your e-mail program and generates a message to your customer.

Clicking the button next to the Web address (as shown here) launches your Web browser and directs it to the customer's Web site. If you plan to e-mail forms (quotes, sales orders, or invoices) to your customers, fill in the e-mail address. See Chapter 13 for information on e-mailing forms.

If you have Microsoft Outlook installed on your system, Peachtree can synchronize with your Outlook contacts folder. Click the Outlook button, as shown in the margin, on the toolbar.

If you don't see the Outlook button, widen the Customer/Prospects window.

4. **If you charge sales taxes, select a Sales Tax applicable to this customer.**

5. **If desired, enter or select a customer type.**

Use the Customer Type field to group similar customers. You can then limit the information on most A/R reports to a specific customer type. For example, you might want to distinguish between wholesale customers and retail customers. The Customer Type field is case sensitive.

6. **Enter any desired information in the Customizable fields.**

When you set up default customer information (see Chapter 4), you create the custom fields for the Maintain Customers/Prospects window.

7. **Click the Save button (as shown in the margin).**

If you have any supplementary documentation — such as, Word or Excel files, images, PDF files, and so forth that pertain to the customer — click the Attachments button (as shown here). If you don't see the Attachments button, widen the Customer/Prospects window. You can then individually add the files you want attached to the customer record.

The Addresses tab

On the General tab, you enter the customer billing address. In the Addresses tab, you can store up to 20 shipping addresses for each customer. Whenever you create a quote, sales order, or invoice, you can choose from the stored shipping addresses, thereby saving data-entry time.

If the customer shipping address is the same as the billing address, you can click the Copy button (as shown in the margin) and copy the billing address to one of the shipping address lines.

The History tab

When you first set up a customer, the History tab doesn't have any information. However, after you record customer sales transactions, the History tab gives you a month-by-month summary of both sales and receipts.

The History tab also shows you how long you've been doing business with the customer. In fact, the Customer Since date is the only editable piece of information on this screen. Everything else is provided for a quick overview of the customer's history.

The History tab also has a Customer Beginning Balance button, which you use in the upcoming section, "Where to begin? Beginning Balances."

If you no longer do business with this customer, select the Inactive check box.

The Sales Info tab

On the Sales Info tab, you can store several additional key pieces of customer information. Peachtree relates many of the fields on this window to the inventory and payroll modules.

1. **Select a default sales rep for this customer by typing the sales rep ID or selecting one from the lookup list.**

   See Chapter 9 for information on creating sales reps. If you don't use sales reps, keep this field blank.

2. **Define a GL Sales account for the customer if it's different from the default account established in the Customer Defaults dialog box.**

   For more information about customer defaults, see Chapter 4.

   When you create an inventory item, you specify a Sales account for the item. When you generate an invoice, the Sales account associated with inventory items overrides the customer Sales account. You can find out how to set up inventory items in Chapter 11.

3. **In the Open PO Number field, enter a purchase order number if your customer has given you a standing purchase order number to use for all purchases from you.**

   This purchase order number appears by default in the Customer Purchase Order field on the Quotes, Sales Orders, and Sales/Invoicing windows.

4. **In the Ship Via field, choose a preferred shipping method.**

   Determine shipping methods in the Maintain Inventory Item Defaults window. If necessary, you can override the preferred method when you generate a customer invoice. You set up shipping methods in Chapter 4.

5. **If the customer does not have to pay sales tax, enter the resale number.**

   Most states require customers to provide you with their resale number for tax-exempt purchases.

6. **Choose the pricing level most often associated with this customer.**

   Pricing levels are tied to inventory items. See Chapter 11 for details on how to assign up to ten prices to each inventory item. Peachtree then automatically charges the customer the price shown in the pricing level you specify here.

7. **Select a preferred form delivery method and options.**

   Forms include Sales Orders, Packing Slips, Invoices, and Statements.

To use the e-mail delivery method in Peachtree, you must use a MAPI-compliant, default e-mail application, such as Outlook or Outlook Express. If your default e-mail system is AOL, you won't be able to send e-mail from Peachtree because AOL is not a fully MAPI-compliant e-mail application.

The Payment & Credit tab

All things not being equal, Peachtree provides the ability to assign different credit terms to different customers. You use the Payment & Credit tab to establish the specific terms for the current customer. If you accept credit cards from your clients, this tab provides a place to store the customer's credit card number and expiration date.

Options in the Receipt Settings area are time-savers. If the Use Payment Method and Cash Account from Last Saved Receipt check box is selected, Peachtree uses the payment method and Cash account you selected on the last receipt you saved for the selected customer. You might want to change this setting if, for example, the selected customer always pays by credit card, but the majority of your other customers pay by check.

Peachtree assumes that each customer uses the default terms you establish when you set up customer defaults. If your customer uses terms different than the default terms, click the arrow next to Use Default Terms and then select Customize Terms for This Customer. You can then edit the terms, indicating whether to charge finance charges, change the customer's credit limit, or determine whether or how Peachtree should notify you about the customer's credit limit status. See Figure 7-6 for an example.

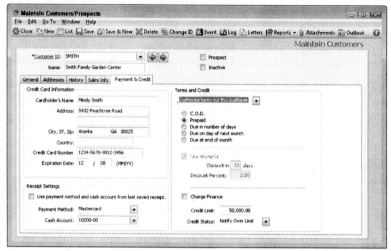

Figure 7-6:
Use this
window to
record
information
about the
customer's
terms.

Use the Credit Status field to place a customer on credit hold. If a customer's status is Always Hold, Peachtree displays a warning message and does not allow you to save an invoice for that customer.

After making any changes, be sure to click the Save button.

After you save the customer record, if you determine that you want to use a different customer ID, click the Change ID button (as shown here). Type the new ID in the Enter New Customer ID field, click OK, and then click the Save button again.

Where to begin? Beginning balances

Chances are that you've been selling your goods and services for a while. You probably haven't been paid yet for all the work you did and the products you sold. You probably gave your customers a specified amount of time to pay their invoices to you. You specify your terms when you set up your default customer information in Chapter 4.

Although some invoices aren't due yet, others might be past due. Either way, the customer owes you money. When you begin using Peachtree, you need to tell Peachtree about those unpaid invoices. Enter these invoices as customer beginning balances.

Entering invoices as beginning balances does not affect the General Ledger.

To enter customer beginning balances, follow these steps:

1. **Choose Maintain⇨Customers/Prospects.**

2. **From the History tab, click the Customer Beginning Balances button (as shown in the margin) to display the Customer Beginning Balances dialog box.**

3. **Double-click the first customer for which you need to enter a beginning balance invoice.**

   Did you think you'd have to re-create your invoices? You don't. Simply provide Peachtree with a few key pieces of information.

4. **Enter the invoice number and the date of the original invoice.**

   The date is needed so that Peachtree can age the invoice properly.

5. **(Optional) Enter the customer's purchase order number for the invoice.**

6. **Enter the invoice amount.**

7. **Enter the A/R account number.**

   The A/R account is the Accounts Receivable account. Notice we say _Accounts Receivable._ We're not talking about the Sales account. It's a common mistake to enter the Sales account number.

8. **Repeat Steps 4–7 for each outstanding invoice for the selected customer.**

   Figure 7-7 shows a sample list of outstanding invoices.

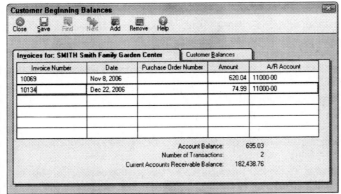

Figure 7-7:
Enter
invoices
dated prior
to your
using
Peachtree.

Technically, Peachtree has no limit to the number of beginning balance invoices you can enter for an individual customer. However, if you exceed 100 invoices, you can enter but not edit or delete the 101st invoice and subsequent invoices.

9. **Click the Save button.**

10. **Click the Customer Balances tab and then select the next customer for whom you want to enter beginning balances.**

11. **After you finish entering beginning balances, click the Close button, as shown in the margin.**

We recommend that you print both an Aged Receivables report to verify the invoice information and dates and a Trial Balance report to make sure that the Aged Receivables balance matches the GL balance.

Bidding with Quotes

Many businesses let their customers know how much a product or service costs by producing a quote before the customer decides to buy. Peachtree allows you to create a quote; after the customer determines he or she does want to buy from you, you can convert that quote to a sales order or an invoice.

Quotes are optional in the Peachtree sales process.

Entering quotes

The top part of the quote window contains header information, such as customer name, address, quote number, date, and other such information. Enter the actual products or services you supply in the body of the quote. In Bonus Chapter 1, located at www.dummies.com/go/peachtreefd, you can find out how to modify the appearance of the Quotes window by using templates.

The steps to create, edit, and print quotes are almost identical to the steps for sales orders and invoices.

To create a quote in Peachtree, follow these steps:

1. **Choose Tasks⇨Quotes/Sales Orders/Proposals⇨Quotes to display the Quotes window, as shown in Figure 7-8.**

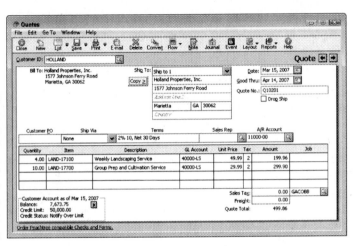

Figure 7-8:
Quotes
inform your
customer in
advance of
the price of
a product or
service.

2. **Type or select the customer ID.**

   You can't enter a quote in Peachtree unless you set up a customer. Peachtree displays the customer's current balance and credit limit in the lower-left corner.

   If you begin typing the customer ID only to find you haven't yet entered the customer into Peachtree, press the plus (+) key while the insertion point is in the ID field. Peachtree displays the Maintain Customers/Prospects window, allowing you to create the customer record. After you close the Maintain Customers/Prospects window, Peachtree redisplays the Quotes window. This procedure works for any lookup list you open in Peachtree. Pressing the plus (+) key opens the appropriate Maintain window: Vendors, Customers/Prospects, Inventory, Employees/Sales Reps, or Chart of Accounts.

3. **Type the recipient Ship To address, or click the arrow next to the Ship To field and then select one of the addresses you entered when first setting up the customer.**

   Peachtree doesn't store a manually entered Ship To address permanently in the customer record. However, Peachtree does store the custom address with the current quote and transfers the address to the resulting sales order or invoice, or both.

   Optionally, click the Copy button to copy the billing address into the Ship To fields.

4. **Enter the date you want printed on the quote in the Date field and a Good Thru date for the quote.**

   Peachtree assumes that the quote is valid for a period of 30 days and prints the ending date on the quote form. If you're giving your customer a longer or shorter period of time, choose a different date in the Good Thru field.

Peachtree doesn't do anything to the quote if the customer doesn't respond in the specified number of days. The date is simply printed on the quote form.

5. **(Optional) Enter a quote number in the Quote No. field.**

   If you're going to print the quote (and usually you do), don't enter a quote number because Peachtree assigns the number when it prints the quote. If you already assigned the quote a number, perhaps from a verbal quote, enter the quote number.

   If you plan to have your vendor ship the item directly to your customer, select the Drop Ship check box.

   It's unlikely that your customer has given you a purchase order number for a quote. After all, if you're quoting it, the customer hasn't yet decided to buy. You can leave the Customer PO field blank.

6. **(Optional) Type a shipping method or select a shipping method from the Ship Via drop-down list.**

7. **(Optional) Change the terms for this order.**

   By default, Peachtree displays the terms you chose when you set up this customer in Maintain Customers/Prospects.

8. **(Optional) Select a sales rep ID from the Sales Rep lookup list.**

   Take a look at Chapter 9 for information on how to set up a sales representative.

   If your company is cash based, the A/R Account field displays <Cash Basis>, and you can't access the Account field. If your business is accrual based, you can select the A/R account from the lookup list for this potential sale although typically you *shouldn't* change the default. If you elect to hide General Ledger accounts in A/R, you won't even see an A/R Account field. See Bonus Chapter 1 on this book's Web site for more information on hiding or showing GL accounts.

9. **In the body of the quote, enter the quantity for the first item on the quote.**

   If you're quoting a service or product that doesn't have a quantity, you can leave the quantity blank.

10. **If you're selling an inventory item, select the item ID.**

    Peachtree fills in the item description, the GL Sales account, the item's unit price, and the tax status. Then Peachtree multiplies the quantity times the unit price for the amount. Read about setting up inventory items in Chapter 11.

11. **If you're quoting or selling a non-stock item or you don't use inventory, leave the Item field blank and fill in the Description, GL (Sales) Account, and Unit Price fields.**

    Peachtree calculates the amount. If you did not enter a quantity in Step 9, you must enter an amount rather than a unit price. Peachtree flags any spelling errors as they occur. See Bonus Chapter 1 on this book's Web site for information on spelling options.

Journal

    Quotes don't affect the General Ledger, but whenever the quote becomes a sale, Peachtree uses the GL account numbers to update your financial information.

    If you have globally hidden General Ledger accounts, Peachtree does not display GL Account fields in the Quotes window. To modify GL accounts used for this transaction, you must click the Journal button (as shown here) on the window toolbar.

12. **If you're quoting a non-inventory item, select the tax type in the Tax field.**

    The Tax field refers to the tax types you determine when setting inventory defaults. Peachtree uses default tax types of 1 for Taxable and 2 for Exempt. If you're using inventory items, Peachtree determines the tax type from the inventory item.

13. **You probably won't have a job number assigned yet because this is still a quote, so skip the Job field.**

14. **Repeat Steps 9–13 for each item you want to quote.**

15. **If you're going to charge shipping charges, enter the estimated amount in the Freight field.**

Note

16. **(Optional) Click the Note button, as shown here in the margin, to store one of three different notes:**

    - *A customer note,* which prints on the actual Quote form

    - *A statement note,* which prints on the customer statement

    - *An internal note,* for internal reference only

    If you later convert the quote to a sales order or invoice, the notes carry over as well.

Save

We're assuming that you need to print the quote; however, if you don't need to print the quote, click the Save button (as shown here). Peachtree saves the quote for future reference. To print or e-mail your quote, click the Print button or the E-mail button. See Chapter 13 for more information about printing forms.

Converting a quote to a sales order or an invoice

Congratulations! You got the sale! Now you're ready to generate a sales order or an invoice from the original quote.

To convert a quote to make the sale, follow these steps:

1. **Choose Tasks⇨Quotes/Sales Orders/Proposals⇨Quotes which displays the Quotes window.**

2. **Click the List button (as shown in the margin) to display a list of previously created quotes.**

3. **Choose the quote you want to convert and then click the Open button.**

   You might have to change the date range to display quotes from a different time period.

   If you don't remember what month you created the quote, try this: In the Date Range list, select All Transactions (at the top of the list). Then click in the Search For field and enter a few characters of your customer's name. Click the drop-down list next to the Search For field and then select Customer/Prospect Name. Click the Search button, and Peachtree locates quotes for only the customer you specify.

4. **Change the date on the quote to the sales order date or invoice date you want to use.**

5. **Click the Convert button (as shown in the margin) to display the Convert Quote dialog box shown in Figure 7-9.**

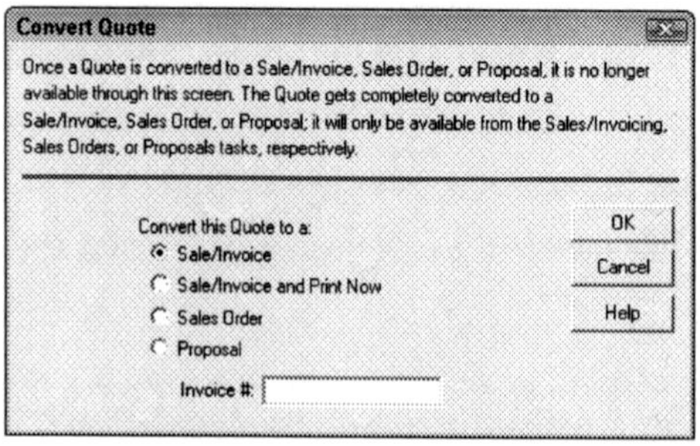

Figure 7-9:
Converting a quote to another document type.

> **Convert Quote**
>
> Once a Quote is converted to a Sale/Invoice, Sales Order, or Proposal, it is no longer available through this screen. The Quote gets completely converted to a Sale/Invoice, Sales Order, or Proposal; it will only be available from the Sales/Invoicing, Sales Orders, or Proposals tasks, respectively.
>
> Convert this Quote to a:
> - Sale/Invoice
> - Sale/Invoice and Print Now
> - Sales Order
> - Proposal
>
> Invoice #: [   ]
>
> OK   Cancel   Help

6. **Select a conversion option.**

   The options, which appear depending on your selection, are as follows:

- *Sale/Invoice:* Select this to convert your quote to an invoice. You get a field prompting you for an invoice number. If you elect not to enter an invoice number, the quote still converts to an invoice, but you'll need to print the invoice at a later time.

- *Sale/Invoice and Print Now:* Select this to convert your quote to an invoice. After you click OK, Peachtree prompts you for a beginning invoice number and other print options and then prints the invoice.

- *Sales Order:* Select this to convert your quote to a sales order. A field appears with the next sales order number displayed. You can change this sales order number if desired.

- *Proposal:* Select this to convert your quote to a proposal. A field appears with the next proposal number displays. You can change the proposal number if you wish.

Proposals are similar to sales orders except that with a proposal, you can bill the customer for a percentage of the amount due, for specific lines of the proposal, or for the remaining unbilled portion of the job. See Chapter 12 for more information on proposals.

7. **Click OK.**

   After you convert a quote, the transaction is no longer available as a quote if you click the List button in the Quotes window. You can, however, see it as a sales order, proposal, or invoice in the Sales Order List window, Proposal List window, or the Sales/Invoicing window.

Working with Sales Orders

Why should you use sales orders? Why not just create an invoice? Well, this choice is really a matter of timing. If your business receives a customer order and ships the product or provides the service within a day or two, you could skip the sales order step and wait to enter the invoice. If a lapse exists between the time when you take the order and when you provide the product or service, however, you might find the sales order feature helpful. The sales order feature lets you enter items for a customer and then invoice and ship the items as they become available, tracking the back orders in the system.

By viewing inventory and sales order reports, you know the number of items back-ordered for your customers, which can help you plan purchases from your vendors.

Sales orders are optional in the Peachtree sales process.

Even though you reference GL accounts when you create a sales order, Peachtree doesn't update the General Ledger from a sales order.

You might find entering data in the Sales Order window similar to creating a quote. To create a sales order, follow these steps:

1. **Choose Tasks⇨Quotes/Sales Orders/Proposals⇨Sales Orders to display the Sales Orders window.**

2. **Fill in the customer information or select the customer ID from the lookup list.**

   If you enter a customer ID not set up in Peachtree, the ID field flashes. When you later save or print the transactions, Peachtree prompts you to save the customer information.

   The lower-left corner displays the customer's current balance, credit limit, and credit status. Click the arrow to display the customer ledger.

3. **Type the Ship To address, or click the arrow next to the Ship To field and then select one of the addresses you entered when first setting up the customer.**

   Peachtree doesn't store a manually entered Ship To address permanently in the customer record. However, Peachtree does store the custom address with the sales order and later transfers the address to the resulting invoice.

4. **Enter the date you want for the sales order and a ship-by date.**

   The ship-by date can appear on several sales order reports to help you better track your customer orders.

   Peachtree automatically assigns the next sales order number, but you can change it if you want.

5. **If you want your vendor to ship the item directly to your customer, select the Drop Ship check box.**

   If you activate the default inventory option in Peachtree Premium or higher to create purchase orders automatically, Peachtree creates a purchase order for the item. See Chapter 4.

   Read the earlier section, "Entering quotes," to review entering line items.

6. **Fill in the body of the sales order, keeping the following variations in mind:**

   • *A sales order does not have a Good Thru field.*

   • *Your customer might not supply you with a customer purchase order number.*

- *If you don't enter a quantity, enter an amount.*

- *If you're using the Peachtree job costing feature, you might have already assigned a job number to the customer order.* If so, be sure to indicate the job ID, and optionally, the phase code and cost code to each sales order line item. Read about setting up jobs in Chapter 12.

Peachtree can play a visual trick on you here. When you click the Job field, it expands backward and covers up part of the Amount field (see Figure 7-10). At first glance, it might appear that some of or all the amount has disappeared, but it's only hidden. When you move the insertion point past the Job field, Peachtree redisplays the Amount field.

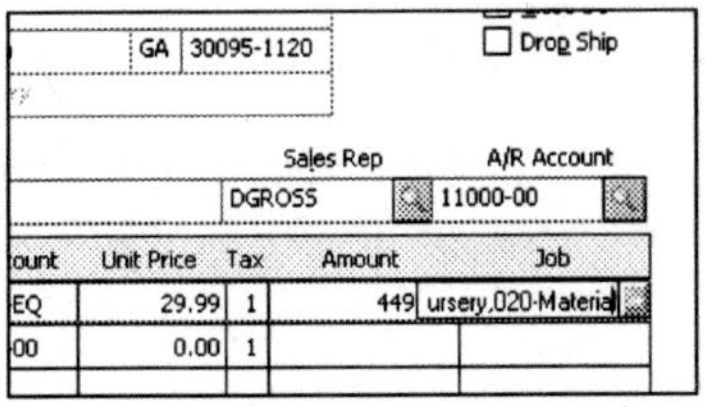

Figure 7-10:
The amount
is not
gone, just
temporarily
hidden.

GA	30095-1120			☐ Drop Ship	
			Sales Rep	A/R Account	
			DGROSS	11000-00	
ount	Unit Price	Tax	Amount	Job	
EQ	29.99	1	449	ursery,020-Material	
00	0.00	1			

- *If you're going to charge shipping charges and you know the amount, enter it in the Freight field.*

- *The Shipped quantity field is unavailable for you to edit.* When you ship the ordered goods (whether partially or completely) and bill them on an invoice, Peachtree tracks the quantity shipped and enters it in this column of the sales order.

7. **(Optional) Click the Note button to store one of three different notes:**

   - *A customer note,* which prints on the actual Sales Order form

   - *A statement note,* which prints on the customer statement

   - *An internal note,* for internal reference only

If you have an electronic copy of the customer's original order, you can click the Attach button to link the original order to the Peachtree sales order.

8. **After you finish entering the sales order, click the Save button to save the transaction or the Print button to print it.**

See Chapter 13 for instructions on printing sales orders.

Generating an Invoice

Finally! Your company has produced the product or performed the service, and you're now ready to collect your money. Most businesses generate an invoice as proof of the sale to give or send to their customers.

If you read the previous sections on creating quotes or creating sales orders, you know quite a bit about creating an invoice. Like with quotes and sales orders, you enter the invoice header and body information. The difference is that when you *do* use sales orders, you enter the information a little differently from the way you enter data if you *don't* use sales orders.

Invoicing against a sales order

In a single transaction, only one sales order can apply to an invoice. However, you can create multiple invoices from a single sales order. To create an invoice and apply it to a sales order, follow these steps:

1. **Choose Tasks⇨Sales/Invoicing to display the Sales/Invoicing window.**

   The Sales/Invoicing window is similar to the Quotes and Sales Order windows.

2. **Type or select the customer ID.**

   You can't create an invoice in Peachtree unless you set up a customer through Maintain Customers/Prospects.

   With the insertion point in the ID field, you can press the plus (+) key to display the Maintain Customers/Prospects window.

   Here's where things get a little different. See Figure 7-11. After you select your customer ID, Peachtree looks for any open sales order for that customer. If an open sales order exists, Peachtree automatically displays the Apply to Sales Order No. tab.

   If the invoice you want to enter does not apply to a sales order, click the Apply to Sales tab and proceed to the information in the next section, "Invoicing against sales."

   If your customer has both open sales orders and open accepted proposals, Peachtree alerts you with a message window. Click OK. See Chapter 12 for information on progress billing against a proposal.

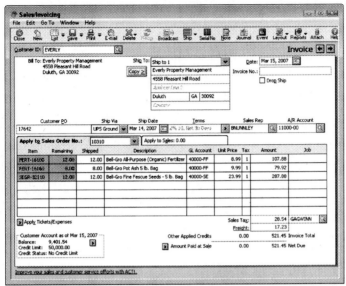

Figure 7-11:
Create an
invoice
for your
customers.

3. **On the Apply to Sales Order No. tab, click the arrow to display a drop-down list of open sales orders.**

4. **Select the sales order you want to invoice.**

   Peachtree fills in the information you supplied when you created the sales order, including Ship To, Customer PO, Sales Rep, and the items ordered.

5. **Enter the invoice date and change any header information.**

   Leave the invoice number blank if you want Peachtree to assign an invoice number when you print the invoice.

   Inventory item numbers on a sales order can't be edited from an invoice. To change item numbers, you must edit the original sales order. You can, however, change the quantities or item description. To add additional items or charges to the invoice, click the Apply to Sales tab and add the items there.

6. **In the Shipped column, enter the quantities shipped. Or if the entire order has been filled, click the Ship toolbar button and then choose All (both shown in the margin).**

   If you click the All button, Peachtree fills in the remaining quantities of the order.

7. **Enter the Freight amount.**

   If you entered freight information when you created the sales order, Peachtree automatically displays it on the invoice *only* if you use the Ship All feature in the previous step. If you make a partial shipment and need to charge freight, enter the freight amount manually.

   If you're going to ship the product via UPS and plan to use the shipping feature available in Peachtree Complete and above, click the Freight link. See "Shipping the UPS Way," later in this chapter, for information on the shipping feature.

8. **(Optional) Click the Note button to store one of three notes:**

   - *A customer note,* which prints on the actual invoice

   - *A statement note,* which prints on the customer statement

   - *An internal note,* for internal reference only

9. **Click the Save button or the Print button (both as shown in the margin).**

   You probably want to print the invoice. If you're not going to print it or if you want to continue entering invoices and print them later in a batch, though, click the Save button to save the invoice. To print your invoices, see Chapter 13.

   When you save or print the invoice, if the current invoice total plus any unpaid invoices for this customer exceed the credit limit determined when you set up the customer, Peachtree might warn you and potentially stop you from proceeding with the invoice.

Invoicing against sales

Your business doesn't use sales orders? You can create an invoice without a sales order. To create an invoice, follow these steps:

1. **Choose Tasks⇨Sales Invoicing to display the Sales/Invoicing window.**

2. **Enter the invoice header information.**

   To review how to enter the header information, see the "Bidding with quotes" section, earlier in this chapter. The header information comprises the invoice date, shipping address, customer's purchase order number (if available), shipping method, terms, and sales rep ID.

3. **If you want your vendor to ship the item directly to your customer, select the Drop Ship check box.**

   If you activate the default inventory option in Peachtree Premium or higher to create purchase orders automatically, Peachtree creates a purchase order for the item. See Chapter 4 for more about setting inventory defaults.

4. **Fill in the line items for the invoice, starting by entering a quantity for the first item on the invoice.**

   You can leave the Quantity field blank when invoicing a service or product that doesn't have a quantity. Then, enter the information for the following if they apply:

   - *If the product is an inventory item, select the item ID.*

     Peachtree fills in the item description, the GL account, the item's unit price, and the tax type. Then Peachtree multiplies the quantity times the unit price for the amount.

     You can tell Peachtree to warn you if you don't have enough stock to sell the item. Read more about this in Chapter 4.

   - *If your product is a non-inventory item or you don't use inventory, leave the Item field blank and enter a description, GL account, and unit price.*

     The Tax field refers to the tax types you determine when setting inventory defaults. If you're using inventory items, Peachtree determines the tax type from the inventory item.

   - *If you don't enter a quantity, enter an amount.*

   - *(Optional) If you're using the Peachtree job-costing feature, select a job.*

     Click in the Job field to display the lookup list button and then select a job from the list.

   - *If you're going to charge shipping charges and you know the amount, enter it in the Freight Amount field.*

   If you're going to ship the product via UPS and plan to use the shipping feature available in Peachtree Complete or Peachtree Premium, click the Freight link. This saves the invoice and opens the Shipping window with the customer information already entered. See "Shipping the UPS Way," later in this chapter, for information on the shipping feature.

5. **(Optional) Click the Note button to store one of three different notes:**

   - *A customer note,* which prints on the actual invoice

   - *A statement note,* which prints on the customer statement

   - *An internal note,* for internal reference only

6. **Click the Save button or the Print button.**

   You probably want to print the invoice; however, if you're not going to print it or if you want to continue entering invoices and print them later in a batch, click the Save button to save the invoice. To print your invoices, see "Printing Forms" in Chapter 13.

   Like with sales orders, if the current invoice total plus any unpaid invoices for this customer exceed the credit limit you established when you set up the customer, Peachtree might warn you and potentially stop you from proceeding with the invoice.

Shipping the UPS Way

This feature is available only in Peachtree Complete and higher.

What happens when you mix brown and peach? No, we're not referring to disintegrating fruit. You get UPS (brown) integration with your Peachtree (peach) software! You might deliver your goods to your clients in many different ways. You might hand-deliver them, the customer might pick them up from your warehouse, or you might ship them by using a common carrier such as a freight line or a parcel delivery service. If you ship your goods through UPS, you can generate and track the shipment information directly through the Peachtree Shipments feature.

A shipment generated through the Shipments feature doesn't have to be for goods you sell. It could be for any document or package you want to ship to anyone, anywhere.

You must have an Internet connection for the Shipments feature to work.

Before you can use the Shipments feature, you must have an account number registered through UPS. Contact UPS at 1-800-PICK-UPS (1-800-742-5877) or www.ups.com to initiate an account. Don't lose the account number, because you need it to register through the Shipping Registration Wizard.

After you have an account number assigned but before you can ship your first package, you must use the Shipping Registration Wizard to activate the link between UPS and Peachtree. Choose Tasks⇨Shipments⇨Shipping Registration Wizard. Follow the steps, which include entering your shipping address, a contact name, your UPS account number, and the billing method you want UPS to use.

The contact person entered in the Shipping Registration Wizard must be set up as an employee in Maintain Employees even if you don't use Peachtree to process payroll. See Chapter 9 for setting up employees.

When you have UPS packages to ship, follow these easy steps:

1. **Choose Tasks⇨Shipments⇨Shipments.**

   Peachtree opens the Shipping window.

2. **(Optional) In the Ship to Type list, select whether you're shipping to a customer, a vendor, or an employee.**

3. **Select the ID. If you're not shipping to a customer, a vendor, or an employee, leave this field blank.**

   If you clicked the Freight link in the Sales/Invoicing window, you see the Shipping window with the customer information and invoice number already entered.

4. **Enter a shipment number.**

   This is a required data-entry field. After you create a shipment number (say, 101), Peachtree remembers the sequence for the next shipment and numbers it (102). Optionally, you could use the customer invoice number as the shipment reference number.

5. **Select the level of UPS service you want.**

   You can select the service level as well as any extras, such as delivery confirmation or COD charges.

6. **(Optional) In the Shipment Description field, enter a brief description of the contents of the shipment.**

7. **Enter the package information, including package type and weight.**

8. **(Optional) Enter the package value and then select whether you want the package to have special handling.**

   Each package going to this recipient must be listed with its own package type, weight, and dimensions. Peachtree lists the standard UPS-provided packages as well as a custom field, where you enter your own dimensions. The length should be the longest dimension in the package.

9. **If you want a cost estimate before shipping this order, click the Estimate button and follow the on-screen instructions.**

   The UPS Estimate Settings field prompts you for the method you plan on using to get the package to UPS and then displays a list of the UPS service level options and their published rates.

10. **Click the Process button.**

    Peachtree registers the shipment with UPS and assigns a UPS tracking number.

    If you're billing the total to the customer invoice and the customer invoice already has an invoice number assigned, Peachtree thinks the invoice is already printed and warns you that proceeding will change the invoice's total amount due.

    A confirmation message appears, stating the total estimated charges, and prompts you to print the shipping labels. Print the shipping label on plain paper and attach it to the package, usually in a special UPS window envelope.

11. **Click OK twice and then click Yes after the label prints.**

    Your UPS account does not get billed until the actual package is scanned by a UPS representative. If you decide to not ship the package, you can void the shipment by locating it through the List button and then clicking the Void button.

You can track the status of your shipment by choosing Tasks⇨Shipments⇨ Track a Package and entering the UPS tracking number.

Editing a Sales Transaction

Like most transactions you enter in Peachtree, quotes, sales orders, and invoices are not written in stone. Peachtree makes it easy for you to modify anything on the transaction — even after it has been printed.

Choose Lists⇨Customers & Sales and then choose the type of document you want to edit: Quote, Proposal, Sales Order, or Sales/Invoicing. Locate the document you want and then click the Open button. Make any desired changes to the transaction by using the steps described in appropriate preceding sections in this chapter. Then click the Print button to reprint the transaction or click the Save button to save the transaction without reprinting it.

Voiding an Invoice

If you generate an invoice and then discover that the invoice needs to be canceled, use the Void Invoice feature. See Chapter 8 if you need to issue a credit memo to the customer.

Although technically, you could delete an invoice to get rid of it, deleting an invoice is not good accounting practice. When you delete transactions, you lose your audit trail of the actions you took. If the original invoice occurred in a previous month, you could hurt the integrity of your reports. Your accountant would not be a happy camper.

When you void an invoice, Peachtree creates several transactions. First, Peachtree creates another invoice with the same invoice number as the original except that it appends a *V* to the invoice number. That invoice amount is a negative dollar amount equal to the amount of the original invoice. For example, if you generate invoice number 1234 for $150.00 that you must cancel, Peachtree generates another invoice 1234V for –$150.00 to void the original.

If the original transaction involves inventory items, Peachtree restores to inventory the items sold. In the General Ledger, Peachtree creates a reversing entry, affecting Sales and Accounts Receivable accounts and (if applicable) Cost of Sales and Inventory accounts. If the original invoice does not come from a sales order, the reversing entry contains negative values for the quantities sold. However, if the original invoice does come from a sales order, the reversing entry contains negative values for the quantities shipped. Peachtree then reopens the sales order.

Next, Peachtree creates a zero-dollar receipt to pay both the original and voided invoices. This receipt clears both transactions from the Aged Receivables report. In other words, if you add the two transactions together, you get zero, and a $0 transaction causes no change in your cash balance. You can view the zero-dollar receipt by clicking the Open button in the Tasks⇨Receipts window and then selecting the appropriate receipt.

To void an invoice, follow these steps:

1. **Choose Lists⇨Customers & Sales⇨Sales Invoices.**

2. **Locate the transaction you want to void and then click the Open button, as shown in the margin.**

   The transaction must appear on the screen before you can void it.

   Optionally, choose a different period from the Date Range drop-down list to find the invoice you want.

3. **Click the Delete button and then choose Void (both as shown in the margin).**

   Peachtree opens a Void Existing Invoice dialog box, such as the one in Figure 7-12.

Figure 7-12:
Peachtree displays the invoice number, date, amount, and customer.

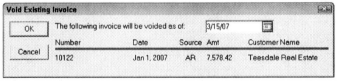

4. **Type the date you want — usually the current date — in The Following Invoice Will Be Voided As Of field.**

5. **Click OK.**

   Peachtree lists the word *Void* beside both the original and reversing invoices and uses the invoice number as the receipt reference number.

Recurring Invoices

In some businesses, you have customers that you bill the same amount every month for the same products or services. By setting up recurring entries, you can save a great deal of time entering these invoices. Even if the amount differs next time, it's helpful to have all the other information filled out for you. Then, you have to change only the amount.

If you're using Peachtree Premium or higher and your company is set up for auto-creation of purchase orders, Peachtree does not automatically create POs for recurring customer invoices. (See Chapter 4.)

Recurring entries can't be created if you generate the invoice by using a sales order.

You also can create recurring purchases, payments, and general journal entries. You can adapt the following steps for these other tasks.

To create recurring invoices, follow these steps:

1. **Choose Tasks⇨Sales/Invoicing to display the Sales/Invoicing window.**

2. **Enter the invoice information as you usually would, but do enter an invoice number or click the Save or the Print button.**

3. **Click the Recur button (as shown here) to display the Create Recurring Sales Invoices dialog box, as shown in Figure 7-13.**

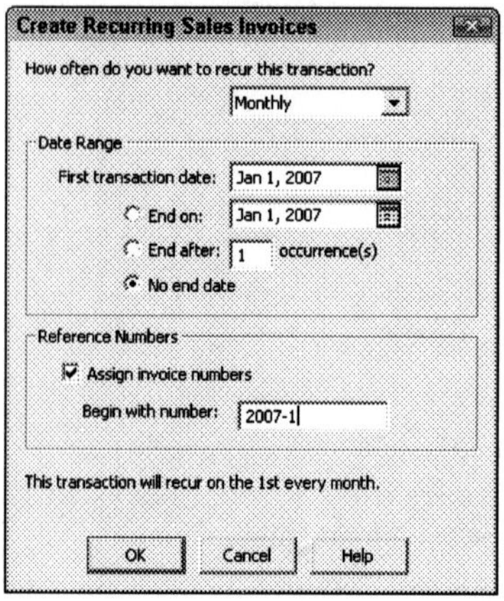

Figure 7-13:
Save data-entry time by creating recurring entries.

> **Create Recurring Sales Invoices**
>
> How often do you want to recur this transaction?
>
> Monthly ▼
>
> **Date Range**
>
> First transaction date: Jan 1, 2007
>
> ○ End on: Jan 1, 2007
>
> ○ End after: 1 occurrence(s)
>
> ● No end date
>
> **Reference Numbers**
>
> ☑ Assign invoice numbers
>
> Begin with number: 2007-1
>
> This transaction will recur on the 1st every month.
>
> OK   Cancel   Help

4. **From the How Often Do You Want to Recur This Transaction? drop-down list, select a time frame for the recurring invoice.**

   You can select Weekly, Bi-Weekly, Every 4 Weeks, Monthly, Per Period, Quarterly, Twice a Year, or Yearly.

5. **Select a beginning and ending transaction date range.**

   If the transactions are infinite, select No End Date.

6. **(Optional) Assign a beginning invoice number by selecting the Assign Invoice Numbers check box.**

Peachtree displays a field to enter a beginning invoice number. All transactions are numbered incrementally. A number of our clients use a system that includes the current year as the first two or four digits of the number, followed by a dash and then the beginning invoice number.

Peachtree doesn't automatically print recurring invoices. If you leave the invoice number blank, you can print the recurring transactions when you use the batch printing method or edit the transaction and then click Print. Chapter 13 discusses how to print batches of forms.

7. Click OK.

Peachtree saves all transactions in the appropriate periods.

If you need to edit or delete a recurring transaction, Peachtree prompts you with the Change Recurring Journal Entries dialog box. You can edit only the current invoice or the current invoice and all future occurrences. Editing a recurring transaction does not affect previous transactions.

Broadcasting Invoices

In the preceding section, you can read about generating recurring invoices for when your customer buys the same product or service on a regular basis; monthly, for example. Suppose, however, that you provide a service for a number of customers, all being charged the same amount. It might be a one-time service for many of these customers, so creating a recurring invoice won't work for you.

The Peachtree broadcast invoicing feature (available in Peachtree Premium and higher) allows you to create one invoice for multiple customers. This can be quite a time-saver compared with creating the invoices one at a time for each customer.

The following steps show you how to broadcast an invoice:

1. Create the invoice that you want to broadcast to multiple customers.

Don't enter information in the customer ID, date, or invoice number fields. Peachtree fills this in for you later.

You cannot broadcast an invoice that contains serialized inventory items.

2. Click the Broadcast button, as shown in the margin.

The Select Customers for Broadcast Invoicing - Filter Selection screen, as shown in Figure 7-14, appears.

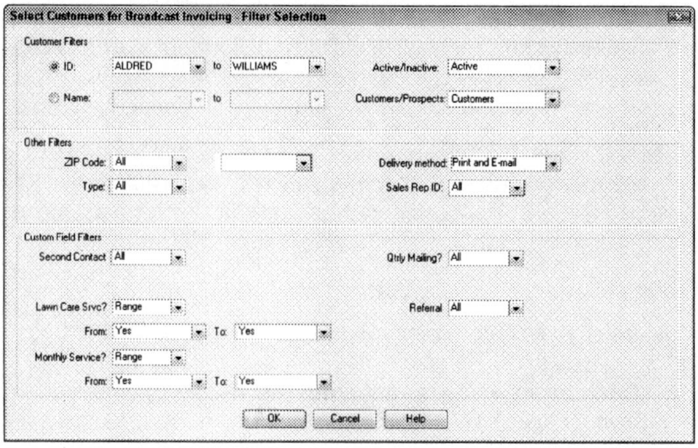

Figure 7-14: Broadcasting a single invoice to many customers.

3. **Choose from the following options to filter to the list of customers you want to use. You can choose a combination of options:**

   • *ID:* To filter by customer ID, select the option button and then choose the beginning and ending customer IDs.

   • *Name:* To filter by customer name, select the Name button; then, choose the beginning and ending customer name.

   • *Active/Inactive:* To filter by whether the customer is active or inactive, click the arrow and then select an option.

   • *Customers/Prospects:* To filter by whether the invoice should go to customers, prospects, or both, click the arrow and then select an option.

   After you create an invoice for a prospect, the prospect is automatically changed to a customer.

   • *ZIP Code:* To filter by Zip code, select All to include customers in all Zip codes or select Mask if you want customers in specific Zip codes. For example, if you want to select customers with Zip code 46239, enter 46239 in the Zip Code field. If you want to filter customers whose Zip code begins with 462, enter "462**" in the Zip Code field.

   • *Type:* To filter customers by type, select Range; then, select the customer types you want. Choose All if you don't want to filter by customer type.

   • *Delivery Method:* To filter customers based on the customer's form delivery method, select Print Only, E-mail Only, or Print and E-mail.

- *Sales Rep ID:* To filter customers assigned to a particular sales rep, select All or Range and then select the sales reps you want.

- *Custom Fields:* To filter customers with a particular value in a custom field, select the value from the From and To lists for the appropriate custom field.

4. **Click OK.**

   [Return to filter screen]

   The Create Broadcast Invoices screen appears with a grid displaying a list of customers that meet the filter criteria. If you need to change the filter criteria, click the Return to Filter Screen button (as shown here).

5. **Verify and, if needed, change the Broadcast Invoice Date.**

   You might see warning messages in the grid next to some customers: for example, if the customer were over the credit limit. Review the messages and decide whether you want to continue sending an invoice to this customer.

6. **Deselect any customer to whom you don't want to send the invoice.**

   Peachtree displays in the lower-right corner the number of invoices you selected and the estimated invoice totals.

   [Create]

7. **Click the Create button (as shown in the margin).**

   Peachtree creates the invoices for each selected customer and then displays a confirmation screen.

   [Print Invoices]

8. **Click the Print Invoices button (as shown here) if you want to print the invoices now. Or, click the Close button if you plan on printing the invoices later.**

   [View Summary]

   Click the View Summary button (as shown here) to see a list of the invoices you just created. You don't have the option to view this report any other time.

   After you finish, you can review the invoices and (if desired) edit them by choosing them from the Lists➪Customers & Sales➪Sales Invoices.

Reviewing Customer Reports

Peachtree offers several useful reports that you can use for listing customer information, compiling tax information, and tracking quotes that you want to turn into sales. In Tables 7-2, 7-3, and 7-4, we provide you with a description of the reports that pertain to selling your goods and services. You can sort the report data in a variety of ways, and you can control how much and which information you want to display on the report. See Chapter 14 to find out how to customize and print reports.

Table 7-2   Reports Related to Quotes and Customers in General

Report Name	What It Does
Customer List	For each customer, lists the ID, name, contact name, telephone number, and resale number.
Customer Master File List	Similar to the Customer List report, but also includes address information, tax codes, and terms.
Prospect List	Lists each prospect with contact and telephone number.
Quote Register	Lists each quote with quote date, expiration date, customer name, and quote amount.

Table 7-3   Reports Related to Sales Orders

Report Name	What It Does
Picklist Report	Lists open sales order items, such as item ID and description, quantity to ship, and warehouse location. Sort this report by sales order number, ship-by date, location, customer ID, or item ID.
Sales Backorder Report	Lists open order items, such as item ID, description, and quantities on order, on hand and on purchase orders. Sort this report by sales order number, ship-by date, location, customer ID, or item ID.
Sales Order Journal	Lists sales orders in journal entry format.
Sales Order Register	Lists each sales order and its status. Sort this report by customer ID, sales order date, or ship-by date.
Sales Order Report	Lists the details of all sales orders by sales order number, ship-by date, customer ID, or item ID.

Table 7-4   Reports Related to Customer Invoicing

Report Name	Description
Customer Ledgers	Shows the transactions and a running balance for each customer for a specified date range.
Customer Sales History	Summarizes, by customer, how much each has purchased.

Report Name	Description
Invoice Register	Lists each invoice number with date, quote number, customer name, and invoice amount. Sort this report by invoice number, customer ID, or invoice date.
Items Sold to Customers	Lists for each customer, the quantity, amount, and profit of both inventoried and non-inventoried items sold.
Sales Journal	Lists transactions as reported to the General Ledger.
Customer Transaction History	Lists, by customer, invoices and invoice-related entries, such as payments and credit memos.
Shipment Register	Lists shipments and to whom they were made. Sort this report by shipment number, shipment date, or ship to ID. (This report is listed under the Inventory category.)
Sales Rep Report	Lists sales statistics by sales rep ID or customer.
Taxable/Exempt Sales	Lists all taxable and exempt sales per tax authority. See Chapter 6 for information on using this report to pay your sales tax.

Don't forget to visit www.dummies.com/go/peachtreefd for more information on Peachtree.

Chapter 8

Collecting the Money

● ●

In This Chapter

▶ Receiving your customers' money

▶ Tracking accounts receivable

▶ Issuing credit memos

▶ Charging finance charges

▶ Printing statements

● ●

*O*ne of our favorite sayings is, "As much fun as I'm having doing what I'm doing . . . I'm still doing it for the money."

Most people *do* find that their preferred part of being in business is collecting the money. Peachtree not only provides you with an easy way to track the money your customers owe you, but it also provides you with a few ways to encourage your customers to pay up.

Peachtree refers to the money you receive from your customers as *receipts*. That sounds logical enough, doesn't it?

Recording Receipts

The Receipts feature allows you to enter all checks, cash, and credit card slips you receive and post them to your checking account. Peachtree provides two ways to account for receipts. The method you use is mostly determined by timing.

One method is used when you receive the customer's money *at the time of the sale.* You enter the receipt right on the invoice and then when you print the invoice, it can also show the funds received.

The other and more commonly used method is to apply the receipt to an invoice through the Receipts window. You can use this method either if the customer pays you at the time of the sale or at a later date.

Applying receipts to an invoice

To apply a receipt to a customer invoice, begin by taking a look at the Receipts window:

1. **Choose Tasks⇨Receipts to display the Receipts window.**

   The Receipts window appears as shown in Figure 8-1.

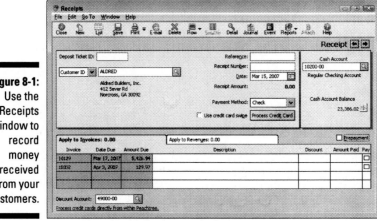

Figure 8-1: Use the Receipts window to record money received from your customers.

2. **If necessary, enter a deposit ticket ID.**

   What appears in the Deposit Ticket ID field of the Receipts window depends on your choice of method for generating these IDs in the Pay Methods tab in the Customer Defaults dialog box (see Chapter 4). If you opted for the Receipts window, Peachtree displays the current date; otherwise this field is blank. If you leave the Deposit Ticket ID field blank, Peachtree can automatically suggest deposit ticket IDs in the Select for Deposit window. We recommend you leave the Deposit Ticket ID field blank and let Peachtree assign a group of deposits together when you actually make the bank deposit.

   For more information about deposit ticket IDs, see "Laughing All the Way to the Bank," later in this chapter.

3. **Select the customer ID.**

   If this customer has unpaid invoices, Peachtree lists them on the Apply to Invoices tab. If the customer has no outstanding balance, Peachtree displays the Apply to Revenues tab.

Double-click any unpaid invoice to see the transaction details.

4. Enter a reference number in the Reference field that helps identify the receipt.

You must enter a reference number, usually the customer's check number. If the receipt was transmitted electronically, you might enter the electronic confirmation number or the date.

5. Enter the date of the receipt in the Date field.

Use this field to record the date you *received* the check, not the date on the check.

6. Select a payment method: Cash, Check, Charge, and so on.

You set up payment methods in the Customer Defaults dialog box. You can find out how to set customer defaults in Chapter 4. You can run some reports based on payment methods. Chapter 14 shows you how to filter reports.

If the customer is paying by credit card, you can store the credit card information or use the Peachtree credit card service to process the credit card. See "Handling Credit Card Receipts," later in this chapter.

7. In the Cash Account field, verify the bank account into which you're depositing the receipt.

Always confirm the Cash account. Peachtree remembers which account you last used in this window.

8. Select the check box in the Pay column beside each invoice being paid by this receipt.

If the amount of the receipt doesn't match the invoice amount, enter the actual amount received in the Amount Paid column.

If, based on the customer terms, the invoice is eligible for a discount, Peachtree automatically displays the discount amount. You can accept that amount, delete it, or enter a different amount. If you offer — and the customer took — discounts, verify the Discount account number at the bottom of the window.

If the amount paid is less than the amount due, Peachtree assumes that the customer still owes the difference. The next time you open the Receipts window for the customer, Peachtree displays the remainder due on the invoice.

If the amount paid is less than the amount due and you're going to write off the difference, enter the full amount of the invoice in the Amount Paid field and then click the Apply to Revenues tab and enter a negative amount for the amount you're writing off. (Make sure the amount you're writing off is not taxed.) Choose your write-off account for the GL account. This process clears the invoice from A/R, posts the correct amount to cash, and charges the unpaid balance on the invoice to the write-off account.

If you're not sure whether you're going to write off an over- or underpayment, go ahead and apply the actual amount received on the Apply to Invoices tab. You can write a credit memo to your client later. See "Giving Credit Where Credit Is Due," later in this chapter.

Journal

If you don't see a field to select the GL account, it means the field is hidden. (See Bonus Chapter 1 on this book's Web site for more information about displaying the GL account fields.) You can click the Journal button, as shown here in the margin, at the top of the window and enter the account numbers you want to use.

If the amount paid is more than the invoice amount, Peachtree automatically creates a credit balance against the specified invoice. The next time you display the Receipts window for this customer, you see a credit balance. If you're going to absorb the overpayment (usually for small amounts), click the appropriate check box in the Pay column, which marks the invoice as paid in full. Then click the Apply to Revenues tab and enter the overpayment amount as a positive number. This clears the transaction from Accounts Receivable.

If you make a direct sale that doesn't require an invoice, click the Apply to Revenues tab and specify a Sales account and an amount. Optionally, enter a quantity, item ID, or description.

The amount Peachtree displays in the Receipt Amount field should match the total amount received from your customer.

Save

9. **Click the Save button, as shown in the margin, to record the receipt.**

Print

You could also click the Print button, as shown in the margin, to print a receipt that you can give to your customer. Printing the receipt saves the receipt.

TIP

The Receipts window also gives you a handy way to write off an entire invoice as a bad debt. In the Receipts window, enter a unique reference number that helps identify the receipt as a write-off. For example, we typically use the letters WO (for write-off) or BD (for bad debt) and the original invoice number as the reference number (BD12345). Click the Cash Account field to select the Bad Debt Expense account. Select the check box in the Pay column for the invoice you want to write off as a bad debt and then click Save. Peachtree clears the transaction from Accounts Receivable and increases the Bad Debt Expense account. Be sure to change the Cash account back to the regular Checking account before closing the window.

Entering receipts from non-established customers

Occasionally, you receive money from a customer you haven't invoiced. Even if the customer isn't set up in your customer list, you can still record a receipt. You can also use this procedure if you receive money from other sources, such as a product rebate or utility deposit refund.

The procedure is the same as applying receipts to an invoice, except you won't enter a customer ID. Skip this field and enter the payer's name in the Name field. Because you haven't entered an invoice, Peachtree displays the Apply to Revenues tab. Select the Sales account (or expense account for a refund), enter the receipt amount, and then click the Save button or the Print button. Again, optionally, enter a quantity, item ID, or description.

Make sure the Tax type field shows the appropriate sales tax type.

Applying receipts at the time of sale

You can apply a receipt also by recording it at the time of sale as you create the invoice. (You see how to create an invoice in Chapter 7.) Using this method allows Peachtree to print the amount received on the invoice.

To apply a receipt at the time of the sale, follow these steps:

1. **Choose the Tasks⇨Sales/Invoicing window to display the invoice window.**

2. **Create an invoice for the customer.**

3. **At the bottom of the invoice, click the Amount Paid at Sale arrow button, as shown here in the margin, to display the Receive Payment dialog box, as shown in Figure 8-2.**

4. **Enter the payment information.**

   Also, be sure to verify the Cash account into which you're depositing the money.

5. **Click OK to close the Receive Payment dialog box.**

6. **Save or print the transaction. In this situation, you're printing the customer invoice.**

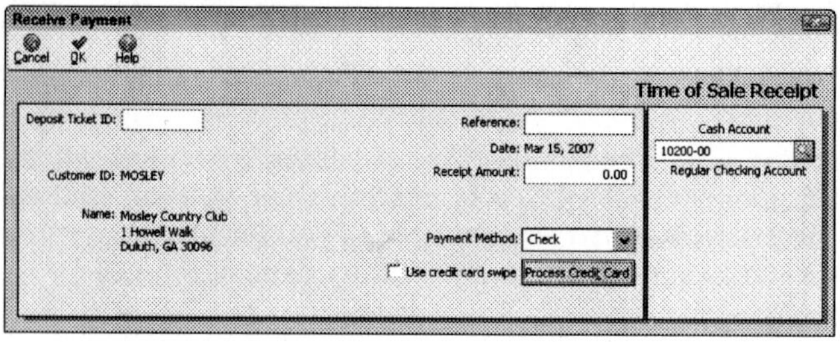

Figure 8-2:
Enter
receipt
information
in the
Receive
Payment
dialog box.

Handling Credit Card Receipts

If your business accepts credit card payments from customers, you can enter and track these transactions in Peachtree. Assuming (we know, there we go assuming again) you have to wait for that time lapse before you receive the money from the credit card financial institution, you can go ahead and record the credit card transactions in Peachtree, but first you need the following items:

✔ **A GL account** in your Chart of Accounts to use for the credit card receivable amount. Create an account in the Accounts Receivable area of your Chart of Accounts, giving it an ID and a description to identify it, such as Credit Cards Receivable. Choose Accounts Receivable as the account type. If necessary, create additional accounts by using the same method. (Chapter 3 shows you how to create accounts.)

✔ **A vendor ID** for the credit card financial institution that processes the credit card transactions. This way, you can record and track processing fee expenses.

To record a credit card transaction, you must follow two sets of steps — one when the transaction occurs and another when you know that the credit card financial institution has deposited the money in your account:

1. **In the Receipts window or the Receive Payments window, record receipt information but don't save or print the transaction yet.**

   You can apply the customer credit card receipts to open invoices or to revenue.

   Use the techniques shown in the "Applying receipts to an invoice," "Entering receipts from non-established customers," or "Applying receipts at the time of sale" sections, earlier in this chapter. *However,* you must use this exception: Enter the credit card receivable GL account as the Cash account.

2. **To keep the customer's account accurate and up-to-date, record the amount paid as the full amount of the credit card charge, regardless of how the financial institution handles processing fees.**

   You enter the processing fees as an expense after your bank statement arrives.

3. **Click the Process Credit Card button, as shown in the margin.**

   The Credit Card Information window appears (see Figure 8-3). If you stored the customer's credit card information when you set up the customer, the stored information automatically appears.

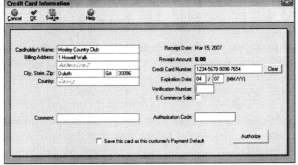

Figure 8-3:
You can store the credit card information as a customer default.

4. **Enter the credit card number and other information pertaining to the customer's credit card, such as name and expiration date.**

   You can store default credit card information in the customer record. See Chapter 7 for more on storing customer information.

5. **If you subscribe to the Peachtree credit card service, click the Authorize button, as shown in the margin, to connect with your online merchant account provider.**

   When authorized, the provider automatically supplies the authorization number. If you don't subscribe to this service, enter the authorization number manually in the Authorization Code field.

6. **Click OK and then click either the Save button or the Print button, as shown here in the margin.**

After the credit card financial institution has notified you that the money has been deposited into your account, you need to create another receipt that transfers the funds from the credit card receivable account to your bank account.

Create a receipt in the Receipts window just as you create any other Peachtree receipt, with the following exceptions:

- ✔ Skip the Customer ID field and enter the credit card company name in the Name field. Because you're not using a customer ID, Peachtree automatically displays the Apply to Revenues tab.

- ✔ On the line item GL Account field, enter the credit card receivable GL account number.

- ✔ Enter the amount actually transferred to your account.

Laughing All the Way to the Bank

When you enter receipts, you decide whether to assign a deposit ticket ID or let Peachtree assign one when you go to the bank. Peachtree lets you group deposited items together by using the Select for Deposit window to greatly speed up the bank reconciliation process.

What's a deposit ticket ID, you ask? Well, Peachtree uses deposit ticket IDs to make account reconciliation easier to manage. You should assign the same deposit ticket ID to all transactions that you deposit on the same deposit ticket. All receipts that use the same deposit ticket ID appear as one lump sum in account reconciliation, making it easier for you to match the deposits the bank records with the deposits you record in Peachtree. (See Chapter 16 for steps to use account reconciliation in Peachtree.)

More often than not, you receive checks daily and enter them into Peachtree daily, but you don't go to the bank until you accumulate several days' worth of checks. The following example lists five checks you receive on three different days but want to lump together into a single bank deposit:

Date	Check Amount
March 16	$125.75
March 16	$28.41
March 17	$722.01
March 18	$549.10
March 18	$100.05

When you go to the bank, you make one deposit of $1,525.32, and that amount appears on your bank statement. Although in Peachtree you have five different receipts, assigning a single deposit ticket ID to these transactions makes the deposit total of $1,525.32 appear in the Account Reconciliation window. If each of these five transactions has its own unique deposit ticket ID, the

Account Reconciliation window would list all five of them independently, making it extremely difficult for you to match Peachtree deposits to the ones listed on your bank statement. You'd have to sit and figure out which Peachtree transactions add up to the ones listed on your bank statement. If you have lots of receipts with separate deposit ticket IDs, you'd spend lots of time trying to reconcile receipts to your bank statement. Therefore, we recommend that you make your bank account reconciliation process easier by *not* assigning a deposit ticket ID on the Receipts window.

You use the Select for Deposit window to combine multiple customer receipts into a single bank deposit. To select receipts to include in a bank deposit, follow these steps:

1. **Choose Tasks⇨Select for Deposit.**

   The Select for Deposit window appears, as shown in Figure 8-4. The window displays the receipts that don't yet have a deposit ticket ID assigned.

   Open

   To review, modify, or print an existing deposit, click the Open button, as shown here in the margin. Existing deposits include receipts that already have a deposit ticket ID associated with them. If you entered a deposit ticket ID when you recorded the receipt, that ID appears in the Deposit Ticket ID field.

Figure 8-4:
Any receipt you posted to this Cash account without a deposit ticket ID already assigned appears here.

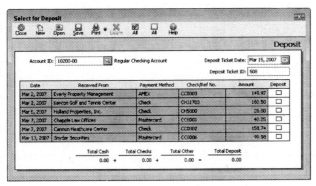

2. **If needed, select a different Cash account from the Account ID drop-down list.**

   If you don't see a receipt that you plan to deposit, you might have entered a deposit ticket ID on the receipt or you might have entered a different Cash account when you recorded the receipt. Edit the receipt to make the correction so that you can include it with the deposit.

3. **Enter the date on which you will make the deposit in the Deposit Ticket Date field.**

4. **Enter or accept the currently suggested deposit ticket ID.**

   Peachtree maintains a numbering scheme based on the last deposit ticket ID entered. Deposit ticket IDs can be alphanumeric and up to eight characters. We recommend using the deposit date and -1, -2, and so on. For example, 031507-1 would be the first deposit made on March 15.

5. **Select the check box in the Deposit column next to the receipts you want included in the current deposit or select all the receipts simultaneously by clicking the All button with the check mark, as shown here in the margin.**

   If you want a receipt to appear as a separate transaction when you reconcile your checking account, select it by itself as its own deposit. You can find out more about account reconciliation in Chapter 16.

6. **Click the Print button to print and save the deposit record, or click the Save button, also shown in the margin, to save the deposit without printing it.**

   Peachtree calls the form a *deposit ticket,* but it does not contain the bank routing information needed to get the money into your account. You might ask your bank whether you can simply attach the report to an actual deposit slip to save you time and effort. It's also helpful to print a copy for your records and attach your bank receipt to it.

Boing! Handling Bounced Checks

One of those nasty facts of life, now and then, is that customers write bad checks, sometimes by accident and sometimes not. In Peachtree, you handle checks returned for nonsufficient funds (NSF) in two simple steps:

1. **Create a new invoice to charge the customer the NSF fees.**

2. **Create a receipt and apply a negative amount for the same amount as the original check.**

   For example, suppose the original (bounced) check is for $147.63. In the example shown in Figure 8-5, we created an NSF invoice number, NSF CK# 13942, for $20.00, which is the amount of the NSF fees. Then, in the Receipts window, we apply a negative $147.63 (which represents the original returned check amount) against the open invoice.

3. **Click the Save button.**

   Peachtree updates the customer balance to reflect the money that the customer once again owes against the original invoice and corrects your bank account balance.

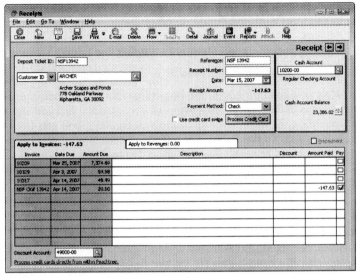

Figure 8-5:
Create a
negative
receipt to
adjust your
bank
balance.

Later, after your customer writes you a second check or instructs you to
redeposit the original check, you will have a second receipt for audit trail
purposes. If the customer writes a second check for the original amount plus
the NSF fee, Peachtree clears the invoice in full. If, however, the customer
instructs you to redeposit the original check, enter only the amount of the
check. After all, the customer still owes you the NSF fee.

We *really* hope you don't have to use this section of our book.

Giving Credit Where Credit Is Due

Unfortunately, products are returned sometimes, or you need to make an
adjustment to a customer invoice. In these situations, you need to create a
credit memo to reduce the amount of money your customer owes.

If you owe money to a customer for overpayment or because you applied a
credit memo to an invoice, you can write a check to the customer for the
refund amount you owe.

Creating a credit memo

You can create a credit memo that refers to an unpaid original invoice, or
you can create an open credit. Additionally, you can create credit memos for

inventoried items or other goods or services. The following steps show you how to use the Peachtree Credit Memo feature:

1. **Choose Tasks⇨Credit Memos to display the Credit Memos window.**

2. **Enter or select the customer ID.**

   After you select a customer, Peachtree fills in the customer name and address. In the lower-left corner of the window, you can see the customer's current balance as of the system date. You can click the arrow button next to the balance to display a Customer Ledger report of the invoices and receipts that make up the balance.

3. **Select a date and enter a Credit No.**

   For the Credit No., we suggest that you use the original invoice number preceded or followed by *CM* to indicate credit memo. This numbering scheme helps you tie the credit memo to a particular sale.

4. **If the credit memo is for an unpaid customer invoice, click the arrow to open the drop-down list on the Apply to Invoice No. tab. Then select the invoice number to which you want to apply the credit memo.**

   Peachtree fills in the lines that appear on the original invoice.

   If you're creating a credit memo for which there's no existing invoice, click the Apply to Sales tab and enter the information for the items to be credited, including quantity, item, price, and (if applicable) job.

5. **In the Returned field on each line of the Apply to Invoice No. tab, type the quantity the customer returned.**

   Enter the returned quantity as a positive number. Peachtree understands that this is a return (see Figure 8-6).

   To quickly fill in the original transaction quantities, click the Return button and then select All.

   If the customer is returning inventory items, Peachtree automatically restores the item quantities to inventory. If the inventory items are damaged, the customer is probably not returning them. Go ahead and record the credit memo, but don't enter any item IDs. This gives the customer a credit for the damaged goods, but does not bring them back into your inventory.

   If a line item was originally assigned to a job, Peachtree also assigns the credit to the same job.

   If the customer is returning serialized inventory items, click the Serial Number button, as shown here in the margin, and then select the serial numbers being returned.

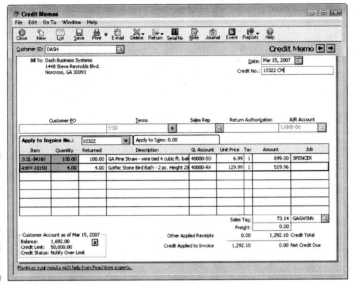

Figure 8-6:
Use this
window to
generate a
customer
credit
memo.

If you charge the customer a restocking fee, click the Apply to Sales tab
and enter it as a negative dollar amount.

6. **Click the Save button to save the transaction, or click the Print button
   to print and save the credit memo.**

   Peachtree applies the credit memo to the open invoice and closes both
   transactions. If you created a credit memo without applying it to an
   invoice, the credit memo appears on the Aged Receivables report. Then,
   when the time comes that the customer makes another purchase, you
   can apply the open credit against the future invoice.

Issuing refund checks for a credit memo

If you owe money to a customer for an overpayment, an open credit, or some
other reason, you can write a check to the customer for the refund amount
owed.

Issuing a refund check is a two-part process. First, you write the check from
the Payments window, and then you apply the check to the credit memo or
overpayment in the Receipts window. This process is based on the assumption that you already created a credit memo or applied the overpayment. See
the preceding section for more information.

Follow these steps to issue a customer refund check:

1. **Choose Tasks⇨Payments to display the Payments window.**

   Click the arrow next to the ID and then select Customer ID, indicating that the check goes to a customer rather than a vendor (see Figure 8-7).

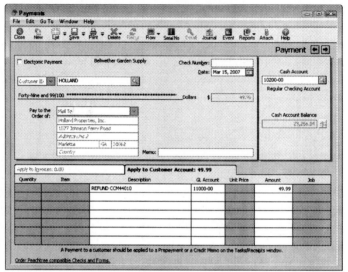

Figure 8-7:
After you
select
Customer ID
from the
drop-down
list,
Peachtree
displays
customer
IDs in the
lookup list.

3. **Choose the customer ID of the customer receiving the refund.**

   Like with generating checks to vendors, don't enter a check number if Peachtree will be printing the check for you. Enter a check number only if you're writing checks by hand (heaven forbid).

4. **Verify the check date and the Cash account from which you're writing the check.**

5. **On the Apply to Customer Account tab, enter a description for the refund.**

   Entering a description helps you remember later, when you're staring at your check register trying to figure out why you wrote a check to a customer, that you issued a refund.

6. **In the line item section of the check, enter or select the GL account to which you want to post the refund amount.**

   Typically, this is your Accounts Receivable account.

7. **Enter the amount of the refund.**

8. **Click the Print button or the Save button.**

   For details on printing checks, see Chapter 6. If you're not going to print the check or you plan to print a batch of checks later, click the Save button.

When you create a check to a customer, Peachtree applies it to the customer account and it appears as a balance due from the customer. To complete the process, you need to apply the refund check to a credit memo or an overpayment.

1. **Choose Tasks⇨Receipts.**

2. **Select the customer ID.**

   The credit memo appears in the invoice listing, along with the refund check.

3. **Select the check box in the Pay column for both the credit memo and refund check.**

   The amount of the receipt displays zero (0.00). Therefore, no money is being applied to the General Ledger. See Figure 8-8.

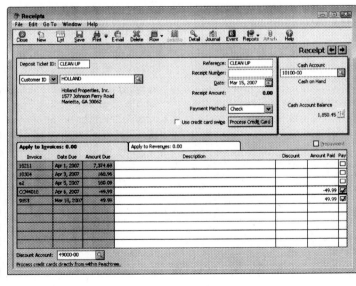

Figure 8-8:
Clear the
credit memo
and refund
check from
the
customer
record.

4. **Enter a receipt reference number in the Reference field, such as the check number you wrote to the customer.**

5. **Click the Save button.**

   Both transactions are cleared from Accounts Receivable.

Entering Finance Charges

Sometimes you want to nudge your customers to pay their bills on time by charging them a late fee or a finance charge if they pay later than the due date. Peachtree can calculate finance charges for all customers who haven't been excluded from finance charge calculations and who meet the filter criteria you determine when it's time to apply the finance charges. Chapter 4 shows you how to set up your default finance charge terms.

How do finance charges work?

To whom does Peachtree charge finance charges? Well, only customers with past due balances who have a check mark in the Charge Finance check box, mentioned in the preceding paragraph. Okay, that's obvious, but what other criteria does Peachtree use? After all, if a customer isn't late paying, you don't want to charge a finance charge.

Peachtree calculates finance charges by using the following formula for *each* overdue invoice:

```
Finance Charge = Number of
    Days Past Due multiplied
    by the Daily Rate
    multiplied by the
    Outstanding Invoice Amount
```

The formula uses these definitions:

✔ **Daily Rate** is the percentage you set divided by 365 days.

✔ **Outstanding Invoice Amount** is the balance remaining unpaid on the invoice.

✔ **Number of Days Past Due** is the number of days between the date that you calculate finance charges and one of the following:

✔ *The invoice date,* if aging is set to Invoice Date in the Customer Defaults dialog box

✔ *The due date,* if aging is set to Due Date in the Customer Defaults dialog box

✔ *The date of the last finance charge calculation*

To clarify these definitions, consider an example: Suppose that today is July 15, and you want to calculate charges for an invoice dated 5/1 (due 5/31) in the amount of $200.00. Your company charges an 18 percent finance charge for invoices 30 days overdue. You age your customer invoices by due date.

The invoice is overdue by 44 days (from May 31 to July 15):

```
(.18/365) x 44 x 200.00 = 4.34
```

The .18/365 is the annual percentage rate divided by 365 days. Multiply that by the 44 days the invoice is past due, and then multiply that times the $200.00 invoice amount. Therefore, a finance charge applied on 7/15 would be $4.34.

If you don't want to charge finance charges to certain customers, you must alter the default terms for those customers. In the Maintain Customers/Prospects window, click the Payment & Credit tab. Then click the arrow, as shown in the margin, next to the Terms and Credit field and then select Customize Terms for This Customer. Then deselect the Charge Finance check box.

Applying finance charges

Okay, now that you understand how the finance charge process works, you can actually apply the charges.

When you decide to apply a finance charge, Peachtree creates but does not print an invoice for the amount due. The charges do appear on customer statements, so you need to apply finance charges before you print customer statements:

1. **Choose Tasks⇨Finance Charge to display the Calculate Finance Charges dialog box.**

2. **(Optional) Select a range of customers for whom you want to calculate finance charges.**

   If you leave the customer range blank, Peachtree assumes you want to calculate charges on all eligible customers (by way of the Charge Finance check box and past due balances).

3. **Enter the date you want Peachtree to use to calculate finance charges and then click OK.**

   The Apply Finance Charges dialog box shown in Figure 8-9 appears.

4. **If you'd like to review the finance charges before Peachtree applies them, select No under Apply Finance Charges. If you'd prefer to just go ahead and apply the charges, select Yes under Apply Finance Charges.**

5. **Select a Report Destination (Screen or Printer), and then click OK.**

   The Finance Charge Report Selection dialog box appears. You don't *have* to print the report, but we recommend that you do.

6. **Click OK to print the report in detail.**

7. **If you elected to review the charges before Peachtree applied them, repeat Steps 1–6, but select Yes in Step 4.**

   Peachtree applies the finance charges to the customer.

Figure 8-9:
The Apply
Finance
Charges
dialog box
allows you
to preview
finance
charges
before
Peachtree
applies
them to the
customer
account.

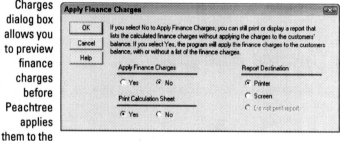

Peachtree generates the finance charges by creating an invoice to the customer by using a reference number that begins with the letters *FC* (for finance charge). Peachtree uses that transaction when recalculating finance charges. Therefore, never enter a customer invoice with a reference number that begins with FC and don't change the reference numbers for the Peachtree-generated finance charge invoices.

Producing Statements

Before you print statements the first time, you might want to determine statement default preferences. Refer to Chapter 4 on how to set statement default options.

To print statements, follow these steps:

1. **Choose Reports & Forms⇨Forms⇨Customer Statements.**

   Peachtree considers a statement a *form*. See Chapter 13 for information on customizing forms.

Preview and Print

2. **In the Forms section, click the statement form you want to use and then click the Preview and Print button, as shown in the margin.**

   The Preview and Print Customer Statements dialog box, as shown in Figure 8-10, appears.

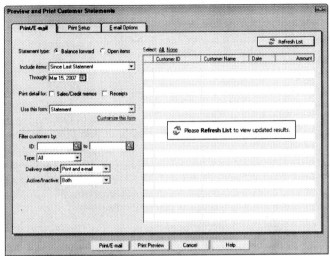

Figure 8-10:
Determine
who should
receive the
statement
and how
you want
the
statement
to appear.

3. **Select any of the following options from the Statement dialog box:**

   - **Statement Type:** On balance forward statements, only the balances left over from previous statements appear, similar to the way information appears on a credit card bill. On open items, the detail for all open (unpaid) items appears. Read Chapter 4 for information on setting a default statement type.

   - **Include Items:** Select a range of transaction dates for which you want to print the statement.

   - **Through:** Select the latest transaction date you want to print on the statements.

   - **Print Detail For:** Choose to print or not print the line item detail information for invoices, credit memos, and receipts. If you don't select the line item detail option, the customer sees a single line entry for each transaction, making the statement much easier to read.

   - **Use This Form:** If you selected the wrong statement form in Step 2, you can click this option and select a different form.

   - **Filter Customers By:** Filter a customer range by specific customer IDs or types. You can also choose the Delivery Method option, which lets you choose how you want to deliver forms to the defined range of customers: as paper copies only, as e-mail attachments only, or as both paper copies and e-mail attachments. If you choose either E-mail or Both, the E-mail tab becomes available, letting you set up more form delivery options. See Chapter 13 for details on printing and e-mailing forms.

4. **Click the Refresh List button, as shown here in the margin.**

Peachtree displays a list of clients who could receive statements based on your settings. You can deselect the check box next to any client to whom you don't want to send a statement.

5. **Click Print/E-mail.**

After the statements finish printing, Peachtree asks you whether the statements printed correctly and whether it's OK to update customer records. If you click Yes, Peachtree stores the statement date in the customer record to use it as the balance forward date the next time you print statements. If you click No or Cancel after printing statements, Peachtree does not update customer records and maintains no record of having printed a statement. That means Peachtree continues to list invoices as open items on any statement you print. If you're using balance forward statements, it's therefore important that you click Yes after statements print successfully.

Reporting on Money Your Customers Owe

Although Peachtree can't guarantee that you make a profit every month, it does give you some ways to show you (or your investors) your various financial reports. We're sure you like to track the money you're taking in so that you can plan your budget or keep your banker happy. So, in Table 8-1, we provide a description of the reports that pertain to collecting your money.

See Chapter 14 to find out how to print reports.

Table 8-1	Reports Related to Collecting Your Money
Report Name	*What It Does*
Aged Receivables	Lists each customer along with outstanding invoices or credits in aging categories
Customer Management Detail Report	Shows customer credit limits and balance information along with unpaid and due invoices
Customer Transaction History	Lists, by customer, invoices and invoice-related entries, such as payments and credit memos
Cash Receipts Journal	Lists the date, amount, description, and General Ledger account number of all receipt transactions created during a specified period

Don't forget to visit www.dummies.com/go/peachtreefd for more information on Peachtree.

Chapter 9

Paid Employees Are Happy Employees

* *

In This Chapter

▶ Setting up employee defaults

▶ Writing and printing payroll checks

▶ Paying commissions or bonuses

* *

*T*hey call it *work* for a reason, some people say. And we can't think of too many people who are willing to work without being paid. If you aren't using an outside payroll service, you might want to consider using the Peachtree payroll features.

The Peachtree payroll features mimic the functions you perform when you prepare payroll checks by hand. However, after you set up basic background information for each employee (yes, you still need to know the employee's gross wages and number of exemptions), we think that preparing payroll in Peachtree is much easier and faster than preparing payroll checks manually. You don't need to look up payroll taxes in the Circular E flyer, also known as IRS Publication 15; you don't need to remember which employees have various deductions; and you don't need to subtract the taxes and deductions to determine the net payroll check. Furthermore, you don't need to keep track of the payroll tax liability amounts that you, as the employer, must pay. Also, if you allow Peachtree to print the checks, you don't need to write them. In this chapter, we show you how to set up your employees and produce paychecks.

Even if you prepare payroll in Peachtree, you're going to have questions about handling various situations. The Circular E booklet that you get from the government every December is your bible for payroll questions. If you don't get a Circular E in the mail, you can download one from www.irs.gov/publications/p15. If you don't understand the Circular E, contact your accountant. If you don't understand your accountant, hire a new one.

If you use an outside payroll service, you might want to consider using the Peachtree payroll features to keep your General Ledger up to date. That way, you can accurately report your company's financial picture. If your outside payroll service provides you with journal entries, you can ignore the Peachtree payroll features and simply enter the journal entries (see Chapter 17). However, if your outside payroll service doesn't provide you with journal entries, you might want to use the Peachtree payroll features to mimic the payroll process and match your records with theirs.

Understanding Payroll Basics

Before you start setting up employees and paying them, you really need to consider some basic information:

- Whom you pay
- When you should start using payroll in Peachtree

Peachtree uses *payroll tax tables* to calculate the amounts you deduct for taxes (federal income tax, Social Security, Medicare, and so on). Sage Software, the company that produces Peachtree, does *not* ship tax tables that calculate federal taxes with the software. To accurately calculate payroll, you must either subscribe to the Peachtree Payroll Tax Update service or create your own tax tables. To order tax table updates, visit the Peachtree Web site, www.peachtree.com, or call 877-231-3761.

Employees and sales representatives

In this chapter, we're talking about paying people who work for you. You can rule out vendors for this discussion. Vendors don't work for you — they just provide you with goods or services. You pay vendors from the Payments, Write Checks, or Select for Payment window, as we describe in Chapter 6.

Both employees and sales representatives work for you. As you see in this chapter, you pay employees from the Select for Payroll window or the Payroll Entry window. Although employees are always employees, sales reps might be employees or independent contractors. The windows in Peachtree that you use to pay sales reps depend on their employment status: employee or independent contractor.

If you're uncertain about an individual's status, check the IRS Web site at www.irs.gov/publications/p15a or check with your accountant. The individual's status is important to the federal government, and choosing the wrong status can cause you trouble that you just don't need.

Employees work for you, so, in this chapter, we're talking about them. And sales representatives who are also employees work for you, so we're talking about them as well. We aren't talking about sales representatives whom you treat as independent contractors; you pay them as 1099 vendors from the Payments window or the Select for Payments window. See Chapter 5 for information on designating a vendor as a 1099 vendor. See Chapter 6 for information on paying vendors.

Most sales reps, whether they're employees or independent contractors, earn commissions. If you want to track commissions in order to make paying sales reps easier, you need to specifically identify sales reps in Peachtree. Interestingly, Peachtree has you set up a sales representative in the same window where you set up employees even though the sales representative might be an independent contractor and not an employee.

Being the logical individual that you are, you ask, "If a sales rep isn't an employee, why should I set up a sales rep in the same window where I set up employees?" Peachtree has you set up sales reps in the Maintain Employees & Sales Reps window for two related reasons:

- ✔ If you set up sales representatives in the Maintain Employees & Sales Reps window, you can include the sales rep on invoices.
- ✔ If you include a sales rep on an invoice, you can produce the Sales Rep report, which shows commissioned and noncommissioned sales amounts per sales rep.

Including a sales rep on an invoice *does not* automatically generate a commission amount for the sales rep. The inventory items sold on the invoice must be subject to commission. In the "Writing and Printing Payroll Checks" section, we tell you how to pay sales representatives who are also employees. In the "Determining commission amounts" section, you see a sample of the Sales Rep report. See Chapter 7 for more information about including sales representatives on invoices. See Chapter 11 for information on making an inventory item subject to commission.

When should you start to use payroll?

You can start using payroll at any time during a calendar year, but you might find it easiest to start using payroll on January 1. If you start using payroll on January 1, you won't have to enter any beginning balance information — information to account for paychecks that you already produced this year that need to be included on payroll tax forms and W-2s at the end of the year.

If you can't start using payroll on January 1, try to start on the first day of any payroll quarter: January 1, April 1, July 1, or October 1. Payroll tax laws require that you file payroll tax returns quarterly, and you need to include information for only the current quarter. If you start using payroll at the beginning of a quarter, you can enter beginning balance information as lump sums for each quarter of the current year in which you produced payroll checks.

As a final resort, if you can't start using payroll on the first day of any payroll quarter, start using payroll on the first day of a month. You need to enter beginning balance information for the other months in the current payroll quarter, but you can enter quarterly amounts for other payroll quarters of the current year in which you produced payroll checks.

Working with Employee Information

In Chapter 4, we show you how the Payroll Wizard walks you through setting up default payroll information for your company. After the default information is in place, you need to set up your employees, establishing individualized information for each of them. For example, different employees claim different withholding exemptions. And some employees might participate in a company retirement plan whereas others do not. Or some might receive a health insurance benefit. To set up employees, choose Maintain⇨ Employees/Sales Reps. Peachtree displays the General tab of the Maintain Employees & Sales Reps window (see Figure 9-1).

Figure 9-1:
Just as you might expect, you supply general employee information on the General tab here.

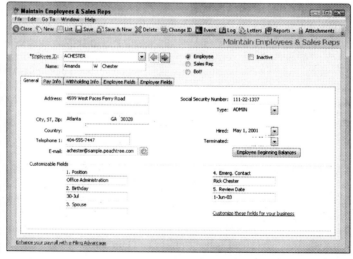

At the top of the window — not associated with any of the tabs in the window — you assign an ID and type in a name. You also can select the Inactive check box after an employee leaves the company to avoid accidentally generating a paycheck.

If you need to change an employee's ID, click the Change ID button, as shown here in the margin.

You can set up each person as an employee, a sales rep, or both. Typically, you deduct payroll taxes for employees, and you don't deduct payroll taxes for sales representatives. If you select Sales Rep, three of the five tabs in the window become gray, and the individual doesn't appear in the Payroll windows when you're paying employees. Choose Both if the individual is both a sales representative and an employee.

We discuss each of the five tabs of the Maintain Employees & Sales Reps window individually.

General employee information

You use the General tab (refer to Figure 9-1) of the Maintain Employees & Sales Reps window to give Peachtree general information about each employee, such as the employee's name, address, and Social Security number. (You need those when you produce W-2s at the end of the year.) You also can supply the employee's telephone number, date of hire, and e-mail address.

Peachtree provides the Type field to give you a way to group employees. If your company pays workers' compensation insurance, you might want to store the workers' compensation categories in the Type field to make it easier to produce a report that helps you pay your workers' compensation liability.

Customizable fields appear at the bottom of the General tab, and you can type the appropriate information for the employee in each field. Custom field information is optional.

Below the Terminated drop-down list, you see the Employee Beginning Balances button. Click this button if you start payroll on any day other than January 1 and you already produced paychecks in the current year. Peachtree displays the Employee Beginning Balances window (see Figure 9-2).

Figure 9-2:
Record
amounts for
paychecks
you wrote
this year
before you
started
using
Peachtree.

	Payroll Field	1 Mar 31, 2007	2 Apr 30, 2007	3	4	5	Total
1	Gross	3,360.00	1,120.00	0.00	0.00	0.00	4,480.00
2	Fed_Income	-395.58	-131.86	0.00	0.00	0.00	-527.44
3	Soc_Sec	-208.32	-69.44	0.00	0.00	0.00	-277.76
4	Medicare	-48.72	-16.24	0.00	0.00	0.00	-64.96
5	State	-145.32	-48.44	0.00	0.00	0.00	-193.76
6	K401	-134.40	-44.80	0.00	0.00	0.00	-179.20
	Net Check:	2,427.66	809.22	0.00	0.00	0.00	

Employee Beginning Balances

Employee ID ACHESTER — Amanda W. Chester

Use the fields in this window to enter the payroll amounts you already paid this year before you started using Peachtree. Each column represents a pay period that you specify: a week, a biweekly or semimonthly pay period, a month, a quarter, or even multiple quarters. For example, suppose that you want to start entering payroll as of July 1, which is the beginning of the third payroll quarter. In the Employee Beginning Balances window, you can enter one column of numbers that represents the sum of all the payroll amounts you paid for the first six months (two quarters) of the year for each payroll field.

Although you can enter amounts for each pay period, we don't recommend that approach because it's cumbersome and time consuming.

At the top of each column you intend to use, right-click to display a calendar and then select the ending date of the timeframe represented by the amounts. Then, in the fields below the date, type the appropriate amounts for each payroll field, entering deductions as negative amounts and earnings as positive amounts. Based on the information in Figure 9-2, we're starting payroll on May 1. In the first column, we include the quarterly amount for the first quarter of the year. In the second column, we include the monthly amount for April, the first month of the second quarter.

Click the Save button and the Close button (both, as shown here) after you finish, and Peachtree redisplays the Maintain Employees & Sales Reps window.

Payroll information

On the Pay Info tab of the Maintain Employees & Sales Reps window (see Figure 9-3), you tell Peachtree the method and frequency you use to pay the employee.

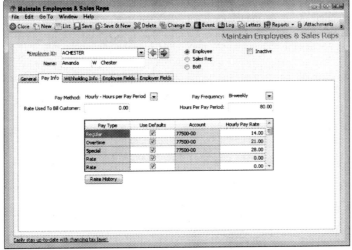

Figure 9-3:
Tell
Peachtree
how often
you want to
pay your
employees.

You can pay your employees by using any of five frequencies:

- Weekly
- Biweekly
- Semimonthly
- Monthly
- Annually

You don't need to pay all your employees by using the same frequency; that is, you can pay some employees weekly, some biweekly, and some monthly. The choice is yours. Most companies tend to pay all employees at the same time, but Peachtree doesn't make you operate that way.

Pay methods tell Peachtree how to calculate wages. Open the Pay Method drop-down list to choose Salary, Hourly – Hours per Pay Period, or Hourly – Time Ticket Hours:

- **Salary:** Pay your employees a flat rate, regardless of the number of hours they work in a pay period.
- **Hourly – Hours per Pay Period:** Pay your employees based on hours they work in a pay period.
- **Hourly – Time Ticket Hours:** Pay your employees for hours they work in a pay period as recorded on time tickets they submit.

You use *time tickets* when you intend to bill your customers for the time that your employees or your vendors work on projects for them. You can, but don't have to, pay employees based on the time tickets they submit. To find out more about this pay method, see Chapter 10.

If you choose Hourly – Hours Per Pay Period, Peachtree displays the standard number of hours associated with the frequency you select:

- ✔ Frequency: Standard hours
- ✔ Weekly: 40
- ✔ Biweekly: 80
- ✔ Semimonthly: 88
- ✔ Monthly: 176
- ✔ Annually: 2112

You can change the value that appears in the Hours Per Pay Period field. For example, you can set the number of hours to zero to ensure that you don't accidentally pay an employee for time not worked.

You indicate the amount, per pay period, that you want to pay the employee. In Figure 9-3, we're paying the employee time-and-a-half for overtime and double-time for special occasions (maybe holidays). For salaried employees, you typically don't see an Overtime field, but you do see the employee's annual salary as well as the salary amount for each pay period.

If you plan to use time tickets to bill your customers for the time an employee works on projects — even if you don't pay the employee based on time tickets — supply an amount in the Rate Used to Bill Customer field.

Peachtree Premium and higher users can track an employee's raise history. Click the Raise History button, and Peachtree displays a dialog box where you can record the following:

- ✔ The raise date
- ✔ The pay rate to which the raise applies (Regular, Overtime, or Special for hourly employees; or Salary, Bonus, or Commission for salaried employees in our sample company).
- ✔ The base amount associated with that pay rate and either the raise amount or the raise percentage (you enter one and Peachtree calculates the other).
- ✔ Any notes you might want to make about the raise. For example, you might want to note that the raise was based on the employee's annual performance review or was an out-of-cycle raise because of the ongoing stellar performance of the employee.

The window also shows the calculated new amount for that pay rate, but Peachtree doesn't change the amount that appears on the Pay Info tab. You must make that change manually.

Withholding information

On the Withholding Info tab, you provide — you guessed it — tax-withholding information, such as the employee's marital status and the number of exemptions he or she claims for federal, state, and local withholding (see Figure 9-4). You also can supply additional federal, state, and local withholding amounts as appropriate, along with the 401(k) deduction percentage if the employee contributes to a company 401(k) plan. Enter the 401(k) deduction amount as a positive percentage — for example, to enter 4 percent, as shown in Figure 9-4, enter **4.0**.

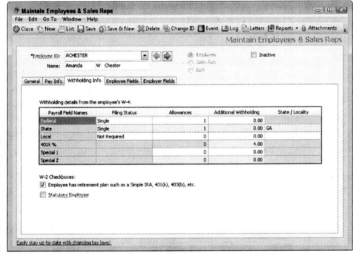

Figure 9-4:
Use the Withholding Info tab to describe the employee.

Peachtree reserves the Special 1 and Special 2 fields for you to use in payroll tax formulas where a value in the calculation is unique for each employee.

Don't forget to select the Employee Has Retirement Plan Such as a Simple IRA, 401(k), 403(b), Etc. check box if your employee participates in a 401(k) or other retirement plan. Select the Statutory Employee check box if IRS guidelines qualify the employee as an employee based on the law. Four categories of independent contractors qualify by law as employees. If you don't know or aren't sure whether you have independent contractors whom you must, by law, treat as employees, ask your accountant.

Employee and Employer fields

You really need to understand only one aspect of the Employee Fields tab of the Maintain Employees & Sales Reps window. You use that tab to indicate anything about the employee that *doesn't* follow the payroll defaults you set up for the company as we describe in Chapter 4.

For example, you might change the GL account to send wages to a different account than the default account. Or, if an employee doesn't participate in the company's dental plan, deselect the check box in the Use Defaults column. If a check appears in the Calc column, deselect it as well. You deselect the check box in the Use Defaults column so that Peachtree allows you to deselect the check box in the Calc column. What's the Calc column? Well, when you select a check box in the Calc column, Peachtree expects to use a payroll tax table to calculate the amount for the field. You deselect the check box in the Calc column under two conditions:

- ✔ When you're not going to use a calculation to figure the amount for the employee, but want to supply a fixed amount in the Amount column instead

- ✔ When you don't want to calculate the field for the employee

If the employee's calculation is different from the calculation used by default for all employees, and you deselect the check box in the Use Defaults column but don't deselect the check box in the Calc column, you can select a different calculation for the employee. Simply click in the Tax Name column to use the lookup list.

If you don't intend to calculate the field for the employee, you must deselect the check boxes in both the Use Defaults column and the Calc column. Otherwise, Peachtree still calculates an amount based on the formula in the payroll tax table.

The Employee Fields tab and the Employer Fields tab in the Maintain Employees & Sales Reps window closely resemble the same tabs in the Employee Defaults dialog box. That makes sense because Peachtree gets the information it displays in the Maintain Employees & Sales Reps window from the information you enter in the Employee Defaults dialog box.

The Employer Fields tab, like the Employee Fields tab, is used to indicate anything about the employer fields that doesn't follow the defaults you set up for the company.

Using the Direct Deposit service

For an additional fee, Peachtree supports use of a direct deposit solution in all versions of Peachtree except Peachtree First Accounting. With direct deposit, you still create paychecks in Peachtree the same way that we describe in this chapter, identifying employees who participate in direct deposit as you create the paychecks. You don't actually print the paychecks to give to employees; instead, through the Direct Deposit service, money is electronically transferred from your bank account to each employee's bank account on payday. You can print a stub for your employees as you create the paychecks. With the Direct Deposit service, employees can select one or more bank accounts into which money can be deposited. Employees can identify fixed amounts or percentages to deposit to each account. Directly deposited paychecks appear in the Account Reconciliation window in lump sums that should match your bank statements. Checks processed through the Direct Deposit service become read-only in Peachtree, and you cannot edit them. For more information or to sign up for Direct Deposit, visit www.peachtree.com.

Writing and Printing Payroll Checks

Now you come to the part that your employees like most — the part where you produce paychecks. You can pay employees *en masse* or one at a time; we walk you through both methods. Typically, you pay groups of employees at the same time, so we think you can make more use of the group method.

 We recommend that you let Peachtree print paychecks for you. You can save lots of time and reduce the possibility of introducing errors because you won't be typing in information.

In this section, we show you how to produce and print paychecks and how to pay commissions and bonuses — two other common payroll needs.

Paying a group of employees

Paying a group of employees is similar to paying a group of vendors. If you write your checks by hand or use an outside payroll service, plan to print the paychecks that Peachtree produces on plain paper because Peachtree posts the information to the General Ledger when you print the checks.

Follow these steps:

1. **Choose Tasks⇨Select for Payroll Entry.**

   Peachtree displays the Select Employees – Filter Selection dialog box, as shown in Figure 9-5, so that you can select the majority of employees you want to pay.

   Try to make the selection include everyone you want to pay even if the selection includes more people than you intend to pay. After you make choices in this dialog box, you have another opportunity to exclude employees.

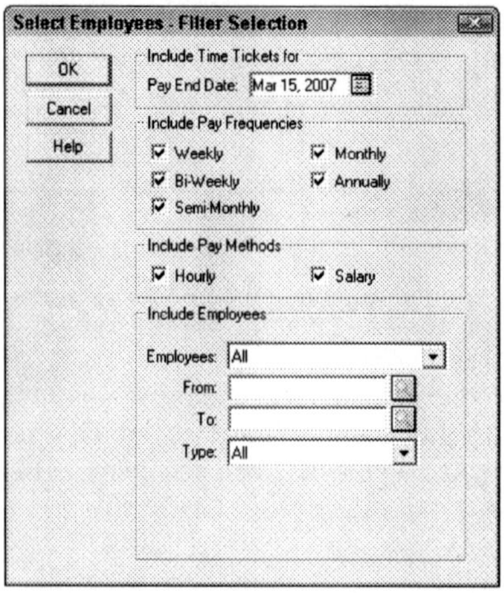

Select Employees - Filter Selection

OK
Cancel
Help

Include Time Tickets for
Pay End Date: Mar 15, 2007

Include Pay Frequencies
☑ Weekly   ☑ Monthly
☑ Bi-Weekly   ☑ Annually
☑ Semi-Monthly

Include Pay Methods
☑ Hourly   ☑ Salary

Include Employees
Employees: All
From:
To:
Type: All

Figure 9-5:
Identify the
employees
you want
to pay.

---

2. **From the Pay End Date field, select the date that represents the last day of the pay period.**

3. **In the Include Pay Frequencies section, select all the check boxes that represent the pay frequencies that you want to include.**

   For example, include employees that you pay weekly. As shown in the dialog box, you can include all pay frequencies. If you don't have any monthly or annual employees, you can leave the check boxes selected without affecting anything.

4. **In the Include Pay Methods section, choose to pay hourly employees, salaried employees, or both.**

5. **Use the Include Employees section to limit the range of employees you pay.**

   If you want to pay all employees who meet the other criteria you establish in this dialog box, simply choose All Employees. Otherwise, in the From field, select the first employee you want to include. Then, in the To field, select the last employee you want to include.

We suggest that you include all employees because you have another opportunity in the next window to exclude an employee.

If you enabled direct deposit, the Employees drop-down list contains two additional choices besides All and Range; you see Direct Deposit Only and Manual Check Only.

6. Click OK.

Peachtree displays the Select Employees to Pay window (see Figure 9-6).

Select

If you don't like the selection you see, click the Select toolbar button (as shown here) to redisplay the Select Employees – Filter Selection dialog box (refer to Figure 9-5).

Figure 9-6:
Confirm that the payroll checks you're about to print are the ones you want to produce.

Employee ID	Employee Name	Check Amount	Field Names	Hours	Salary	#Weeks	Pay
ACHESTER	Amanda W. Chester	809.22	Regular	80.00		2	☑
			Overtime				☐
			Special				☐
ADUKE	Al L. Duke	379.50	Regular	40.00		1	☑
			Overtime				☐
			Special				☐
AHECTER	Anthony H. Hecter	787.54	Regular	80.00		2	☑
			Overtime				☐
			Special				☐

Check Date: Mar 15, 2007   Pay End Date: Mar 15, 2007   Cash Acct: 10300-00

These Employees have: 1) Pay Frequencies of Weekly, Bi-Weekly, Semi-Monthly, Monthly, and Annually 2) Pay Types of Hourly or Salaried.

Payroll Checking Account Balance: 93,444.06
Total Checks: 34,285.19
Balance After Checks: 59,158.87

The Select Employees to Pay window has some options you should keep in mind:

✔ You can avoid paying an employee by deselecting the check box in the Pay column.

✔ You can change the Cash account from which the checks are written by using the Cash Acct field in the upper right of the window.

✔ An asterisk next to an employee's name signifies that you set up the employee's pay method as Hourly – Time Ticket Hours, and that the employee's paycheck is based on the number of time ticket hours in the current pay period. Find out more about time tickets in Chapter 10.

✔ If you enabled direct deposit, you see an extra column AD to the right of the Pay column in the Select Employees to Pay window. A red check mark in this column identifies employees who are set up to use direct deposit. You can remove the check mark, but you cannot add a check mark to anyone who isn't set up to use direct deposit.

✔ You can change the number of hours worked for hourly employees or the salary amount for salaried employees by clicking in those columns and typing. Peachtree recalculates the taxes and net check amount.

✔ You can change the number of weeks in the pay period. Typically, you see 1, 2, 12, or 52 in the #Weeks column; these numbers indicate the frequency with which you pay each employee (weekly, biweekly or semimonthly, monthly, or annually). Changing the number of weeks in the pay period affects the pay period beginning date on the paycheck stub. Peachtree calculates the beginning date by subtracting the number of weeks from the pay period ending date.

You can print the pay period beginning date on a paycheck stub. You need to customize the payroll check form to add the field. See Chapter 13 for information on customizing forms.

Viewing the details

You can view and make changes to the details of any employee's check. Click the employee and then click the Detail button on the toolbar. Peachtree displays the Select Employees to Pay – Detail window. After you finish viewing or changing details, click OK to redisplay the Select Employees to Pay window.

Don't change Social Security or Medicare amounts. If you do, you'll find discrepancies on your payroll tax reports, and the 941 quarterly payroll tax return won't be accurate. You can, however, change the federal income tax and state income tax amounts with no side effects. Make changes to the hours/salary first and the taxes second; if you make the changes in the opposite order, Peachtree recalculates the taxes and ignores your tax changes.

Allocating time to jobs

If you use jobs and want to allocate an employee's time to various jobs, follow the steps in "Paying a group of employees" to display the Select Employees to Pay window. Then follow these steps:

For more information on jobs, see Chapter 12.

1. **In the Select Employees to Pay window, click the employee.**

2. **Click the Jobs button, as shown here in the margin, to display the Labor Distribution to Jobs window (see Figure 9-7).**

3. **Click in a blank field in the Job column to display a lookup list button and then select a job.**

4. **In the Hourly Field column, select the type of pay you want to allocate: Regular, Overtime, or Special.**

5. **In the Hours column, assign hours to that job.**

   Peachtree assigns the hours to the selected job and adjusts the unassigned hours accordingly.

6. **Repeat Steps 3–5 as needed to continue distributing hours or dollars.**

7. **Click OK after you finish to redisplay the Select Employees to Pay window.**

Labor Distribution to Jobs

Cancel   OK   Row   Help

Hours Assigned to Jobs

Job	Hourly Field	Hours	Amount
CHAPPLE,01-Design	Regular	45.00	630.00
	Regular	35.00	490.00
		0.00	0.00
	Total Assigned	80.00	1,120.00

Hours Not Assigned to Jobs

Hourly Field	Hours	Amount
Regular	0.00	0.00
Overtime	0.00	0.00
Special	0.00	0.00
Total Unassigned	0.00	0.00
Total for check	80.00	1,120.00

Figure 9-7:
Allocate
employee
hours to
jobs.

If you're distributing labor for a salaried employee: you select a type of Salary Field instead of a type of Hourly Field in Step 4; and you enter dollars, not hours, in Step 5.

Listing the checks that you plan to print

Wouldn't it be nice to know how many checks Peachtree is planning to print? (You might have noticed that you don't see that number in the window anyplace.) Well, if you click the drop-down arrow on the Print button and then click Report (both, as shown here), Peachtree prints a report that shows you the details of checks you're printing. At the end of the report, you also find the number of checks you're printing. To preview checks on-screen, click the drop-down arrow on the Print button and then choose Preview. See Chapter 13 for details on printing forms. (Checks are considered forms in Peachtree.)

Printing checks

If you click the Print button (not the drop-down arrow beside the Print button) in the Select Employees to Pay window, Peachtree displays the Print Forms: Payroll Checks window. From this window, you can confirm (or change) the first check number, select a check form, identify the number of copies to print of each check, and select a printer.

If you click the Print Sample button, you can print practice checks to see Xs and 9s on the form where words and numbers will appear. Click the Print button, and Peachtree prints the checks and displays a dialog box asking you to confirm that the checks printed properly. Click Yes to post the checks; click No if you need to reprint the checks for any reason — such as a printer jam.

Paying employees individually

If you need to pay only one or two employees, use the Payroll Entry window and follow these steps:

1. **Choose Tasks⇨Payroll Entry.**

   Peachtree displays the Payroll Entry window (see Figure 9-8).

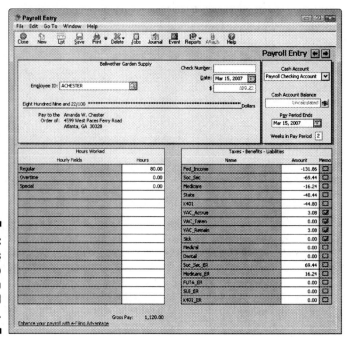

Figure 9-8:
Use this window to pay an individual employee.

2. **Use the lookup list button (as shown here) next to the Employee ID field to select an employee to pay.**

   Peachtree fills in the employee's regular payroll information.

   On the left side of the window, Peachtree displays pay level information, such as hours worked or salary amount. On the right of the window, Peachtree displays payroll fields (such as the employee's taxes and deductions) as well as other payroll liabilities you incur (such as federal unemployment tax).

3. **If necessary, change the information.**

   Set the Pay Period Ends date and the Cash Account.

   If an hourly employee doesn't work all the hours in the pay period, adjust the number of hours on the left of the window.

   Don't change Social Security or Medicare amounts. If you do, you'll find discrepancies on your payroll tax reports, and the 941 quarterly payroll tax return won't be accurate. You can, however, change the federal income tax and state income tax amounts with no side effects. Make changes to the hours/salary first and the taxes second; if you make the changes in the opposite order, Peachtree recalculates the taxes and ignores your tax changes.

4. **To assign the employee's hours to a job, click the Jobs button (as shown here) at the top of the screen.**

   For details, see "Allocating time to jobs," earlier in this chapter.

5. **Click the Print button, as shown in the margin, to print the check.**

   Peachtree displays the Print Forms: Payroll Checks window.

   You can preview checks before printing them from the Payroll Entry window by clicking the drop-down arrow on the Print button and choosing Preview. In the Print Forms: Payroll Checks window, click Print Preview.

   Don't assign a check number before clicking the Print button. If you do, Peachtree prints "Duplicate" on the check because it assumes you already wrote the check. Leave the Check Number field blank, and Peachtree assigns the check number to the check when you print it. Read Chapter 13 to find out how to eliminate the Duplicate message.

6. **Confirm (or change) the first check number, select a check form, identify the number of copies to print of each check, and then select a printer.**

   For details on selecting and printing a form, see Chapter 13. If you click the Print Sample button, you can print practice checks to see Xs and 9s on the form where words and numbers will appear.

7. **Click the Print button.**

   Peachtree prints and posts the checks, updating the employee's record and the General Ledger.

   If you don't print checks — say, because you're entering after-the-fact payroll information provided by a payroll service — you can click the Save button to save the check. If you save the check instead of printing it, assign it a check number.

Paying commissions, bonuses, or other additions

Many companies pay employees bonuses at the end of the year. And employees who act as sales representatives usually earn commissions. It might seem strange to you that we're talking about two different situations in the same breath, but Peachtree handles both situations the same way. In fact, you can use the technique we show you here to handle any form of additional lump-sum income that you must pay through payroll, such as jury duty or maternity leave. We refer to these lump-sum income amounts as *payroll additions*.

Setting up payroll addition items

You can use a pay level to record a bonus or commission, but we recommend that you use the technique we describe here for three reasons:

✔ You can control whether to include the payroll addition in gross pay when calculating payroll taxes or other payroll fields, such as retirement contributions. (Peachtree automatically includes pay levels in gross pay when calculating payroll fields.)

✔ The payroll addition appears as a separate item on payroll reports, making the payroll addition easier to track.

✔ Setting up a payroll addition item is less work than setting up a pay level.

Follow these steps to set up a payroll addition item for commissions:

1. **Choose Maintain⇨Default Information⇨Employees.**

   Peachtree displays the Employee Defaults dialog box.

2. **Click the EmployEE Fields tab and scroll down to find a blank line.**

3. **In the Field Name column, type the name of the payroll addition.**

   The name you use appears on the paycheck stub.

4. **Assign the line to a General Ledger account — usually your Wage Expense account.**

Because commissions (and bonuses, jury duty pay, maternity leave pay, and so on) vary from employee to employee, you don't select a check box in the Calc column and create a payroll tax table to calculate the amount. You also don't need to supply an amount in the Amount column. You need to tell Peachtree only whether to include additional pay when Peachtree calculates gross wages for each tax. For example, you might want Peachtree to include commission pay in gross wages when calculating FIT, Social Security, and Medicare. At the same time, you might want Peachtree to exclude commission pay in gross wages when calculating a pension plan deduction.

Suppose that you want Peachtree to include additional pay in gross wages when calculating federal income tax. Follow these steps:

1. **If you closed the Employee Defaults dialog box from the preceding set of steps, choose Maintain⇨Default Information⇨Employees.**

2. **On the EmployEE Fields tab, scroll up to find the Federal Income Tax entry.**

   It's probably called Fed_Income.

3. **In the Adjust column, click the button beside Fed_Income.**

   Peachtree displays the Calculate Adjusted Gross dialog box (see Figure 9-9).

Figure 9-9:
Identify the amounts Peachtree should add together to calculate adjusted gross income before calculating the selected tax.

Calculate Adjusted Gross

Define adjusted gross for the **Fed_Income** payroll field.

Many payroll fields use "Adjusted Gross" when calculating their respective amounts during payroll entry. Adjusted gross is the sum total of the payroll fields selected below. For example, you may want certain payroll field amounts deducted or added to gross pay prior to calculating tax for the **Fed_Income** payroll field (i.e., pre-tax deductions).

Select the Use check box for each payroll field to define adjusted gross when calculating this payroll field amount during payroll entry. The **Fed_Income** payroll field cannot be selected.

EmployEE Field Names:

Use	Field Name	Add	Deduct
☐	Medicare	☐	☑
☐	State	☐	☑
☑	K401	☐	☑
☐	VAC_Accrue	☐	☐
☐	VAC_Taken	☐	☐
☐	VAC_Remain	☐	☐
☐	Sick	☐	☐
☐	Medical	☐	☐
☐	Dental	☐	☐
☑	Commission	☐	☐

EmployER Field Names:

Use	Field Name	Add	Deduct
☐	Soc_Sec_ER	☐	☑
☐	Medicare_ER	☐	☑
☐	FUTA_ER	☐	☑
☐	SUI_ER	☐	☑
☐	K401_ER	☐	☑
☐		☐	☐
☐		☐	☐
☐		☐	☐
☐		☐	☐
☐		☐	☐

OK
Cancel
Help

4. **If necessary, scroll down in the EmployEE Field Names area on the left side of the dialog box until you see Commission.**

5. **Select the check box in the Use column next to Commission to have Peachtree add commission pay to gross wages before calculating federal income tax.**

   If you're not sure whether you want Peachtree to include a payroll addition when calculating adjusted gross wages, ask your accountant.

6. **Click OK to redisplay the Employee Defaults dialog box.**

   You need to repeat these steps for each payroll field for which the calculation of adjusted gross wages should include the payroll addition — at a minimum, Social Security and Medicare.

If you adjust the gross wage calculation for Social Security and Medicare, be sure that you click the Adjust button for these payroll fields on *both* the EmployEE Fields tab and the EmployER Fields tab.

   7. Click OK to close the Employee Defaults dialog box.

You can include an employee's commission (or bonus or other addition) on his or her paycheck. Simply fill in the amount in the field when you create the paycheck, and Peachtree adjusts appropriate taxes, based on settings you established in the various Calculate Adjusted Gross dialog boxes.

Don't change the Social Security or Medicare amounts on paychecks. If you do, you might find discrepancies on your payroll tax reports and the 941 quarterly payroll tax return won't be accurate. You can, however, change the federal income tax and state income tax amounts on paychecks with no side effects.

The W-2 form and commissions

If you want, you can show commissions in Box 14 on the W-2. The assignment is optional; that is, Peachtree includes the commission wages in Boxes 1 (gross wages), 3 (Social Security wages), and 5 (Medicare wages) automatically. Showing the wages in Box 14 simply identifies the component of Gross Wages (Box 1) that were commissions.

To include commissions in Box 14, follow these steps:

   1. Choose Maintain⇨Default Information⇨Employees.

   Peachtree displays the General tab of the Employee Defaults dialog box.

   2. Click the W-2s button.

   Peachtree displays the Assign Payroll Fields for W-2s dialog box (see Figure 9-10).

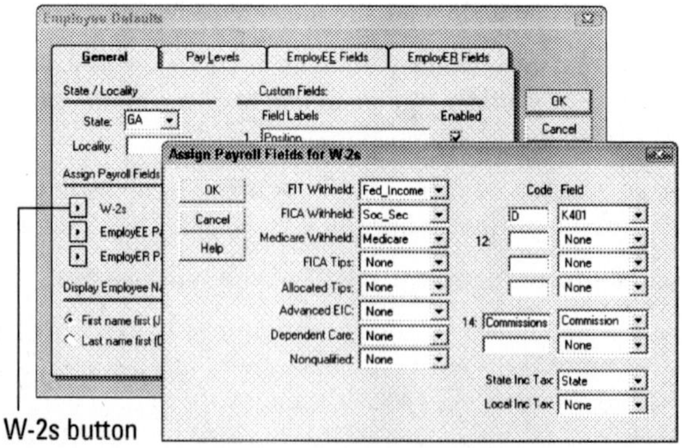

Figure 9-10:
Use this dialog box to report commissions in Box 14 of the W-2 form.

W-2s button

3. **In the text box next to number 14, type the name of the payroll field.**

4. **From the drop-down list, select the appropriate field to print in Box 14.**

   In the example, we use Commission.

5. **Click OK twice to save the changes.**

Determining commission amounts

With respect to commissions, one burning question pops immediately to mind: How do you know how much commission to pay an employee?

When you produce an invoice that contains items that are subject to commission *and* you assign a sales rep to the invoice, the Peachtree Sales Rep report shows you the commissioned sales for each sales rep. Choose Reports & Forms⇨Accounts Receivable. From the Report List on the right, select Sales Rep Reports. You can print this report (see Figure 9-11) for any date range. See Chapter 7 for more information on invoicing and Chapter 14 for more information on printing reports.

Figure 9-11: Use the Sales Rep report to help you identify commission amounts to pay.

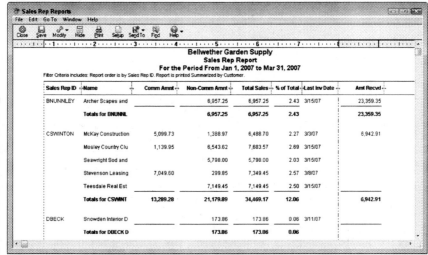

In Figure 9-11, Colista Swinton (CSWINTON) made three sales that contained both commissioned and non-commission inventory items and two sales that contained only non-commission inventory items. As her employer, you'd multiply the commissioned amount by Colista's commission rate and pay her the resulting number.

Peachtree doesn't provide a way to actually calculate commissions. However, you can send the Sales Rep report to Excel and set up the calculations.

Customer returns usually affect commissions due. We have a few recommendations concerning paying commissions:

- ✔ Print the Sales Rep report only once each month and pay commissions only once each month for the *preceding* month — to make sure that you process all invoices for the month.

- ✔ Add the Amt Recvd field to the report, as we did in Figure 9-11, and summarize the report by customer so that you see the invoices that have been paid and pay commissions only on paid invoices. See Chapter 14 for information on how to summarize a report and add a field to a report.

- ✔ Understand that the Total Sales column on the report does *not* include sales tax, but the Amt Recvd column *does* include sales tax. When you calculate the commission amount, be sure to calculate it on the Total Sales column.

- ✔ Hold back a specified amount from each rep's commission and pay that amount when the sales rep decides to leave your company. This practice protects you if you pay a commission for a sale that you later determine you won't collect. Be sure to include this policy in your employee information packet because you can be sure your employees are tracking the commissions due them.

- ✔ Remember that reversing a commission for a merchandise return isn't a problem. Simply enter a credit memo and assign the sales rep to the credit memo. Reversing a commission for a return where you don't get any merchandise back is a little trickier. We suggest that you set up a non-stock inventory item that you assign to your Sales Returns and Allowances account, making sure to set the item up as subject to commission. When you issue the credit memo, use the non-stock, subject-to-commission inventory item.

For more information on entering credit memos, see Chapter 8. For more information on setting up inventory items, see Chapter 11.

Dates for credit memos should be in the period when you enter the credit memo — which is not necessarily the period in which you sell the item. That way, you're always able to pay commissions for a specified period, and you pay a net amount.

Writing the Payroll Tax Liability Check

You have to pay the payroll tax liability, and the IRS frowns greatly if you don't pay it in a timely fashion. The IRS classifies each employer as either a semiweekly or monthly depositor, and your classification determines when your payroll tax deposit is due after a payday. You make your federal tax deposit at any bank, and you complete Form 8109 as your deposit ticket. On Form 8109, you specify the amount of the deposit, the type of tax (such as 941), and the period for which the tax applies (first quarter, second quarter, third quarter, or fourth quarter).

For simplicity's sake, we strongly urge you to write your federal payroll tax liability check and make your payroll tax deposit *at the same time* that you generate paychecks. That way, you can't get into trouble regardless of whether you're a semiweekly or monthly depositor. You also can sign up to pay your payroll taxes online at www.eftps.gov.

You write your payroll tax liability check from the Payments window. The only tricky part is determining how much you owe.

Use the Payroll Tax Liability report to easily determine the amount of your payroll tax liability. Choose Reports & Forms⇨Payroll. From the Report List on the right, choose Tax Liability report and then click the Options button, as shown here in the margin. Peachtree displays a dialog box where you can select printing options; to set up this report, focus your attention on the Filter section.

If you print the default version of the report, you see each tax name listed and each employee under that tax name, along with the amount withheld and the liability amount for one month. We like the summary version of this report for determining the amount of the tax liability check. For monthly depositors, the summary version is easier to read than the 941 Worksheet. Semiweekly depositors don't need to mess with the 941B form anymore; simply use the Tax Liability report for the specified time frame.

Although Peachtree prints all taxes on the report by default, you also can print the Tax Liability report for only one kind of tax: federal, state, or local. Use the Tax drop-down list (it's on the Filter tab when you set up printing options for the report) to choose to print only federal, state, or local taxes. If you leave the Tax list set to print all taxes and then select the Print Report in Summary Format check box, you can produce a report that looks like the one shown in Figure 9-12.

Use the totals in the Tax Liability column for each tax to determine the amount of money you owe for each of your payroll tax liabilities. Then open the Payments window and write a check to your local bank. Set the GL account on the Apply to Expenses tab at the bottom of the window to your payroll tax liability account(s) (not your payroll tax expense accounts) and the Cash account to the account from which you're writing the check. You might use a payroll checking account (if you have a separate account) or an operating checking account.

Tax Liability Report

File Edit Go To Window Help

Close Save Modify Hide Print Setup Send To Find Help

Bellwether Garden Supply
Tax Liability Report
For the Period From Mar 15, 2007 to Mar 31, 2007
Filter Criteria includes: Report order is by Employee ID. Report is printed in Summary Format.

Tax Description	Gross	Taxable Gross	Tax Liability
FUTA	65,809.52	48,449.52	387.60
940 Total			**387.60**
FIT Wages	64,314.57	64,314.57	11,623.20
Social Security Wages	65,809.52	65,809.52	1,052.95
Social Security Tips			
Medicare Wages & Tips	65,809.52	65,809.52	1,052.95
941 Total			**13,729.10**
GA State Taxes			
GASUI ER	65,809.52	49,949.52	1,498.49
GASIT	64,314.57	64,314.57	3,104.69
GA State Total			**4,603.18**
Report Total			**18,719.88**

Figure 9-12:
A summarized version of the Tax Liability report.

Paying your payroll tax liability doesn't affect the numbers that appear on the Tax Liability report. The report shows what you *should* pay and doesn't consider what you already paid, which is *another* good reason to pay your tax liability at the same time you generate paychecks.

Exploring Payroll Reports

Besides the Payroll Tax Liability report we describe in "Writing the Payroll Tax Liability Check," Peachtree offers several reports that you can use for a variety of tracking needs. Table 9-1 shows you a description of the reports that pertain to payroll. See Chapter 14 to learn how to print reports.

Table 9-1	Other Reports Related to Payroll
Report Name	*What It Does*
Payroll Check Register	Lists each paycheck with the check number, payee, and the amount.
Current Earnings Report	Shows, for the current period, much of the same information on the Payroll Register: breakdowns (by payroll field) of each paycheck. The Current Earnings report, however, subtotals each employee.

Report Name	What It Does
Employee Compensation Report	Available only in Peachtree Premium or higher. Lists, for each employee, the raise date, the pay level on which the raise was based, the pay level amount before the raise, the raise amount and percentage, the new pay level amount, and any raise notes you supplied.
Employee List	For each employee, lists the ID, name, contact name, address, Social Security number, and pay type.
Exception Report	Shows the difference between the tax amount Peachtree calculates and the tax amount withheld for each specified payroll tax.
Payroll Journal	Shows the accounts Peachtree updated for each paycheck in the period.
Payroll Register	Lists every paycheck in the specified time period; provides the same information as the Current Earnings report but without subtotaling each employee.
Payroll Tax Report	Shows, for the selected tax, each employee, Social Security number, the number of weeks worked, the gross, the taxable gross, the excess gross, and the tax amount. You can print this report for every payroll tax for which you set up a calculation and selected the Appears on Payroll Tax Report Menus check box.
Quarterly Earnings Report	Shows the same information as the Current Earnings report but for the current quarter.
Yearly Earnings Report	Shows the same information as the Current and Quarterly Earnings reports but for the year.

Visit this book's Web site at www.dummies.com/go/peachtreefd for more information on Peachtree.

Chapter 10

Billing for Your Time

• •

In This Chapter

▶ Setting up time and expense items

▶ Entering time and expense tickets

▶ Paying employees for hours worked

▶ Using tickets to create customer invoices

• •

*Y*ou've probably heard the saying, "Time is money." Some companies (particularly those employing service-oriented professionals such as accountants, consultants, lawyers, and architects) bill their customers for the time spent to complete projects. These companies often have employees track time and expenses, such as travel, for each of their projects. Then the employer bills the customer for the employee time and expenses. In some cases, the companies also pay employees based on time worked.

In this chapter, we show you how Peachtree Complete and higher support these billing functions — complete with a clock that lets you time your activities.

See Chapter 12 to find out how you can use jobs in Peachtree to create reimbursable expenses — expenses you incur that might have nothing to do with time spent by anyone but that you want to include on an invoice. Using time and expense tickets provides an alternative — and possibly better — method for creating reimbursable expenses if you don't need jobs for any other reason. (Chapter 12 lists information concerning the restrictions imposed if you use Peachtree jobs.) If you find that your time and billing needs are more extensive than can be met by the features provided by Peachtree, you might consider Timeslips, which links with Peachtree. See Bonus Chapter 4 on this book's Web site, www.dummies.com/peachtreefd, for details on TAL, the program that links Peachtree and Timeslips.

Time and billing functions are not available in Peachtree First Accounting or Peachtree Pro Accounting.

Creating Time and Expense Items

If you plan to use the time and expense features in Peachtree, you need at least two (but probably more) inventory items. (Yeah, we know that it's weird to use inventory items for time and expense features, but it's true.) You use inventory items with an item class of Activity Item to enter time-related activities, and you use inventory items with an item class of Charge Item to enter expense activities.

See Chapter 11 for details on inventory in Peachtree.

To create inventory items to use on time activities, follow these steps:

1. **Choose Maintain⇨Inventory Items to display the Maintain Inventory Items window (see Figure 10-1).**

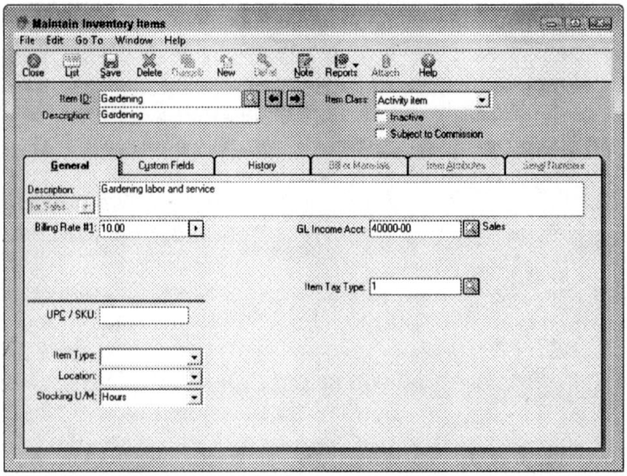

Figure 10-1:
Set up at least one activity item and one charge item if you intend to record both time and expenses.

2. **In the Item ID field, type a label that identifies the item.**

3. **From the Item Class drop-down list, select Activity Item for a time activity or Charge Item for an expense activity.**

4. **In the Description field below the Item ID field, supply a description.**

   This description appears on reports but not on invoices to your customers.

5. **In the Description field on the General tab, fill in the description that you want to appear on customer invoices for time spent on this activity.**

The description in this longer description field appears on the customer's bill unless you choose to display the description from the time ticket. For details on the time ticket's description block, see the "Entering Time Tickets" section.

6. **Enter up to ten billing rates for the activity by clicking the button beside the Billing Rate field.**

   You might assign more than one billing rate to an employee or a vendor so that you can bill the same employee's or vendor's work at different rates for, say, different customers or different situations.

7. **Use the lookup list button, as shown in the margin, to select a GL Income Account for the activity.**

8. **Use the lookup list button to select an Item Tax Type for the activity.**

   UPC/SKU, Stocking U/M, Item Type, and Location are all optional fields.

9. **Click the Save button, as shown here in the margin.**

Entering Time Tickets

The Peachtree Time Tickets feature eliminates the need for timecards and old-fashioned push-in, punch-out tracking of employee hours. You can use Peachtree time tickets to

- ✔ Record time spent by employees or vendors so that you can bill to a customer or job.
- ✔ Track the cost of employee time spent on jobs.
- ✔ Provide employees with a method to track time so that you can pay them based on time worked.

Chapter 9 provides information about one pay method, Hourly – Time Ticket Hours, which you can use to pay your employees based on the hours entered on time tickets. If you pay an employee based on time worked, you also need a way to account for employee time that you don't intend to charge to a customer or job — such as overhead time spent doing marketing or bookkeeping. Although you won't be billing the time to a customer, you need to include overhead hours on the employee's paycheck, or the employee will get angry.

Peachtree allows you to enter overhead time tickets and marks any overhead time you record as non-billable. And, as you might expect, you aren't able to include that time on a bill.

If you don't pay your employees based on time tickets, you don't need to assign time to overhead activities.

Follow these steps to enter a time ticket:

1. **Choose Tasks⇨Time/Expense⇨Time Tickets to display the Time Tickets window (see Figure 10-2).**

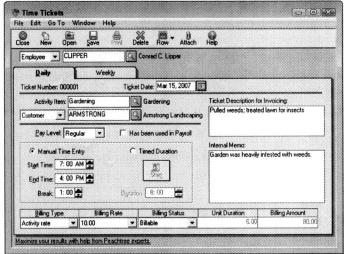

Figure 10-2:
Use this window to enter time tickets.

2. **In the upper-left drop-down list, select either Employee or Vendor, and then click the lookup list button and select an employee or vendor.**

3. **In the Ticket Date field, enter the date you performed the work.**

4. **Next to the Activity Item field, click the lookup list button to select an activity.**

5. **In the drop-down list below Activity Item, select Customer, Job, or Administrative. If you select Customer or Job, select the appropriate customer or job by using the lookup list button.**

   If you select Customer or Job, you can include the time ticket on a customer invoice; if you select Administrative, Peachtree considers the time ticket non-billable.

6. **In the Ticket Description for Invoicing text box, you can enter up to 160 characters of text to display on the customer's invoice instead of the activity name.**

7. **In the Internal Memo text box, you can provide up to 2,000 characters of descriptive information.**

   You can't include the Internal Memo description on a customer's invoice, but Peachtree prints it on reports. Use it to provide details about the work performed.

To start a new paragraph while typing in the Internal Memo text box, press Ctrl+J.

8. **If you're entering a time ticket for an employee, select a pay level.**

Don't mess with the Has Been Used in Payroll check box; let Peachtree fill it in. If the check box is selected, you paid the employee for the time ticket; deselected means that you haven't included the time ticket on a paycheck yet.

9. **Select either the Manual Time Entry or Timed Duration radio button and then do the following:**

   - *Manual Time Entry:* Supply a start and stop time as well as a break time, if appropriate.

   - *Timed Duration:* Click the Start button when you're ready to start timing.

     Peachtree runs a timer. The Start button toggles to a Stop button.

   Regardless of your choice, Peachtree calculates the duration of the time ticket.

You can't save a time ticket or close the time ticket window while the timer is running.

10. **Select a Billing Type:**

    - *Employee Rate:* Uses the Hourly billing rate you entered on the Pay Info tab when you set up the employee in the Maintain Employees/Sales Reps window

    - *Activity Rate:* Uses the rate you entered when you set up the activity in the Maintain Inventory Items window

    - *Override Rate:* Ignores both the employee and activity rates and allows you to enter any rate you want

    - *Flat Fee:* Ignores the duration (and value) of the time ticket and allows you to establish an amount for the ticket

All billing types are available for employees, but only some are available for vendors.

11. **Select a Billing Rate.**

    The available rates depend on the choice you make for Billing Type in Step 10. For example, you can establish only one employee rate, so if you select Employee Rate as the Billing Type, you can't change the billing rate. However, you can establish up to five rates for an activity, so you can choose a billing rate if you select Activity Rate as the Billing Type. For Override Rate, you must type a Billing Rate.

12. **Select a Billing Status: Billable, Non-Billable, Hold, or No Charge.**

   Billable and Non-Billable are self-explanatory. If you select Hold, you can't bill the ticket to a customer until you change the ticket's status. If you select No Charge, Peachtree changes the ticket's value to $0, so you can show your customer on the invoice that you performed work but didn't charge for it.

13. **If you choose Flat Fee as the Billing Type (see the choices in Step 10), enter a Billing Amount.**

   For all other Billing Types, Peachtree calculates the Billing Amount.

14. **Click Save.**

Whew! This process seems like a lot of steps to enter a ticket, but it goes quickly. The daily Time Ticket window appears in Figure 10-2, but Peachtree also provides a weekly view. You can enter time tickets in the weekly view, and you can print the weekly timesheet by clicking the Print button (as shown here) in the window.

The columns in the weekly view aren't terribly wide, and most contain lookup list buttons. As you enter information for a particular column, the fields extend to cover up columns to the right of the current column. The visual effect might make you think that columns have disappeared — but they haven't.

Entering Expense Tickets

Okay, good news here. Almost everything in the preceding section about time tickets applies to expense tickets as well. For example, you can enter expense tickets for both employees and vendors. And you can assign an expense ticket to a customer or job so that you can recover the expense. Or you can assign an expense ticket to overhead, making it non-billable.

If you assign an expense ticket to an employee, you also can select the Reimbursable to Employee check box. Peachtree prints reimbursable expense tickets on the Reimbursable Employee Expense report, making it easy for you to pay employees for their expenses. If an expense is reimbursable and you don't select this check box, the expense doesn't appear on the Reimbursable Employee Expense report.

Choose Tasks⇨Time/Expense⇨Expense Tickets to display the Expense Tickets window. In the Ticket Description for Invoicing text box, you can type up to 160 characters, which can print on the customer's invoice. In the Internal Memo text box, you can type up to 2,000 characters.

Unit Price is tied to the charge item you select; you might see up to ten available unit prices. And you have the same four Billing Status options for expense tickets that you have for time tickets: Billable, Non-Billable, No Charge, and Hold.

Paying Employees

Suppose that you pay employees from time tickets. You can use either of the payroll windows we describe in Chapter 9. Figure 10-3 shows the Payroll Entry window (choose Tasks⇨Payroll Entry). After you set the Pay Period Ends date, Peachtree automatically calculates the paycheck by using time tickets from that pay period that are assigned to Customer or Administrative (in that unnamed list we mention in Step 5 in the "Entering Time Tickets" section).

If your employee assigned the time tickets to Job instead of Customer or Administrative, you need to click the Jobs button when you're paying the employee to see and then select those time tickets.

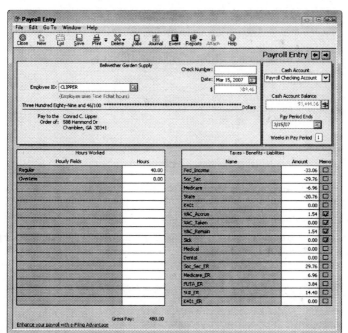

Figure 10-3: Paying an employee for time worked.

Repaying employees for reimbursable expenses

Peachtree doesn't try to repay your employees automatically for expense tickets. You must print the Reimbursable Employee Expense report for the specified pay period to identify expenses for reimbursement. Choose Reports & Forms⇨Time/Expense. On the right side of the Select a Report window that appears, select Reimbursable Employee Expense and then click the Preview button. See Chapter 14 for details on printing reports.

Then you can repay the employee in one of two ways:

✔ **Use the Payments window** (choose Tasks⇨ Payments) to write a separate expense reimbursement check to the employee. If you want to track the reimbursable expense

checks to the employee, set the employee up as a vendor.

✔ **Include the reimbursement in the employee's paycheck** by setting up a payroll field as an addition. See Chapter 9 for details on setting up additions. You need to assign the reimbursement to a General Ledger account but probably *not* to your Wage Expense account. Also, because reimbursements aren't usually subject to payroll taxes, you need to click the Adjust button for each payroll tax and make sure that you're not including the reimbursement item. When you pay the employee, type a positive amount for the reimbursement to add it to the paycheck.

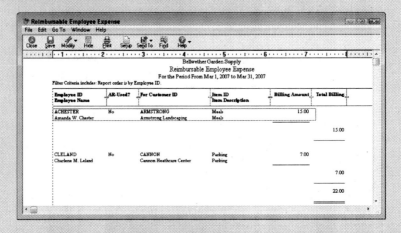

Using Tickets to Bill Customers

If your employees or vendors assign time or expense tickets to customers or jobs, you can bill the customers for those costs. Follow these steps to bill customers by using tickets.

To be sure you don't forget to bill your customers for time or expense tickets, print the Aged Tickets report before you create invoices.

1. **Choose Tasks⇨Sales/Invoicing to display the Sales/Invoicing window.**

2. **Complete most of your invoice as usual.**

   Select a customer by using the lookup list button next to the Customer ID field and assign shipping information, terms, and line item information if you're invoicing this customer for other things besides reimbursable time and expense tickets. For details on entering invoices, see Chapter 7.

3. **In the lower left of the window, click the Apply Tickets/Expenses button.**

   Peachtree displays the Apply Tickets/Reimbursable Expenses window (see Figure 10-4).

   You can view available time tickets on the Time Tickets tab and expense tickets on the Expense Tickets tab. To find out more about the Reimbursable Expenses tab, see Chapter 12.

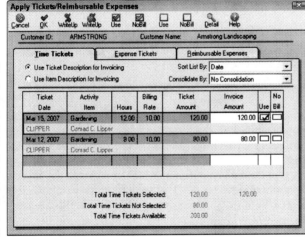

Figure 10-4: Use the tabs here to select time tickets and expense tickets to include on a customer's invoice.

4. **To include a ticket on the invoice, select the Use check box next to the ticket on the appropriate tab.**

5. **In the Invoice Amount column, verify or change the figure.**

   To build some profit into a ticket or a reimbursable expense, you change the amount in the Invoice Amount column. To mark up costs or reduce a group of tickets or reimbursable expenses, click the WriteUp button (as shown here) to display the Select Tickets to Write Up/Down dialog box. You can adjust tickets up or down by a dollar amount or a percentage. To mark up, supply a positive number; to mark down, supply a negative number. Click OK after you finish.

If you change your mind and decide that you don't want to mark tickets up or down, click the Remove WriteUp button, as shown in the margin, in the Apply Tickets/Reimbursable Expenses window.

6. **At the top of the tab, select a description for the ticket to appear on the invoice.**

   The first option, Use Ticket Description for Invoicing, tells Peachtree to use the description supplied on the time ticket. The second option, Use Item Description for Invoicing, tells Peachtree to use the description supplied when you set up the item in inventory.

   If you leave the Consolidate By list set at No Consolidation, Peachtree creates separate lines on the invoice for each ticket you choose to bill. If you select more than one entry containing the same activity item and you choose to consolidate, Peachtree displays only one line for all selected entries and reduces the number of lines on the invoice.

7. **Click OK.**

   The reimbursable expenses appear on the customer's invoice.

8. **Supply GL accounts, select a job if appropriate, print, and post the invoice as usual.**

   See Chapter 7 for details on completing an invoice.

When you print tickets as separate lines on the invoice, Peachtree prints the description you supplied on the expense when you created it. You see either ticket descriptions or item descriptions on the customer's invoice, depending on the selection you make in the Apply Tickets/Reimbursable Expenses window. When you consolidate items, Peachtree prints the information associated with the consolidate choice you selected. For example, if you consolidate by Employee/Vendor ID, Peachtree prints the employee name or the vendor name.

If you choose Consolidate All in the Consolidate By list, Peachtree does not supply a description on the invoice. Instead, Peachtree prints the name of the GL account assigned to the items as the description on the invoice along with the total of all the tickets. If you want, you can type a description on the line for the consolidated tickets in the Sales/Invoicing window, and Peachtree uses that description instead of the GL account name.

Keep the following notes in mind when you work with tickets:

✔ You can delete tickets from the Apply Tickets/Reimbursable Expenses window if you decide not to invoice the client for them. Select the No Bill check box to the right of the ticket or expense. Deleting the ticket does *not* delete the transaction that created the ticket; instead, deleting a ticket in the Apply Tickets/Reimbursable Expenses window disconnects the ticket and the customer.

✔ Be aware that using a ticket makes it disappear from the Apply Tickets/Reimbursable Expenses window. If you subsequently delete the line from the invoice, the reimbursable expense does not reappear in the window. If you mistakenly use the ticket and post the invoice, delete the invoice and reenter it to make the ticket available again.

✔ You can edit a ticket you intend to bill to a customer. You can find the transaction by opening the Time Tickets window or the Expense Tickets window and then clicking the Open button.

Tracking Ticket Traffic

(Say that section title three times fast!)

The Reimbursable Employee Expense report, shown earlier in this chapter, is one example of the reports Peachtree offers to help you keep track of time tickets. Table 10-1 provides you with a description of the other reports that pertain to time and expenses. You can print these reports by choosing Reports & Forms⇨Time/Expense. See Chapter 14 for more details on printing reports.

Table 10-1	Other Reports Related to Time and Billing
Report Name	*What It Does*
Aged Tickets	Shows unbilled tickets and how old they are based on the aging brackets you set up in the Customer Defaults dialog box
Employee Time	Lists, by employee, tickets and billing status
Expense Ticket Register	Lists, by ticket number, detailed information about expense tickets

(continued)

Table 10-1 *(continued)*

Report Name	What It Does
Tickets Recorded By	Lists the tickets entered for each employee or vendor
Tickets Used in Invoicing	Lists tickets that were included on customer invoices
Tickets by Item ID	Shows tickets organized by item ID so that you can see which activities are being used the most
Time Ticket Register	Lists, by ticket number, detailed information about time tickets
Ticket Listing by Customer	Lists each ticket assigned to the customer in the specified time period
Payroll Time Sheet	Shows you the tickets entered by employee for the specified time period

Don't forget to visit www.dummies.com/go/peachtreefd for more information on Peachtree.

Chapter 11

Counting Your Stuff

· ·

· ·

*T*his chapter is about stuff. Many businesses sell stuff you can touch whereas others sell stuff you can't touch. Some stuff is made up of pieces of other stuff. Peachtree lets you sell all these kinds of stuff. Okay — enough stuff.

Of course, we're talking about inventory. And not just the goods you place on your shelves but other kinds of nonphysical items, such as services, labor, activities, and items you charge to your customer's bill.

We'll just warn you up front: The material in this chapter is rather dry, and you probably won't consider it too funny. However, inventory management is typically a crucial part of keeping your books. Peachtree makes handling inventory a lot easier than trying to track it all by hand.

Creating Inventory Items

When you create inventory items, you set up the goods and services you sell. You set a price (actually, you can set up to ten prices) at which you want to sell your product and the account that you want Peachtree to adjust when you sell this item or service. However, before you can set up selling prices, you need to supply basic information about the item.

To set up your inventory items, follow these steps:

1. Choose Maintain⇨Inventory Items.

Peachtree displays the Maintain Inventory Items window, as shown in Figure 11-1, with multiple tabs for each item. The header information consists of the item ID, description, and class.

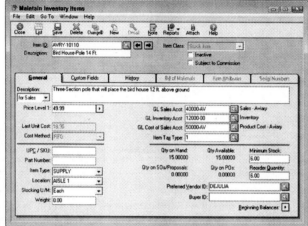

Figure 11-1:
Setting up
a new
inventory
item.

2. In the Item ID field, type an item ID.

Keep in mind that the item ID appears in lookup lists for sales transactions and so on. Peachtree allows item IDs with up to 20 alphanumeric characters.

Item IDs are not case sensitive, but they can't contain an asterisk (*), a question mark (?), or a plus symbol (+). And although technically you can use the inch mark symbol ("), we **STRONGLY** recommend you don't use it in the item ID or any other field, including descriptions. If you ever have to export or import your inventory items, the process will fail if there are inch mark symbols in your inventory IDs, descriptions or any inventory field.

3. Enter a description containing up to 30 characters.

This description appears in the item lookup lists. In the next section, you can read about how to type descriptions that you can use for sales or purchase transactions. For example, in the lookup description, you might refer to a specific birdbath as *Con PBB w/birds,* but when you sell this item, you should be a little more descriptive, such as *Concrete birdbath with two bluebirds on pedestal base.*

If you discontinue an inventory item, you can mark it inactive; redisplay the item in the Maintain Inventory window and then select the Inactive check box.

4. **Select an item class to identify the type of inventory item.**

   Selecting the right classes for your inventory items helps ensure that Peachtree meets your business needs. Peachtree Premium and above support 11 item classes, Peachtree Complete supports 9 item classes, Peachtree Pro supports 7 item classes, and Peachtree First Accounting supports 4 item classes. Chapter 4 provides more information on the different Peachtree inventory classes, but these are the basics:

   - *Stock:* Inventory items you want to track for quantities, average costs, vendors, low stock points, and so on. Stock items are available in Peachtree Pro Accounting and higher.

   - *Non-stock:* Items such as service contracts that you sell but don't put into your inventory.

   - *Master Stock:* Items that consist of information shared by a number of substock items. See the "Whoa, Nellie! Working with Master Stock Items" section. Peachtree Complete Accounting and higher support master stock items.

   - *Serialized Stock:* Items that have serial numbers that you plan to track. Serialized stock items appear only in Peachtree Premium and higher.

   - *Assembly:* Items that consist of components that must be built or unbuilt (dismantled). See the "Putting 'Em Together, Taking 'Em Apart" section. Assembly items are available in Peachtree Pro Accounting and higher.

   - *Serialized Assembly:* Items that consist of serialized components that you plan to build or unbuild. Serialized assembly items appear only in Peachtree Premium and higher.

   - *Service:* Services provided by your employees that you bill to your customers.

   - *Labor:* Charges that you bill to a customer for subcontracted labor on that customer's projects.

   - *Activity:* Records of how time is spent when employees or vendors perform services. Activity items appear only in Peachtree Complete and higher. Chapter 10 gives you more information on setting up activity and charge items.

   - *Charge:* On-the-job expenses of an employee or vendor. Charge items appear only in Peachtree Complete and higher. Chapter 10 gives you more information on setting up activity and charge items.

   - *Description Only:* Time-saver when you track nothing but the description.

If you save an item as a stock item, an assembly item, an activity item, or a charge item, you can't change its item class. Although you probably wouldn't want to, Peachtree does allow you to interchange the item class between non-stock, description, labor, and service items.

5. **Select the Subject to Commission check box if you want to track the sales of the item and have it reported on the Accounts Receivable Sales Rep report.**

When your company no longer carries a particular product, you can select the Inactive check box.

General options

You enter basic item information such as descriptions, account numbers, sales prices, and pricing methods on the General tab.

Why does Peachtree list different description lines? Well, the first description — the one you enter in the header information (refer to Figure 11-1) — appears when you open the inventory item lookup list.

Peachtree also provides a drop-down list where you can select the Description for Sales and the Description for Purchases fields (up to 160 characters for each field). The description you enter for sales appears on quotes, sales orders, sales invoicing, and receipts. The purchases description appears on purchase orders, purchases/receive inventory, and payments. You can modify either the sales description or the purchases description when you create a transaction.

Follow these steps to enter general inventory information:

1. **Click the arrow next to the drop-down list under Description (as shown in the margin) to select the description you want to enter.**

2. **Enter a description as you want it to appear on transactions.**

   Entering information in the Description for Sales and Description for Purchases fields is optional. If you don't specify a sales description, Peachtree uses the lookup description when you enter a quote, a sales order, an invoice, or a receipt. If you don't specify a purchases description, Peachtree uses the sales description when generating purchase orders, purchases, or payments.

3. **Type the price you want to charge.**

   Peachtree refers to the amounts that appear on your quotes, sales orders, and invoices as *sales prices*. The sales pricing levels correspond with those you assign your customers in the Maintain Customers/Prospects window (see Chapter 7).

If you charge only one price for this item, no matter which customer makes the purchase, enter only Price Level 1. To enter additional sales prices, click the arrow next to the Price Level 1 field (as shown here). The Multiple Price Levels dialog box appears, as shown in Figure 11-2.

See Chapter 4 for information on renaming price levels and setting up other inventory default options.

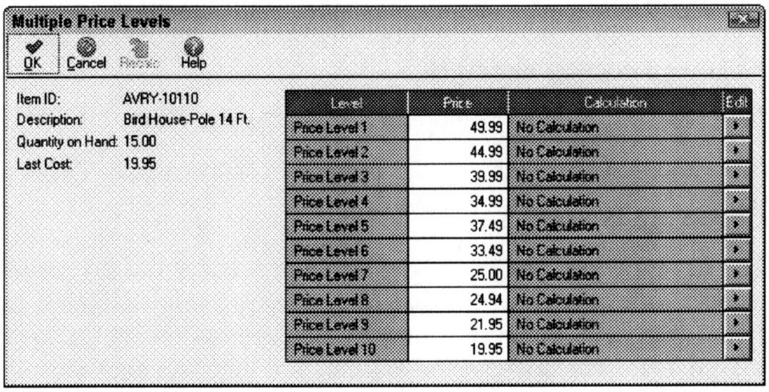

Figure 11-2:
Set up to ten
sales prices
for each
item.

Level	Price	Calculation	Edit
Price Level 1	49.99	No Calculation	▶
Price Level 2	44.99	No Calculation	▶
Price Level 3	39.99	No Calculation	▶
Price Level 4	34.99	No Calculation	▶
Price Level 5	37.49	No Calculation	▶
Price Level 6	33.49	No Calculation	▶
Price Level 7	25.00	No Calculation	▶
Price Level 8	24.94	No Calculation	▶
Price Level 9	21.95	No Calculation	▶
Price Level 10	19.95	No Calculation	▶

Item ID: AVRY-10110
Description: Bird House-Pole 14 Ft.
Quantity on Hand: 15.00
Last Cost: 19.95

Be consistent when entering item sales price levels (for example, from lowest to highest or highest to lowest). See Chapter 4 for information on naming the price levels to something more specific for your business.

Items prices can be a static number you assign, or you can create a calculation that uses the current price or the last cost as the foundation of the formula. By default, Peachtree uses the pricing calculation you entered when creating inventory defaults. (See Chapter 4.)

You can, however, click the arrow button in the Edit column (as shown here) to display the Calculate Price Level dialog box and create a different calculation. You can increase or decrease the price by a percentage or an amount. After you finish, click OK twicwwe to close both the Calculate Price Level dialog box and the Multiple Price Levels window.

4. (Optional) In the Last Unit Cost field, enter the last price you paid for this item.

After you enter transactions against the inventory item, the Last Unit Cost field becomes unavailable. Peachtree automatically updates the Last Unit Cost field as you enter purchases, payments, adjustments, or beginning balances, calculating the amount based on the costing method you select in Step 5.

5. If necessary, select a different costing method.

The Cost Method is a *very important* field. You can't change a costing method after an inventory item is saved.

Costing methods apply only to stock items, master stock items, assemblies, serialized items, and serialized assemblies. In addition to tracking serialized items and serialized assemblies by their specific unit cost, Peachtree supports three other costing methods: average cost, LIFO (last in, first out), and FIFO (first in, first out). The sidebar, "How do inventory costing methods work?" gives you more information on what these methods mean. Typically, you set all inventory items to use the same costing method, so you probably determined a default method when you set up the default inventory item information in Chapter 4. If you're not sure, check with your accountant for advice about different inventory costing methods.

6. **If necessary, change the GL accounts for the item.**

   You can read about setting up default GL accounts in Chapter 4.

7. **Choose an item tax type.**

   The tax type you select applies when you enter the inventory item on quotes, sales orders, invoices, or receipts. If you assign an exempt tax type to an item, Peachtree never calculates sales tax for the item. If you assign a taxable tax type to an item, you can still exempt the item from sales tax in the Maintain Customers/Prospects window or when you create an invoice.

8. **(Optional) Enter a part number.**

   An example might be the part number your vendor uses. The Part Number field is available only in Peachtree Premium and higher.

9. **(Optional) Enter a UPC or SKU number for your barcoded items.**

   In Peachtree Premium or higher, when printing customer or vendor forms, you have the option of replacing the item ID with the part number or the UPC/SKU number.

10. **(Optional) Enter an item type.**

    You'll appreciate this field when you're generating reports. Grouping items on reports is much easier when they're marked, for example, as *supplies* or *raw materials.*

11. **(Optional) Enter a storage location for the unit.**

    Someday you might need to know where the unit is located, such as Bin 17 or Shelf B3 or in Mom's garage. The storage location is helpful when doing a physical inventory as well.

12. **(Optional) Select a unit of measure from the Stock U/M drop-down list.**

    You might sell your products on an individual basis (each), in pairs, per dozen, per pound or kilogram, or per ounce.

    Peachtree Premium for Distribution, Peachtree Premium for Manufacturing, and Peachtree Quantum include the ability to purchase and sell your products in different units of measure.

13. **(Optional) Enter an item weight.**

14. **(Optional) In the Minimum Stock field, enter the quantity at which you want Peachtree to remind you that it's time to reorder the item.**

    When the quantity on hand reaches the minimum stock quantity, Peachtree prints the item on the Inventory Reorder Worksheet.

    Although entering a minimum stock point is optional, you need to enter a minimum stock point if you want Peachtree Premium or higher to automatically create a purchase order when the stock gets low. See Chapter 5 for more information about purchase orders.

15. **(Optional) Enter a reorder quantity.**

    Reorder quantity is the quantity you generally purchase when you order the inventory item. Entering a reorder quantity point is also optional, but again ,you need to enter a reorder quantity if you want Peachtree Premium or higher to automatically create a purchase order when the stock gets low.

16. **(Optional) Tell Peachtree where you prefer to buy this item by selecting the vendor ID in the Preferred Vendor lookup list.**

    Selecting a Preferred Vendor doesn't mean that's the *only* vendor from whom you can purchase the item. It just means that this vendor is your *favorite* vendor for this item. You must supply a Preferred Vendor if you want Peachtree Premium or higher to automatically create purchase orders for reorder or for drop-ship transactions and non–drop-ship transactions.

17. **(Optional) Select the employee who is the usual buyer for this item.**

    The information can appear on the Buyer report and can be used to select items for automatic purchase orders.

18. **If you're not creating an assembly item, a master stock item, or a serialized item and are ready to move on, click the Save button (as shown here) to save the inventory item.**

    Later in this chapter, we show you how to set up serialized items. Additionally, you see how to set up a bill of materials for an assembly item and master stock items with their substock items.

If you enter the item ID incorrectly, after saving the item, click the Change ID button (as shown in the margin) and enter a new inventory item ID.

Whew! That's a *lot* of stuff to enter for one item! Fortunately, the rest of the Maintain Inventory Items window is easy and doesn't involve too many tough decisions.

How do inventory costing methods work?

If you're not sure which option to choose in the Cost Method field, you might want to know how Peachtree handles these options. Peachtree supports three main inventory costing methods: Average, FIFO (first-in, first-out), and LIFO (last-in, first-out). (Those terms kinda remind us of Jack and the Beanstalk — Fee Fie Foe Fum. . . .) Peachtree also supports Specific Unit as a costing method. That method, though — available only in Peachtree Premium and higher — applies only to those items with a serialized inventory class.

If you use the Average costing method, Peachtree adds the total amount paid for the items and divides that by the total units on hand. The average is recalculated each time you purchase more of the item. Remember that Peachtree calculates costs on a daily basis. For example, say you have on hand five widgets for which you paid $6 each and three more widgets for which you paid $7 each. That's a total of $51

for the eight widgets, or an average of $6.375 each.

If you use the FIFO costing method, Peachtree calculates costs at the *earliest* purchase price, inventory increase adjustment, build, sales return, or assembly unbuild (for the component item) for a particular item. FIFO produces the lowest possible net income in periods of falling costs, and the cost of the most recently purchased item most closely approximates the replacement of the item.

If you use the LIFO costing method, Peachtree calculates costs at the most recent *(last)* purchase price, inventory increase adjustment, build, sales return, or assembly unbuild (for the component item) for a particular item. LIFO produces the lowest possible net income in periods of rising costs, and the cost of the most recently purchased item most closely approximates the replacement of the item.

Custom fields

If you use other Peachtree modules (such as Accounts Receivable, Accounts Payable, Payroll, or Job Cost), you've seen custom fields. Use custom fields to store miscellaneous pieces of information about the inventory item that just don't seem to fit anywhere else in the Maintain Inventory Items window. Examples of such items are the product average shelf life and information about an alternate vendor for the product. One of our clients uses a custom field to store the chemical makeup of each item.

History

The History tab displays a summary of inventory transactions for stock, assembly, and serialized items for past periods. Peachtree shows units sold and received as well as sales and costs by accounting period. Peachtree does not retain history for non-stock, service, and the remaining class items.

Serial numbers

The Serial Number tab is one location where you can view the in-stock serial numbers of the current item as well as determine whether you provide a warranty with the item. The Serial Number tab becomes available only if you class the inventory item as a serialized stock item or a serialized assembly item.

Only Peachtree Premium and higher support serialized inventory items.

Peachtree assigns a status that you cannot manually change, to each serial number except by entering transactions such as buying or selling. Table 11-1 shows the different statuses and what they mean.

Table 11-1	Serialized Inventory Item Status Codes
Status	*What It Is*
Available	Serial numbers with this status are available for selection on transactions.
Sold	Serial numbers with this status are no longer available because the serial number for the item has been removed from inventory by a transaction such as a sale.
Adjusted	Serial numbers with this status have been taken out of inventory because of an inventory adjustment.
Returned	Serial numbers with this status have been returned to the vendor by using a credit memo.
In Progress	Serial numbers with this status have been added to work tickets that haven't yet been closed. This status is available only in the Peachtree Premium for Distribution, Peachtree Premium for Manufacturing, and Peachtree Quantum editions.
New	Serial numbers with this status have been added to the system by a transaction, but the transaction hasn't been saved.
Error	Serial numbers with this status have been imported into Peachtree with an on-hand quantity. However, the transaction that added the serial number to the system (the originating transaction) is missing.

The Peachtree Premium for Distribution, Peachtree Premium for Manufacturing, and Peachtree Quantum editions also include work tickets to help track the build progress of an assembled item. Work tickets contain information about what's needed to build an assembly and whether all the items are available. Work tickets follow a build through its process, and you can check off the build steps as they're completed.

Serial number statuses are displayed on the Serial Numbers tab in the Maintain Inventory Items window, on the Serial Number Entry window, and on the Serial Number Selection window. Serial number statuses are reported on the Serial Number History report.

Also on the Serial Numbers tab, you can indicate whether the current item has a warranty and determine the length of the warranty period (see Figure 11-3). Peachtree allows up to 90 days, months, or years for a warranty period.

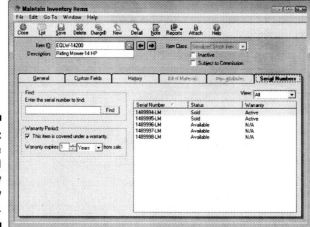

Figure 11-3:
Enter the
serialized
inventory
warranty
period.

You can customize your invoice to display the warranty information and warranty expiration date. See Chapter 13 for information on customizing forms such as invoices.

Whoa, Nellie! Working with Master Stock Items

If you have a lot of items and each of those items comes in a different flavor such as color, size, or condition, you can end up with an out-of-control inventory list. To help you harness your inventory list, Peachtree uses another inventory class called master stock. You use master stock items when you have several variations of similar items, such as T-shirts in various colors and sizes, or both new and used lawn mowers (as shown in Figure 11-4).

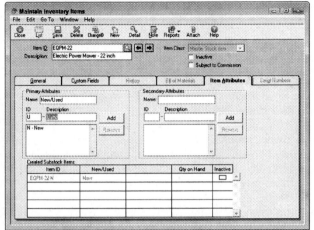

Figure 11-4: Peachtree automatically creates substock inventory items.

Master stock items are available only in Peachtree Complete and higher editions.

When you create a master stock item and designate its various attributes, Peachtree creates substock items for each category you determine. In our example, instead of creating new and used versions of each lawn mower, we can set up one master stock item, assign it to either the new or used version of the Sales and Cost of Sales accounts, and then use the Item Attributes tab to create new and used versions of the item. The Item Attributes tab becomes available only if you're working with a master stock item. Use the following steps to create a master stock item:

1. **Click the Item Attributes tab.**

2. **In the Name field under Primary Attributes, type a name that describes the distinction you're making for the item.**

   In the example, we used New/Used.

3. **In the ID field, type an ID that identifies the substock item.**

   Peachtree appends this ID to the ID of the master stock item.

4. **In the Description field, type a description for the substock item.**

   We used N for the ID and New for the description for the first substock item and U and Used for the second substock item.

5. **Click the Add button, as shown in the margin.**

   Add

   The ID and description appear in the field immediately below the ID and Description fields, and the full item ID appears in the bottom of the window in the Created Substock Items list.

6. **Repeat Steps 2–5 for each substock item.**

   Peachtree creates separate entries for each substock item; you see these entries if you click the lookup list indicator next to the Item ID field at the top of the window. This method makes creating items with similar characteristics quick and easy.

7. **Click the Save button to save both the master stock items and each of the substock items you created.**

You can't sell master stock items; instead, you sell one of the substock items. Because you don't sell master stock items, Peachtree doesn't track the last unit cost, the UPC/SKU, or any quantity information shown on the General tab of the Maintain Inventory Items window.

During reporting, you can summarize report information for substock items by filtering most inventory reports to show only master stock items. For example, if you print the Inventory Profitability report and filter it for master stock items, you see the master stock item and numbers that are the totals for all associated substock items. On reports, you can't filter for particular substock items.

In the Beginning (Balance, That Is)

Chances are that you've been in business for some time and have a current stock of inventory goods. If so and if you're setting up your Peachtree company for the first time, you need to enter beginning balances for the items you have on hand.

To enter inventory item beginning balances, follow these steps:

1. **Choose Maintain⇨Inventory Items.**

   The Maintain Inventory Items window appears.

2. **From the General tab, click the arrow button next to Beginning Balances (in the lower-right corner of the window), as shown here in the margin.**

   The Inventory Beginning Balances dialog box appears, as shown in Figure 11-5.

3. **From the list, select the inventory item.**

   The item appears at the top.

Figure 11-5:
Only stock
items,
substock
items,
serialized
items, and
assemblies
appear
here.

Inventory Beginning Balances					
Cancel	OK	Find	Next	Serial No	Help

Item ID	Description	Quantity	Unit Cost	Total Cost
EQPM-22-N	Electric Power Mower - 22 inch	2.00	219.75	439.50

Item ID	Description	Quantity	Unit Cost	Total Cost
EQLW-14220	Gas Backpack Blower	0.00	0.00	0.00
EQLW-14230	Cordless Mower	0.00	0.00	0.00
EQPM-22-N	Electric Power Mower - 22 inch	2.00	219.75	439.50
EQPM-22-U	Electric Power Mower - 22 inch	0.00	0.00	0.00
EQWT-15100	Drip Irrigation System	10.00	59.95	599.50
EQWT-15110	Garden Hose - 50 ft	20.00	11.95	239.00
EQWT-15120	Garden Hose - 75 ft	24.00	15.95	382.80
EQWT-15130	Hose Hanger - Wall Mount	15.00	7.95	119.25
EQWT-15140	Hose Reel Cart	11.00	19.95	219.45

Total Beginning Balances: 19,037.69

4. **Enter the quantity and the *unit cost* (the price you paid for the unit).**

   If you bought the items at a lot (bulk) price and don't know the cost of each one, skip the unit cost and enter the total cost you paid for the goods. Peachtree divides the total cost by the quantity and displays the result in the Unit Cost field.

Serial No

5. **If the item is a serialized item, click the Serial No button, as shown in the margin, and enter the serial number you want to add.**

6. **Repeat Steps 3–5 for each inventory item for which you have stock.**

OK

7. **Click the OK button (as shown here) to update the inventory balance and close the Inventory Beginning Balances window.**

Putting 'Em Together, Taking 'Em Apart

Some stuff is made up of pieces of other stuff. Peachtree calls the pieces *components* and the complete items *assemblies.* Maybe your company sells bird feeders as a stand-alone product or as part of a package deal that includes a post, a hook, and birdseed. The package deal is an assembly. Or maybe you sell a "doobob." (Elaine, that one's for you!) This doobob is made up of several thingamajigs and a couple of whatchamacallits. You don't actually sell thingamajigs or whatchamacallits (components) to your customers, but you still need to keep track of their quantities so you know how many doobobs (assemblies) you can make. In either situation, you create the assembled items by building them out of a list of component parts, both in your physical inventory and in your virtual store.

Peachtree Premium for Distribution, Peachtree Premium for Manufacturing, and Peachtree Quantum editions also offers work tickets to help track the build progress of an assembled item. Work tickets contain information about what's needed to build an assembly and whether you have all the items available. You can use work tickets to follow a build through its process, and you can check off the build steps as they are completed.

Creating a bill of materials

The *bill of materials* is a list of the individual parts that make up assemblies. Before you can create an assembly item, you need to make sure that each component part is set up in Peachtree.

Create a bill of materials by following these steps:

1. **Choose Maintain⇨Inventory Items to display the Maintain Inventory Items window.**

2. **Create the assembly items inventory item ID, description, and other information.**

   Make sure that you select Assembly as the item class.

3. **Click the Bill of Materials tab to display a screen like the one in Figure 11-6.**

   Because assemblies are made up of other components, you need to use the Bill of Materials tab to list the component items. Assemblies must have at least one component (item ID) listed in the bill of materials.

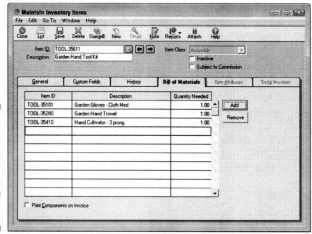

Figure 11-6: Assemblies must have at least one item listed in the bill of materials.

4. **Select or enter the first item ID you want to include in the assembly.**

   Peachtree automatically fills in the description, but you can change the description.

5. **Enter the quantity needed to build one assembly.**

6. **Repeat Steps 4 and 5 for each component item.**

   If you run out of lines on the Bill of Materials list and have additional components, click the Add button. Peachtree inserts a blank line above the current item.

7. **If you want Peachtree to print the list of the individual components on the invoice, select the Print Components on Invoice check box.**

8. **Click the Save button to save the assembly item.**

After you use an assembly on a transaction, you can't add or remove component items from the bill of materials. You need to create a new assembly item to change component parts unless you're using Peachtree Premium for Distribution, Peachtree Premium for Manufacturing, or Peachtree Quantum editions. In these three products, you can revise the original bill of materials with the following stipulations:

✔ Up to a maximum of 99 revisions per assembly item

✔ One revision per assembly item per day

Building assemblies

When you build an assembly item, Peachtree takes the individual components and reduces their quantity on hand. Peachtree does not allow negative component quantities when building assemblies — that's only logical. Therefore, you need enough component parts in stock to build the requested number of assemblies.

Be sure to build assemblies before you sell them. Although Peachtree technically allows you to sell an assembly before you build it, you shouldn't. Selling the assembly before it's in stock can greatly distort your inventory costing.

Follow these steps to build assemblies:

1. **Choose Tasks⊏>Assemblies.**

   The Build/Unbuild Assemblies dialog box, as shown in Figure 11-7, appears.

2. **In the Item ID lookup list, select the assembly item ID.**

   Peachtree displays each assembly component along with the current quantity on hand.

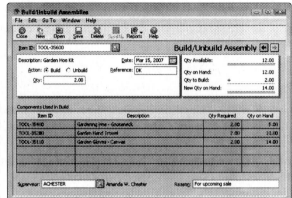

Figure 11-7:
Using
components
to build
assemblies.

3. **In the Reference field, enter an optional reference number or any piece of information to identify this transaction, perhaps your initials and the date.**

Many Peachtree windows don't require reference numbers, but making sure that every transaction you enter into Peachtree has some type of a reference number is a good idea.

4. **Choose the transaction date, which is typically the date the changes in your inventory occurred.**

5. **Next to Action, select Build or Unbuild.**

You might want to unbuild an assembly, for example, if you need to sell the individual components.

6. **Enter the build or unbuild quantity.**

Whether you're building or unbuilding, enter a positive number. As you enter the quantity you want to build, the assembly New Qty on Hand amount changes, as well as the component quantity required. If you're unbuilding assemblies, Peachtree shows the components quantity returned to stock.

7. **In the lower-right corner, enter a reason to build the assemblies.**

You don't *have* to enter a reason. Undoubtedly, you know exactly right now why you're building them, but will you remember six months from now?

Optionally, select an employee name from the Supervisor list. The *supervisor* is the person overseeing the assembly build or unbuild. Supervisors must be set up as employees. See Chapter 9 for information on setting up employees.

8. **Click the Save button to record the transaction.**

Making Inventory Adjustments

Face it: Inventory counts get out of whack sometimes. Items get damaged, lost, or stolen. Sometimes, for reasons unknown, you might find several products that you didn't know you had, stashed away in a corner. So periodically, you need to adjust your inventory.

Whether you take a physical inventory count of all your goods or just need to adjust the quantity on hand of a single product, you use the Peachtree Inventory Adjustment feature.

Follow these steps to make adjustments to your inventory:

1. **Choose Tasks⇨Inventory Adjustments to display the Inventory Adjustments window you see in Figure 11-8.**

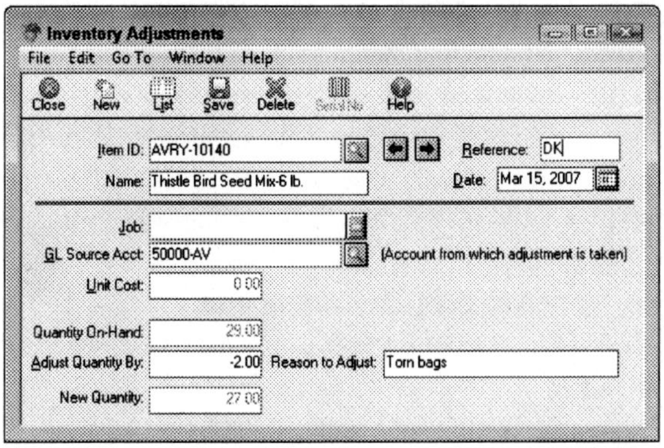

Figure 11-8: Make inventory adjustments using this window.

2. **Enter a reference number or any piece of information to identify this transaction — perhaps your initials and the date.**

   Many Peachtree windows don't require reference numbers, but making sure that every transaction you enter into Peachtree has some type of a reference number is a good idea.

3. **Select a date for the inventory adjustment.**

4. **If you use the Peachtree job-costing feature, select the job (and optionally, the phase or cost code) to which you want to charge the adjustment.**

   Chapter 12 tells you all about job costing.

5. **Choose the GL Source account you want to charge for the adjustment cost.**

If you decrease the item quantity, Peachtree debits the GL Source account and credits the Inventory account you listed in the Maintain Inventory Items window for the item. If you increase the item quantity, Peachtree credits the GL Source account and debits the item's Inventory account.

6. **Enter a unit cost.**

   The Unit Cost field defaults to the last purchase price you entered in the system. If you use the Inventory Adjustment transaction to increase your inventory count, you can change the unit cost. If you're reducing the quantity on hand, however, the Unit Cost field becomes disabled. Peachtree determines the cost of the adjustment based on the item's costing method at the time of the adjustment.

   The unit cost is very important! Not putting in a cost when increasing inventory can throw off your entire inventory valuation.

7. **In the Adjust Quantity By field, type a quantity to adjust.**

   Enter the quantity as a negative number if you need to decrease your quantity on hand. Peachtree displays the new quantity on hand.

8. **(Optional) In the Reason to Adjust field, describe why you're creating the transaction (for example, damaged or annual inventory).**

   You might know quite well why you're creating this adjustment, but will you remember later when your accountant asks you about this transaction?

9. **Click the Save button to save the transaction.**

Adjusting Prices

One day, you suddenly realize you haven't raised the prices on your products for a long time. Your costs have gone up, and you know you have to pass some of that increase on to your customers. We know this isn't a step you take lightly. After all, you still want to be competitive, but you're in business to *make* money — *not lose it* — so you make the decision to increase your prices.

Originally, you enter the sales prices when you create the inventory item in the Maintain Inventory Items window. You *could* go back to the Maintain Inventory Items window and pull each item up individually, change the sales prices, and then save the inventory item again.

"Oh no!" you say. "I have too many inventory items to change the prices individually. Isn't there a faster way?" Yes. Peachtree provides an easy way to update prices on all your inventory items, a range of items, or a single item. For example, you can mark up sales prices for all your stock items by 10 percent. You can even adjust the prices for only the products you purchase from a specific vendor. Peachtree allows you to adjust the item sales prices up or down.

Make a backup before you change item prices.

To adjust sales prices, follow these steps:

1. **Choose Maintain⇨Item Prices to display the Maintain Item Prices – Filter Selection dialog box, as shown in Figure 11-9.**

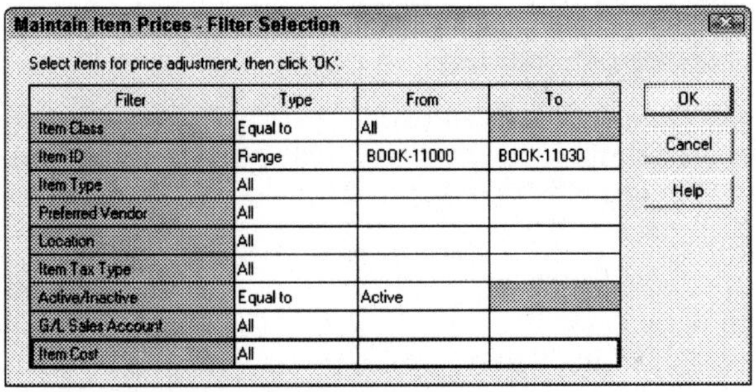

Figure 11-9:
Adjust inventory sales prices for all or some of your items.

Maintain Item Prices - Filter Selection				
Select items for price adjustment, then click 'OK'.				
Filter	Type	From	To	OK
Item Class	Equal to	All		Cancel
Item ID	Range	BOOK-11000	BOOK-11030	Help
Item Type	All			
Preferred Vendor	All			
Location	All			
Item Tax Type	All			
Active/Inactive	Equal to	Active		
G/L Sales Account	All			
Item Cost	All			

2. **Enter any desired filter information.**

   This dialog box gives you lots of different ways to select the products that need a price increase. If you don't choose any settings, Peachtree assumes you want to change the prices of all your products. However, you can select just stock items, or stock items you purchase from vendor JONES-01, or only the products that cost more than $10 but less than $50, or . . . you get the idea. You can select any of these combinations. In Figure 11-9, we changed the price on only our gardening books.

3. **Click OK to display the Maintain Item Prices window, as shown in Figure 11-10.**

4. **Because Peachtree assumes that you want to change all ten pricing levels, you have to deselect the check box next to each price level that you don't want to change.**

   Now you have to make some decisions regarding your method of adjustment. Do you want to adjust your price levels manually or through calculations?

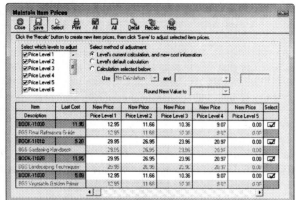

Figure 11-10:
Peachtree
displays
items based
on your filter
selection.

5. **Select an adjustment method:**

   • *Level's Current Calculation, and New Cost Information:* Selected price levels and items that use cost or Level 1 in calculating the price are recalculated based on the current cost or the updated Level 1 price.

   • *Level's Default Calculation:* Each price level and item selected are recalculated using the calculation in the Inventory Item Defaults dialog box. This method overrides any customized calculations you might have set up for individual items in the Maintain Inventory Items window.

   • *Calculation Selected Below:* If you use a calculation for changing your prices, select the Calculation Selected Below radio button. Then click the arrow next to the Use drop-down list and select an adjustment method: Current Price or Last Cost. Some companies mark up their products by a flat percentage — say, 25 percent over cost. In that case, they'd select the Last Cost option. If you want to increase the current sales price — say, a $1 item that you now want to sell for $1.15 — choose the Current Price option.

6. **If you select the Calculation Selected Below method, follow Steps 7 and 8. If not, jump ahead to Step 9.**

7. **Choose a markup method and enter an amount or percentage to mark up the item.**

   Peachtree allows you to change prices on the selected items by an amount or a percentage. If you select Amount, enter the amount as a positive or negative dollar amount. If you select Percent, enter the amount as a positive or negative percentage (for example, enter **6** for a 6 percent markup).

Enter a negative number if you want to mark down the current price.

8. **From the Round New Value To drop-down list, select a method for rounding the new prices:**

   - *Next Dollar:* Peachtree rounds the item prices up to the nearest dollar amount. For example, if you increase the price of a product you previously sold for $11.60 by 15 percent, the calculated price is $13.34, but Peachtree rounds the new price up to $14.

   - *Specific Cent:* Use this if you want to round all prices up to a specified cent level. For example, at a 95-cent price level, your products would sell for $5.95, $7.95, $11.95, and so on. If you choose Specific Cent, specify the cents (95, in our example) in the Amount field.

   - *Do Not Round:* Select this if you don't want the prices rounded.

9. **Click the Recalc toolbar button (as shown here) to see the new item prices.**

   You can also manually change individual prices by simply typing in a new price in the appropriate price box.

   Click the Detail button, as shown in the margin, to display additional information about an item or click the Print button to print a report of your proposed price adjustments.

10. **Click the Save button to record the new prices.**

11. **Click the Close button to close the Maintain Item Prices dialog box.**

When Does Peachtree Assign a Cost to Items?

We'll be honest here. This section is Booooring with a capital *B*. You certainly don't have to read this information, but our experience shows that many clients want to know how the Peachtree inventory system works — not just the mechanics of entering items or transactions, but what's happening behind the scenes. We don't give you any steps or tasks to accomplish — just some plain old facts about inventory.

This whole inventory state of affairs can be confusing. You probably already noticed that the Peachtree inventory module is perfect for a *buy/sell situation* — where you purchase a product and then resell it — but it doesn't work very well for tracking raw materials used in production, especially if scrap is involved. Add that factor to all the different item transactions that can affect the cost, and sometimes the entire picture becomes blurred.

Peachtree calculates the value of inventory items on a daily basis. To ensure that increases to inventory are posted before decreases to inventory, Peachtree posts transactions in the following order:

1. **Purchases**

2. **Payments**

3. **Increase adjustments**

4. **Assembly builds (for an assembly item)**

5. **Sales returns**

6. **Receipts return**

7. **Assembly unbuilds (for a component item)**

8. **Purchase returns**

9. **Payment returns**

10. **Assembly unbuilds (for an assembly item)**

11. **Sales**

12. **Receipts**

13. **Decrease adjustments**

14. **Assembly builds (for a component item)**

Peachtree creates three types of system-generated adjustments: the purchase return adjustment, the assembly unbuild adjustment, and the system cost adjustment. You can't erase these types of adjustments. They appear in the Inventory Adjustment Journal and on the Item Costing report. The reference for a system cost adjustment is SysCost, the reference for a purchase return adjustment is the reference number of the purchase transaction (usually the invoice number), and the reference for the assembly unbuild adjustment is the reference number of the assembly unbuild transaction.

Figure 11-11 shows an inventory adjustment journal with a system-generated cost (SysCost) adjustment.

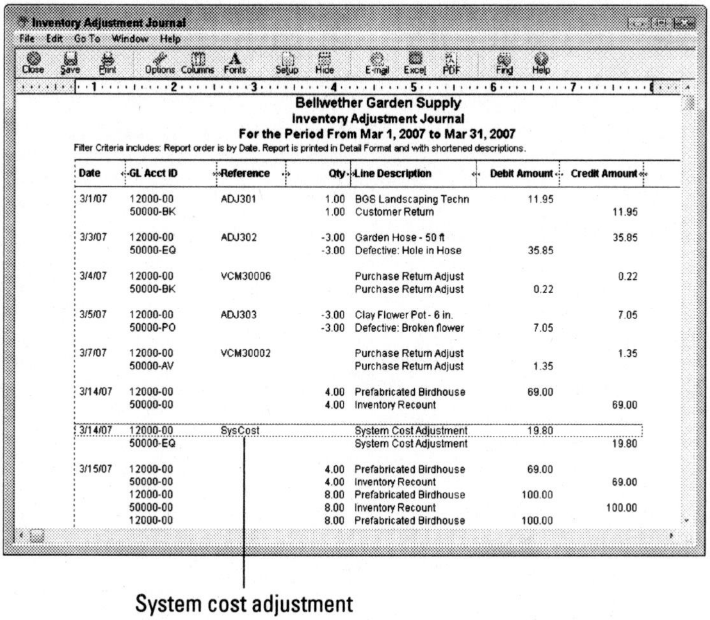

Figure 11-11: See system-generated adjustments in the Inventory Adjustment Journal.

System cost adjustment

Reporting on Your Inventory

Here comes the spiel you see in many other chapters: Although it would be nice to print a sample of every report Peachtree offers (especially in this chapter because Peachtree has a number of valuable inventory reports), there simply isn't space in this book to do so. In Table 11-2, we provide you with a description of the reports that pertain to maintaining your inventory. (Chapter 14 describes how to print and customize reports.) Many inventory reports offer only stock and assembly item information.

Table 11-2	Reports Related to Inventory
Report Name	*What It Does*
Assemblies Adjustment Journal	Shows built and unbuilt assembly transactions in journal format.
Assembly List	Lists each assembly with the components that make up the assembly.
Bill of Materials Report	Lists each assembly with its components, the cost of each component, and an estimated cost to build the assembly.

(continued)

Table 11-2 *(continued)*

Report Name	*What It Does*
Buyer Report	Lists each item along with the buyer. You can sort this report by buyer ID, item ID, item description, or preferred vendor ID.
Component Use List	Lists component items and the assemblies on which they are used. Sort by component item or assembly item ID.
Cost of Goods Sold Journal	Shows, in journal format, the cost of goods sold.
Inventory Adjustment Journal	Lists, in journal format, inventory adjustments.
Inventory Profitability Report	Lists each item with units sold, cost, gross profit, adjustments, and percent of total.
Inventory Reorder Worksheet	Displays reorder amounts for inventory items when they fall below the specified minimum stock amount.
Inventory Stock Status Report	Lists items, quantity on hand, and reorder quantity.
Inventory Unit Activity Report	Lists the item's beginning quantity; units sold, purchased, adjusted, and assembled; and an ending quantity on hand.
Inventory Valuation Report	Shows the quantity on hand, value, average cost, and percent of inventory value for all in-stock items.
Item Costing Report	Lists each inventory item with costing information for quantities received and sold.
Item List	Lists each item, item description, class, type, and quantity on hand.
Item Master List	Lists items with detail information as entered in the Maintain Inventory Items window.
Item Price List	Lists each item with quantity on hand and each available sales price.
Physical Inventory List	A worksheet you can use to check the actual quantity of items on hand versus what the system reports on hand.
Serial Number History Report	Lists serialized items along with their status. Sort this report by item ID or description or by serial number.

One report you should definitely know is the Inventory Valuation report, which shows the quantity on hand, value, average cost, and percent of inventory value for all in-stock items. To arrive at the percent of inventory value, Peachtree takes the value of the item divided by the total value of items that have a positive item value. The example in Table 11-3 shows you how the percent-to-total value works.

Table 11-3		Sample Inventory Valuation	
Transaction #	*Quantity*	*Total Item Value*	*% of Inventory*
1	4	10.00	33.33
2	1	−5.00	
3	2	20.00	66.67
	Total	25.00	

In Table 11-3, Peachtree calculates the percent of inventory on the percent of the positive item values (items 1 and 3), which equal $10 + $20, or $30. Therefore, the 33.33% of inventory means that the $10 total value for those items are one-third of the $30 total, and the 66.67% of inventory shows the $20 total is two-thirds of the $30 total.

Don't forget to visit www.dummies.com/go/peachtreefd for more information on Peachtree.

Chapter 12

Tracking Project Costs

Some businesses lend themselves well to organizing work by projects. For the purposes of this discussion, *project* is synonymous with *job.* In particular, these companies perform the same general type of work for each customer — that is, all their projects are similar. Companies that use *job costing* (assigning costs to jobs) in their business want to track expenses and revenues for each job so that they can determine the net profit from the job. These companies often bid for the services they sell by providing a proposal that estimates the cost of performing the work. Then, if they get the work, they want to compare the estimated costs with the actual costs so that they can improve their estimating skills for future jobs and thus increase revenues.

In this chapter, we describe the job-costing features available in Peachtree Complete and higher. In Peachtree Pro Accounting, you can create jobs but not *phases* or *cost codes,* which are fields that enable you to capture more details about jobs. Peachtree First Accounting doesn't support job costing. One of the vertical market Peachtree products, Peachtree for Construction, contains even more job-costing features than described here.

Understanding Job Costing

What kinds of companies use job costing? Well, job costing is widely used in the construction industry, but it also can be used by a variety of other businesses, such as convention planning, party planning, landscaping, cleaning services, and printing (like when producing letterhead).

Do you need to use job costing? If the jobs you perform tend to stretch out over time, particularly across accounting years, you're more likely to use job costing. However, if you complete a job in a short period of time — a week or less — you probably don't need to use the Peachtree job-costing feature because the time you'd spend entering job information would exceed the value you'd receive from that information.

Creating custom fields for jobs

In Chapter 4, we set up defaults for other areas of Peachtree; for jobs, you can establish only custom fields because this feature has no other preferences to set. Choose Maintain⇨Default Information⇨Jobs to display the Job Defaults dialog box. Place a check mark next to any of the five field labels to enable the custom field. Then type a label description for each custom field. Click OK when you're finished.

Reviewing job examples

Before you dive in and start creating things, we think you'd benefit by examining a few examples that will help you better understand the order in which we choose to create things after you read these examples.

Jobs are a method of organizing accounting information. Throughout this chapter, we explain the various facets of jobs by using a running example: a company that builds swimming pools. Consider each swimming pool that the company builds as a separate job.

Phases

You can use *phases* to further break down the costs of a project. Phases are optional; use them only if you want to organize your project in some way and look at costs and revenues at a more detailed level. In the case of our swimming pool builder, we might use five phases:

- Design
- Permits
- Site preparation
- Installation
- Finishing/landscaping

Peachtree allows you to assign each phase to a cost type: Labor, Materials, Subcontract Labor, Equipment Rental, and Other.

Cost codes

If you need a further breakdown of any of these cost types for a particular phase — for example, if you need to track the costs of specific materials, such as concrete and tile — you can create *cost codes*. If you choose to create cost codes for a phase, you won't assign a cost type to the phase. Instead, you can assign a cost type to each cost code; Peachtree uses the same cost types for cost codes and phases.

Cost codes, like phases, are optional. You might find that you need cost codes for only one cost type, such as Labor. You can set up specific cost codes for Materials — such as tile, lumber, and concrete — and then assign those cost codes as needed to phases. For phases that don't need a cost code, you can simply use the phase — and its cost type.

If you use cost codes, we recommend that you try to use the same ones for every project. That way, you can set up one set of cost codes and assign them, as needed, to any phase of any project. You might also be able to use the same phases (or a subset of phases) for each project.

Consider one more example. Suppose that you manage an apartment complex, and you want to monitor the costs associated with each building on the property. You could set up each building as a job. Then, as you make purchases for a particular building, you can assign the purchases to that building. Your job reports show you the costs of each building in the complex. Note that we haven't suggested using phases or cost codes because they're optional.

Suppose, however, that you want to track costs for the complex at a more detailed level — say, by apartment. In that case, you could set up the apartments in each building as phases and assign expenses to particular apartments.

"So what's your point? Why are you telling me all this now?" you ask. Well, when setting up a job in Peachtree, you must decide whether the job uses phases. Similarly, when setting up a phase, you must decide whether the phase uses cost codes. You need to understand what each entity is so that you know what to create and the order in which to create things.

Creating Cost Codes

After you understand what cost codes are, you can use the following steps to create them if you need to use them:

1. **Choose Maintain➪Job Costs➪Cost Codes.**

   Peachtree displays the Maintain Cost Codes window (see Figure 12-1).

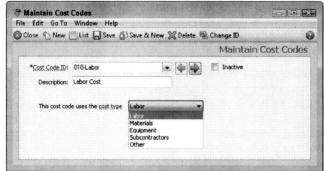

Figure 12-1:
Create a
cost code.

2. **In the Cost Code ID text box, type an ID (up to 20 alphanumeric characters).**

   You can change the ID later by using the Change ID button on the window toolbar.

3. **In the Description text box, type a description for the cost code.**

4. **Select a cost type for the cost code to categorize it in a general way.**

   You can select Labor, Materials, Equipment, Subcontractors, or Other.

5. **Click the Save button (as shown here).**

Repeat these steps to set up other cost codes you need for your phases.

If you no longer need a cost code, you can mark it inactive. To do so, redisplay the cost code in the Maintain Cost Codes window and select the Inactive check box.

Establishing Phases

If you decide to use phases for your jobs, use these steps to create a phase:

1. **Choose Maintain⇨Job Costs⇨Phases.**

   Peachtree displays the Maintain Phases window (see Figure 12-2).

2. **In the Phase ID text box, type an ID (up to 20 alphanumeric characters).**

   You can change the ID later by using the Change ID button on the window toolbar.

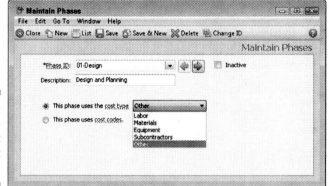

Figure 12-2:
Create a
phase that
uses cost
codes.

3. **In the Description text box, type a description for the phase.**

4. **Decide whether to use cost codes:**

   • *If you don't plan to use cost codes:* Select the This Phase Uses the
     Cost Type radio button and then select a cost type for the phase to
     categorize it in a general way. You can select Labor, Materials,
     Equipment, Subcontractors, or Other.

   • *If you plan to use cost codes for the phase:* Select the This Phase
     Uses Cost Codes option. Peachtree disables the ability to select a
     cost type.

5. **Click the Save button.**

Repeat these steps to set up other phases you need for your jobs.

If you no longer need a phase, you can mark it as inactive. To do so, redisplay
the phase in the Maintain Phases window and add a check mark to the
Inactive check box.

Creating Jobs and Estimates

To use jobs in Peachtree, you need to set up at least one job. To set up a job,
follow these steps:

1. **Choose Maintain⇨Job Costs⇨Jobs.**

   Peachtree displays the Maintain Jobs window (see Figure 12-3).

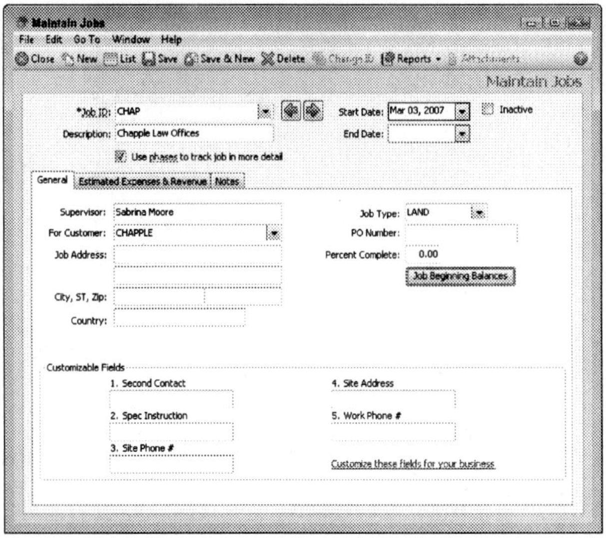

Figure 12-3:
Set up a job
in this
window.

2. **Type the job ID.**

   You can use up to 20 alphanumeric characters, excluding an asterisk (*),
   a question mark (?), and a plus sign (+). IDs are not case sensitive, so
   POOL-1 is the same as pool-1. See the sidebar, "Job reports and masking"
   for hints on assigning job IDs.

   You can change the job ID later by redisplaying the job and then clicking
   the Change ID button (as shown here). Peachtree displays the Change
   Job ID dialog box, which shows you the current job ID and lets you enter
   a new one.

3. **In the Description text box, provide a description for the job.**

4. **If the job uses phases, select the Use Phases check box.**

5. **(Optional) On the General tab, fill in any pertinent information.**

   Peachtree doesn't limit the number of jobs you can assign to customers,
   but you don't *need* to assign jobs to customers. If you don't need jobs
   for any reason other than charging customers for expenses, you can use
   time and expense slips. See Chapter 10 for details.

6. **If you work on the job before you enter it in Peachtree and you have
   historical revenues and expenses for the job, do the following:**

   If you use phases and cost codes with your job, you can enter beginning
   balances by phase and cost code instead of by job.

a. *Click the Job Beginning Balances button to display the Job Beginning Balances window. Use the Job Entries tab of the Job Beginning Balances window to enter beginning balances.*

From the Job Balances tab of the window, you can view the beginning balance of all jobs in the system.

b. *To enter a beginning balance, enter a date for the balance you intend to enter and a beginning balance in either the Expenses column or the Revenues column.*

You can enter balances for more than one date.

For reporting purposes, put the phase expenses on one line and the phase revenues on another line.

7. **When you finish entering beginning balances, click Save to redisplay the Maintain Jobs window.**

8. **Click the Estimated Expenses & Revenue tab to enter estimated expenses and revenues.**

These estimates are optional. In Figure 12-4, you see the Estimated Expenses & Revenue tab for a job that uses phases. If you don't use phases with your job, you see only two text boxes: one for total estimated expenses and one for total estimated revenues.

9. **Click Save to store the job's information.**

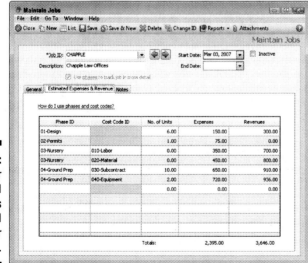

Figure 12-4:
Enter estimated expenses and revenues for the job.

Job reports and masking

Some job reports enable you to filter jobs using a job mask, which can be useful if you have several different characteristics about each job that you want to track. For one type of information you want to track, you can use the Job Type field. For the rest, you can use a coding scheme for the job ID.

Suppose, for example, that you work in three cities — Phoenix, Glendale, and Scottsdale — doing design, planting, and maintenance. You also want to differentiate jobs for residential and commercial customers. You can use the Job Type field to store the information about design, planting, and maintenance. Then you can create a coding scheme for the job ID that will enable you to use masking to print reports that display information on a subset of jobs. In the example, you might want to create a ten-character job ID that is composed of one character (P, G, or S) representing the city, one character (C or R) representing commercial or residential, four characters representing the customer's name, and four characters representing a job number. On most job reports, you can filter by Job Type and then mask for Phoenix jobs by typing P********* in the Job Mask field. You could mask for commercial jobs in Scottsdale by typing SC******** or residential jobs in Glendale by typing GR********. To use the mask, you supply asterisks for the characters that can change; the total number of characters you type is equal to the length of the job ID.

When you complete a job, you can mark it inactive. To do so, redisplay the job in the Maintain Jobs window and select the Inactive check box.

Assigning Jobs When You Buy

Suppose that you're buying something to use on a job and you want to assign the expense to the job. To do so, use the Purchase Orders window, the Purchases/Receive Inventory window, or the Payments window. The method is the same, regardless of the window you choose. In the following steps, we show you the process in the Purchases/Receive Inventory window:

1. **Choose Tasks⇨Purchases/Receive Inventory.**

   Peachtree displays the Purchases/Receive Inventory window (see Figure 12-5).

2. **Fill in the purchase information at the top of the window, like you would for any purchase.**

   See Chapter 5 for details on completing a purchase.

3. **In the bottom portion of the window, enter the information for the item that you're purchasing.**

   You can't purchase a stock inventory item to use on a job. If you already own a stock item that you want to use on a job, you can enter an inventory adjustment (see Chapter 11), or you can place the item on the customer's invoice. If you invoice the customer, you don't need to make the inventory adjustment.

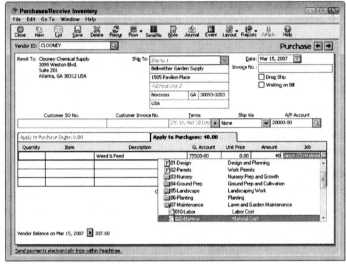

Figure 12-5: Assign a job to a purchase of anything but stock inventory items.

4. **In the Job column, click the list indicator and make a selection to assign the line to a job.**

   If the job uses phases or cost codes, you see a folder (as shown here) in the list representing the job. You need to click the folder to open it and select the appropriate phase or cost code.

   As you can see in Figure 12-5, when you open the Job list, it partially overlays the Amount box.

5. **Continue entering lines as needed.**

   You can include lines that you assign to jobs and lines that you don't assign to jobs on the same purchase.

6. **Click the Save button (as shown here) to save the purchase.**

Invoicing Customers' Jobs

By default, Peachtree creates reimbursable expenses for purchases you assign to jobs, and you can include these reimbursable expenses on an invoice to a customer. You also can choose not to include these reimbursable expenses on customer invoices.

Follow these steps to work with reimbursable expenses generated by assigning jobs to purchases or payments:

1. **Choose Tasks⇨Sales/Invoicing.**

   Peachtree displays the Sales/Invoicing window.

2. **Fill in the invoice information at the top of the window, like you would for any invoice.**

   For details on filling in an invoice, see Chapter 7.

3. **In the bottom portion of the window, enter one line of information for each of the items that you're selling.**

4. **In the Job column, click the list indicator to assign the lines to a job, as appropriate.**

5. **To include a reimbursable expense on an invoice, click the Apply Tickets/Expenses button in the lower left of the window.**

   Peachtree displays the Apply Tickets/Reimbursable Expenses window (see Figure 12-6).

   You won't know whether reimbursable expenses exist for a customer until you click the Apply Tickets/Expenses button.

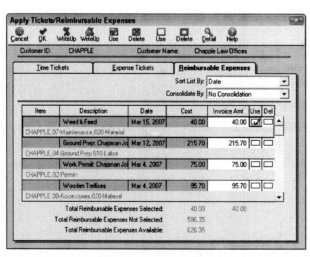

Figure 12-6:
Bill the selected customer for any or all of these re-imbursable expenses.

6. **Click the Reimbursable Expenses tab to see expenses you entered and assigned to a job in the Purchases/Inventory window and the Payments window.**

   If you ignored our advice and assigned an expense to a job in the Write Checks window, that expense will also appear on the Reimbursable Expenses tab.

7. **To include a reimbursable expense on the invoice, select the Use check box next to that reimbursable expense.**

8. **To build some profit into a reimbursable expense, change the amount in the Invoice Amt column.**

   To mark up or down a group of reimbursable expenses, click the WriteUp toolbar button (as shown here) to display the Select Reimbursables to Write Up/Down dialog box, where you can identify reimbursable expenses to mark up or down by either a dollar amount or a percentage.

   If you change your mind after marking up reimbursable expenses, you can click the Remove WriteUp button (as shown here) that appears immediately to the right of the WriteUp button. (We know it's confusing because they both seem to be called WriteUp, but you can point your mouse at each button to display a ToolTip that describes each button's function. The Remove WriteUp button image is the universal No sign.)

When you use reimbursable expenses, keep these points in mind:

✔ You can delete reimbursable expenses from the Apply Tickets/Reimbursable Expenses window if you decide not to bill the client for them. Place a check mark in the Del check box to the right of the expense. Deleting the reimbursable expense does *not* delete the transaction that created the reimbursable expense. Instead, deleting in the Apply Tickets/Reimbursable Expenses window breaks the tie between the reimbursable expense and the customer.

You can't undo deleting here. After you delete a reimbursable expense, the connection between the reimbursable expense and the customer is *permanently broken* unless you erase the purchase or payment that created the reimbursable expense and reenter it.

✔ Be aware that deleting or using a reimbursable expense makes it disappear from the Apply Tickets/Reimbursable Expenses window. If you use a reimbursable expense and subsequently delete the line from the invoice, the reimbursable expense *does not* reappear in the window. If you mistakenly use a reimbursable expense and post the invoice, delete the invoice and reenter it.

✔ You can edit a reimbursable expense you intend to bill to a customer by editing the purchase or payment that assigns the expense to a job. To find the transaction, open the window where you first created it — for example, the Purchases/Receive Inventory window — and click the List button.

Progress Billing

In Peachtree Premium and higher, you use proposals when you want to bill a customer based on the progress of a job. *Proposals* function in much the same way that quotes and sales orders function: They are documents you prepare prior to actually selling something and they do not update your General Ledger accounts. See Chapter 7 for details on using quotes and sales orders.

Proposals differ from quotes and sales orders after a customer accepts a proposal and you want to prepare the customer's invoice. The proposal gives you added flexibility that you don't have when you invoice from a quote or a sales order. When you invoice from a proposal, you can bill the customer for a percentage of the amount due or for specific lines of the proposal; or, you can bill your customer for the remaining unbilled portion of the job.

Initially, you prepare a proposal the same way that you prepare a quote. In Figure 12-7, you can see a completed sample of an accepted proposal in the Proposals window. To view this window, choose Tasks⇨Quotes/Sales Orders/Proposals⇨Proposals.

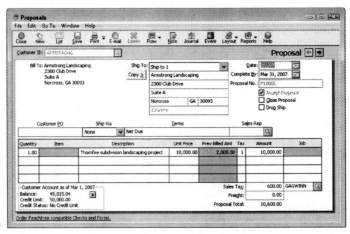

Figure 12-7:
A typical
proposal.

You can assign lines of the proposal to jobs the same way that you assign lines to an invoice, as described in the preceding section, "Invoicing Customers' Jobs." In fact, if you intend to use jobs, you must include the job line assignments on the proposal; you won't have an opportunity after you mark a proposal as accepted by a customer. You can, of course, wait to make job assignments until you're ready to mark a proposal as accepted. However, make sure that you edit the proposal *before* you accept it to assign jobs to lines of the proposal.

You can print or e-mail proposals the same way that you can print or e-mail quotes or sales orders. If you intend to print a proposal, don't assign a number; Peachtree will assign the number when you print the document.

The two options of most interest on a proposal appear just below the proposal number. You edit a proposal and select the Accept Proposal check box when the customer agrees that you should provide the goods or perform the services on the proposal. After you enable this check box, Peachtree makes the proposal available for invoicing in the Sales/Invoicing window.

Select the Close Proposal check box after you complete invoicing the proposal and it still contains goods or services that you won't provide. If you invoice for all the items listed on the proposal, Peachtree automatically closes the proposal for you.

Like with other documents in Peachtree, you can display a list of proposals either by clicking the List button in the Proposals window or by choosing Lists⇨Customers & Sales⇨Proposals. We suggest that you add the Accept Proposal column to the Proposal List window so that you can see at a glance whether a proposal has been accepted. See Bonus Chapter 1 on this book's Web site for details on customizing a list window to add or remove columns.

To invoice for a proposal, open the Sales/Invoicing window and select the customer for whom a proposal exists. You might see a message indicating that the customer has open and accepted proposals; click OK.

If both proposals and sales orders exist for the customer, Peachtree displays the Apply to Sales Order No. tab; otherwise, you see the Apply to Proposal No. tab. Open the list box on the tab and select the proposal you want to invoice (see Figure 12-8).

When both proposals and sales order exist, you can view proposals by clicking the list box beside the tab name and selecting View Proposals; then reopen the box and select the appropriate proposal number.

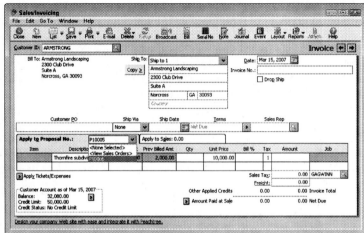

Figure 12-8:
Click here to
view open
and
accepted
proposals.

After you select a proposal to view, Peachtree displays the Select Percentage to Bill dialog box, as shown in Figure 12-9. If you select either of the first two options in this dialog box, Peachtree fills in appropriate amounts for you on the invoice. If you select the last option, you must manually fill in either a percentage or an amount for each line of the proposal that you want to bill.

If you select the first option, Peachtree transfers the freight amount, if any, from the proposal to the invoice.

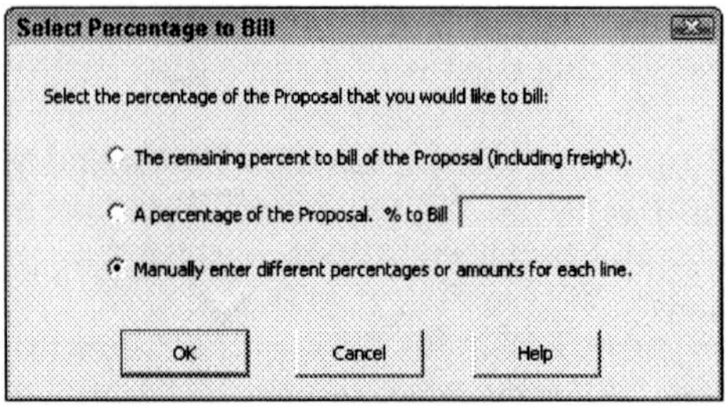

Figure 12-9:
Select a
billing
option.

Regardless of the option you select in the Select Percentage to Bill dialog box, you cannot assign lines of the invoice to a job. You need to edit the proposal *before* you accept it to assign jobs to lines of the proposal.

Adding Overhead to a Job

To run your business, you incur certain expenses that accountants call *overhead* — expenses such as telephone, postage, and electricity. You can think of overhead expenses as expenses you incur even if you don't sell anything. (Of course, you wouldn't incur overhead for long if you didn't sell anything — because you'd go out of business! — but you get our drift.)

If your company uses job costing, you probably want to divide your overhead and assign it to jobs. There's no standard method to do this in Peachtree unless you use the Construction version of Peachtree Premium or higher, but you *can* do it. The method we describe assumes that you know the amount of overhead to add to each job. It could be a percentage of the expenses you incur or an hourly rate. If you don't know, you need to ask your accountant to figure out the overhead burden rate for you.

After you have the rate from your accountant, you need to know your expenses by job so that you can apply the overhead burden rate to each job.

We suggest that you customize the Job Ledger report. Choose Reports & Forms⇨Jobs, select the Job Ledger report, and click Options. In the Other Options section, click Columns. On the Columns tab, include the following fields: Job ID, Job Description, Phase ID, Cost Code ID, Transaction Date, Transaction Description, Actual Expenses, and Hours with Totals. When you print the report, you have all the information you need to apply the burden rate to your expenses and then assign the overhead to various jobs. You might want to export the report to Excel and calculate the burden amount there (you know, burden rate × expense amount). For more information on customizing reports, see Chapter 14.

Okay. After you calculate the overhead amount, enter the amount into Peachtree by using a journal entry.

For this task, you need a suspense account. We use a suspense account to handle amounts that are temporary in nature. You can set up a suspense account as any kind of account: asset, liability, income, or expense. We suggest that you make it an account you're likely to notice if it appears on reports because, ultimately, your suspense account shouldn't have a non-zero balance. For help in creating an account, see Chapter 3.

Add your suspense account to the accounts you display in the Business Status center so that you can see at a glance whether it has a non-zero balance. See Bonus Chapter 2 on this book's Web site for details on adding an account to the Business Status center.

To assign overhead to a job, you make a journal entry. Don't worry — it's easy. (For more details on entering journal entries, see Chapter 17.) Follow these steps:

1. **Choose Tasks⇨General Journal Entry.**

   Peachtree displays the General Journal Entry window (see Figure 12-10).

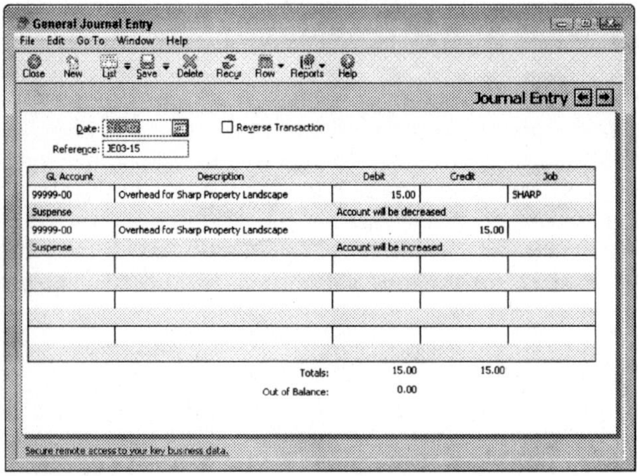

Figure 12-10: Create the journal entry to assign overhead to jobs.

2. **Supply a Date and a Reference number for the journal entry but ignore the Reverse Transaction check box.**

3. **Supply two lines of the same amount for every overhead amount you want to assign, choosing the Suspense account on both lines.**

4. **Assign the job to the Debit line, not the Credit line.**

5. **Click Save to save the entry.**

This journal entry debits and credits the same account, which makes the entry have no effect on your books. However, assigning the job to the debit side of the transaction allocates the overhead expense to the job.

Reporting on the Job

Table 12-1 shows a list of the other reports that relate to job costing. You can exclude balance forward information on the Job Ledger, the Job Profitability report, and the Job Register. See Chapter 14 to find out how to print reports.

Table 12-1	Other Reports Related to Job Costing
Report Name	*What It Does*
Cost Code List	Lists all defined cost codes, along with their description and cost type.
Estimated Job Expenses	Shows estimated expenses, actual expenses, the difference by job, and (if appropriate) the difference by phase and by cost code. Along with other filters, you can filter this report by cost code ID and by using a job mask.
Estimated Job Revenue	Shows estimated expenses, actual revenues, the difference by job, and if appropriate, the difference by phase and by cost code. Along with other filters, you can filter this report by cost code ID and by using a job mask.
Job Costs by Type	Shows estimated and actual expenses by cost type for jobs that have phases.
Job Estimates	For each job (and, if appropriate, phase and cost code), lists estimated units and expenses. Along with other filters, you can filter this report by cost code ID and by using a job mask.
Job Ledger	Shows all transactions that you've assigned to each job. Along with other filters, you can filter this report by cost code ID, using a job mask, and vendor ID.
Job List	Lists each job's ID, description, the starting and ending dates for the job, the customer to whom you assign the job, and the percentage complete.
Job Master File List	Lists all the details you entered in the Maintain Jobs window for each job.
Job Profitability Report	Shows the actual expenses and revenues for each job (and phase and cost code, if appropriate). Along with other filters, you can filter this report by cost code ID, using a job mask, and vendor ID.
Job Register	Shows an overview of job transaction dollars as of a certain date. Along with other filters, you can filter this report by cost code ID, using a job mask, and vendor ID.
Phase List	Lists all defined phases, along with their description, cost type, and whether the phase uses cost codes.

(continued)

Table 12-1 *(continued)*

Report Name	What It Does
Proposal Register	This report, found in the Accounts Receivable report group, lists the status of proposals: open or closed.
Proposal Report	This report, found in the Accounts Receivable report group, shows billing information about open, accepted proposals. The report includes the proposal amount, previously billed amount, and the amount remaining to be billed.
Unbilled Job Expense	Helps you identify existing reimbursable expenses that you can bill to a customer. Along with other filters, you can filter this report by cost code ID, using a job mask, and vendor ID.

Part III
The Fancy Stuff

The 5th Wave   By Rich Tennant

"I'm not sure — I like the mutual funds with rotating dollar signs, although the dancing stocks and bonds look good too."

In this part . . .

*I*n this part, we cover many of the tasks you don't do
every day. First, we show you how to customize forms
and produce and modify reports. After all, you put information *into* Peachtree, so you should be able to get it out
and see the effects of your business habits. Then we cover
reconciling the bank statement and the stuff you do
monthly, quarterly, or annually. This part also contains a
chapter that shows you how to easily keep your accounting information safe — a *very* important chapter. Why?
Because you spend so much time putting stuff into
Peachtree that it would be criminal to lose it just because
your hard drive crashes or your office is robbed.

Lastly, we provide some real-life situations encountered
by people just like you and suggest ways you might
handle similar situations.

Chapter 13

Working with Forms

In This Chapter

▶ Previewing and printing forms
▶ E-mailing your forms
▶ Customizing your forms

*U*nderstanding the differences among the types of information you produce with Peachtree is important. Peachtree provides three types of documents: forms, reports, and financial statements. In this chapter, we discuss *forms,* which Peachtree defines as documents you exchange with your customers, vendors, or employees.

Reports are typically specific to a module such as Accounts Payable or Payroll and provide feedback about one or more customers, vendors, employees, or inventory items. *Financial statements* tell you the overall value of your company and whether the company as a whole made or lost money. You can find out about reports in Chapter 14 and financial statements in Chapter 15.

You can print forms on preprinted forms or on blank paper. You can purchase preprinted forms from your local printer, or you can use the offers you receive in your Peachtree software box. Chapter 21 lists Web contact information on Deluxe Forms, a great source for all types of forms and envelopes.

If you contact Deluxe Forms at 800-328-0304 and reference this book and discount code R03578, you'll receive 20 percent off your first order.

Printing Forms

You use essentially the same steps for printing all forms whether you're printing a quote, purchase order, check, or customer invoice. Peachtree can print your forms one at a time or together in a batch. Peachtree also provides forms for printing customer, vendor, and employee labels as well as collection letters, 1099s, and various payroll forms, such as W-2s and 941 reports.

A variety of forms are available, and you can customize almost any form.

Previewing forms in the document window

Because Peachtree has several forms, you might want to see what your quote, purchase order, check, or invoice would look like in each form. You can use the Preview feature to examine the transaction:

1. **Display the transaction you want to preview on the screen.**

   If necessary, click the List button, as shown in the margin, and then select a previously posted transaction.

2. **Click the drop-down arrow on the Print button (as shown here) and then choose Print Preview.**

   The Preview Forms dialog box appears, listing the available forms (see Figure 13-1). The forms listed vary depending on the transaction type.

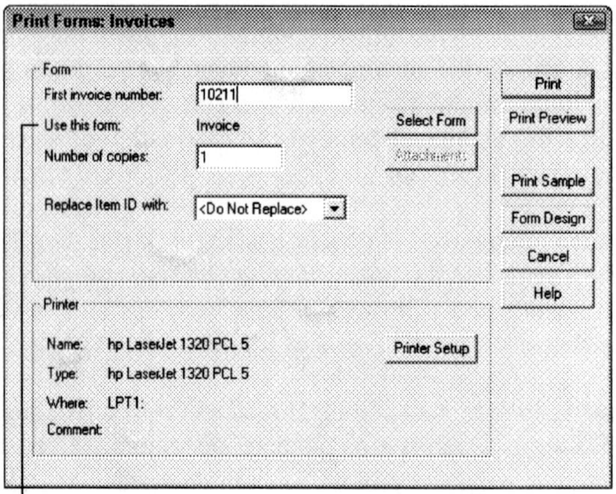

Figure 13-1:
Choose the
form that
best suits
your needs.

Form being used

3. **If you want to change the form, do the following:**

   a. *Click the Select Form button (as shown in the margin).*

      Peachtree assumes that you want to use the same form you used the last time you printed, but the Select Form button lets you select a different form. The Preview Forms dialog box appears.

   b. *Select the form you want to print and then click OK.*

4. **Click Print Preview.**

5. **Click anywhere on the form to enlarge the view; click a second time to enlarge the view even more (see Figure 13-2).**

   No need to strain your eyes. Whenever the mouse pointer turns into a magnifying glass, you can click to zoom in or out on the form.

   You can click the Close button (as shown here) if you need to make changes to the transaction. Peachtree redisplays the transaction window.

6. **To print the transaction on the selected form, click the Print button, as shown in the margin.**

   Peachtree prints the form, saves the transaction, and returns you to a blank transaction window.

Printing from the document window

In the preceding section, you discover how to preview and then print a document from the preview window. If you don't want to preview the document, you can print directly from the data entry window.

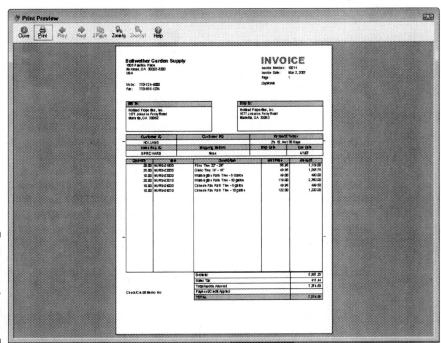

Figure 13-2:
Click on the document to enlarge or reduce the view.

To print a form, follow these steps:

1. **With a document displayed in the window, click the Print button (or press Ctrl+P).**

   You see the Print Forms dialog box, like the one shown in Figure 13-1.

2. **Verify the transaction number, printer, number of copies, and form name.**

   If you didn't manually enter a transaction number in the data entry screen, Peachtree automatically uses the next number.

   Peachtree maintains a different series of numbers for each form type. For example, checks have a different numbering system from purchase orders or customer invoices.

   If you are using Peachtree Premium or higher and you want to replace the inventory item ID on your form with either the item's UPS/SKU number or part number, select an option from the Replace Item ID With drop-down list. See Chapter 11 for more information about inventory item IDs and UPC/SKU and part numbers.

   Print Sample

   To test the form alignment, click the Print Sample button (as shown here) to print practice forms. You see Xs and 9s on the form where words and numbers will appear.

   Print

3. **Click the Print button, as shown in the margin.**

   Peachtree automatically saves a transaction after printing. Saving a transaction posts the transaction, and if applicable, updates the General Ledger as well.

Printing forms in a batch

Sometimes, when you're entering data such as invoices, you don't want to stop and go through the steps to print each invoice separately. In this case, you might like the Peachtree batch printing feature.

If you want to print several invoices at the same time, create each invoice without assigning an invoice number and then click the Save button. Whenever you're ready to print your transactions, Peachtree can print all unnumbered invoices at the same time. You can batch print any form *except* receipts and deposit tickets.

The following steps show you how you can batch print forms, such as statements, quotes, sales orders, purchase orders, and checks:

1. **Click Reports & Forms⇨Forms and then select the form type you want to print.**

   Peachtree displays the Select a Report or Form window.

2. From the Forms section, select the form you want to use.

A sample of the form previews on the right side of the dialog box.

Preview and Print

3. Click the Preview and Print button, as shown in the margin.

The Preview and Print dialog box specific to the form you selected appears. The appearance of the dialog box varies based on the form you select.

Refresh List

4. Click the Refresh List button, as shown here.

A list of all the unprinted transactions matching your selection appears. (See Figure 13-3.)

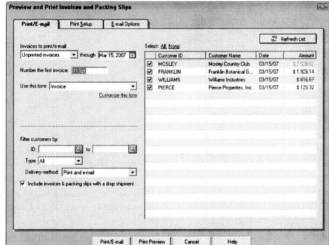

Figure 13-3: Select printing options from this dialog box.

If you don't want to print a specific transaction, deselect the check box next to the transaction.

5. Verify the beginning transaction number and that the correct form name appears in the Use this form box.

6. (Optional) In the lower-left portion of the dialog box, set any desired filter options.

You can select a forms printing method from the Print dialog box as well and select to send only e-mailed forms, only paper forms, or both. Peachtree looks at the default method for sending forms assigned to each vendor (Chapter 5) or customer (Chapter 7). The next section shows you how Peachtree handles e-mailing forms.

Click the Refresh List button again to update the transaction list.

7. **Click the Print Setup tab, and if desired, change the printer or number of copies.**

8. **(Optional) If you're e-mailing forms, click the E-mail Options tab and review the e-mail actions and options.**

   If you're printing checks, the E-mail Options tab isn't available.

9. **Click the Print/E-mail button, as shown in the margin.**

   After printing the forms, Peachtree displays a dialog box asking whether the forms printed properly.

10. **Answer the dialog box by clicking Yes or No:**

    - *Yes:* Peachtree assigns the numbers to the forms.

    - *No:* The forms remain unnumbered, and you need to reprint them.

11. **Click the Close button.**

    The Select a Report or Form window closes.

E-mailing Forms

Some customers or vendors prefer that you e-mail their forms instead of making the trek to the mailbox (or even worse, the post office). Many transaction windows allow you to send e-mail copies in place of or in addition to paper forms. Peachtree provides a place to store an e-mail address in the Maintain Customer or the Maintain Vendor screen. You have the option of e-mailing the form to the stored address or to one you type in when e-mailing the form.

Most forms are eligible for e-mailing. You can e-mail invoices, statements, collection letters, sales orders, and purchase orders. You can't e-mail deposit tickets, receipts, customer or vendor labels, any payroll forms, and (for obvious reasons) vendor or payroll checks.

To generate e-mail in Peachtree, you use a MAPI-compliant, default e-mail application such as Outlook or Outlook Express. If your default e-mail system is AOL, you won't be able to send e-mail alerts from Peachtree because AOL isn't a fully MAPI-compliant e-mail application.

During batch printing, if you're e-mailing forms, Peachtree provides several additional options. The E-mail Options tab, available with most forms, addresses how you want Peachtree to manage the printing. To see the options, click the E-mail Options tab of the Preview and Print option window. (See Figure 13-4.) You decide: whether you want to e-mail only the form, both e-mail the form and generate a paper copy, or print only a paper copy.

Additionally, you can assign a different e-mail numbering system to e-mailed invoices and you can select the Show Me Each E-mail Before Sending option which allows you to see and optionally manually edit the individual e-mail messages before they are sent. We recommend you leave this option checked.

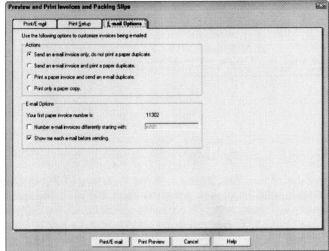

Figure 13-4:
Change
e-mail forms
options.

If you're not batch printing the forms you want to e-mail, you need to display the transaction:

1. **In a transaction window — for example, the Sales/Invoicing window — click the E-mail button (as shown here).**

   The E-Mail Forms window appears so that you can confirm the transaction number and the form name. You can assign a different numbering sequence to e-mailed forms.

2. **Click the Send button.**

   Peachtree launches your e-mail program and automatically inserts the recipient information as stored in your Peachtree customer or vendor file. If your Peachtree options specified to send a copy to a sales or buyers representative, their e-mail information appears in the Cc line (see Figure 13-5).

3. **To change the recipients, type a different e-mail address, or if available, click the address book icon and then select a recipient from the address book.**

4. **Click the Send button.**

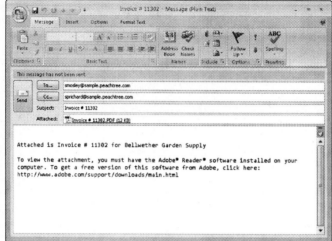

Figure 13-5:
Send forms
directly to
your
customer's
e-mail
address.

When e-mailing a form, Peachtree sends the form as a PDF (Portable Document Format) attachment. To view or print the form, the recipient must have the Adobe Reader software, which is a free download from the Internet at www. adobe.com/reader. The e-mail body also contains a link to obtain the free PDF reader.

Customizing Forms

You can customize any form to better meet your needs. You can move, add, or delete fields; change fonts; and even add graphical images. You begin by taking a standard form and customizing it the way you want. After customizing the form, you save it with a different form name. Peachtree protects the original forms by not letting you save changes to the original form name.

Exploring the Form Design window

The Forms Design window enables you to create customized forms or edit existing forms to match the needs of your business. To use the Forms Design window, follow these steps:

1. **Choose Reports & Forms⇨Forms and select the form type you want to modify.**

   The Select a Report or Form window appears.

2. **In the Forms list, select the form you want to modify.**

3. **Click once on the form you want to modify and then click the Customize button, as shown in the margin.**

The selected report appears in Forms Design view (see Figure 13-6).

If you accidentally double-click the desired form, Peachtree assumes you want to print it, not modify its design. It displays a dialog box containing filter and format options that you can set before printing. Click the Cancel button, and be sure to click only once on the form that you want to modify. Then you can click the Customize button.

Maximize the design window for optimal viewing.

The design window has two main parts: the toolbars and the design area, which displays the fields and objects currently in use. The design area contains Peachtree data field objects, text objects, and other objects such as rectangles or pictures. Four of the five forms toolbars appear in the design window. Each toolbar has a specific function:

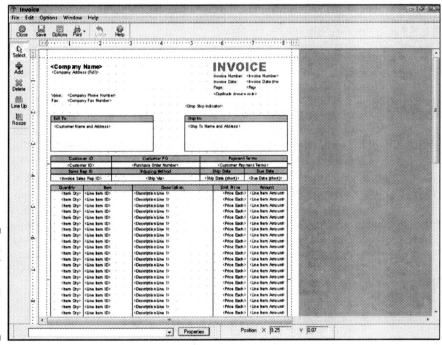

Figure 13-6:
A customer invoice in Forms Design view.

✔ **Main toolbar:** Located at the top of the Forms Design window. Use this toolbar to accomplish many common steps, including saving the form and closing the design window.

✔ **Object toolbar:** Use this toolbar, located on the left of your screen, to select, insert, delete, align, or resize form objects.

Use the Select tool, the first tool on the Object toolbar, to select objects that you want to move, modify, or delete.

✔ **Properties toolbar:** Use this toolbar to determine an object's content, size, order, position, and appearance. The Properties toolbar resides along the bottom of the design window.

✔ **Cursor Position toolbar:** Located next to the Properties toolbar along the bottom edge of the window. Use this toolbar to determine the mouse pointer position. You find this helpful when sizing or aligning objects.

✔ **Formatting toolbar:** Use the Formatting toolbar to change the font, color, or background of the selected form object. The Formatting toolbar appears in the middle of your screen and might not be on by default.

You can turn on and off any toolbar at any time by selecting an option from the Options menu.

Everything on a form is a type of object. You can find data field objects, text objects, shaped objects, and even grouped objects. The two main object types you find on a form are

✔ **Data field object:** This is the most common object you see. When printing the form, Peachtree obtains information, either from the Maintain window or from the Tasks window, and places it in the data field objects. Peachtree displays data field objects with brackets around them, such as <Customer Name and Address>. In Figure 13-6, you see the data field <Company Name>.

✔ **Text object:** This is the second–most-common form object. This is text that always prints the same specific words, such as *Sold to* or *Thank you for your business*. You can easily identify text objects because you just read them on the screen, and they don't have brackets around them. In Figure 13-6, you see the words Invoice Number which is a text object.

Modifying screen options

You can control how the Forms Design window appears. Click the Options button on the Main toolbar, as shown here in the margin. The Forms Design Options dialog box appears with two tabs. If you click the Display tab, you can make the following choices:

- ✔ **Ruler:** Choose this option to display a ruler on the top and left sides of the Forms Design window.

- ✔ **Placeholder Text:** Choose this option to display sample placeholder text in the form of xXXXX for text fields, or -NNNN.nn for numeric fields.

- ✔ **Fold Marks:** Choose this option to print fold *marks* on the form, which are small dashes that show you where to fold the printed form in order for it to fit into a standard envelope.

- ✔ **Commands:** Choose this option if you want to display command objects as a red C in a small gray box on the form you're working with. Commands do not print on the form. Command objects tell the printer to read the next line of data or that you are finished with the form and are ready to print the next form.

- ✔ **Margin Cropping:** Choose this option to trim objects outside the margins of the form. We don't recommend you use this option. Instead, if an object hangs over the margin, resize or move the object.

- ✔ **Outline OLE Objects:** Choose this option to place a non-printing border around graphic OLE objects, such as logos.

- ✔ **Order Number:** Choose this option if you want to display the order numbers next to each object. Order numbers appear as red numbers in a yellow block and represent the order in which the fields appear on the form.

Click the Grid/Copies tab to manage the ruled grid that appears on the window. You can also enter the default number of copies to print.

Selecting objects

You can select multiple form objects to perform a common task in a single step. For example, you might want to copy a group of objects, move them, align them, change their font, or change their color. Peachtree provides two ways to select multiple objects:

- ✔ **With the Selection tool:** Click the first object with your mouse pointer, and then hold down the Ctrl key and click a second object. Each selected object displays a blue outline with blue boxes or size handles around it. Continue holding down the Ctrl key and select as many objects as you want; then release the Ctrl key.

- ✔ **With the Selection tool:** Click and drag an imaginary box around the group of objects you want. When you release the mouse button, all the objects within your marquee border are selected.

If you want to select all the objects on your form, press Ctrl+A or choose Edit⇨Select All. If you select the wrong object, click anywhere in a blank area of the window to deselect the object.

Moving form objects

You won't throw your back out moving form design objects. You can move an object by selecting it and dragging it to a new location.

You can move an object also by selecting it and using your arrow keys to move it to a new position. This technique works well when you want to move the object only a little bit.

Deleting form objects

Deleting objects is easy, too. If you want to get rid of something on a form, click the object to select it and then press the Delete key. Poof . . . it's gone! For example, if you don't want the word *Duplicate* to print on a check to which you assign a check number, delete the Duplicate Check Message field in the check form that you use.

If you delete the wrong object, immediately choose Edit⇨Undo or press Ctrl+Z to reverse the last step you took.

Adding data field objects

If you want to add data field objects to a form, you need to tell Peachtree where you want to place the field and which field you want to add. To do so

1. **Click the Add button on the Object toolbar, as shown in the margin.**

   A submenu appears.

2. **Choose Data from Peachtree.**

3. **Click OK at the Add Data Confirmation dialog box.**

   The Add Field dialog box appears, as shown in Figure 13-7.

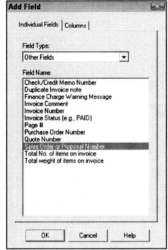

Figure 13-7:
Select the
field type
and field
name you
want added
to your form.

4. **From the Field Type drop-down list, select the type of data you want to add.**

   You might have to look at the available field names for each data type until you find the item you want.

5. **From the Field Name list, click the data field you want to add and then click OK.**

   Peachtree adds the data field along the top of the form.

6. **Move the data field object into the desired position.**

   See "Moving form objects," earlier in this chapter.

Adding text objects

Data field objects contain variable information that . . . well, varies, or changes from one document to the next. Text objects are static. The information doesn't change; the same words appear on each and every document that uses this form. Follow these simple steps to create a text object:

1. **Click the Add button on the Object toolbar.**

2. **Choose Text and then click OK at the confirmation message.**

   A text box with a blinking cursor appears at the top of the form.

   Select Do Not Display Again to disable the confirmation message.

3. **Type the text that you want to appear on the form.**

The text box expands to accommodate the text you enter, as shown in Figure 13-8.

4. **After you finish typing, click anywhere outside the text box.**

5. **Click and drag the data field object to move it into the desired position.**

Resizing an object

If an object is too long, too short, too narrow, or too wide, resize it with your mouse:

1. **Select the object you want to resize; then position the mouse over one of the object's sizing handles.**

   As you do so, the mouse pointer turns into a double-headed black arrow.

2. **Drag the handle in the direction you want to resize the object.**

   As you drag the handle, you see the box boundaries resize.

3. **When you reach the desired size, release the mouse button.**

To quickly change an object to its default height and width, right-click the object and then choose AutoSize.

Peachtree also provides an easy way to make multiple objects the same size. You can make them the same height, the same width, or both. You must have at least two objects selected. To select multiple objects, hold the Ctrl key and then click each object you want to modify as a group. Then, from the Object toolbar, click the Resize button (as shown here) which displays a menu of sizing options from which you can select.

Formatting field properties

How do you know which font and other attributes are assigned to the form objects? Well, you examine the object's properties. The properties tell you what field each object represents as well as its size and appearance. You can modify properties for both data field objects and text objects.

Properties

To view or modify object properties, you must first select the object you want to modify. With the object selected, click the Properties button (as shown here) on the Properties toolbar. Peachtree then displays a dialog box that varies depending on the object type you select. In Figure 13-9, you can see the Data Field Options dialog box for the Invoice Amount field.

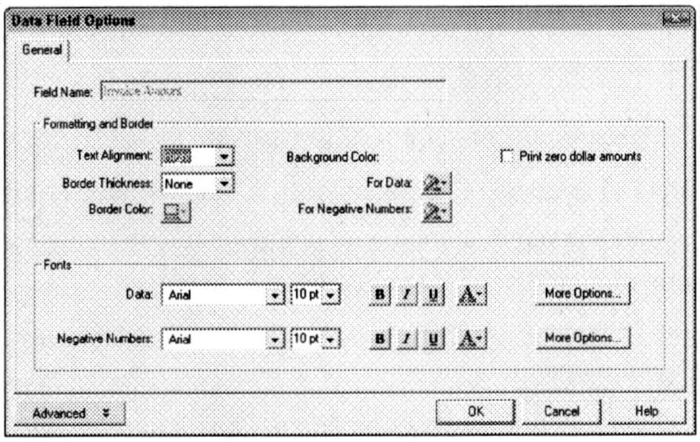

Figure 13-9: Change the object's appearance through this dialog box.

From this dialog box, you can choose a specific font, size, alignment, border, and color for each object.

Advanced ¥

If you're working with a data field object and want to control how the numbers appear, click the Advanced button, as shown in the margin. This expands the dialog box, as shown in Figure 13-10, so you can change how you want numbers to print.

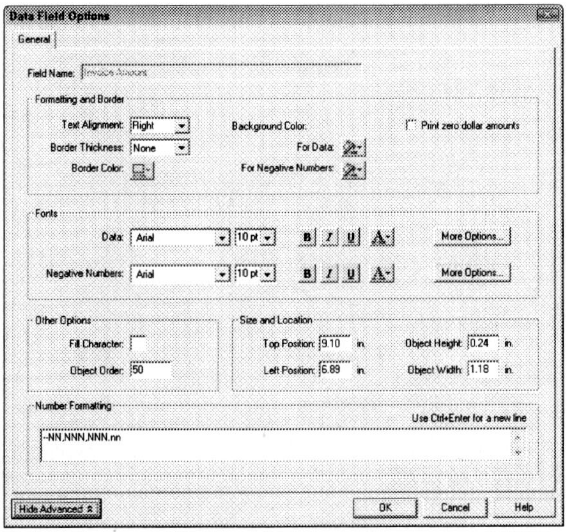

Figure 13-10: Make your numbers appear the way you want.

In the Number Formatting field located at the bottom of the dialog box, you see a series of upper- and lowercase *N*s. Peachtree designates numbers that appear before the decimal point with a capital *N* and numbers that appear after the decimal point with a lowercase *n*. Suppose that you want standard decimal points and commas. If you use NNN,NNN.nn as your template, one thousand prints as 1,000.00, and ten thousand prints as 10,000.00. To change the number format for the selected field, change the contents to match the appearance you want. There are several key notes you should know about managing numeric formats:

- ✔ You can place plus or minus signs either before or after the numbers.

- ✔ If a minus sign (–) is used, it appears only if the number is negative.

- ✔ If the plus sign (+) is used, a minus sign appears if the number is negative and a plus sign appears if the number is positive.

- ✔ If parentheses (( )) or angle brackets (< >) are used, they appear only if the number is negative.

- ✔ If the sign is doubled before the number — for example, two minus signs (—) or two dollar signs ($$) — the sign appears right next to the number. When you use a single sign, a space appears between the sign and the number.

In Table 13-1, we show the values 1234.56 and –1234.56 in various formats.

Table 13-1	Number Samples	
Format	*Positive*	*Negative*
NNN,NNN.nn	1,234.56	–1,234.56
NNN,NNN.nn–	1,234.56	1,234.56–
(NNN,NNN.nn)	1,234.56	(1,234.56)
–NNN,NNN.nn	1,234.56	–1,234.56
+NNN,NNN.nn	+ 1,234.56	–1,234.56
—NNN,NNN.nn	1,234.56	–1,234.56
++NNN,NNN.nn	+1,234.56	–1,234.56
$NNN,NNN.nn	$ 1,234.56	$ –1,234.56
$$NNN,NNN.nn	$1,234.56	$–1,234.56
NNN,NNN.nn+	1,234.56+	1,234.56–

Aligning objects

When you select multiple objects in the Forms Design window, Peachtree can align those objects in relation to each other. You can align their top, bottom, left, or right edges together, or you can choose to align the centers vertically or horizontally. To align multiple objects

1. **Click the Selection tool and then select the objects you want to align.**

   You must have at least two objects selected. To select multiple objects, hold the Ctrl key and then click each object you want to align. To select contiguous objects, hold down the Shift key and then click the first and last objects you want to modify.

2. **From the Object toolbar, click the Line Up button and then select an alignment choice.**

   You can line up the objects' left, right, top, or bottom edges; or you can center them vertically or horizontally. Peachtree aligns the objects to the one you selected last — we call it the "foundation" object.

Adding a logo

Adding your company logo or any other graphic image to your form is as easy as A-B-C. The forms use images in a bitmap, JPEG, or GIF format, which are all common graphic formats. Just follow these steps:

1. **Select the Add button on the Object toolbar.**

2. **Select Logo or Image from the Add submenu.**

   An Open dialog box similar to the one shown in Figure 13-11 appears.

Figure 13-11: Personalize your forms by adding your company logo.

3. **Locate and select the logo or image file you want.**

4. **Click Open.**

   The image should appear on the form.

5. **(Optional) Resize the image by using the image sizing handles, and then move the graphic to the desired location on the form.**

Creating a grouped data table

When you have a series of rows of data, such as the body lines of an invoice, customer statement, or purchase order, instead of creating each field individually, use the Column Data command to list data fields displayed in a table format using columns and rows.

To create a table object, follow these steps:

1. **Select the Add button on the Object toolbar and then choose Column to Table.**

   The Add Field dialog box opens on top of the Column Data Options dialog box. See Figure 13-12.

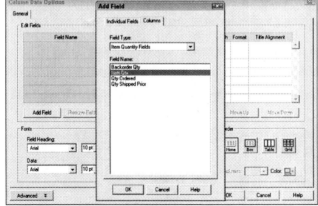

Figure 13-12: Select the fields you want to add to your table.

2. **From the Columns tab of the Add Field dialog box, select the first field that you want to add.**

   You might have to look through the various Field Type options to locate the field you want.

3. **Click OK.**

   The field now appears in the list of fields on the Column Data Options dialog.

Add Field

4. **Click the Add Field button, as shown in the margin, and repeat Steps 2 and 3 to add additional fields as needed. See Figure 13-13.**

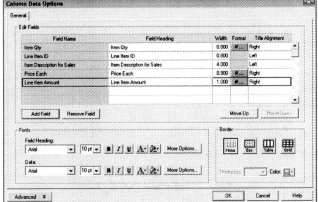

Figure 13-13:
Setting your table appearance options.

5. **Set any desired table options. From the Column Data Options dialog box, you can:**

   Move Up

   ✔ *Select a field and change its order in the table.* Click the Move Up button (as shown here) or the Move Down button.

   - *Change the field heading that appears at the top of the column.* Select the existing heading text and replace it with your own, or leave it blank.

   ✔ *Change the number format.* Click the # button (as shown here) on the numeric field you want to modify and make any desired changes. See "Formatting Field Properties."

   - *Set field heading and data font options.* Select the options in the Fonts section of the dialog box.

   - *Modify the column width.* Change the field width to the desired value.

   - *Add a border or grid around the table.* Select any desired setting from the Border section.

   - *Set advanced options such as Row Spacing or Column Margins.* Click the Advanced button to reveal the options. By defining the Row Spacing, you determine the spacing between rows of data in the table. For example, if you use a 10-point font for data and you want the data rows double-spaced, enter **10** in the Row Spacing field.

6. **Click OK to close the Column Data Options dialog box and place the table on your form.**

Double-click the table or click the Properties button to redisplay the Column Data Options dialog box.

You can move or resize the entire table as you would a text object, data field object, or graphic object.

Saving forms

After you modify a form, you'll want to save it. In fact, we recommend that you save the form *as* you're modifying it. Then resave it again every few steps or so. To save a form:

1. **Click the Save button to display the Save As dialog box.**

2. **Enter a name for the form.**

   You can't use the same name as one of the Peachtree standard forms. You must give your form a unique name.

3. **(Optional) In the Description field, type a description of the form.**

4. **Click Save to save the form for future use.**

   Peachtree identifies custom forms by a blue tool on the form icon.

Delete any customized form by highlighting the form name in the Select a Report window and then clicking the Delete button, as shown in the margin.

We would have loved to include a discussion of Shapes, Commands, Field Order, and OLE objects. Unfortunately, these topics are beyond the scope of this book, but you can find information about them in your User Manual available under the Help menu.

Don't forget to visit www.dummies.com/go/peachtreefd for more information on Peachtree.

Chapter 14

Making Reports Work for You

....

....

*P*eachtree includes over 100 standard reports, ranging from a list of your Chart of Accounts to a Check Register to a Job Profitability report. In each chapter in Part II, you can find a list of the standard reports that Peachtree supplies, appropriate to the subject of the chapter. In this chapter, we show you how to show the reports on-screen, or print them to your printer, a PDF file, an e-mail, or an Excel workbook. We also show you how to modify and save reports. We even show you how to merge information with Microsoft Word.

Previewing Standard Reports

Save a tree! You might find that you want to take only a brief look at your information. Peachtree allows you to preview any report to the screen before or instead of printing it.

To preview reports on your screen, follow these steps:

1. **Choose Reports & Forms and then select the report area you need, such as Accounts Payable.**

   The Select a Report or Form window (see Figure 14-1) appears with an alphabetical listing of available reports.

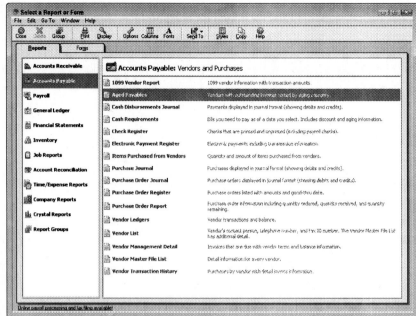

Figure 14-1:
Select
reports to
preview.

2. Click the report to view.

3. Click the Display button (as shown in the margin).

The selected report appears on your screen using any default options determined on the report.

In most displayed reports, you can drill down to view the details of a transaction. When you move the mouse pointer over a transaction, the pointer changes to a magnifying glass that contains a *Z* (for zoom). Double-click that, and Peachtree displays the transaction in the window where you entered it. You can make changes to the transaction and save it; Peachtree automatically updates the report to reflect the changes.

Printing Reports

After you preview your report on the screen, you might decide that you want a paper copy or need to send the report to someone.

Peachtree provides several ways to transmit a report. You can print it, send it by e-mail, or print it to a PDF file. You access these different methods through the report toolbar, which is shown in Figure 14-2.

Figure 14-2:
The report
toolbar.

To print the report, click the Print button. You see a dialog box where you can select which printer you want to use as well as which pages to print and how many copies to print.

To print the report to a PDF file, click the PDF button. The Save As dialog box appears. You can specify the PDF filename and location.

PDF stands for Portable Document Format. To view or print the report in PDF, you must have the Adobe Reader software, which is a free download from the Internet at www.adobe.com/reader.

To e-mail the report, click the E-mail button. A window from your default e-mail program appears with the report as a PDF attachment (see Figure 14-3). Peachtree fills in the e-mail Subject line, and also the message body with information pertaining to the creation date and report title. Enter the recipient's e-mail address and then click Send.

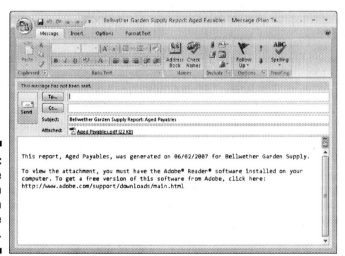

Figure 14-3:
Peachtree
can e-mail a
report as a
PDF file
attachment.

You can additionally send a report to an Excel file. See the section, "Excel with Peachtree," later in this chapter.

Finding the Facts

Some reports can be quite lengthy, and locating a specific number can look like a total blur. While previewing a report, you can click the Find button (as shown here) to search for specific text or numbers. Peachtree then displays the Find on Report dialog box, as shown in Figure 14-4.

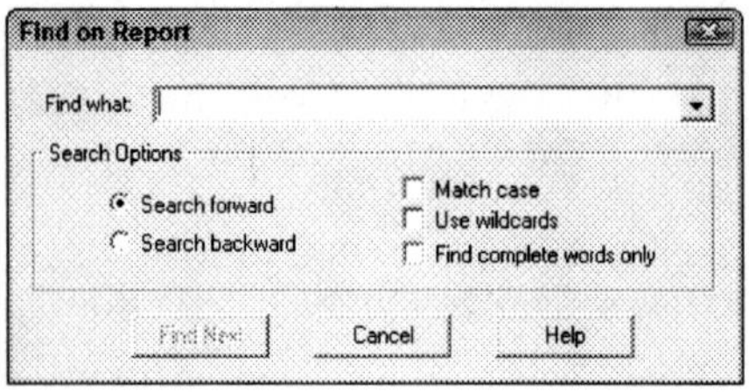

Figure 14-4:
Use this window to search for data within a previewed report.

> **Find on Report**
>
> Find what: [_____] ▼
>
> ─ Search Options ──────────────────
>   ⦿ Search forward   ☐ Match case
>   ○ Search backward   ☐ Use wildcards
>   ☐ Find complete words only
>
>   [Find Next]   [Cancel]   [Help]

You can make several search option selections:

- ✓ **Find What:** Use this text box to enter the information for which you want to search.

- ✓ **Search Forward:** Select this option if you want to search down the report, from the location of the *selected line,* which is the line with the thin blue border around it.

- ✓ **Search Backward:** Select this option if you want to search backward in the report, based on the location of the selected line.

- ✓ **Match Case:** Select this check box if you want your search to be case sensitive. Peachtree will search only for text that matches the case of whatever you enter in the Find What text box. For example, if you enter **SMITH** and select Match Case, Peachtree searches for any occurrence of *SMITH* but will not search for *smith* or *Smith.*

- ✓ **Use Wildcards:** Peachtree recognizes the ? and the * characters as *wild-cards,* meaning that you can use them in the search to indicate unknown characters. The question mark (?) represents a single character, and the asterisk (*) can represent any number of characters. Here's an example, using the sample Aged Receivables report: Select the Use Wildcards check box and type **a?m** in the Find What text box, and Peachtree could find *armstrong, alma, palm,* or any other similar combination. If you type **a*m**, Peachtree would find all the words we just listed, along with *Natasha Cannon, M.D.* and *Dash Business Systems.*

✔ **Find Complete Words Only:** Select this check box to tell Peachtree that you want to be specific and to locate exactly what you type. For example, if you select this check box and type **build** in the Find What text box, Peachtree locates only the word *build,* not *builders* or *building.* You can use this option along with the Match Case option.

If you use the Find What text box to search for text or numbers, even on a different report or financial statement, Peachtree stores the previous 20 values used during the current Peachtree session. You can choose one of your previously entered values by selecting it from the drop-down list.

Enter the text or numbers you want to locate, select any desired options, and then click Find Next. Peachtree locates and highlights the first occurrence of the item. Click Find Next again to locate the next occurrence. Peachtree displays a message box when no more occurrences are found. Click OK and then click Cancel.

Customizing Reports

Sometimes, the standard reports don't contain enough information to meet your needs. Or perhaps they contain more information than you're looking for. Maybe you want to see the information only for a particular customer or vendor and over a different time frame than that specified in the report. You can modify the date range, field information, font, and page layout of any report.

Using filters

Filtering restricts the report data to a different set of specifications than Peachtree shows in standard reports. Suppose that you need to take a standard report — for example, the Customer Ledgers — and view it a little differently.

In Figure 14-5, you can see the Modify Report–Customer Ledgers dialog box with its default options. By default, the standard Customer Ledgers report shows all activity for all customers for the current month. But what if you want to see the transactions (both sales and receipts) for the entire year for customer Cummings Construction? By using filtering, you can have Peachtree display only that information.

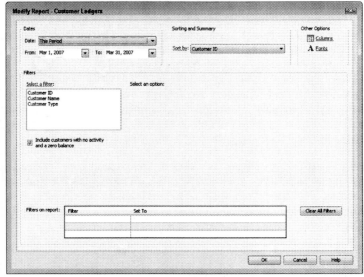

Figure 14-5:
Choose
sorting
options,
time frame,
and other
limits for a
selected
report.

To use a filter, follow these steps:

1. **Choose the report name that you want to filter.**

   In the example, we chose the Customer Ledgers report under Accounts Receivable.

2. **Click Options (as shown in the margin).**

   A Modify Report dialog box appears in which you can set a variety of options for the report you want to display. The first thing you want to change is the time frame. By default, this report displays the current month, but we want to see the transactions for the entire year.

3. **From the Date text box, change the date to represent the period you want.**

   In our example, we want This Year. You can enter a more specific date range by entering the beginning and ending dates in the From and To text boxes.

4. **From the Sort By option, select a method you want for sorting your report.**

   The options available vary with the report that you're using.

5. **In the Filters section, click Customer ID.**

   On the right side of the dialog box, a list of all your customers appears along with filtering options.

6. **Select the Range radio button. Then, in the From text box, type (or look up and select) the first customer you want to view.**

   In this example, we use CUMMINGS.

7. **Click in the To box and type (or lookup and select) the last customer you want to view.**

   If you're looking for a specific customer, enter the same ID in both the From and To text boxes. If you want to see a list of IDs from a certain point down through the list, enter only the From ID and leave the To ID blank. For example, if you want to see every customer from SMITH through WILLIAMS (last customer on the list), enter **SMITH** in the From text box and leave the To text box empty.

   Some reports allow you to select multiple IDs that are not contiguous. When using the One or More option, select the check box for each customer that you want to view on the report.

   Figure 14-6 illustrates the Modify Report dialog box after setting our filtering options.

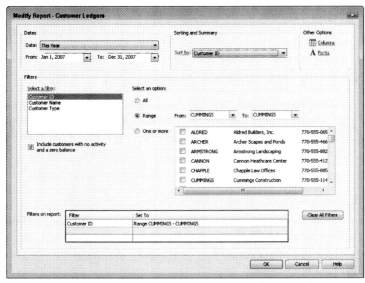

Figure 14-6:
The Modify Report dialog box after determining filtering options.

8. **Click OK to display the report on-screen.**

   Peachtree displays transactions for the specified time frame and the specified customers.

9. **Click Close (as shown here) when you finish reviewing the report.**

Adding, deleting, and moving report fields

Reports in Peachtree consist of data fields. Those data fields come from the various modules in Peachtree. For example, information on an Aged Receivables report contains information from a variety of Customer and Sales fields, and the payroll register displays information from a variety of Employee and Payroll entry fields. You have the option of including or excluding any available fields to create a customized report.

For example, we want to add a field to the Cash Requirements report — a field that indicates whether we're still waiting on a bill from the vendor. We also want to remove the Age field. To customize a report, just follow these steps:

1. **Choose Reports and Forms and select the module containing the report you want to modify.**

   In this example, we chose Accounts Payable.

2. **Locate and click the report that you want to modify.**

   In this example, we're modifying the Cash Requirements report. A standard Cash Requirements report displays eight columns: the vendor ID, vendor name, invoice number, invoice date, due date, amount due, discount amount, and invoice age.

Columns

3. **Click the Columns button (as shown here).**

   The options for the selected report appear. You can display any field in the dialog box on the selected report. You might find that some fields appear dimmed, which indicates that they can't be changed. Dimmed fields usually appear when the filter screen has the report set to display in a summarized format. The fields currently being displayed have a green check mark in the first column (the Show column).

4. **Select the check box of the field you want to add.**

   For this example, select the Show check box next to the Waiting on Bill from Vendor field (see Figure 14-7).

5. **Clear the Show check box of the field you want to remove.**

   In this example, we cleared the check box beside the Age field. Removing the check mark removes the field so that it no longer appears on the report. When you remove a field from a report, the columns previously displayed to the right of the removed field move to the left. In this example, when we added the Waiting on Bill from Vendor column, it became the eighth column; but when we remove the Age column, Waiting on Bill from Vendor becomes the seventh column.

   We want the Waiting on Bill to appear next to the Invoice/CM# field. No problem! We just use the Move Up command to change its location.

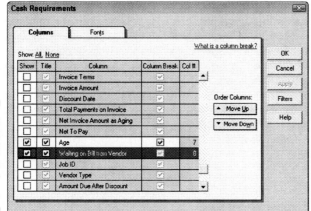

Figure 14-7:
You can add
additional
fields to
your
reports.

6. **Click the field name you want to move.**

   Use caution not to click the Show column, or you'll turn off the display of the field. When you select a field, a red border appears around the entire selected line.

7. **Click the Move Up button (as shown here) to move the field up one column at a time.**

   Conversely, click the Move Down button to move the field down one column at a time. Continue clicking the Move Up or Move Down button until the field appears in the location you want.

   Select the check box in the Column Break section to make the selected field appear on a new column on the report. If you want to place more than one field in a column, first make sure that you select the Show check box and then remove the check from the Break check box. Doing so means that Peachtree doesn't place a break (a column) between the fields.

8. **Click OK.**

   The report redisplays with the changes you selected.

Changing column width

Adding too many columns can cause some to fall off the edge of a page. Well, they don't really fall off, but it does cause the report to print two or more pages in width. You have several choices at this point. You can print the report in landscape mode, print multiple pages in width, remove some report columns, stack some of the columns as described in the previous section, or — and this is probably the best choice — change the column widths.

Here's how to change the column width. With the report on your screen, notice the blue column marker lines that appear at the right of each column, as shown in Figure 14-8. Position your mouse over the arrows on the column marker until the mouse pointer turns into a double-headed arrow. You can then drag the column markers to the left to make a column narrower, or to the right to widen a column.

If you see a long red vertical dashed line on the right (also shown in Figure 14-8), your report prints multiple pages wide. You'll know that the report fits on one page when the long red dashed line disappears.

Column Markers

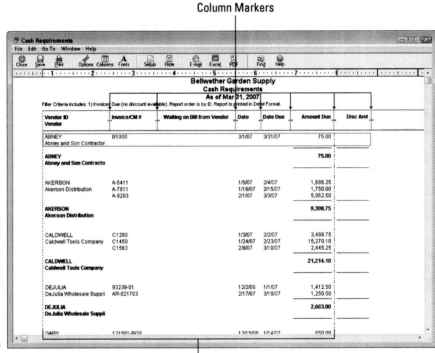

Figure 14-8:
Drag the
column
markers to
change the
column
width.

Page Break

Keeping in style

What's your style? Classic, Elegant, Contemporary, or Professional? By default, Peachtree uses its Professional style, which simply means that all reports print in an Arial font. You can display any or all of your reports in any of the aforementioned styles. Here's a description of the Peachtree-furnished styles:

✔ **Classic:** The entire report uses a Times New Roman (black) font.

✔ **Contemporary:** The report heading appears as an Arial (red) font, the data uses a Times New Roman (black) font, and the report totals appear in Times New Roman (red) font.

✔ **Elegant:** The entire report uses a Garamond font. Headings and report totals appear in navy blue, and the body data appears in black.

✔ **Professional:** The entire report appears in an Arial (black) font.

If you have a color printer, the reports print in the same colors that appear on the screen.

Here's an easy way to modify a report style:

1. **Select the report you want to modify and click the Fonts button (as shown here).**

   The Fonts tab of the report options appears, as shown in Figure 14-9.

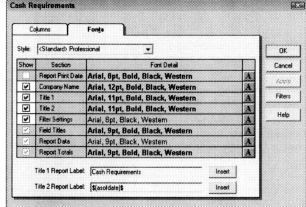

Figure 14-9: Select the fonts you want to use in your report.

2. **Click the down arrow to the right of the Style box to display a list of available styles.**

3. **Click the style you want for this report and then click OK.**

   The report redisplays on the screen with the new style.

Saving a customized report

Sometimes you customize reports for a one-time use, but you use other reports frequently. To save yourself the trouble of re-creating the customized report each time you want to display it, save the report with a name that you'll recognize.

To save a customized report, follow these steps:

1. **Display the customized report on the screen.**

2. **Click the Save button (as shown here).**

   The Save As dialog box appears.

3. **Enter a name for the report.**

   You can't use the name of a Peachtree standard report. You must give it a unique name. For example, you might call a customized Chart of Accounts report *My COA*.

4. **(Optional) In the Description text box, type a description of the report.**

5. **Click Save.**

   The report is saved for future use.

6. **Click Close to close the report window.**

 You can identify custom reports by the blue wrench symbol (as shown here) that Peachtree places on the report icon.

 Delete any customized report by highlighting the report name and then clicking the Delete button (as shown here).

 You can copy customized reports from one company to another. For instructions, see Chapter 15.

Mail Merge

One common marketing tool is to offer existing customers a discount to encourage them to purchase again. Make your customers feel really special by sending them a personalized letter with this distinctive offer. What? You don't have time to send them a personalized letter? It takes only a few minutes to send such letters when using the Peachtree Mail Merge feature.

You can use one of the standard letters included with Peachtree or create your own letter. Just combine the letter and the customer contact information that you already have in Peachtree. In a very short time, you can have a personalized letter for every customer in your database. Don't want to send this letter to everyone? That's okay. You can choose which customers should receive the letter.

This type of mailing is called a *mail merge* because you're merging the generic letter and the variable customer information. Peachtree includes a variety of mail merge letters for customers, vendors, or employees. The underlying engine for this mail merge uses Microsoft Word. If you're already familiar with the Word Mail Merge feature, you can even customize your own letters to merge with your Peachtree data.

You must have both Excel and Word installed on your system for the Peachtree mail merge process to work correctly. Supported versions include Excel and Word 2000, 2002, 2003, and 2007.

Perhaps you're in the process of setting up a new employee and want to send a letter welcoming him or her to your firm. As you enter the new employee information in Peachtree, creating a welcome letter is just a click away. Follow these steps:

1. **Choose Tasks➪Write Letters➪Employee Letters.**

   The Select a Report or Form window appears, as shown in Figure 14-10.

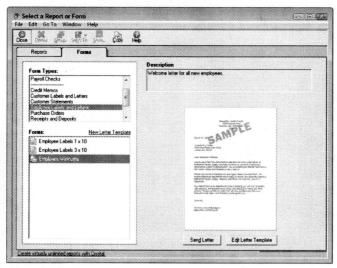

Figure 14-10: Send mail merge letters to customers, vendors, or employees.

2. **In the Form Types section, click the form type you want to use.**

   In this example, we chose Employee Labels and Letters.

3. **Select the letter you want to use.**

   Peachtree separates letters from forms by including an envelope on the icon next to letters. In this case of the employee letters, there's only one example.

4. **Click the Send Letter button (as shown here).**

   A filter dialog box opens from which you can select the specific IDs, date ranges, and other criteria.

5. **Select the filter criteria you want to use.**

   Refer to the "Using Filters" section earlier in this chapter.

6. **Click the Word button (as shown here).**

   Microsoft Word opens with all the completed letters ready for you to print or further modify if desired. (See Figure 14-11.)

   Optionally, click the E-mail button (as shown here) to e-mail the letter instead of opening it in Word.

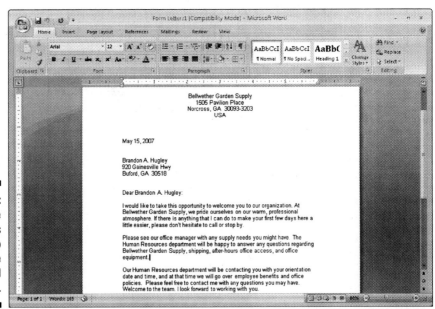

Figure 14-11:
Peachtree
interacts
with Word to
create
personalized
letters.

You can also create letters for customers, vendors, or employees from the respective Maintenance window. Select the customer, vendor, or employee to whom you want to send a letter and then click the Letters button (as shown here).

Excel with Peachtree

If you have Excel, you can send any report — including financial statements — to an Excel workbook.

Why would you want to send a report to Microsoft Excel? Well, perhaps you'd like to sort the report in a different manner than Peachtree offers, total a report that Peachtree can't total, or add a column based on a calculation. How about creating a chart based on the data? We like to use the Excel function to copy customer sales information that can be sorted and ranked in Excel. Those are just a few things you can do by copying a report to Excel.

Follow these steps to copy report data to Excel:

1. **Display the Peachtree report on your screen.**

2. **Click the Send To button on the report toolbar (refer to Figure 14-2) and then click the Excel button (as shown here) from its menu.**

   The Copy Report to Excel dialog box appears, as shown in Figure 14-12.

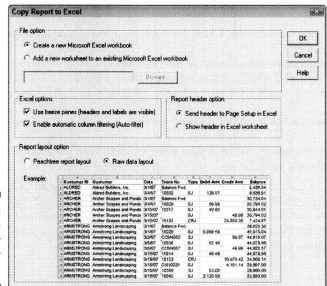

Figure 14-12:
Send reports
to Excel for
further
modification.

3. **Select the File Option that you want use to copy the report to Excel. Your two choices are**

   - *Select the New Microsoft Excel Workbook radio button.*

   - *Select the Add a New Worksheet to an Existing Microsoft Workbook radio button.*

     This option appends the report to an existing Excel file. Click the Browse button to select an existing file.

4. **Select any other desired Excel options.**

   You can determine where Excel should place the report header information: in the worksheet header area or in the worksheet itself. You can also decide whether you want Excel to freeze the heading rows and optionally add filter arrows.

5. **Select a report layout.**

   Select Peachtree Report Layout to display the report in Excel exactly as you see it in Peachtree, or select Raw Data Layout to display the data in standard Excel column layout.

6. **Click OK to copy the report to Excel.**

   Peachtree copies the data including formulas to Excel.

Stay in a Group, Now

If you have a number of reports that you need at the same time, you can create a report group to print them all at once. Report groups print directly to the printer or Microsoft Excel; they can't be previewed on the screen.

In Chapter 17, we suggest reports that you should print at the end of the month. Placing those reports in a report group will make the report printing process much easier.

Follow these steps to create a report group:

1. **From anywhere in the Select a Report window, click the Group button (as shown here).**

   The Report Groups window appears, as shown in Figure 14-13. All standard and custom reports appear in the Report Index list. To help you find a particular report, you can limit the reports you see in the Report Index list to only the reports for a particular module. Click the Report Index drop-down arrow and select the module.

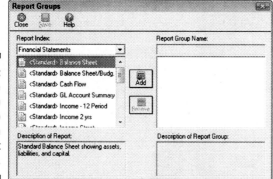

Figure 14-13:
Select the
reports you
want to
include in
the report
group.

2. **To build a report group, select the first report that you want to include in the group in the Report Index list and then click the Add button (as shown here).**

   Added reports appear on the right side of the window. Peachtree prints the reports in the order that they appear on the right side of the window.

3. **Add any additional reports to the group.**

   You can mix and match report categories. For example, you might want to print an Aged Payables report and an Aged Receivables report.

4. **When you finish adding reports to the group, click the Save button.**

   The Save As dialog box appears.

5. **Enter a name for the group, such as Monthly Reports.**

6. **(Optional) In the Description text box, type a description of the reports.**

7. **Click Save (as shown here) to save the report group.**

8. **Click Close to close the Report Groups window.**

When you're ready to print the report group, click Report Groups in the Select a Report window, and then click the name of the report group to print.

Click Print to print the reports to the printer with no further action on your part, or click the Send button to send the reports to Microsoft Excel, a PDF file, or as an e-mail PDF attachment. If you send the reports to Excel, Peachtree opens each report in its own workbook.

Don't forget to visit www.dummies.com/go/peachtreefd for more information on Peachtree.

Chapter 15

Reviewing the Financial Picture

* *

In This Chapter

▶ Printing financial reports

▶ Printing financial statements

▶ Creating a departmentalized income statement

▶ Copying reports and statements

* *

*B*efore you advance to the next Peachtree accounting period, you'll prob- ably want to print a series of reports for your records and possibly for your accountant. Reports that you might find useful include the General Ledger, Trial Balance, Balance Sheet, and Income Statement. Peachtree pro- vides lots of other reports you may want, but these are the most common ones. You'll probably want to include them in a report group. (See Chapter 14 for creating a report group.)

The preceding reports fall into two categories: General Ledger reports and financial statements. We begin by taking a look at the General Ledger reports.

Reviewing Standard General Ledger Reports

Two of the standard reports that you'll use frequently are the General Ledger and Trial Balance. Peachtree lists both of these reports in the General Ledger report area of the Select a Report or Form window. (You can find out how to display, filter, and customize reports in Chapter 14.)

The General Ledger report is the mother of all accounting reports. This report lists all transactions you enter into Peachtree *that affect the general ledger.* Figure 15-1 shows a sample General Ledger report. Note the column titled Jrnl. The reference in this column represents the source of the transac- tion. Table 15-1 lists the different Jrnl codes and their source.

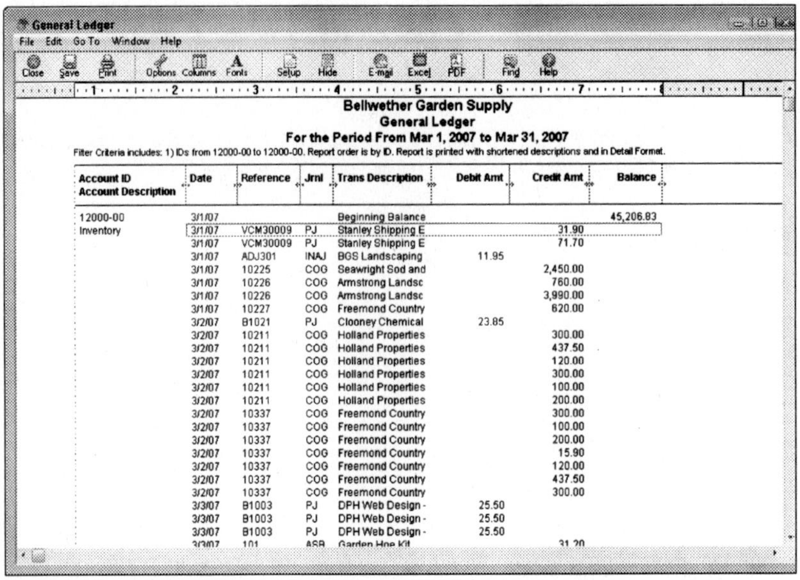

Figure 15-1:
See all
transactions
affecting
your
accounts in
the General
Ledger
report.

Table 15-1	General Ledger Source Codes	
Jrnl Code	*Stands For*	*Source*
SJ	Sales journal	Sales/Invoicing
CRJ	Cash receipts journal	Receipts
PJ	Purchase journal	Purchases/Receive Inventory
CDJ	Cash disbursements journal	Payments and Write Checks
PRJ	Payroll journal	Payroll entry
INAJ	Inventory adjustment journal	Inventory Adjustments
COG	Cost of goods sold journal	Sales/Invoicing
ASB	Assemblies adjustment journal	Assemblies
GEN	General journal	General Journal entry

Purchase orders, quotes, and sales orders don't affect General Ledger accounts, so you won't see them on the General Ledger report.

When printing or previewing the General Ledger report for multiple months, you might find the option Hide Period Totals on Multiple Period Report useful. You can select this check box on the Modify Report screen when you set up the report's options.

Like most Peachtree reports, you can double-click a line to open the window in which Peachtree created the original transaction.

Peachtree provides two Trial Balance reports. The first report, General Ledger Trial Balance, shows each account and its balance as of the date or period you choose. The report displays the account ID and description as well as the debit or credit balance.

The other Trial Balance report is Working Trial Balance. This report provides a worksheet where you can list adjusting entries. Each account includes the current balance and a series of lines where you can write down any necessary adjusting amount. Referring to your handwritten trial balance entries speeds up data entry when you need to make adjusting entries. Your accountant will like this report; he or she can use it to provide you with adjusting entries before closing the year.

Using Segments and Masking

In Chapter 3, we show you how to set up your Chart of Accounts to better track departments or locations. In that chapter, you can see how important the numbering sequence is when setting up the Chart of Accounts, especially if you want to report on your different company areas or segments.

In Peachtree Premium or higher, you can formally divide your accounts into segments. In other Peachtree editions, you set up your accounts in a pattern where you could utilize report masking. *Masking* is the ability to limit information in certain reports to a single division, department, location, or type code.

You can use masking and segmenting in most General Ledger reports and in financial statements.

For a review of designing your Chart of Accounts for masking or segmenting, see Chapter 3.

Report masks use a wildcard character — an asterisk (*) — to represent all the other digits of the account number *except* the digits you want on the report. For example, Bellwether Garden Supply references two departments as Aviary and Landscape Services; these departments are represented as AV and LS in the Chart of Accounts. 40000-AV is the account number for the Aviary sales account, and 40000-LS is the account number for the Landscape Services sales account. So, a mask for the Aviary department looks like *****-AV, and a mask for the Landscape Services appears as *****-LS. On many standard General Ledger reports, you can use the mask when you set the report options.

If you're using Peachtree Premium or higher, you can take advantage of the segments feature. Using segments over masking means that you don't have to remember the wildcard character or the number of digits. You need to remember only what you called the segments, such as *department* or *location*.

From the Select a Report or Form window, select the General Ledger report you want to view. Click the Options button (as shown here) to display the Options dialog box. You'll see an options dialog box, such as the one shown in Figure 15-2. From the Select a Filter list, select Account Segment. Then, on the right, select the segment type that you want to review. Finally, in the From and To drop-down lists, select the segments you want.

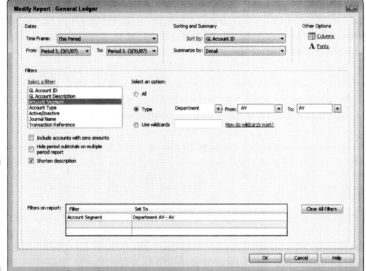

Figure 15-2:
Select the segment on which you want to report.

If you don't use segments or your Peachtree version doesn't support segments, the Account Segment option doesn't even appear in the Filter list. You can still use wildcards and the Peachtree Department mask feature. Instead of choosing Account Segment from the Filter list, choose Department Mask and set masking options, using wildcards.

Producing Financial Statements

You display or print financial statements through the Select a Report or Form window the same way you display or print other reports. Peachtree provides a number of predefined financial statements, including a Balance Sheet and an Income Statement. Similar to other reports, you can preview them, print them to a printer or a PDF file, e-mail them, or send them to Excel.

Table 15-2 provides a list of all the Peachtree-provided, predefined standard financial statements. If none of these statements fit your needs, look in the next section to find out how to customize them.

Table 15-2	Furnished Financial Statements
Report Name	*What It Does*
<Standard> Balance Sheet	Lists your company assets, liabilities, and capital.
<Standard> Balance Sheet/Budg.	Lists actual and budget amounts for all assets, liabilities, and capital accounts as of a specific date. This report comes standard only with Peachtree Premium or higher.
<Standard> Cash Flow	Shows the cash receipts, cash payments, and change in cash in a business.
<Standard> GL Account Summary	Shows the account number and description, beginning balance, activity, and ending balance for each account.
<Standard> Income – 12 period	Shows income and expenses with values for each month.
<Standard> Income 2 yrs	Compares revenue and expenses for the current month totals with the same month last year, and the current year's totals with last year's totals.
<Standard> Income Stmnt	Sometimes referred to as a P&L (profit and loss) statement. Shows income and expenses and the difference between them.
<Standard> Income/2 Budget-Per	Available in Peachtree Premium or higher, compares period income and expenses with two different budgets.
<Standard> Income/2 Budget-YTD	Available in Peachtree Premium or higher, compares year with date income to two different budgets.
<Standard> Income/Budget	Compares income and expenses balances with the budgeted amounts.
<Standard> Income/Budget-Per	Compares current actual income and expenses with a budget and the previous year actual amounts. Available in Peachtree Premium or higher.

(continued)

Table 15-2 *(continued)*

Report Name	What It Does
<Standard> Income/Budget-YTD	Compares year to date actual income and expenses with the year-to-date budgets and the previous year actual amounts. Available in Peachtree Premium or higher.
<Standard> Income/Earnings	Shows income and expense activity as well as retained earnings information.
<Standard> Retained Earnings	Shows beginning and ending retained earnings amounts, adjustments to retained earnings in the period, and the detail for all Equity-gets closed accounts.
<Standard> Stmnt Changes	Describes changes in a company's overall financial position.

As we mention earlier in this chapter, the two most frequently used financial statements are the Balance Sheet and the Income Statement. Here are a few suggestions to assist you when working with your financial statements:

✔ All financial statements appear for the current fiscal period unless you select a different date range in the Options dialog box; however, financial statements are always listed by fiscal periods. You cannot select a specific date range, such as March 3 through March 21.

✔ Open any financial statement by double-clicking the desired report. The report Options dialog box, like the one shown in Figure 15-3, appears. Make the desired changes, such as the date range or segments, and then click OK.

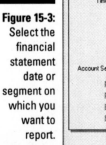

Figure 15-3:
Select the financial statement date or segment on which you want to report.

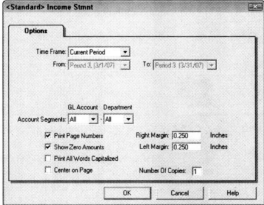

✔ Double-clicking an account while viewing the financial report on-screen displays the underlying details for the selected account through the General Ledger report.

✔ The option to select a segment does not appear if you don't have segments set up in General Ledger defaults.

Modifying Financial Statements

In this section, we take a look at the Financial Statement designer.

You can create customized financial reports by using the Financial Statement Wizard or by the conventional method of customizing a statement yourself in the Financial Statement Design window. The Financial Statement Design window gives you more control over each individual aspect of the financial design process, but the Financial Statement Wizard provides a grasp of the basic elements of a statement and how to put them together effectively.

Using the Financial Statement Wizard

The Financial Statement Wizard can assist you with great detail in creating a financial statement. At every point in the process, the wizard makes your choices clear so you know what effect each choice has on the finished statement. The following steps show you how to use the Peachtree Financial Statement Wizard:

1. **In the Select a Report window, choose Financial Statements.**

2. **Click the Financial Statement Wizard link (as shown here), located at the top right of the window.**

   An introduction screen appears, showing you the processes that you can specify by using the wizard.

3. **Click Next to see the Financial Statement Name screen.**

   Similar to customized forms and reports, customized financial statements must have their own name. Additionally, you start customization by basing your report on one that already exists, as shown in Figure 15-4. This saves you *tons* of time!

4. **From the Financial Statement Template drop-down list, choose an existing financial statement design to use as the model for your new statement. Then type a unique name for the new statement.**

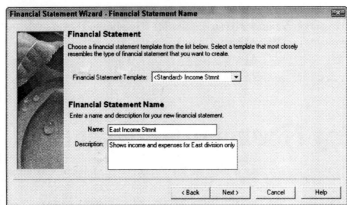

Figure 15-4:
The
Financial
Statement
Name
screen.

Although a report description is optional, we encourage you to supply one. That way, when you click the report in the Select a Report or Form window, you'll see a reminder of the report's purpose.

5. **Click Next.**

Each screen of the Financial Statement Wizard defines a specific area of your financial statement:

• *Headers and Footers:* Enter the text of each header and footer you want to include.

• *Dates and General Ledger Account Masking:* Choose the range of dates you want the statement to cover. If you set up your General Ledger accounts for account segments, you can enter an account segment that limits reporting to just one of your departments. If you're not using segments, the screen provides options for creating an account mask.

• *Column Properties:* Select the type and properties of data that appears in as many as 30 columns.

• *Column Options:* For each type of column you set up in your statement, you can determine secondary titles, width, and alignment for the column.

• *Fonts:* You can choose the fonts that Peachtree uses to display or print each of the sections of your statement.

• *Formatting and Default Printer:* You can tell Peachtree which printer you want to use, whether you want to print page numbers, to show zero dollar amounts, to center the report on the page, and so forth.

- *Congratulations:* Decide whether you want to display the newly created statement, modify the new statement in the designer window,
or create another financial statement with the Financial Statement
Wizard.

6. **Click Finish.**

   The Financial Statement dialog box appears.

7. **Click OK.**

   The designed financial statement appears for your review on your
   screen.

Creating customized financial statements

Earlier in this chapter, we talk about how you can use the Financial Statement
Wizard to create customized financial statements. However, you can also
manually customize any financial statement.

As a simple example, suppose that you want to compare the current period
with the year-to-date information for only one department. The standard
Income Statement compares current period information with year-to-date
information for your entire company. The upcoming steps outline how to
create a departmental version of the standard Income Statement, using the
department mask.

Creating a new financial statement by using an existing financial statement as
a model is always easiest. To avoid accidentally damaging the model, make a
copy by saving it under a new name in the Design window. Then, modify the
properties of the column heading to include a department mask.

For a review on designing your Chart of Accounts for masking, see Chapter 3.
The following steps show you how to create a customized financial statement:

1. **Choose Reports & Forms⇨Financial Statements.**

   Peachtree displays the available financial statement report formats in
   the Select a Report window.

2. **Select the financial statement you want to modify and then click the
   Design button (as shown here).**

   In the example, we're using the <Standard> Income Statement.
   Peachtree's Financial Statement Designer window for the Income
   Statement appears (see Figure 15-5).

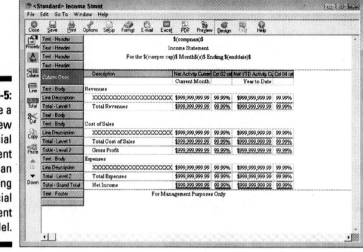

Figure 15-5:
Create a
new
financial
statement
by using an
existing
financial
statement
as a model.

3. **Double-click the Column Desc. button (as shown here)**

   The Column Description dialog box appears, as shown in Figure 15-6.

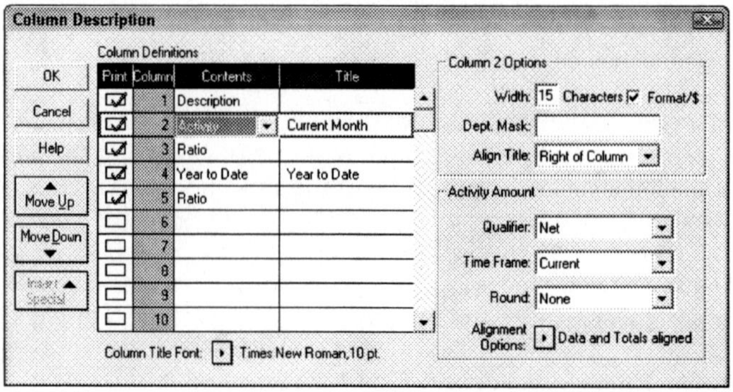

Figure 15-6:
Add a
department
mask to
print this
report for
only one
department.

4. **Click the row for Column 2 Activity to select it and display the Dept. Mask field.**

   Just like in the earlier section, "Using Segments and Masking in Reports," you create the mask by using an asterisk (*) wildcard character to represent all the other digits of the account number *except* the digits you want displayed.

5. **Add an appropriate mask.**

   To mask for just the Aviary department, for example, enter *******-AV**.

6. **Repeat the mask for other activity columns, such as Column 4 Y-T-D Activity.**

7. **Click OK to redisplay the report design.**

8. **Click the Save button (as shown here) to display the Save As dialog box.**

   Peachtree will not allow you to overwrite a <Standard> financial statement. You must supply a different name.

9. **In the Name text box, type a new name for the report.**

   For example, you might type **Income Statement — Aviary**.

10. **(Option) Enter a description.**

11. **Click OK.**

    Peachtree changes the report title in the title bar.

Now when you print or preview the report, it includes information only for the department you specified.

Delete any customized financial statement by highlighting the financial statement name and then clicking the Delete button (as shown here).

You can be very creative when designing financial statements; however, there's just not enough room in this book to go into great detail. If you would like more information, feel free to contact the nice folks at Wiley Publishing and let them know you want them to hire us to write a *Peachtree Bible*.

Copying Reports and Financial Statements

You'll find customized reports (in any report area) and financial statements available only in the company you created them in. However, you can copy reports and financial statements that you create in one company to another company. This feature comes in particularly handy if you create a second company and would like to use a customized report or financial statement that you created in the first company.

Peachtree makes customized forms (invoices, checks, purchase orders, and so on) available in *all* companies, regardless of which company you used to create them.

To copy reports or financial statements between companies, begin by following these steps:

1. **Open the company that doesn't have the necessary report.**

2. **Choose Reports & Forms and select any module.**

   For example, select Financial Statements or Accounts Payable. The Select a Report or Form window appears.

3. **Click the Copy button (as shown here).**

   The Copy Reports, Financial Statements & Letter Templates dialog box opens.

4. **From the Select a Company to Copy From drop-down list, select the company containing the report you want to copy. See Figure 15-7.**

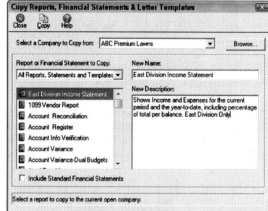

Figure 15-7:
Use this box to copy custom reports and financial statements from one company to another.

5. **From the Report or Financial Statement to Copy drop-down list, select the report you want to copy.**

6. **Enter a name for the report and then click the Copy button.**

   You can use the name Peachtree suggests or you can change it. You can also modify the description if desired.

7. **Click the Close button (as shown here) to close the dialog box.**

   Your newly copied financial statement or report now appears in the current company list.

Chapter 16

When the Bank Statement Arrives

● ●

In This Chapter

▶ Choosing an account to reconcile

▶ Marking cleared items

▶ Printing the results of reconciliation

● ●

*E*ach month, the mailman delivers an envelope from your bank. In that envelope, you find a statement that lists deposits and withdrawals you made, along with checks or copies of checks you wrote to others.

So why is the bank sending you this information? Well, the bank is obligated to tell you each month how much money you have in your account. "Uh . . . okay, so what?" you ask.

Well, if you're smart, you want to make sure that the bank thinks you have the same amount of money that you think you have. After all, banks make mistakes, and you wouldn't want to give your money away to the bank just because you didn't take the time to check its accounting and find its error. Comparing the bank's balance with yours is *reconciling*.

Face it; accounting isn't exactly a barrel of laughs. And reconciling your bank statement probably wins the award for the least fun thing you can do when working with your company's books. However, reconciling is an important function because it's the only way to confirm that you and the bank agree on the amount of money you have in your account.

Anyone who ever tried to reconcile a bank account knows that the process can be tedious at best — and at worst, a nightmare when you just can't make the bank's numbers match yours. When you reconcile your bank statement by using paper and pencil, you add *time-consuming* to the list of negative adjectives.

Let Peachtree help you. At least when you reconcile your bank statement by using the Peachtree Account Reconciliation feature, you finish more quickly. This chapter shows you how to use the Account Reconciliation feature — and how to track down problems when things don't balance on the first try.

Understanding the Concept of Balancing

The statement that you receive summarizes the transactions the bank processed for you during the month. These transactions include checks you wrote, deposits you made, and actions the bank took, such as charging your account for checks you ordered or adding interest to your account.

You need to use the statement to compare the account balance that the bank says you have with the account balance that you think you have. In the best of all worlds, they should match. If they don't match, you need to figure out why they don't match and then take some action (which we talk about later in this chapter) to make them match — that's the part that most people think isn't fun.

After you record the transactions the bank has entered (check order charges, service charges, and the interest), the difference between your account balance and the bank statement's balance should be the total of the uncleared transactions. *Uncleared transactions* are any checks you wrote or deposits you made after the cutoff date on the bank statement. Think of uncleared transactions as transactions about which the bank doesn't know — that is, according to the information on the statement. To reconcile a bank account, you add to the bank statement balance any deposits you made after the bank prepared the statement. Similarly, you subtract from the bank statement balance any checks you wrote after the bank prepared the bank statement.

Typically, the bank's cutoff date for a business checking account is the last day of the month; this date coincides with the end of an accounting period for most businesses. So, when you reconcile your bank statement, you effectively determine your actual cash balance as of the last day of the accounting period. Your accountant needs to know your cash balance on the last day of the accounting period to prepare accurate financial statements, so reconciling your bank statement helps your accountant prepare financial statements.

When you reconcile using paper and pencil, you list and total all checks you wrote that don't appear on the bank statement as well as all deposits that you made that don't appear on the bank statement. Then you can subtract and add them to the bank's ending balance to determine whether you and the bank agree on your account balance. Initially, the listing and totaling is the most time-consuming part of the process. (If your account doesn't balance, finding the error can become the most time-consuming part of the process.) Peachtree shortens the listing and totaling part of the process by doing the math for you.

Before You Start Reconciling

Before you start reconciling, you need to address two issues. First, after you receive your statement from the bank, make sure you're working in the accounting period covered by the bank statement. The accounting period appears at the top of any of the Navigation Centers.

If you need to change the accounting period, follow these steps:

1. **Click the button above the Navigation Centers that displays the current period.**

2. **Click the period you want to reconcile.**

3. **Click OK.**

   If you see a prompt asking whether you want to print invoices, checks, or reports, click No. Typically, this prompt appears when you change the period to a higher number, not to a lower number.

For details on changing the accounting period, see Chapter 17.

Second, for deposits, some bank statements list individual items instead of the deposit ticket total. (Most banks, however, list deposit ticket totals instead of individual items.) If your bank lists individual items and you group receipts by using the deposit ticket ID field available in the Receipts, Receive Payments, and Select for Deposit windows, you can print the Bank Deposit report (as shown in Figure 16-1) to match individual items to deposit ticket totals.

For details on grouping deposits, see Chapter 8.

Figure 16-1:
This report lists the individual items that are included on each bank deposit ticket.

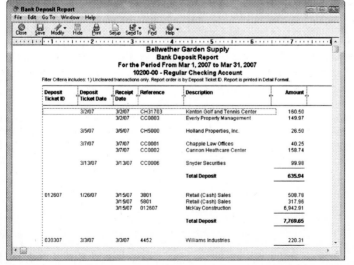

In the Account Reconciliation window, Peachtree lists individual items if you don't fill in the deposit ticket ID field or if you have items you haven't yet selected for deposit. If you fill in the deposit ticket ID field, Peachtree lists the deposit ticket total rather than each individual item. The Bank Deposit report helps you tie the individual items to a particular deposit so that you can properly identify deposits that clear the bank. To print the report, follow these steps:

1. **Choose Reports & Forms⇨Account Reconciliation.**

    The Select a Report window appears, showing the available account reconciliation reports.

2. **On the right side of the window, select Bank Deposit Report.**

3. **Click the Print button, as shown in the margin.**

4. **In the Cash Account ID field, select the correct Cash account.**

5. **Click OK.**

The Bank Deposit report doesn't display deposits recorded using journal entries.

Manually Marking Cleared Transactions

In the previous section, which we strongly suggest that you read, we discuss two housekeeping tasks you should complete to prepare for reconciliation. With those two housekeeping tasks out of the way, you're ready to reconcile. It won't be painful. Honest. Or at least it won't be as painful as it used to be.

You use a combination of your bank statement and the Account Reconciliation window to reconcile a bank account. The bank statement shows checks and deposits that have cleared the bank, along with those other miscellaneous transactions that the bank might have recorded (service charges, interest, and so on). The Account Reconciliation window shows the transactions in the selected account that are available for reconciliation for the period (see Figure 16-2).

You can maximize this window to see more information, and you can sort the information in the window by any column in the window — just click the column heading. If you're looking for a particular transaction, you can click the Find button (as shown here) on the Account Reconciliation window's toolbar to search for it.

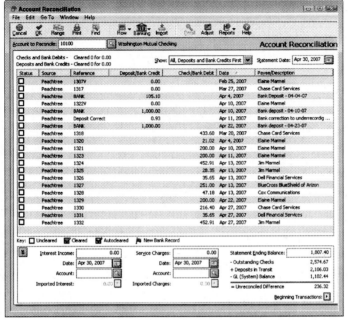

Figure 16-2:
The
Account
Reconcil-
iation
window
displays
transactions
you can
clear.

When you compare your bank statement with the Account Reconciliation window, you see some transactions in Peachtree that don't appear on the bank statement, and you might also see some transactions on the bank statement that don't appear in Peachtree.

You need to mark the transactions that appear on the bank statement as cleared in the Peachtree Account Reconciliation window. You can match cleared checks on the bank statement to checks in Peachtree by using the number that appears in the Reference column. Most people use amounts to match deposits on the bank statement to deposits in Peachtree. If you have trouble matching deposits, Peachtree probably grouped a deposit differently than the deposit you presented at the bank. You can double-click to drill down on a deposit in the Account Reconciliation window to open it in the Select for Deposit, Receipts, or Receive Payment window (wherever it was created). Then, if necessary, change the deposit ticket ID number so that all items you deposited in the bank on the same deposit ticket have the same deposit ticket ID number in Peachtree. Also, use the Bank Deposit report (refer to Figure 16-1) to help identify the receipts included in each deposit in Peachtree.

Reconciling for the first time

If you just started using Peachtree and this is the first time you're reconciling, you might find checks and deposits on your bank statement that you haven't entered in Peachtree because the transactions occurred before you started using Peachtree. Your very first action after opening the Account Reconciliation window should be to enter these outstanding transactions. In the Account Reconciliation window, click the arrow button next to Beginning Transactions in the lower-right corner of the window. Peachtree displays the Beginning Transactions dialog box, as shown in the figure here.

Enter unreconciled transactions that appear on your bank statement but occurred before you started using Peachtree. In the top portion of the window, enter unreconciled checks that were written before you started using Peachtree. Remember that unreconciled checks include those checks remaining unreconciled from prior bank statements *as well as* checks that appear on the bank statement you're about to reconcile. In the lower portion of the window, enter unreconciled deposits that were made before you started using Peachtree. Like unreconciled checks, unreconciled deposits include deposits remaining unreconciled from prior bank statements *as well as*

deposits that appear on the bank statement that you're about to reconcile.

For checks, assign the check number as the reference number. For deposits, the reference number doesn't really matter; just make sure that you enter the deposit amount as it appears on your bank statement. Click OK after you finish. The transactions you entered appear in the Account Reconciliation window so that you can mark them as cleared and reconcile your bank statement.

If you've been using Peachtree for a while — oh, say, maybe ten years — and you're just now deciding that you're going to use Peachtree to reconcile, you have a fairly big project ahead of you. You see, all the checks and deposits you entered after you started using Peachtree still appear in Peachtree — unless you've purged unreconciled transactions, which only complicates the matter further. To make reconciliation work, you have two choices:

✔ **The "long but accurate" choice:** You can pull all your old bank statements and reconcile, month by month. If you've purged unreconciled transactions, you can't use this method.

Beginning Transactions

Cancel   OK   Row   Help

| Account to Reconcile: | 10100 | Statement Date: | Apr 30, 2007 |

Beginning Withdrawals

Amount	Description	Reference	Date
25.43	Office supplies	1234	Feb 18, 2007

Beginning Deposits

Amount	Description	Reference	Date
4,650.00	Various customers	022807	Feb 28, 2007

✓ **The "shorter but potentially problematic" choice:** You can perform a dummy reconciliation. Suppose that it's May 2007, you received your April 2007 bank statement, and you want to reconcile it. Perform a dummy reconciliation that clears all transactions older than April 1 that don't appear on the April bank statement and have appeared on older bank statements. To make the Unreconciled Difference field equal 0, you need to enter a dummy number in the Statement Ending Balance field. That dummy number is the part that can get you in trouble down the road.

You might want to consider hiring a Peachtree Certified Consultant, such as Diane (one of the co-authors of this book), to help you reconcile for the first time after using Peachtree for years. You can contact her at `diane@thepeach treelady.com.`

Follow these steps to reconcile a bank account:

1. **Choose Tasks⇨Account Reconciliation to display the Account Reconciliation window.**

2. **Click the lookup list indicator (as shown here) beside the Account to Reconcile field to display the list of your accounts.**

3. **Click the account that you want to reconcile.**

   In Peachtree, you can balance any account, not just a checking account. For example, you can balance savings accounts, petty cash accounts, and credit card accounts.

4. **At the bottom of the window, fill in the following:**

   • *Interest Income and Service Charges fields:* Record any interest you earned and any bank service charges you incurred. For both fields, assign the date of the bank statement and then select the appropriate account.

   • *Statement Ending Balance field:* Enter the ending balance that appears on the bank statement.

5. **Select the check box in the Status column at the left edge of each entry that appears on the bank statement.**

   Peachtree places a blue check mark in the check box, indicating that the bank has processed the item.

Range

   You can mark consecutive groups of transactions by using either the reference number or a date range. Click the Range button (as shown here), and in the Clear Transactions dialog box that appears, enter the range of reference numbers or transaction dates for Peachtree to mark.

   If most transactions cleared the bank, you can mark all the transactions cleared and then unclear the ones that didn't clear. Click the Row drop-down button and then click the All button. Peachtree marks all transactions cleared. You can then remove check marks by deselecting the check boxes for the transactions that did not clear the bank.

6. **Check the Unreconciled Difference value in the lower right of the window.**

   Your goal is to make that value equal to 0.

   - *If the Unreconciled Difference value equals 0:* You've reconciled, and you're finished (pat yourself on the back). Just click the OK button to save your work.

   - *If the Unreconciled Difference value doesn't equal 0:* Read the upcoming section, "When the Account Doesn't Balance." (And we're sorry.)

Automatically Marking Cleared Transactions

If you're using Peachtree Complete or higher, you can download transactions from your bank and let Peachtree match cleared transactions for you — saving even more time in the reconciliation process.

Peachtree refers to this feature as *online banking,* and you can use it with any bank that lets you download transactions. Some banks interface directly with Peachtree, but you can import bank transactions even if your bank doesn't interface with Peachtree — just as long as your bank lets you download transactions and save them to an OFX (Microsoft Money) file or a QFX (QuickBooks) file.

The list of banks that interface directly with Peachtree appears in the Import Statement Wizard. If your bank doesn't interface directly, go to your bank's Web site and follow its procedures to download your bank statement. If you have a choice between an OFX and a QFX file, choose OFX. Save the file to your hard drive and note the location. You're now ready to use the Import Statement Wizard.

When you use the Import Statement Wizard, Peachtree imports statement information provided by your bank and then *auto-clears* records: that is, matching the bank's transactions with transactions in Peachtree. Your job becomes reviewing the work Peachtree has done to make sure it's accurate. This method can save you *lots* of time because Peachtree is pretty good at matching transactions. To import bank statement information, follow these steps:

1. **Choose Tasks⇨Account Reconciliation.**

   Peachtree displays the Account Reconciliation window (refer to Figure 16-2).

2. **Select your bank account in the Account to Reconcile field.**

3. **Click the Import button.**

   Peachtree displays the Welcome screen of the Import Statement Wizard.

4. **Click Next to choose how to import your statement (see Figure 16-3).**

   Select the Automatically Connect to My Bank and Import a Statement option if your bank appears in the Bank list box. Enter your bank-supplied user ID and password.

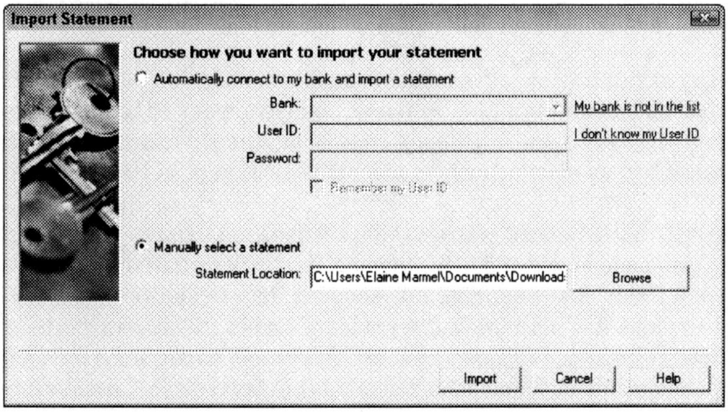

Figure 16-3:
Select a method to import your bank statement into Peachtree.

   Select the Manually Select a Statement option if your bank doesn't appear in the Bank list box. Then click the Browse button to navigate to the location on your hard drive where you saved your downloaded bank statement information.

5. **Click Import.**

   Peachtree imports bank statement information. When Peachtree finishes, you see the Import Summary screen, which shows the statement date and number of records, debits, credits, interest, and service charges imported.

   If your company uses more than one bank account, you see the Select Account dialog box, where you need to select the bank account for which you're importing information.

6. **Click Finish.**

   Peachtree auto-clears records, matching Peachtree transactions to bank statement transactions. When the process finishes, Peachtree redisplays the Account Reconciliation window, showing you the results. A key appears below the list of transactions, describing the status of each transaction.

7. **Fill in the Statement Ending Balance field and note the Unreconciled Difference amount.**

   • *If the Unreconciled Difference value equals 0:* You reconciled, and you're finished (pat yourself on the back). Just click the OK button to save your work.

   • *If the Unreconciled Difference value doesn't equal 0:* Read on; you might need to do a little manual matching.

Most of the time, Peachtree is pretty good at matching transactions. Occasionally, though, you have to do some matching. It really isn't tough, so don't worry.

The key at the bottom of the list of transactions helps you identify transactions that haven't been matched. In particular, you want to handle transactions marked with a red flag. These are New Bank Record transactions that Peachtree has identified as existing only at the bank — and not in your Peachtree company.

If the New Bank Record transactions really don't exist in your Peachtree company, you need to enter them because the bank updated your account balance by using them. Just minimize the Account Reconciliation window — you don't need to close it — and enter the transactions in the appropriate Peachtree window. For example, choose Tasks⇨Payments to record a check by using the Payments window. When you redisplay the Account Reconciliation window (you can click the Account Reconciliation button on the Windows taskbar), Peachtree has updated it, and you can manually match the records.

If the New Bank Record transactions do exist in your Peachtree company, manually match them by following these steps:

1. **Click a New Bank Record transaction.**

   Peachtree adds the Quick Action buttons to the transaction (see Figure 16-4).

2. **Click the Manual Match button.**

   Peachtree displays the Manual Matching dialog box (see Figure 16-5).

3. **Select the Peachtree transaction that should match the New Bank Record transaction.**

4. **Click the OK/Next button to continue matching other New Bank Record transactions.**

   You might see a message explaining why Peachtree didn't originally match the transactions and asking whether you're sure that they match. Click Yes.

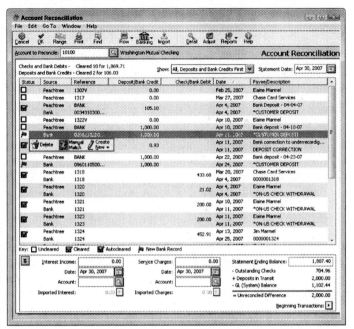

Figure 16-4:
Manually
matching
trans-
actions.

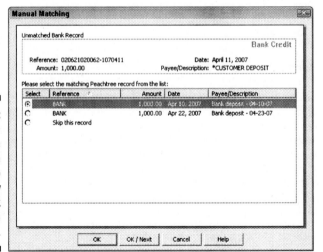

Figure 16-5:
Select a
Peachtree
transaction
to match to
the New
Bank
Record
transaction.

If Peachtree incorrectly matches an imported bank record to a Peachtree transaction, you can unclear it and then manually match it to the correct transaction. Click the transaction in the Account Reconciliation window, and then click the Unclear Quick Action button that appears when you select the transaction. Then, follow Steps 2–4 to manually match the bank record to the correct Peachtree transaction.

5. **Repeat Steps 3 and 4 as necessary.**

   Peachtree displays a message indicating that all transactions have been matched. When you click OK, Peachtree redisplays the Account Reconciliation window.

6. **Check the Unreconciled Difference value.**

   Your goal is to make that value equal to 0.

   - *If the Unreconciled Difference value equals 0:* You reconciled, and you're finished (pat yourself on the back). Just click the OK button to save your work.

   - *If the Unreconciled Difference value doesn't equal 0:* Read the following section, "When the Account Doesn't Balance." (Sorry.)

When the Account Doesn't Balance

What do you do when you marked everything but the Unreconciled Difference doesn't equal 0? Well, you do a little detective work. Go dig your detective hat and magnifying glass out of the closet so you can prepare to snoop around. We'll wait. . . .

Items to review

The Unreconciled Difference might not equal 0 for several reasons:

- ✔ **The bank might have recorded a transaction that you didn't record in Peachtree.** Look for bank charges, such as check reorder charges, other service charges, or interest payments (assuming that your account is interest bearing). Or, occasionally, you'll write a check and forget to post it in Peachtree, and the check will clear the bank.

- ✔ **The bank might have recorded a transaction for a different amount than you recorded in Peachtree.** Compare the amounts of checks that you recorded in Peachtree with the amount the bank cleared for the check. Similarly, compare deposit amounts you recorded in Peachtree with deposit amounts on the bank statement.

Add the digits of the unreconciled difference and see whether they equal nine or a multiple of nine. If so, the odds are good that you transposed the digits when recording one or more checks or deposits. We don't know why this works, but it does.

✔ **You might have cleared a transaction that didn't clear the bank.**
Review the transactions you have cleared. If you used the Range button, double-check the check numbers in the range both in Peachtree and on the bank statement. When you mark a range, finding that transaction can be difficult.

✔ **You might have recorded the Statement Ending Balance incorrectly.**
Make sure you typed the amount correctly.

If you determine that you need to correct an existing transaction or enter a check or receipt, you can leave the Account Reconciliation window open while you edit or add the transaction in the appropriate window. Repeat: *There is no need to close the Account Reconciliation window.* To edit a check or deposit, double-click it in the Account Reconciliation window; Peachtree opens it in the window where you created it. To enter a check or deposit, just ignore the Account Reconciliation window for a minute and choose Tasks⇨ Payments to open the Payments window, or choose Tasks⇨Receipts to open the Receipts window. If you determine that you need to record either a bank service charge or an interest payment, you can make an adjustment — read on.

Making adjustments

You can make an adjustment when you can't find the problem and you decide to write it off as a lost cause.

Accountants don't frown on adjusting to reconcile the account when the difference is small (less than $5). You need to weigh the trade-offs: Is it worth spending hours to find a nickel? We have to believe that your time is better spent if you're doing something other than looking for a dime or a quarter. On the other hand, don't write off large unreconciled differences and don't make a practice of writing off unreconciled differences because they will eventually come back to haunt you.

To record an adjustment, follow these steps:

1. **Click the Adjust button to open the General Journal Entry window.**

   Yep, that's right, adjustments are journal entries. Don't panic.

2. **Record a journal entry.**

   On one line of the entry, select the Cash account you're reconciling for the GL account. On the other line of the entry, select an Income or Expense account for the GL account. Record additional withdrawals for check reorder charges as credits to the Cash account, and additional deposits such as interest earned as debits to the Cash account.

Record the same amount on the other line that contains the Income or Expense account. For additional withdrawals, select an Expense account such as Bank Charges. For additional deposits, select an Income account such as Interest Income. If you aren't sure which account to select, ask your accountant.

What about when you're off by a small amount that you want to write off? Remember this rule: If the Unreconciled Difference is negative, you need to record a journal entry that credits the Cash account for the Unreconciled Difference amount. If the Unreconciled Difference is positive, you need to record a journal entry that debits the Cash account for the Unreconciled Difference amount. To record the other side of the entry, set up an Expense account called something like Bank Over/Short.

3. **After you finish, click the Save button and then click the Close button to redisplay the Account Reconciliation window.**

4. **Select the check box next to each adjusting entry to mark it as cleared and to balance your account.**

   Each debit or credit on the journal entry that affects the Cash account appears as a separate entry in the Account Reconciliation window.

5. **When the Unreconciled Difference equals 0, you can consider the account reconciled. Click the OK button to close the Account Reconciliation window.**

If you later find the source of the problem that caused you to make the adjustment and you want to delete or change the adjustment, choose Lists⇨General Journal Entries. Select the period in which you posted the adjustment, click the transaction, and click the Open button. While viewing the transaction in the General Journal Entry window, edit and save the transaction or delete it.

Printing the Reconciliation Summary

After all your hard work, you'll want to print a record of the balanced reconciliation. Follow these steps:

1. **Choose Reports & Forms⇨Account Reconciliation.**

   The Select a Report window appears, showing the available Account Reconciliation reports.

2. **From the list on the right, select Account Reconciliation.**

3. **Click the Print button to produce a paper copy of the report.**

   Peachtree prints a report similar to the one you see in Figure 16-6, showing that the Unreconciled Difference is 0.

Figure 16-6:
This report shows the matching ending balances as well as deposits and checks that haven't yet cleared the bank.

```
Account Reconciliation
File   Edit   Go To   Window   Help
Close  Save  Modify  Hide  Print  Setup  Send To  Find  Help

                        Bellwether Garden Supply
                         Account Reconciliation
                            As of Jan 31, 2007
                   10200-00 - Regular Checking Account
                    Bank Statement Date: January 31, 2007
  Filter Criteria includes: Report is printed in Detail Format.

  Beginning GL Balance                              11,326.55

  Add: Cash Receipts                                31,113.93

  Less: Cash Disbursement

  Add (Less) Other

  Ending GL Balance                                 42,440.48

  Ending Bank Balance                               15,410.48

  Add back deposits in transi
                     Jan 15, 2007   011607   27,030.00

  Total deposits in transit                         27,030.00

  (Less) outstanding checks

  Total outstanding checks

  Add (Less) Other

  Total other

  Unreconciled difference                               0.00

  Ending GL Balance                                 42,440.48
```

You might have noticed other available reports when you printed the Account Reconciliation report. You don't really need the Deposits in Transit, Outstanding Checks, or Outstanding Other Items reports because all that information appears on the Account Reconciliation report. We discuss the Bank Deposit report in the "Before You Start Reconciling" section earlier in this chapter; the Account Register report lists individual deposits and withdrawals in the selected account.

In transit refers to checks you've written or deposits you've made that haven't yet cleared the bank.

You can see the same information that appears on the Account Register report in the Account Register window. Choose Tasks⇨Account Register to display the window. (The window reminds us of the register you use with a personal checking account to record deposits and withdrawals.) For the current period, it lists only transactions that affect the Cash account. You can switch to a different Cash account, and you can change the time frame displayed in the window. To see the details of any transaction, double-click to drill down on it; Peachtree displays it in the window where you created it.

Visit this book's Web site for more information on Peachtree.

Chapter 17

When Accounting Cycles End . . . and Other Miscellaneous Stuff

....

In This Chapter

▶ Changing accounting periods

▶ Making general journal entries

▶ Preparing the payroll quarterly report

▶ Completing year-end tasks

....

A lot of stuff happens at the end of an accounting period — whether that period is a month, a quarter, or a year. Most of it deals with finishing the transactions that belong in the period that's ending. But you need to start working in a new period before you finish working in the old period because you won't have all the necessary information to finish working in a period on the last day of the period. For example, you won't be able to reconcile your bank statement on the last day of the period because the bank hasn't mailed it to you yet.

In this chapter, we talk about the things you do at the end of each period — and some other topics that just don't fit well in any other chapter, such as (and here come those words!) making journal entries.

Changing Accounting Periods

When you open Peachtree, note the date that appears in the middle of the Button Control Bar, next to the current accounting period. The date matches the system date on your computer, and Peachtree uses that date as the default date for every transaction you enter.

This is true except when the accounting period changes. Look at an easy example: You use standard months in the calendar year for accounting periods, and your fiscal year matches the calendar year.

Fiscal year refers to the year your business uses. The fiscal year can be the same as the calendar year, running from January 1 to December 31. Or the fiscal year might run from April 1 to March 31 or from July 1 to June 30. You and your accountant establish your fiscal year with the IRS.

So, assume that the current accounting period is January. All through the month, Peachtree defaults transaction dates to the current day of the month in January. On February 1, Peachtree will correctly report the date in the Button Control Bar, but the default date for transactions will not be February 1 because you haven't changed the accounting period. The default date on transactions will be January 1 — and will remain January 1 for all subsequent days — until you change the accounting period.

So, what's the big deal? Well, you might be sitting around posting February transactions in the accounting period that runs from January 1 through January 31. That, of course, will misstate the financial condition of your business for both January and February. You need to change the accounting period on the first day of each new period.

"Is this a difficult thing?" you ask. Nope. "Don't you need to wait to change the accounting period until you've posted everything in the current period?" Nope. You can switch back to any open period at any time. "You mean that changing the accounting period doesn't close it?" Yes, that's what we mean. In fact, in Peachtree, you can't close a single accounting period; you can close only a fiscal year, a subject we talk about later in this chapter.

Although you can change to a prior accounting period, we don't recommend that you make changes to transactions in a prior period after giving your data to your accountant. Such actions tend to strain relationships.

If you enable security in Peachtree Complete or higher, a padlock symbol appears in the Change Accounting Periods dialog box next to prior periods. You can allow users to view prior period transactions but prevent them from editing those transactions using Peachtree's security settings. In the User Security window, click the Company tab. Then, under Tasks, open the Transactions in Prior Periods list box and choose Read. For more information on Peachtree and security, see Chapter 18.

When you move forward to a new accounting period and operate on an accrual basis, Peachtree asks you whether you want to print invoices, checks, and reports before changing the period. (If you operate on a cash basis and have printed all checks and invoices, Peachtree asks only about reports.) If you haven't finished entering transactions for the period, you don't need to print anything. However, we suggest that you simply answer no to these questions, even if you've entered all transactions. Then when you've finished entering everything for a period, use the Reports menu to print all the reports for the period — the journals discussed at the end of the chapters in Part II and the financial reports discussed in Chapter 14.

To make the report-printing process easier, create a report group that contains all the reports you want to print at the end of a period. Then you won't need to select and set up each report. To find out how to make a report group, see Chapter 14.

So, why do we suggest that you print reports using the Reports menu before you change the accounting period? Well, the window you see when you're selecting reports to print while changing the accounting period doesn't include a few reports that you might find useful, such as the Balance Sheet, Income Statement, and Trial Balance reports. And although you can print these reports at any time for any period, printing them for an accounting period while you're working in that accounting period is easiest.

Second (for reasons we don't understand), when you print reports while changing the period, Peachtree displays reports from prior periods as well as reports from the current period. You might think the reports appear because you've changed a transaction in a prior period, but we can't prove that. We've found that printing reports using a report group is faster and easier.

Follow these steps to change the accounting period if you operate on an accrual basis:

Period 3 · 03/01/07–03/31/07   **1. Click the Period button (as shown here) on the Button Control Bar or choose Tasks⇨System⇨Change Accounting Period.**

The Change Accounting Period dialog box appears (see Figure 17-1).

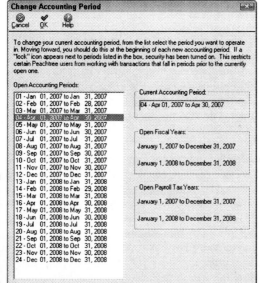

Figure 17-1: Use this dialog box to switch to a different period.

2. **Click the new period you want to use and then click OK.**

   Peachtree might display a dialog box asking whether you want to print invoices or checks. If the dialog box appears, we suggest that you click No and print invoices or checks using the batch printing method described in Chapter 13.

   When you select No, Peachtree displays another dialog box asking whether you want to print reports. Again, we suggest that you click No and create a report group to print reports as described in Chapter 14.

   Peachtree changes the accounting period; you'll see the new period reflected at the top of the screen.

If you operate on a cash basis and have no unprinted invoices or checks, Peachtree doesn't ask whether you want to print invoices and checks, but it does ask whether you want to print reports. Again, we advise that you *not* print reports at this time. Instead, see Chapter 14 to learn how to create a report group to print the necessary end-of-period reports.

Making General Journal Entries

Okay, don't be freaked by the title of this section. *Journal entries* are nothing more than another type of transaction to enter in Peachtree. You just won't use journal entries as often as you do other types of transactions. In fact, here's a good rule to follow:

Don't enter journal entries unless your accountant tells you to make the entry and you *really* know what you're doing.

You see, the truth is, you can usually find another way to enter the information. For example, when you pay your telephone bill of $57.50, you spend money from your Cash account and identify what you spent the money on by making an entry in your Telephone account. Although you can use the General Journal Entry window, it's much easier to write a check from the Payments window or the Select for Payment window.

By the way, this example also demonstrates what accounting types mean when they talk about *double-entry bookkeeping*. The term simply means that each transaction conducted by your business causes you — and your accounting software — to make at least two entries. And here come those dreaded words: One entry is a *debit,* and one entry is a *credit*. The most important thing to know about debits and credits is that they must equal each other. Do you *need* to know this? No. When you use Peachtree's various Task windows, Peachtree does the work for you. Can it *hurt* you to know this? No. Who knows . . . knowing may even help you.

So, when would you use the General Journal Entry window? Well, you'd use it to record the depreciation of assets. Most businesses let their accountants figure the amount of the depreciation — and then the accountant gives you the journal entry information so you can enter the transaction. Or, if you use job costing (see Chapter 12), you can add overhead to a job using a journal entry.

If you're interested in the how-and-why of debits and credits, read Bonus Chapter 5, "The Accounting Equation — Whom to Blame and How It Works," which you can find on this book's Web site, www.dummies.com/go/peachtreefd.

Okay, now that you understand to *not* make journal entries unless you really need to make them, we'll show you how to make them:

We set the window display to show two lines for each entry so that you can see the account name below each line along with the other information for the line. To set your display to show two lines per entry, see Bonus Chapter 1 on this book's Web site, www.dummies.com/go/peachtreefd.

1. Choose Tasks⇨General Journal Entry.

Peachtree displays the General Journal Entry window (see Figure 17-2).

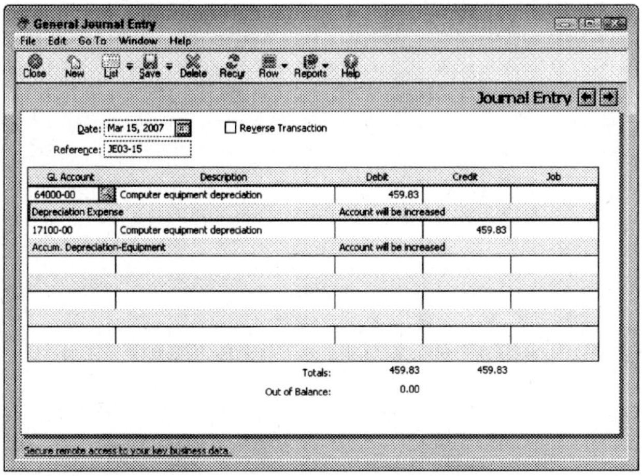

Figure 17-2: To be able to record a journal entry, it must be in balance.

2. If necessary, change the date.

3. Enter a reference number to identify the transaction.

We use JE (for Journal Entry) and then the month and date (refer to Figure 17-2). And yes, you can use the same reference number more than once.

4. **In the GL Account column, click the lookup list button (as shown here) to select the first account you want to change.**

   Accountants like for you to list debits first and then credits. Doing so is not a rule, but this habit will make you look more professional. We're going to assume that you want to look professional, so enter the debit first and then the credit.

5. **In the Description column, enter the reason for the transaction.**

   Peachtree copies these words to the next line for you, saving you the typing. You can change them on the next line if you want.

6. **In the Debit column, enter the amount.**

7. **If necessary, assign a job to the entry.**

8. **Repeat Steps 4–7, but in Step 6, enter the amount in the Credit column.**

   When you finish, debits should equal credits. If they don't, the amount that you're out of balance appears at the bottom of the window. If you're out of balance, fix things before you try to save. Peachtree won't let you save the entry if it's out of balance.

9. **Click Save (as shown here) to save the journal entry.**

For some journal entries, you might need to enter multiple debits to offset one credit or multiple credits to offset one debit, or even multiple debits and multiple credits to offset each other. That's fine. A journal entry consists of a set of debits and credits that equal each other. Also, your accountant might send you a list of entries to make before you close the fiscal year. You can make all the entries in one General Journal Entry transaction — maybe even with a description such as *"Adjustment per CPA."* That is, you can keep entering lines in the General Journal Entry window using only one reference number.

Accounting Behind the Screens

If you chose the Hide General Ledger Accounts option for your company in the Maintain Global Options dialog box, your transaction windows don't look like the ones we show throughout this book. In particular, you don't see any General Ledger accounts in your transaction windows. See Bonus Chapter 1 on this book's Web site, www.dummies.com/go/peachtreefd, for a comparison of what windows look like when you hide or display General Ledger accounts.

In Chapter 5, we allude to a neat way to identify the accounts Peachtree updates while you enter transactions even if you don't display the General

Ledger accounts in your transaction window. Click the Journal button in the window (as shown here), and Peachtree displays the Accounting Behind the Screens dialog box shown in Figure 17-3.

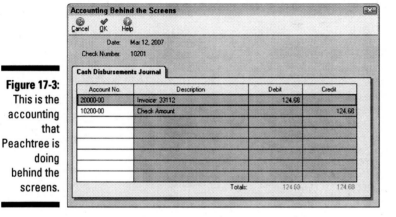

Figure 17-3: This is the accounting that Peachtree is doing behind the screens.

And yes, you *can* make changes in this dialog box to modify one or more of the accounts Peachtree updates for this transaction, but we don't recommend it. Notice that you can't change a debit to a credit or vice versa; if you change the accounts and you don't know what you're doing, you'll really mess up your company's books.

Batch Posting

Don't read this section if you're using real-time posting. You'll just waste your time.

People who like batch posting typically work in a multi-user environment and want to review transactions before updating the General Ledger. When you use batch posting in Peachtree, you save transactions as you enter them, but they don't update your accounts — or appear on reports — until you post. You choose batch or real-time posting in the Maintain Company window. See Chapter 2 for more information.

You can't create purchase orders behind the scenes if you use batch posting.

Okay, so you know you need to post to update your accounts. You also need to make sure you post all journals before you try to change the accounting period. If you use batch posting, follow these steps to post:

1. **Choose Tasks⇨System⇨Post.**

   Peachtree displays the Post dialog box shown in Figure 17-4.

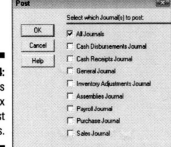

Figure 17-4:
Use this
dialog box
to post
journals.

2. **Select the journal you want to post, or leave the check mark in All Journals to post everything.**

3. **Click OK.**

   Peachtree displays a bar across the screen while it posts and then redisplays the main Peachtree window when posting finishes.

Before producing many reports, Peachtree asks batch posting users whether they want to post before viewing the report.

Preparing the Payroll Quarterly Report (941)

This one's easy. You're gonna love it. As long as you subscribe to any Peachtree Payroll Solution, you just print a form. You can print the form onto plain paper, and the IRS will accept the form in lieu of the preprinted form that it sends you each quarter, or you can file it electronically *(e-filing)*.

We recommend that you print the 941 Worksheet (or the 941B Worksheet if appropriate) before you print the Federal Form 941; choose Reports & Forms⇨Payroll. The worksheet will show you the amount you were supposed to deposit during the quarter — and we assume that you make your payroll tax deposits in a timely fashion, as required by law. You'll need the amount you deposited to print an accurate Federal Form 941.

To print an Employer's Quarterly Federal Tax Return, follow these steps.

1. **Choose Reports & Forms⇨Forms⇨Tax Forms.**

   Peachtree displays the Select a Report or Form window. In the Form Types list, Peachtree selects Tax Forms and displays available tax forms.

2. **In the Forms list, select Payroll Tax forms.**

   Peachtree displays a sample Federal 940; don't let that throw you.

3. **Click the Print Preview button.**

   Peachtree displays the Payroll Tax Form Selector dialog box (see Figure 17-5.

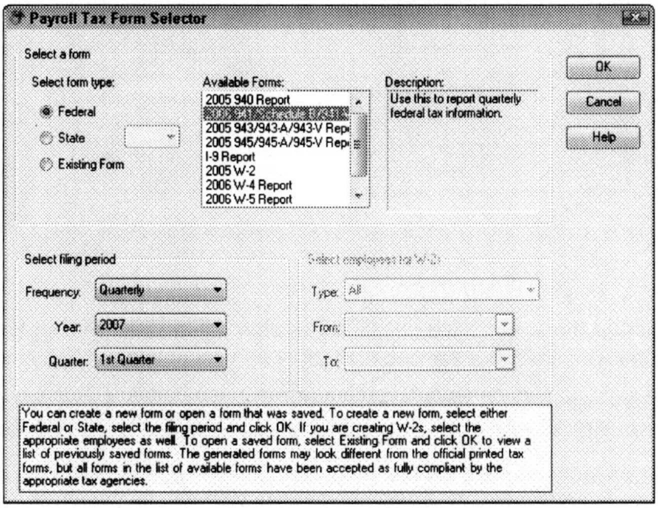

Figure 17-5: Use this dialog box to select the payroll tax form you want to print.

4. **In the Select Form Type section, select the Federal option button.**

5. **From the Available Forms list, choose the 941/Schedule B form for the appropriate year.**

6. **In the Select Filing Period section, click the Quarter drop-down list arrow and select the quarter for which you're reporting.**

7. **Click OK.**

   Peachtree opens the form on-screen (see Figure 17-6) and displays the Report Steps dialog box, which explains the steps you need to take to complete the form. Click OK to dismiss the dialog box. The Red Fields dialog box appears to remind you to fill out each field surrounded by a red flashing box. Click OK to dismiss the dialog box.

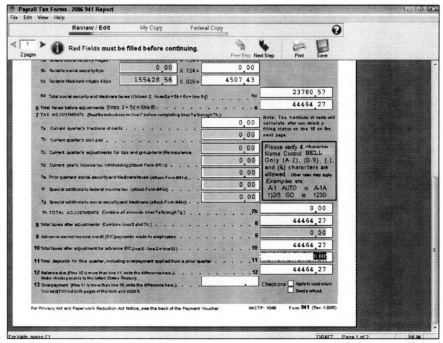

Figure 17-6:
Complete
this 941
form that
Peachtree
displays.

You can make changes to fields highlighted in blue, but we don't recommend that unless your accountant tells you to make changes.

8. Fill out each field that Peachtree highlights with a red flashing box. Press Tab to move to the next field surrounded by a red flashing box.

The choices in Part 2, Line 15 determine whether Peachtree also displays the Schedule B. If Peachtree displays the Schedule B, continue filling in the fields surrounded by red flashing boxes. When you finish filling fields surrounded by red flashing boxes, Peachtree displays a blue flashing box around your company name.

9. To print a copy of the report for your records, click the Next Step button (as shown here) on the toolbar above the report.

Peachtree displays a message that indicates that you won't be able to make changes to the report if you continue. The message offers you the opportunity to double-check your work (by clicking the Double Check button). Or click the Agree button to continue with the printing process.

10. Click the Print button (as shown here) to print your copy.

Peachtree prints the form. If your printer cuts off any portion of the form, you should e-file the form.

11. **Click the Next Step button again.**

    Peachtree displays the Filing Options dialog box.

12. **Click the e-File button to file the report electronically or click the Print button to print a copy of the report that you can mail to the IRS.**

Printing W-2s

You must print W-2s before you close the Payroll Tax year. To print W-2s, you follow Steps 1–7 in the preceding section, selecting W-2s in Step 5. A wizard then displays a checklist that you can print of things you need to verify. The wizard then walks you through the process of verifying employee information, such as name, address, Social Security number, and wage information, and company information and printing W-2s. After you dismiss that dialog box, you begin the verification process. In Figure 17-7, we're printing only one W-2, just to give you an idea. By default, Peachtree automatically includes all employees whom you've paid during the current year when you choose All employees, even if you've marked an employee as inactive.

You mark an employee inactive in the Maintain Employees/Sales Reps window when the employee no longer works for you. If the employee worked for you during any part of a calendar year, though, you must provide the employee with a W-2. Also, by marking the employee inactive, you make the employee a candidate for purging, which we talk about later in this chapter.

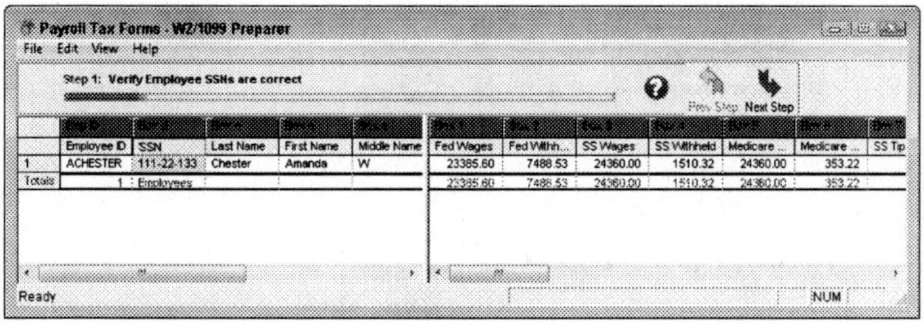

Figure 17-7:
Verify
information
highlighted
in yellow.

	Employee ID	SSN	Last Name	First Name	Middle Name	Fed Wages	Fed Withh...	SS Wages	SS Withheld	Medicare ...	Medicare ...	SS Tip
1	ACHESTER	111-22-133	Chester	Amanda	W	23385.60	7488.53	24360.00	1510.32	24360.00	353.22	
Totals	1	Employees				23385.60	7488.53	24360.00	1510.32	24360.00	353.22	

Click the Next Step button at the top of the window until you complete the review process. Peachtree asks you to review all employee information first and then all company information. After you finish reviewing information, Peachtree gives you the option to e-file W-2s or to print your own. If you choose to print W-2s, Peachtree displays them on-screen (see Figure 17-8), and you can use the Print Final button at the top of the window to print the W-2s. After you print W-2s, the wizard prompts you to print the W-3 Transmittal of Wage and Tax Statements form that accompanies W-2s when you submit them.

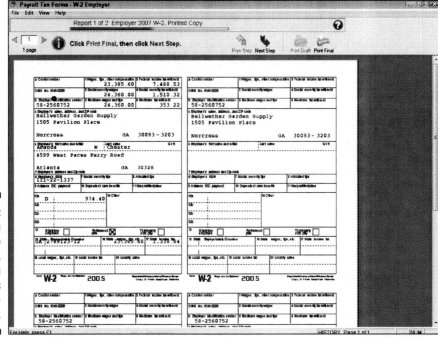

Figure 17-8:
If you choose to print W-2s, Peachtree displays them on-screen.

Printing 1099s

You'll need to purchase 1099 forms and load them into your printer.

You can purchase your forms from your local office supply store or printer (the people, not the machines), or you can use the offers you receive in your Peachtree software box. Chapter 21 lists Web contact information on a few sources for forms. (If you contact Deluxe Forms at 800-328-0304 and reference this book and discount code R03578, you'll receive 20 percent off your first order.)

You follow the same steps to print 1099s that you follow to print the Federal Form 941, outlined in the earlier section, "Preparing the Payroll Quarterly Report (941)." Follow Steps 1–7, but, in Step 2, select the appropriate 1099 form: 1099-MISC Preprinted or 1099-INT Preprinted.

Peachtree displays the Preview and Print 1099 Forms dialog box, where you select the year for which you're printing the forms and the vendors for whom you want to print the form. By default, Peachtree automatically includes all vendors who meet both of the following criteria:

> ✔ You select Independent Contractor or Interest in the 1099 Type field of the Maintain Vendors window.
>
> ✔ You paid more than $600.00 or more than $10.00 in interest during the calendar year.

Read Chapter 5 for information on setting up vendors and the 1099 Type field.

You must print 1099s before you close the payroll year. You can modify the form if necessary; see Chapter 13.

Peachtree supports producing 1099s for only two types of vendors: Interest (1099-INT) and Independent Contractors (1099-MISC). If you need to produce 1099s for more than two types of 1099 vendors, workarounds exist, but they are beyond the scope of this book. So, once again, if you *like* this book, contact Wiley and tell them that you want them to hire us to write a *Peachtree Bible*.

Updating Payroll Tax Tables

To calculate payroll accurately, Peachtree uses tax tables. Each tax table is associated with the current year. The name of the table ends with the last two digits of the current year, which means that as you begin a new calendar year, you must have new tax tables with names that include the last two digits of the new year. In addition, the calculations in the tax table might have changed, and you need to make sure that the tax tables will calculate correctly.

So, how do you do this? We suggest that you subscribe to one of the Peachtree Payroll Solutions. Whenever the government makes changes to payroll tax tables or payroll forms, the Peachtree updates your tax tables via electronic download. For more information on the services and subscribing, visit www.peachtree.com.

As an alternative, you can manually update the User-Maintained tax tables in Peachtree. Because most tax tables you see in the User-Maintained Payroll Tax Tables window don't change drastically from year to year, you can use last year's tax table as a model to create this year's table.

If you start a new payroll year and attempt to process payroll without creating new tables for the new year, Peachtree displays a message indicating that it couldn't find tax table calculations and offers to update your User-Maintained tax tables for you by creating new tables using last year's tables as models.

For details on creating a User-Maintained tax table, see the section on union dues in Chapter 19. However, be aware that out of the box, Peachtree doesn't come with tax tables needed to calculate federal income tax, Social Security, and Medicare. To use payroll, you *must* have these tables. So, either set them up yourself as User-Maintained tax tables or pop for one of the Peachtree Payroll Solutions. Further, even if you set up these tax tables yourself, you won't be able to produce the payroll forms we describe earlier in this chapter: namely, the 941 and the W-2. To produce those forms, you need to subscribe to one of the Peachtree Payroll Solutions.

"If I can't print payroll forms without subscribing to a Peachtree Payroll Solution, why would I bother to set up User-Maintained tables?" you ask. If you're recording after-the-fact payroll — say, an outside service prepares all your payroll information for you — setting up User-Maintained tables will suit your needs and make your payroll entry easy.

Understanding Closing

Closing the Payroll Tax Year and the Fiscal Year are not difficult or time consuming. The activities that you should complete before closing, however, can indeed be time consuming. Before we jump into describing those activities, you should understand what happens when you close in Peachtree.

Closing in Peachtree automatically does the equivalent of manually preparing and posting closing entries to the General Ledger. In addition, Peachtree resets all your vendors', customers', and employees' year-to-date totals to zero. That way, you can begin monitoring the new year's purchases with each vendor; sales with each customer; and wages, benefits, deductions, and taxes with each employee.

Why does Peachtree enable you to close the payroll tax year separately from the fiscal year? The payroll tax year is based on a calendar year. When you close the payroll tax year, Peachtree zeros-out year-to-date wage and tax information for employees and year-to-date purchasing information for vendors — the information that appears on W-2s and 1099s. However, your fiscal year might or might not be a calendar year. When you close the fiscal year, Peachtree zeros-out other information (such as year-to-date customer information) and closes everything, including the General Ledger. If your fiscal year is the same as your calendar year, you still need to let Peachtree close both years to close everything.

Even if you don't use payroll, you need to close the payroll year to zero-out year-to-date vendor purchase information.

When you close, Peachtree automatically closes the first 12 periods, which make up the oldest open year. Timing is everything when you talk about closing. Typically, no one is ready to close a year on December 31. But because Peachtree allows you to have two years — 24 periods — open simultaneously, you should have no trouble moving forward to the new year while leaving the prior year open. Therefore, closing should not become a pressing issue unless you find that you're working in Period 24 and need to move to a new open period. If you find yourself in this situation, you need to close both the Payroll Tax Year and the Fiscal Year. Then, Peachtree will close Periods 1–12 and then renumber so that the periods that used to be 13–24 become 1–12.

To identify the years you have open, click the Period button on the Button Bar to display the Change Accounting Period dialog box (refer to Figure 17-1). The open Fiscal and Payroll Tax Years appear on the right side of the box.

Payroll housekeeping tasks

Before you close the payroll year in Peachtree, you must finish payroll processing for the year you intend to close. You should check employee background information, wage information, and tax information. Printing W-2s should be the last task you perform for the year you intend to close so that you can be sure that the information on the forms will be accurate.

If you have adjustments or fringe benefits that should be reflected on W-2s, you can include them in the last payroll of the year, or you can run a separate payroll. We recommend that you try to include them in the last payroll of the year. See Chapter 9 for information on setting up and paying bonuses.

Because Peachtree keeps open two payroll years, you can prepare payroll for the new calendar year before you close the old calendar year as long as the period assigned to the January of the new calendar year is Period 13. Before you prepare payroll in the new calendar year, you'll receive a Peachtree Payroll Tax Service Update that contains information relevant to both the year you're finishing and the year you're starting. You'll want to install that update before you print payroll tax and vendor 1099 forms and calculate fixed asset depreciation for the year you're finishing.

Non-payroll area housekeeping tasks

Before you close a year, take the time to complete general housekeeping tasks in Peachtree before you purge old, unnecessary data from your Peachtree company. And, you don't need to worry about losing information if you purge; even though Peachtree purges inactive transactions, the program retains enough information to produce comparative financial statements. You read about purging later in this chapter.

Review Table 17-1 for ideas on the year-end housekeeping tasks you should consider for other accounting areas besides payroll.

Table 17-1   Year-end Housekeeping Tasks for Non-Payroll Areas

Accounting Area	Considerations
Accounts Payable	In addition to printing 1099s before closing the payroll year, consider identifying any vendors with whom you no longer do business and marking them inactive in the Maintain Vendors window. Also review open purchase orders and close any that you know you won't fill, making them candidates for purging along with inactive vendors.
Inventory	Although there are no special year-end procedures for inventory in Peachtree, many businesses perform a physical inventory count at this time of year. The Peachtree Physical Inventory List report contains space for you to enter actual counts, which makes taking physical inventory easier. Be sure to print an Inventory Valuation Report after you adjust your quantities to the physical count.
Accounts Receivable	Review customers; and, in the Maintain Customers/Prospects window, mark inactive those with whom you no longer do business. Review open quotes and sales orders and close any that you know you won't fill, making them candidates for purging. You should also review your Aged Receivables report for possible bad debts and write off any amounts that you know you won't collect.
Job Cost	Job costing helps you track costs and revenues over the life of a project. By its very nature, job costing doesn't run on a calendar or fiscal year basis and has no end-of-year procedures. Still, you should review existing jobs and mark appropriate ones as inactive from the Maintain Jobs window.
Account Reconciliation	Reconcile your December bank statements before you close the fiscal year to make reconciled checks and deposits candidates for purging. Unreconciled transactions remain in the system.
General Ledger	Make year-end adjustments before closing; you get those from your accountant after he or she has prepared the income tax return for the business. Also review your Chart of Accounts for accounts you're no longer using and mark those accounts inactive.

Checking your data for common accounting mistakes

You can use the Peachtree Internal Accounting Review feature at the end of each month — or, at a minimum, before you close the year — to double-check your company for common mistakes. For example, the Internal Accounting Review checks for payments or checks that don't credit a cash account, like most checks normally do. The Internal Accounting Review checks for 15 common mistakes in accrual-based companies and 11 common mistakes in cash-based companies. You can run the Internal Accounting Review by choosing Reports & Forms⇨Internal Accounting Review. Peachtree displays the Internal Accounting Review window, as shown in Figure 17-9.

Areas with transactions that are atypical appear with a red flag in the right side of the window, and areas where no potentially problematic transactions exist appear with a green check in the right side of the window.

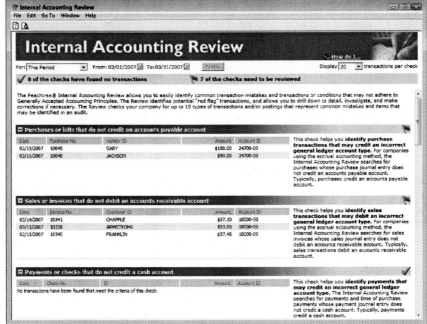

Figure 17-9:
The Internal Accounting Review helps you identify and correct common mistakes.

You can click any potentially problematic transaction, and Peachtree displays it in the window where you created it, leaving the Internal Accounting Review window in the background. Inspect the transaction, makes changes as appropriate to correct the transaction, and then save it.

When you redisplay the Internal Accounting Review window, click the Refresh button in the upper left of the window to recheck your data.

Peachtree doesn't make you fix the transactions it identifies; it's quite possible that the transactions are correct as is. You, as the human in the equation, have the final say. If you are unsure whether to correct a transaction, discuss it with your accountant.

When you change the accounting period or close a year, Peachtree offers you the opportunity to run the Internal Accounting Review.

Archiving your data

If you're using Peachtree Premium or higher, you can archive your company data at any time, but the end of the year is a good time to create an archive copy of your company data. When you archive data, Peachtree creates a read-only copy of your company that you can use to print reports and review transactions. From your accountant's perspective, the good news is that you can't add, change, or delete anything in an archived company. Accountants really *don't* like it when you make changes to a closed period (it kind of makes them nuts). And, if you create an archive copy of your data to use for prior-year research right before you close, you will make your accountant *very* happy.

You might want to change the period to the last month (typically December) of the year you're archiving before you create the archive file. If you change periods like we suggest, Peachtree displays that month when you open the archive file.

Although you get the opportunity to create an archive company while you close your year, we find separating the two processes easier to understand. To create an archive company, choose File➪Archive Company. In the Archive Company window, supply a name for the archive company. Peachtree suggests the name Archive-XXXXXX, where the Xs represent the date in six-digit format, which works for us. Then, click Archive, and Peachtree creates the archive company.

If you archive multiple companies, include the company name after "Archive" so that you can easily identify a particular company archive file.

To use an archived company, choose File⇨Open Archived Company. Peachtree displays the Open Archived Company dialog box, which lists all archived companies you've created. Select the one you want to open and then click OK. Your company name along with the archive date appear in the title bar of the window.

After you review reports or transactions, choose File⇨Open Previous Company to view a list of companies you can open. Select your company from the list. Note that archive companies do not appear in this list.

Peachtree stores archived companies in a folder called Archives, which appears inside your company folder after you create your first archive company. Should you happen to be housecleaning and get the urge, you can delete old archives from the Archives folder. However, the government often tasks two or three years to question a tax return or payroll tax filing, so use the same record-keeping rules for archive files that you use for other documentation that supports your tax returns. Typically you should keep three years' worth of documentation. If the IRS suspects you of committing fraud, they may want to look back seven years, so, if you're committing fraud, keep at least seven years worth of archive files.

Using the Year-End Wizard

We suggest that you print any year-end reports you want before you start the Year-End Wizard. When you close the payroll tax year, Peachtree doesn't prompt you to print any reports. And when you close the fiscal year, Peachtree selects the reports for you that you can print. To retain some choice in this matter, print all your reports before you start the Year-End Wizard. See Chapter 14 for details on printing reports.

You can't cancel the year-end closing process after you click the Begin Close button in the Year-End Wizard. Restoring from a backup becomes the only way you can "undo."

In addition to the backup that Peachtree will force you to make before closing, we suggest that you use the archiving feature available in Peachtree Premium and higher, as we describe in the earlier "Archiving your data" section, so that you'll have access to reporting and transaction details in closed years. If you're using other versions of Peachtree, we suggest that before closing, you create a prior-year company (see Chapter 19) so that you can print reports and view transaction details in closed years.

The closing process closes the first 12 periods. By the time you close these periods, you won't be working in them anymore; instead, you'll be working in Period 13 or later. It's safe to close the first 12 periods if you've finished all the work for those periods.

Closing the payroll year

Peachtree asks you to back up during the closing process, so make sure you have disks or a flash drive available.

Even if your company's fiscal year doesn't match the calendar year, payroll always operates on a calendar-year basis. Therefore, sometime in January, after you create your last payroll for the preceding year, confirm that your payroll data is complete, and print your W-2s, you're ready to close your payroll information for last year.

You won't be able to cancel this process after the first screen.

Follow these steps to close the payroll year:

1. **Choose Tasks⇨System⇨Year-End Wizard.**

   Peachtree displays the current open years. Fiscal years appear on the left side of the window, and payroll tax years appear on the right.

2. **Click Next to display the Close Options dialog box, as shown in Figure 17-10.**

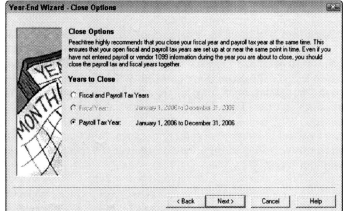

Figure 17-10:
Identify
what you
want to
close.

3. **Select the Payroll Tax Year option button and then click Next.**

   Payroll Tax Year is not an option if the oldest open year is the current year.

If you have any unprinted payroll checks or if you have not yet printed W-2s or 1099s, Peachtree prompts you to print them before you continue. Click Cancel, print the appropriate forms, and restart the closing process. After you close, you won't be able to print them.

Peachtree displays the Internal Accounting Review window. You can skip this process at this time if you ran the review, as we describe earlier in this chapter in the section, "Checking your data for common accounting mistakes."

4. **Click Next.**

Peachtree displays the Back Up Company Data window.

5. **Click the Back Up button.**

Peachtree displays the Back Up Company window, where you can choose to include your company name in the backup filename and other backup options. For details on creating the backup, see Chapter 18.

When Peachtree finishes the backup, you see the Back Up Company Data window again.

6. **Click Next.**

If you use Peachtree Premium or higher, the Archive Company window appears, where you can archive your data before you close. See "Archiving your data," earlier in this chapter, for details on archiving. Then click Next.

Peachtree displays a window where you can confirm that you are closing the payroll tax year for the previous year.

7. **Click Next.**

The Begin Close-Year Process window appears. This is your final chance to cancel before closing.

8. **Click Begin Close.**

Peachtree closes the oldest open payroll tax year and displays a window where you see the new open years, both fiscal and payroll.

9. **Click Finish.**

You can now continue to enter payroll information into the next year.

Closing the fiscal year

When you finish processing and made all adjustments to a fiscal year — adjustments typically identified by your accountant while processing your tax return — you need to close that fiscal year in Peachtree. You'll probably postpone closing a fiscal year until well after you start a new one. For example, if your fiscal year matches the calendar year, you probably won't close last year any earlier than March of the current year.

We suggest that you print any reports for the year that you're closing before you start the closing process. Although you can print reports during the process, they are the reports Peachtree selects — not necessarily the ones you would select.

In addition, before Peachtree will let you close a fiscal year, you must not have any purchases that are "Waiting on Bill" from the vendor in the year that you want to close. Typically, you will have received all bills by the time you want to close the fiscal year. If you haven't, you should change these transactions. We suggest that you create a custom Aged Payables report that includes the Waiting on Bill field and print the report for the entire year. From the report, you can drill down and view transactions that display a Y in the Waiting on Bill From Vendor column and edit them appropriately.

Depending on the amount of data in your company, closing can take awhile. You can't interrupt the process.

To close the fiscal year, follow these steps:

1. **Choose Tasks⇨System⇨Year-End Wizard.**

   Peachtree displays the current open years. Fiscal years appear on the left side of the window, and payroll tax years appear on the right.

2. **Click Next to display the Close Options window.**

3. **Select Fiscal Year and then click Next.**

   If you didn't previously close the payroll tax year, select the Fiscal and Payroll Tax Years option button.

4. **Click Next.**

   If you have any unprinted checks, Peachtree prompts you to print them before you continue. Click Cancel to print them and then restart the closing process. You won't be able to print them after you close the Peachtree Fiscal Year-End Reports window.

5. **If you follow our advice and printed all your reports before you started, click the Check None button and then click Next.**

   If you use Peachtree Premium or higher, the Internal Accounting Review window appears. Click Next and see the section, "Checking your data for common accounting mistakes."

   Peachtree displays the Back Up Company Data window.

6. **Click the Back Up button.**

   Peachtree displays the Back Up Company window, where you can choose to include your company name in the backup filename and select other backup options. See Chapter 18 for details on backing up.

When Peachtree finishes the backup, you see the Back Up Company Data window again.

7. Click Next.

If you use Peachtree Premium or higher, the Archive Company window appears, where you can archive your data before you close. See the "Archiving your data" section for details on archiving. After you make choices in this window, click Next.

Peachtree displays a window where you can view and change the new open fiscal years. Usually, it is *not* necessary to change any of these dates because Peachtree adjusts them for you.

8. Click Next.

Peachtree displays the New Open Fiscal Years window where you see the dates for your next fiscal year. Although you can change these dates, it usually isn't necessary.

9. Click Next.

Peachtree displays the Confirm Close window, where you review one last time the fiscal year you're closing as well as the fiscal years that will be open when you complete the process.

10. Click Next to display the Begin Close-Year Process window.

This window presents your final chance to cancel before closing.

11. Click Begin Close.

Peachtree closes the oldest open year(s) and displays a window where you see the new open years, both fiscal and payroll.

12. Click Finish.

Purging

You can purge information from your company data files at any time, but most people like to tie purging with other year-end activities. Peachtree lets you purge transactions in only closed years of your company, and you can purge payroll and 1099 transactions only after you close both the fiscal and payroll tax years during which you entered those transactions. So, purging after closing is the way to go.

Purging can take quite a long time, depending on the size of your data, the speed of your computer, and the age of the transactions you choose to include in the purge. Peachtree's purge process doesn't have a limit to the number of passes it makes, or the time it takes to go through the journal file. We strongly recommend that you start this process before leaving for the night or weekend.

If your Peachtree journal file is large, you might want to purge every month. To determine the size of your journal file, choose Help⇨Customer Support and Service⇨File Statistics and look at the Size in Kbytes column for the Jrnl Rows file. If this file is larger than 50MB, you'll probably want to purge in small increments.

Peachtree purges two types of data:

✔ **Transactions:** Quotes, invoices, sales orders, receipts, purchases, purchase orders, payments, paychecks, and general journal entries from previous years that are no longer needed. If you use Peachtree Complete or higher, Peachtree also purges time and expense tickets.

✔ **Inactives:** Customers, vendors, employees, inventory items, jobs (and phases and cost codes if you use Peachtree Complete or higher), and General Ledger accounts that you've marked as Inactive in the Maintain windows.

If you plan to purge inactives, you should also purge transactions because Peachtree won't purge inactives if any transactions apply to them.

Follow these steps to purge information:

1. **Choose Tasks⇨System⇨Purge Wizard.**

   Peachtree displays a screen that tells you the earliest date you can use to purge data.

2. **Click Next.**

   Peachtree displays the Back Up Company Data window.

3. **Click the Back Up button.**

   Peachtree displays the Back Up Company window, where you can choose to include your company name in the backup filename, For detailed instructions on creating a backup, see Chapter 18.

   When Peachtree finishes the backup, you see the Back Up Company Data window again.

4. **Click Next.**

   Peachtree displays the Old Transactions window, as shown in Figure 17-11.

5. **Select the date Peachtree uses to identify transactions to purge as well as the types of transactions to purge.**

   The choices concerning Audit Trails and Tickets appear only if you're using Peachtree Complete or higher.

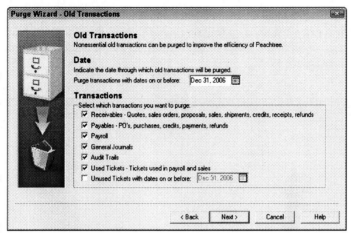

Figure 17-11:
Identify the
ending date
for selecting
transactions
along with
the type of
transactions
to purge.

6. **Click Next.**

   The Account Reconciliation window appears.

7. **Identify accounts that you reconcile. Most people reconcile Cash accounts at a minimum, but you can also reconcile other accounts.**

   Double-click the arrow in the Use column for any account type to display the account numbers. Then add a check mark next to each account you reconcile. Peachtree purges all unreconciled transactions dated earlier than the purge date you establish in Step 5.

8. **Click Next.**

   The Inactive Maintenance Records window appears.

9. **Select the check box next to each type of inactive maintenance record that you want to purge.**

   Maintenance records are the ones you create for customers, vendors, employees, General Ledger accounts, inventory items, and jobs in the windows that open when you select a command on the Maintain menu.

10. **Click Next.**

    The Summary of Options window appears, and you see a list of the choices you made in the wizard.

11. **Click Begin Purge.**

    You can stop a purge as long as the Stop button is available in the Purge Is in Progress window. When that button appears dimmed, you can't safely interrupt the purge. Yes, that means turning off your computer at this point is *not* recommended.

12. **When the purge finishes, click Close.**

You can click the Log button to see a file in the Windows Notepad listing your selection criteria and information about what did and did not purge (see Figure 17-12).

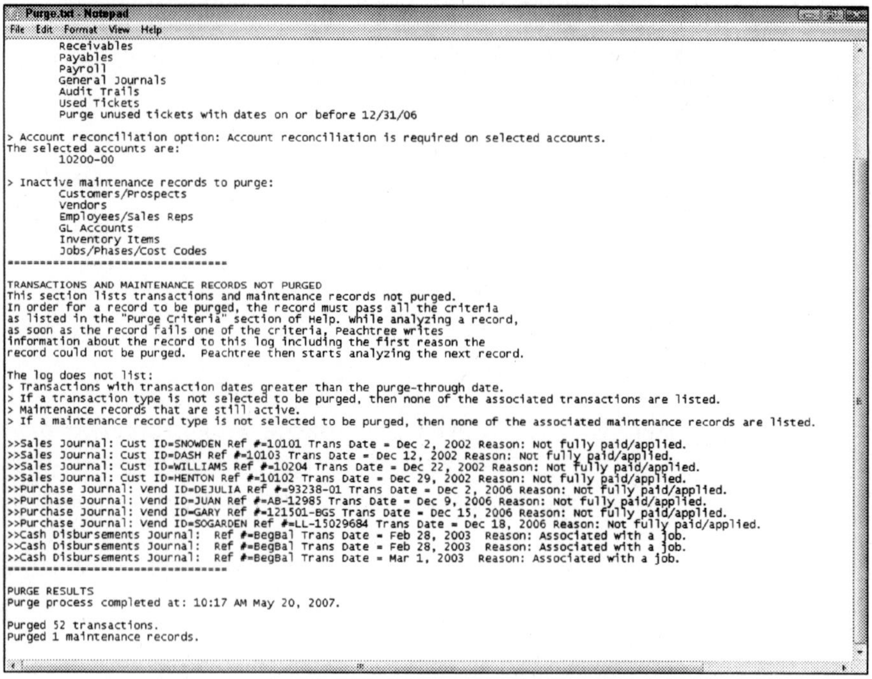

Figure 17-12:
The purge log shows you what information was and wasn't purged.

When Stuff Doesn't Purge

Sometimes, after purging, you'll find information still in the system that you think should have been purged. Peachtree follows some extensive rules when selecting information to purge.

We don't have room to list all the rules Peachtree follows, but we do list the ones that we believe affect the majority of transactions that don't purge. Anything that Peachtree leaves in your database, we call a *saved transaction*. We refer to the date you specify while setting up a purge (the one that identifies the latest transaction date Peachtree will purge) as *the Purge Through date*. Peachtree saves the following:

- ✔ All transactions dated later than the Purge Through date

- ✔ All transactions in any open year

- ✔ All inventory adjustment transactions

- ✔ Purchases and invoices that are not completely paid as of the Purge Through date

- ✔ All cash disbursements or receipts applied to a saved purchase or invoice

- ✔ All purchases and invoices that are related to saved cash disbursements or cash receipts

- ✔ Purchases or invoices related to unpurged jobs

- ✔ Open sales orders and purchase orders

- ✔ All quotes with a transaction date or good-through date later than the Purge Through date

- ✔ Unreconciled transactions (as of the Purge Through date) associated with an account you designate as one you reconcile

- ✔ For Peachtree Complete and higher, time or expense tickets dated later than the Purge Through date or available as reimbursable expense tickets

  If you haven't chosen to purge unused time tickets, Peachtree also saves unused tickets for employees paid using time tickets and tickets tied to customers where the ticket status is HOLD.

- ✔ Inactive jobs (and phases and cost codes for users of Peachtree Complete and higher) with saved transactions that refer to the inactive job

Use the purge log to review what Peachtree purged and what it didn't purge. The log will even tell you why an item wasn't purged. Peachtree stores the purge log (purge.txt) in your company data folder. You can open it at any time by locating and double-clicking it.

Visit this book's Web site, www.dummies.com/go/peachtreefd, for more information on Peachtree.

Chapter 18

Keeping Your House Safe

● ●

In This Chapter

▶ Backing up and restoring data

▶ Setting up user security

▶ Using the audit trail

● ●

*L*ike with any financial software, a business has a lot at stake with Peachtree data. After all, it holds the financial picture of the business. In this chapter, we show you how to protect that data. You discover how to protect your data from computer failure as well as from unauthorized entry. We even show you how to play detective and snoop on what others are doing to your financial data. (However, we don't provide the detective hat, overcoat, and spyglass. Those you need to provide for yourself.)

Backing Up Your Data

Prepare yourself. We're going to nag at you here.

You know the silly (but popular) little saying, "Stuff happens." (That's not exactly how it goes, but you get the idea.) Well, it's true. Things happen. Now, we don't mean to sound pessimistic, but computers do fail, data gets deleted or corrupted, and disasters (such as fire or theft) can occur.

Well, you can always get another computer and reload Peachtree. Even millions of dollars, though, can't buy back all the work that you've put into Peachtree. That's why backing up your company data files on a regular basis is important. You can then restore your data if necessary.

Even if your network administrator backs up to a tape every day, you still should make your own Peachtree backup. This is our years of experience talking here.

By backing up company data within Peachtree, your company data files and customized forms are backed up using the Peachtree format. You can save your Peachtree backup to another hard drive; or other mediums, such as Flash drives and recordable CDs. Personally, we recommend that you use a Flash drive because they are reliable, inexpensive, fast, and very portable.

If you choose to back up your company data to a tape device, you must exit Peachtree and use the tape backup to copy the company files. To make backups to those mediums, refer to the tape instruction manual. However, we really don't recommend this method. And don't forget to look up how to restore those tape backups: The non-standardization of tape backup functioning is one of the reasons we really don't recommend this method.

Establish a regular policy for backing up your data. Backups are the only way to guarantee the safety of the accounting records that you create in Peachtree. Without backups, you run the risk of losing weeks, months, or even years of work. Do you really want to take that kind of risk?

The general rule is that if you used Peachtree that day, back it up that day. Backing up data doesn't take long, and in case of a catastrophe, you'll be glad you did. Backup media is inexpensive, especially when compared with the costs of reconstructing and reentering data.

In Table 18-1, we show you an ideal plan for backing up. That's the one that we really suggest that you use. However, we're also realistic. We show you an absolute minimum strategy for backing up in Table 18-2. If you don't follow Plan A (the ideal), follow Plan B (the minimum) at the very least. Believe us — you won't regret it. Backing up is the cheapest form of insurance that you can have.

When we refer to backup disks, they can be Flash drives, CDs, DVDs, Zip disks, floppy disks, or tapes.

Table 18-1	Plan A: An Ideal Backup Strategy
Number of Disks	*Backup Plan*
10 disks	Back up onto a different disk each day (Monday through Friday) for two weeks, and then begin again with the same set of disks.
12 monthly disks	At the end of each month, back up to one of these disks. Keep the monthly disk sets off site.

Label each disk with the day of the week. If a backup uses more than one disk, be sure to number the disks so that you know which disk is Disk 1 of the backup.

Table 18-2	Plan B: The Minimum Backup Strategy
Number of Disks	*Backup Plan*
5 daily disks	Use one disk for each day of the week and then start reusing them again the following Monday.
2 monthly disks	At the end of each month, back up to one of these disks. Again, alternate them. For example, use one disk in January, and then use the second disk in February. Reuse the January disk in March. Keep the monthly disk sets off site.

To back up your Peachtree data and customized forms, use the following procedure:

1. **Choose File⇨Back Up or press Ctrl+B to display the Back Up Company dialog box.**

   No other users can work in Peachtree during the backup process.

   Select the Reminder check box if you want Peachtree to prompt you to back up in a specified number of days. When the specified number of days elapses, Peachtree displays a reminder message when you close the company or exit the program.

   In a moment, Peachtree suggests a name for the backup file. First, though, Peachtree wants to know whether it should include the company name as part of the backup filename. We recommend that you *do* include it, especially if you have multiple companies. That way, you won't confuse the backups of one company with another. If you do want to include the company name as part of the backup, select the Include Company Name in the Backup File Name check box.

   Peachtree can also back up your archived data if any is available. Find out more about archiving data in Chapter 17.

Back Up

2. **Click the Back Up button (as shown here) to display the Save Backup As dialog box.**

3. **In the File Name text box, type a filename for the backup set or leave the one Peachtree suggests.**

   Peachtree backup files use the `*.ptb` (for *Peachtree backup* — clever, huh?) file extension. Peachtree automatically adds the current date to the backup filename. If you elect to not include the company name as part of the backup filename, Peachtree includes the letters *BU* as part of the filename. (In case you're wondering, BU stands for *backup* — also clever.)

4. **From the Save In list box, choose a location for the backup set.**

   We recommend backing up to a Flash drive or CD drive, a Zip disk, floppy disks, or a different computer.

For data protection, don't back up the Peachtree data to the same hard drive where the current data resides. If the hard drive crashes, you'll lose both your original company data and your backup, and that won't do you one bit of good.

5. Click the Save button.

Peachtree displays the estimated size in megabytes (MB) of your backup. Or, if you're backing up to a floppy disk, Peachtree displays the estimated number of floppy disks needed for the backup.

6. Click OK.

Depending on the medium you're using for backup, Peachtree might prompt you to insert the first disk.

7. Click OK.

The system displays the backup progress.

Depending on the quantity of data, the speed of your computer, and the backup device that you use (floppy drives back up more slowly than any other kind of device), the backup process might take several minutes to complete. Don't interrupt the process. Interrupting the backup process could corrupt the data — and then you'd have a useless backup.

If you're backing up to a Flash drive, CD, or Zip disk, the disk might become too full at some point to hold another backup, so you'll want to erase the oldest backup file. Refer to your Windows documentation for directions on deleting files.

If you're backing up to floppy disks, you probably need to erase those disks before you use them again. Refer to your Windows documentation for procedures on erasing floppy disks.

If you have a server making automated backups for you, be sure that you don't make incremental backups of Peachtree data. You cannot back up individual files because each file relates to another. You must back up the entire Peachtree company data. In fact, we suggest that you let the server back up everything and that you back up Peachtree independently by using the steps that we provide. This approach is safer, and we're all about safety, especially when it's Peachtree data we're discussing.

Restoring Information

We sincerely hope that you never ever have to restore your data. If you do, it probably means that something really bad happened, and we just don't want those kinds of incidents to materialize.

But if something does happen, you'll be so glad that you read this chapter and found out how to back up and restore your data.

If you back up company data by using an alternate utility (for example, a tape program), you must use that program to restore your company data.

No other users can use Peachtree during the restore process. Use the following steps to restore your data:

1. **Open the company that you want to restore.**

   Any data that you entered after making the backup isn't part of the backup — and, thus, is lost.

2. **Choose File⇨Restore to launch the Restore Wizard.**

   Peachtree displays the Select Backup File window, as shown in Figure 18-1.

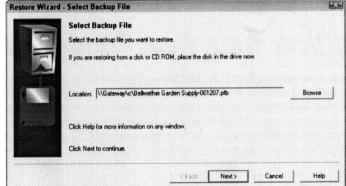

Figure 18-1: Select the file you want to restore.

If the file that you want to restore doesn't appear, click the Browse button (as shown here) and then locate and click the name of the backup file that you want to restore. Peachtree backup files use the `*.ptb` file extension.

Many compression programs, such as WinZip, can open and extract PTB files.

3. **Click Next.**

   The Select Company screen appears. You can restore the backup file on top of the currently open company data, or you can restore it to a new separate company folder.

4. **Select the option that you want and then click Next.**

   What data gets restored? When you restore data, you're restoring *all* the information that was previously backed up: all the Receivable, Payroll,

Payable, Inventory, and Job Cost information together. *Everything.* The process replaces all the current data files with those that have been previously backed up. You cannot restore individual files because each file relates to another. However, you can restore your customized forms, such as invoices or checks, separately from your data.

5. **Click the options that you want restored and then click Next.**

   A confirmation screen appears.

6. **Click Finish.**

   Peachtree displays the progress of the restoring data files. Peachtree might prompt you to insert disks as needed.

Depending on the quantity of data, the speed of your computer, and the backup device that you use, the restoration process could take several minutes to complete. Don't interrupt the process. Interrupting the restoration process could corrupt the data.

Securing Your Data from Prying Eyes

Because accounting data is highly sensitive and confidential, you might want to prevent unauthorized persons from accessing your data. Peachtree includes a security system that allows you to set accessibility parameters for each user that you identify. Peachtree security makes use of user IDs and passwords and uses what Peachtree calls a Named User philosophy. Named users are those who have assigned privileges to access the Peachtree data.

Setting up users

Peachtree can allow tailored access for different individuals. With the security feature activated, Peachtree requires each user to enter his or her user name and password before opening and working with company data. With the correct user name and password, users can access the areas of the program to which they have rights.

All Peachtree versions support setting up multiple users. However, unless you purchase a multi-user Peachtree version, only one user at a time can access Peachtree. Multiple user versions are available in Peachtree Complete and higher.

The multi-user versions of Peachtree Complete and all the Peachtree Premium flavors allow five licensed users to access the data simultaneously. Peachtree Quantum allows for ten licensed users.

When you set up users, you must set up at least one user with full administrative rights. Typically, this user is a system administrator who has the access rights to all Peachtree features, including setting up and maintaining company users and their passwords.

While setting up or maintaining user accounts, no other users can use Peachtree. To set up users, follow these steps:

1. **Choose Maintain⇨User Security.**

   The User Security dialog box appears.

New User

2. **Click the New User button (as shown here).**

   The Create Administrator dialog box opens. The first user must be an administrator with full administrative rights.

3. **Enter a user name or accept the default user name Admin.**

   User names are not case sensitive and each must be unique: For example, Joe, joe, and JOE are all the same user name.

4. **In the Choose Your Password, enter your password.**

   The password can be up to 16 alphanumeric characters. Don't use a slash (/) as part of the password. Passwords are case sensitive, and two users cannot have the same password.

   Unlike passwords in many other programs, when you create the user, the Peachtree passwords *do* display on the screen. Make sure that no unwanted eyes are peeking. The passwords don't display when the user logs on to Peachtree.

Save

5. **Click the Save button (as shown here).**

   The administrative user appears in the User Security dialog box.

6. **To enter additional users, click the New User button.**

   The User Rights dialog box, as shown in Figure 18-2, appears.

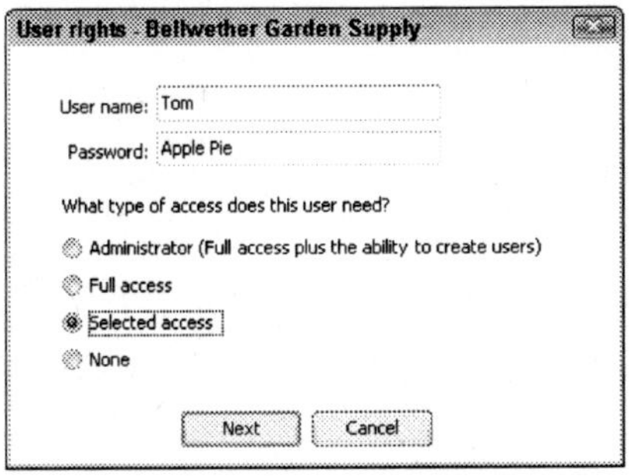

Figure 18-2:
Assign a new user name and password here.

7. **Enter the next user name and its corresponding password.**

8. **Choose an access type.**

   • *Full access* allows access to all features except user security.

     If you select Full or Administrator access, the Save button appears.

   • *Selected access* allows you to precisely define areas the user can access.

     If you enable Selected access, the Next button appears.

9. **Click Save or Next (as shown here).**

   • *If you choose Save:* The User Security dialog box reappears.

   • *If you choose Next:* The Selected Access dialog box appears.

   Continue with the next section on customizing user rights.

Customizing user rights

When setting up users, you can select an access level to each program area for an individual user. For example, if you have a clerk who mainly makes Accounts Receivable entries, you might want to restrict that clerk from accessing Accounts Payable, Payroll, or General Ledger information. Perhaps you have a person who receives inventory, but you want to restrict him or her from editing the information after it's entered or from printing Inventory Valuation reports.

By customizing the user rights, you give each user specific access. The rights vary depending on the feature. Through the Selected Access dialog box, you can choose from the following options when deciding how much access you want to allow a user:

✔ No Access at All to the Feature

✔ Only the Ability to View the Data

✔ To View and Add to the Data

✔ To View, Add to, or Edit the Data

✔ Full Rights (which allows the user to view, add, edit, or erase data)

The security that we describe here is for the Peachtree Complete and above editions. If you're using Peachtree First or Pro Accounting, your choices are limited to setting security selections for an entire module (Accounts Receivable, Accounts Payable, Payroll, and so on).

We recommend that you have only one administrative user with access to the Maintain Users window. This setup prevents multiple users from accessing other users' passwords, changing other users' security settings, or inadvertently erasing users.

You can quickly restrict access to a primary program area, such as Payroll. Along the left side of the window, select the tab for the program area you want to restrict. Then, at the top of the right side on the window, select a control level. For example, in Figure 18-3, we restrict all rights to Payroll by choosing Payroll on the left side and also choosing No Access from the Employees & Payroll Access drop-down list.

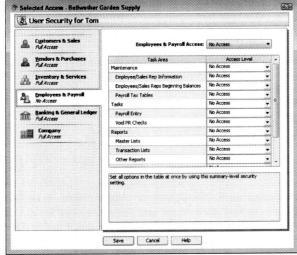

Figure 18-3:
The user named Tom can't access any feature of Payroll.

Follow these instructions to be more specific regarding user accessibility:

1. **Click the module for which you want to set restrictions.**

   Peachtree displays a list of the task areas.

2. **Scroll through the task area until you locate the feature you want restricted.**

3. **Click the Access level you want to modify.**

   The access choices vary depending on the feature. For example, if you click the Customer & Sales area and open the Access Level drop-down list for Receive Money, you find that you can select Full, No Access, Read, Add, or Edit. But if you open the Access Level drop-down list for Master Lists under the Reports program area, you can select only Full or No Access. In Figure 18-4, the user named Alex can view or add Inventory items and adjustment but cannot edit or erase them.

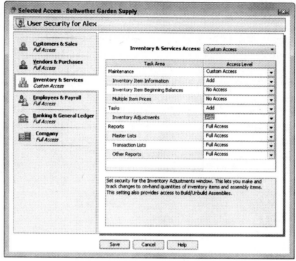

Figure 18-4:
Each user
can have
specific
access to
individual
areas of
Peachtree.

4. **Click Save.**

   The User Security dialog box reappears with a list of user names and
   their access areas.

   Select a user and click Edit User's Rights (as shown here) to modify the
   user password or access.

   To create another user with the same access rights as an existing
   user, click the current user name and then click the Copy User button
   (as shown here). Peachtree prompts you for another user name and
   password.

   You can set up as many user names as you like, but you can license only
   five users (ten if you're using Peachtree Quantum) at one time. If you
   have more users than licenses, the administrator must uncheck the
   license for one user to allow another user access. You can check and
   uncheck the license allowances as needed, but Peachtree will never
   allow you to check more than the maximum your license allows. See
   Figure 18-5.

5. **Click the Close button to close the User Security dialog box.**

   Any changes that you make take effect the next time you open the company.

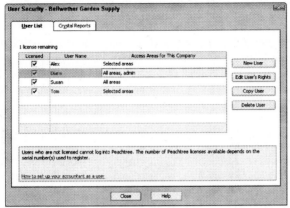

Figure 18-5:
Peachtree
multi-user
versions
have a
restricted
number of
licenses.

Removing users

By deleting users, when someone leaves or changes positions, you can stop him or her from accessing Peachtree data. If you have multiple companies, deleting a user from the current company doesn't affect his or her rights in other Peachtree companies. If you want the user completely deleted from the system, you must remove that user from each company independently.

To remove a user, choose Maintain⇨User Security to display the User Security window. Select the user record that you want to remove, and then click the Delete User button. A warning message appears. Click OK to delete the user.

If multiple users still exist and you attempt to delete the only administrative user with access to Maintain Users, Peachtree displays an error message. You cannot remove the administrative user until you remove all other user records.

Any changes that you make take effect the next time you open the company.

Logging on as a user

After user security is enabled, when you or anyone on your Peachtree network (if you're on a network, that is) tries to open your Peachtree company files, Peachtree prompts you for a user name and password.

Enter your user ID in the User Name text box, enter your password in the Password text box, and then press Enter.

Don't lose the password! If you do lose your user name or password and no one else can open the Peachtree company, you have no back-door way to access the passwords. You'll need to back up your data and send it into a Peachtree-certified consultant or to Peachtree technical support for them to locate the information.

The user ID system works like this: Say you give user Bob no access to Payroll, but user Alex does have Payroll access. No matter whose computer Bob uses — his own computer or Alex's computer — he doesn't have access to Payroll when he logs on as Bob.

To prevent unauthorized access to your data, exit the Peachtree program when you leave your computer unattended.

Using the Audit Trail Report to Track Actions

Peachtree includes an audit trail security feature that tracks when a person enters new transactions, edits existing records or transactions, or removes data. The audit trail provides accountability of users, discourages users against fraudulent activity or mistakes, and tracks transaction history. The Audit Trail report traces all activity and adjustments; from this report, you might find that transactions were completed without your knowledge.

Only the Peachtree Complete and above editions contain the audit trail feature.

The audit trail is automatic in Peachtree and cannot be disabled, except in older versions. In older versions of Peachtree, you activate or deactivate the audit trail through Maintain⇨Company Information.

The Audit Trail report displays the date and time of each Peachtree action. If you have user security enabled, you can also see who did it.

To view the Audit Trail report, choose Reports & Forms⇨Company to display the Select a Report or Form dialog box, and then double-click the Audit Trail report to display the report on-screen.

By default, this report displays only the transactions that took place on the current date, but you can click the Options button to select a different time frame. You can even specify the user ID that you want to review.

Like other Peachtree reports, you can customize the Audit Trail report. See Chapter 14 for instructions on customizing reports.

Chapter 19

Real-Life Ways to Use Peachtree

● ●

In This Chapter

▶ Dealing with customer prepayments

▶ Making a prior-year company

▶ Moving to a new computer

▶ Handling retainage

▶ Organizing employee loans, garnishments, and other odds and ends

● ●

*T*his book wouldn't be complete if we didn't provide you with solutions for some common situations. Given the limited space we have in the book to present Peachtree to you, we worked really hard to make room for these real-life situations.

Handling Customer Prepayments

Under certain conditions, your customers might pay you before you actually deliver the goods or services you promise. For example, in the building business, customers often provide down-payments that builders use to purchase construction materials. Some service providers, such as lawyers and CPAs, request retainers before performing work. If your customers pay you in advance, you're accepting money that you must account for as a liability until you deliver the promised goods or services.

Deposits and *prepayments* — interchangeable terms — are, by definition, payments received before you deliver goods or services. Your method of accounting — cash or accrual basis — has no bearing on how you handle these prepayments. Prepayments from customers are actually your liabilities. Because you receive the money before you supply the goods or services, you now have an obligation (a liability) to the customer to complete the transaction. The money that you accept in advance of providing goods and services is unearned revenue.

First, you need a G/L account in which to record customer prepayments when you receive them. To handle customer deposits, from the Maintain Chart of Accounts window, set up Customer Deposits as an Other Current Liability type account. (See Chapter 3 to review adding accounts.)

Second, set up a non-stock inventory item for deposits. Use the Customer Deposits G/L account you created for all three G/L accounts (Sales, Salary/Wages, and Cost of Sales), and be sure to select an exempt Item Tax Type. See Chapter 11 to review setting up inventory items. When you receive a prepayment from your customer, create a receipt to track the deposit by following these steps:

1. **Choose Tasks⇨Receipts to display the Receipts window.**

2. **Enter the deposit ticket ID, customer ID, receipt number, date, payment method, and Cash account just like you normally enter receipts.**

   Refer to Chapter 8 for details on entering receipts.

3. **On the Apply to Revenues tab, enter a quantity of 1.**

4. **In the Item drop-down list, select Deposits.**

5. **Enter the amount of the deposit.**

6. **Click Save (as shown here) to save the transaction.**

This transaction debits Cash and credits Customer Deposits. The balance sheet shows the Customer Deposits account as well as the Cash account increased by the amount of the prepayment.

After you perform the work, you want to send your customer an invoice. Add a final line item on the invoice showing a quantity of –1 by using the Deposits item for the amount of the prepayment (see Figure 19-1). On the line showing the deposit, be sure to enter a negative number (–1) for the quantity but use a positive number for the unit price amount. Peachtree automatically converts the total amount to a negative number.

If the amount of the invoice you create equals the amount of the prepayment, the customer owes you nothing. If the invoice amount exceeds the prepayment amount, the customer owes you the difference between the invoice amount and the prepayment amount.

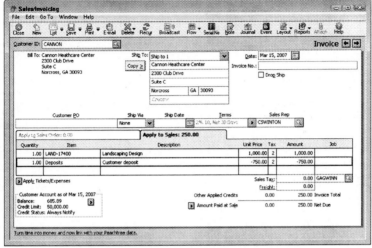

Figure 19-1:
The deposit
reduces the
amount
owed
against the
invoice.

Creating a Prior-Year Company

When you close and purge a fiscal year, the transactions and reports are no longer accessible. Before you close your year, you should archive your company data if you're using Peachtree Premium or higher. If you're using any other edition of Peachtree, you can create a prior-year company so that you can print reports, look for transactions, and so on. The big picture? You create a backup of your existing company; create a new, empty company; and then restore the backup into the new, empty company.

To find out how to close and purge a fiscal year, turn to Chapter 17.

Follow these steps before you close the fiscal year.

1. **Open your company in Peachtree.**

2. **Choose File⇨Back Up, select backup options, and then click Back Up.**

   See Chapter 18 for details on backup options.

   The Save Backup For dialog box appears.

3. **In the File Name text box, leave your company name but replace today's date with the last open fiscal year (so that you can easily identify the data in the backup).**

4. **Use the Save In drop-down list to select the folder on your C: drive where you store your Peachtree company data.**

   If you work in a network, save the backup to the My Documents folder on your C: drive.

5. **Click Save to back up.**

When the backup is complete, you need to restore it and simultaneously create a new company.

The following technique works with Peachtree 2004 or later. If you have an older version of Peachtree, you need to create a new, empty company before you restore; then restore the backup into that company.

Follow these steps:

1. **Choose File⇨Restore to start the Restore Wizard.**

2. **On the Select Backup File screen, click Browse and navigate to the location where you stored the backup.**

3. **Select the backup file and click Open.**

4. **Click Next to display the Select Company screen.**

5. **Click the A New Company option button and then click Next.**

6. **On the Restore Options screen, select all appropriate check boxes and then click Next.**

   Peachtree automatically selects the Company Data check box; if you have Customized Forms or Web Transactions, select those check boxes as well.

7. **On the Confirmation screen that appears, click Finish.**

   Peachtree creates a new company for you and restores the backup into it.

8. **When Peachtree finishes the process, choose Maintain⇨Company Information and change the name of the new company.**

   Use an obvious name, such as FY*XXXX* Company Data, where *XXXX* is the last open fiscal year in the company. This step makes the second copy of your company appear as a separate name in the Open Company window.

You can now open your regular current company by choosing File⇨Open Company. When you need to refer to the prior-year company, you can find it in the Open dialog box.

Handling Retainage

Suppose that you receive partial payment at the beginning of a job and the balance when the job is completed. If you work this way, you have *retainage,* and you need to know how to correctly bill customers and track both billed and unbilled amounts owed to you.

You need only one extra account on your balance sheet — an Other Current Assets account, called Retainage Receivable. See Chapter 3 to review adding accounts.

Suppose that the terms of your contract specify that you will earn $10,000 and get paid 90 percent at the beginning of the job, with 10 percent ($1,000) held as retainage. You need to prepare an invoice for $9,000 and account for the $1,000 retained by the customer:

1. **Choose Tasks⇨Sales/Invoicing to display the Sales/Invoicing window and select the customer for whom you need to prepare the invoice.**

2. **In the line item section of the invoice, create two lines.**

3. **Fill in the total sale amount ($10,000 in our example) and post the line against an income account.**

4. **On the second line, post the retainage amount as a negative number to the Retainage Receivable account and then save the invoice.**

This transaction credits an Income account for $10,000, recognizing the revenue you will generate from the contract. It also debits Accounts Receivable for $9,000 (the amount the customer owes immediately) as well as Retainage Receivable for $1,000 (the amount the customer will pay when the job is completed).

When the customer pays you for the original invoice — $9,000, in this example — record the receipt in the same way that you'd record any receipt in the Receipts window. When you finish the job, you need to bill the customer for the final amount — the retainage amount of $1,000 in this example. Record an invoice, posting the line item for the retainage amount as a positive number against the Retainage Receivable account. As a result of this invoice, Peachtree debits the Accounts Receivable account and credits the Retainage Receivable account, reducing the amount of retainage the customer owes but increasing the customer's regular Accounts Receivable balance.

TIP

To use the following method to track retainage balances, we suggest that you use an invoice number for the retainage bill that is the same as the original invoice number, followed by an *R*.

When the customer pays this bill, record the receipt the same way you would record any receipt in the Receipts window.

To help you identify clients who have unbilled retainage amounts, we suggest that you take advantage of the Peachtree Account Reconciliation feature. (See Chapter 16 for details on account reconciliation.) You can use the Account Reconciliation feature to reconcile *any* account, not just bank accounts:

1. **Choose Tasks⇨Account Reconciliation to display the Account Reconciliation window.**

2. **Select the Retainage Receivable account as the account to reconcile.**

   Note that some amounts appear in both the Deposit/Bank Credit and Check/Bank Debit columns of the window and the Payee for those amounts is identical. The entry in the Check/Bank Debit column occurs when you prepare the original invoice that held back the retainage amount. The entry in the Deposit/Bank Credit column occurs when you bill the retainage.

3. **When you see a pair of like entries in both the Deposit/Bank Credit column and the Check/Bank Debit column, select their respective check boxes in the Status column (shown in Figure 19-2) because they represent billed retainage amounts.**

   You don't need to enter the Statement Ending Balance because you don't have a statement. The Unreconciled Difference should always be zero because you're checking off matching entries in the Account Reconciliation window.

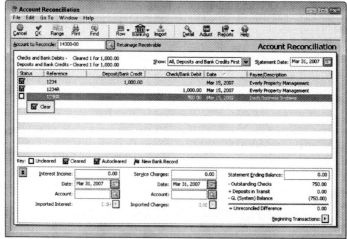

Figure 19-2: Match entries by retainage amounts to help identify billed retainage.

4. **When you finish marking off matched pairs, click OK (as shown here).**

Use the Account Reconciliation Other Outstanding Items report to identify the clients and retainage amounts you didn't mark off in Account Reconciliation. These are the amounts that you have not yet billed. Choose Reports & Forms⇨Account Reconciliation and highlight the Other Outstanding Items report. On the Filter tab, choose the Retainage Receivable account. When you print the report, you'll see only retainage amounts that you haven't yet billed.

Paying for Purchase Orders by Credit Card

Here's the situation: You ordered goods via a purchase order and, at the time that you placed the order, you hadn't made a decision about how you wanted to pay for the goods. The goods arrive, and you now decide that you want to pay for them with a credit card. You need to make sure that you account for everything properly in Peachtree.

We assume that you have a Credit Card Payable account — an Other Current Liabilities account — on your Chart of Accounts so that you can record credit card purchases in Peachtree. If you don't have a Credit Card Payable account — yours might be called Visa Payable or American Express Payable — set one up from the Maintain Chart of Accounts window.

The process starts when you decide to buy a product and you issue a purchase order. You create the purchase order the same way that you create any purchase order. Some time passes, and the goods you ordered arrive. You need to receive the goods into inventory and establish that you owe the vendor money. Enter a purchase against the purchase order in the same way that you enter a purchase against any purchase order.

So far, you haven't done anything unusual. When you pay for the goods using a credit card, though, you need to make some changes from your usual procedures. Follow these steps:

1. **Choose Tasks⇨Payments to display the Payments window.**

2. **Select the vendor.**

3. **Find the appropriate purchase to pay and click in the Pay column.**

4. **Click the lookup list button (as shown here) to change the Cash Account from your checking account to the Credit Card Payable account (see Figure 19-3).**

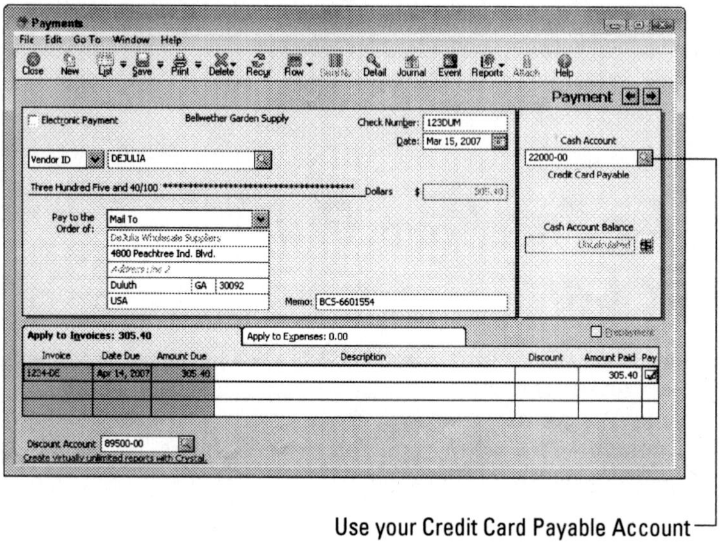

Figure 19-3:
Apply the
payment
to the
purchase
and select
your Credit
Card
Payable
account.

Use your Credit Card Payable Account

5. **Enter a dummy check number and then click Save to save the transaction.**

Don't forget to change your Cash account back to your regular checking account. Peachtree remembers the last account you selected until you change it.

When the credit card bill arrives, you need to make sure that you post the items on it correctly in the Purchases/Receive Inventory window. Typically, you post each line item to its appropriate expense account. But for goods you ordered on a purchase order and paid for using a credit card, you need to assign the purchase order charge on the credit card bill to the Credit Card Payable account (see Figure 19-4).

When you're ready to pay the credit card bill, use the Payments window or the Select for Payment window. Make sure that you use your regular Cash account when you print the check to pay this bill.

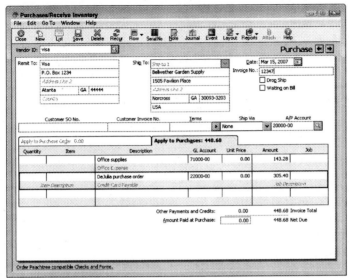

Figure 19-4:
Assign card
transactions
for
purchase
order goods
to the Credit
Card
Payable
account.

For those of you who care, we'll explain the debits and credits posted to the General Ledger with these transactions. If you don't care, you can quit reading here:

- ✔ Entering the purchase order had no effect on the General Ledger; no purchase order affects the General Ledger. When we entered the purchase to receive the goods into inventory and post a payable for the vendor, we debited Inventory or Expense accounts and credited Accounts Payable.

- ✔ When we paid the vendor's bill, we debited Accounts Payable (reducing our debt to the vendor and washing out the Accounts Payable account) and credited the Credit Card Payable account (increasing the credit card liability).

- ✔ When we recorded the line on the bill from the credit card company for the goods purchased using the purchase order, we debited the Credit Card Payable account (washing out the Credit Card Payable account) and credited Accounts Payable (increasing our debt to the credit card vendor).

- ✔ Finally, when we paid the credit card bill, we debited Accounts Payable (reducing Accounts Payable and washing out the balance owed to the credit card vendor for the credit card bill), and we credited Cash (reducing the balance in our checking account).

For you visual people, Table 19-1 summarizes the debits and credits.

Table 19-1	Debits and Credits for Paying Purchase Orders by Credit Card	
Action	*Debit*	*Credit*
Recording the purchase for goods on the purchase order	Expense	A/P
Paying the vendor's bill by credit card	A/P	Credit Card Payable
Recording the credit card bill for the goods purchased on the purchase order	Credit Card Payable	A/P
Paying the credit card bill	A/P	Cash

Real-Life Payroll Situations

Of the dozens of real-life payroll situations, we picked the ones we figure occur most frequently and therefore would be of the most use to you. In the sections that follow, we show you how to set up some common payroll deductions and taxes.

Payroll deductions, in general

For all payroll deductions, you need at least two elements: the payroll field for the deduction and a General Ledger account that you tie to the field. Because you assign a General Ledger account to a payroll deduction, we usually suggest that you first set up the General Ledger account and then set up the deduction.

In many cases, you also need a third element: a user-maintained payroll tax table to calculate the amount of the deduction. And you assign a payroll tax table to a deduction. So, when a deduction requires a payroll tax table, we suggest that you first set up the General Ledger account, then set up the user-maintained payroll tax table, and finally set up the deduction.

"But what does a payroll tax table have to do with a deduction?" you ask. Well, Peachtree uses payroll tax tables to calculate more than just federal, state, or local taxes due. The name *payroll tax table* is somewhat of a misnomer because these tax tables store calculations that you need for payroll, even if the calculation is not for a tax. You can set up payroll tax tables to calculate 401(k) deductions, health insurance deductions, union dues deductions, vacation, and sick leave. You can see where we're going with this concept.

Finally, you also need to define the elements of Adjusted Gross Income so that Peachtree can calculate payroll deductions or additions. In the upcoming section, "Health insurance," you can see examples of deductions that affect the calculation of adjusted gross wages. Read the sidebar, "Calculating Adjusted Gross," for more information about adjusted gross wages.

Peachtree simplifies the process of tracking employee vacation and sick leave if you use the Payroll Setup Wizard — and we highly recommend this approach. It's very straightforward and self explanatory. Good wizard. Similarly, Peachtree simplifies setting up a 401(k) plan using the Payroll Setup Wizard, and we like the Payroll Setup Wizard for this deduction, too. In the upcoming section, "Adding a 401(k) plan to an existing company," we show you a modification you can make *after* you let the wizard set up your 401(k) deduction that will simplify the other steps needed to finish setting up the 401(k) plan in Peachtree.

Employee loans

Suppose that you loan money to an employee. You can set up a payroll deduction so that the employee can repay the loan from his or her paycheck. And, depending on the repayment amounts, you can either manually enter the repayment amount on each paycheck, or Peachtree can automatically deduct a fixed amount from each paycheck until the loan is repaid.

The General Ledger

You need two elements for a payroll deduction for an employee loan: the General Ledger account and the deduction. To track a loan, set up an Other Current Assets account on your Chart of Accounts and then call the account something like Employee Loans or Employee Advances.

If you intend to loan money to more than one employee, we suggest that you use Peachtree's masking feature (if you're using Peachtree Premium or higher, use the segmenting feature) and set up individual accounts for each loan that would roll up into the Employee Advances account. For example, if you created 14100 for your Employee Advances account, the account number for a loan to Dorothy Beckstrom might be 14100-01, and the account number for a loan to Elliot Adams might be 14100-02. See Chapters 3 and 15 for information on masking.

Writing a loan check

When you write the check for the employee's loan, use the Payments window. You don't need to set up the employee as a vendor; simply type the employee's name in the Pay to The Order Of box. On the Apply to Expenses tab of the Payments window, fill in the employee's loan account as the G/L account.

The payroll field

You need to use the manual repayment method if the repayment amounts differ from paycheck to paycheck.

Set up a payroll deduction for the loan by following these steps:

1. **Choose Maintain⇨Default Information⇨Employees.**

2. **Click the EmployEE Fields tab and scroll to the bottom.**

3. **In the Field Name column, add a field called Loan (see Figure 19-5).**

   The name must not contain spaces. Use the underscore (_) character if you need space between words. The name you use will appear on the paycheck stub.

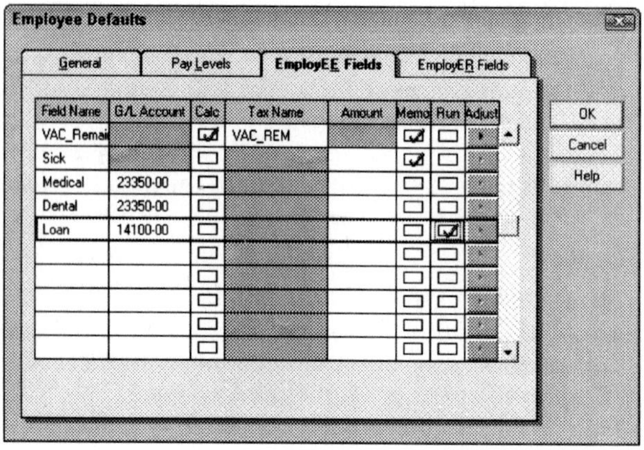

Figure 19-5:
Setting up a payroll field.

4. **In the G/L Account list, select the main account you set up for employee loans.**

   In our example, we selected 14100-00.

5. **Place a check mark in the Run column.**

   Peachtree will now maintain a running total for the deduction even after you close the payroll year.

6. **Click OK.**

Next, use these steps to assign the loan payroll field to the employee to whom you are making the loan:

1. **Choose Maintain⇨Employees/Sales Reps.**

2. **Select the employee to whom you are making the loan.**

3. **Click the Employee Fields tab and remove the check mark from the Use Defaults column (see Figure 19-6).**

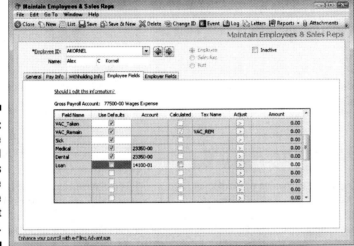

Figure 19-6: Override the standard defaults for the employee taking out the loan.

4. **Change the G/L account to the account for the employee.**

5. **Click Save (as shown here).**

Repaying the loan

When you create a paycheck for the employee, fill in the repayment amount on the paycheck as a negative number. To track the amount the employee has repaid, customize the Yearly Earnings report. On the Fields tab, show only the payroll field for the loan and the Amount field. On the Filter tab, select the Show Totals Only check box.

TIP

If you can divide the loan amount into equal installment payments, you can let Peachtree automatically record the loan payment on the employee's paycheck. Set up the General Ledger account and the deduction as we describe. However, when you edit the employee's record in the Maintain Employees/Sales Reps window, also fill in the loan repayment amount as a negative number in the Amount column on the Employee Fields tab.

Garnishments

Occasionally, you need to hold back money from an employee's check as a legal garnishment. Garnishments are another form of payroll deduction similar to employee advances; however, garnishments typically use all three elements of the payroll deduction. For the General Ledger account, use an Other Current Liabilities account in the case of a garnishment instead of the Other Current Assets account you set up for an employee loan. You also need to set up the payroll deduction that you'll probably name *Garnishment,* and you'll probably use a payroll tax table to calculate the garnishment amount. In the upcoming sections, "Health insurance" and "Union dues," you see some examples of setting up payroll tax tables.

Different states have different requirements for garnishments; the garnishment might be a percentage of adjusted gross pay or a percentage of net pay. Check with your accountant to determine the correct way to calculate the garnishment.

Health insurance

For health insurance deductions, you need two elements: the General Ledger account and the payroll deduction. However, health insurance deductions come in two basic types: after-tax deductions (non-qualified plans) and before-tax deductions (qualified plans, such as cafeteria plans). And for cafeteria plans, you need to take an extra step and include the field when Peachtree calculates the adjusted gross amount it uses for taxes.

As the employer, you must pay the amount you deduct for health insurance to the insurance company that supplies the plan. Therefore, the amount is a liability to you, and you need to set up an Other Current Liabilities account in your Chart of Accounts.

You set up the health insurance deduction in the same way that you set up the deduction for an employee loan. In the Employee Defaults dialog box, on the EmployEE Fields tab, type a name (no spaces allowed) for the health insurance deduction. Remember that the name you type will appear on the paycheck stub. Supply the liability account for health insurance.

You handle this next part in the same way you handle employee loans, as we describe in the preceding section. If you deduct the same amount for most employees, enter the amount in the Amount column on the EmployEE Fields tab of the Employee Defaults dialog box as a negative number. To supply amounts for employees who don't pay the standard amount or who don't pay anything, open the Maintain Employees/Sales Reps window and select the employee. Click the EmployEE Fields tab and remove the check mark from the

STD column for the health insurance deduction. Then supply the appropriate amount as a negative number in the Amount column (refer to Figure 19-6).

A new payroll field can affect the calculation of existing payroll fields. Whenever you add a tax-sheltered deduction or an addition that is taxable, you need to click the Adjust button for *other payroll fields* that are affected by the new field — not the field you are setting up. For example, tax-sheltered deductions — such as a health insurance deduction for a cafeteria plan — are typically deducted from gross pay before calculating taxes. So you need to click the Adjust button next to Federal Income Tax, Social Security, Medicare, and any state and local taxes. In the Calculate Adjusted Gross dialog box, shown in Figure 19-7, you select the Use check box next to the health insurance deduction. Then Peachtree will subtract the health insurance deduction from gross pay before calculating taxes. If you're not sure whether a deduction is taxable, check with the plan administrator.

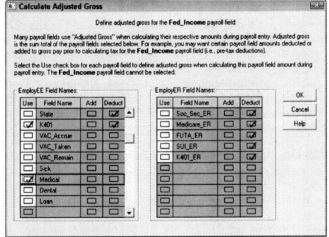

Figure 19-7:
Selecting the payroll elements Peachtree should include when calculating adjusted gross income.

Union dues

Deducting union dues from an employee's paycheck can be tricky simply because so many different ways exist to calculate union dues. In this section, we examine how to set up payroll to calculate and deduct union dues, and examine four different ways of calculating the amount:

✔ Deducting a flat amount per month

✔ Deducting a number of hours of pay per month

✔ Using an hourly rate based on hours worked

✔ Using a percentage of gross pay

Calculating Adjusted Gross

You'll find ADJUSTED_GROSS in the formulas of many payroll tax tables. When you use one of these payroll tax tables, you need to identify the fields that Peachtree should include when calculating ADJUSTED_GROSS to make Peachtree actually calculate something. You identify these fields by clicking the Adjust button next to the new field you're adding and then selecting the Use check box next to the fields that Peachtree should add or subtract when calculating ADJUSTED_GROSS for the new field. As a rule, whenever you create a payroll field for which you don't supply an amount in the Amount column, you should always click the Adjust button for the new field and select the Use check box for the Gross field. The Gross field is the first field in the left column — you can't see it in Figure 19-7. A formula that includes ADJUSTED_GROSS in its calculation makes Peachtree calculate something; if the formula doesn't include ADJUSTED_GROSS, you won't hurt anything.

If you must deduct a flat amount per month, regardless of the number of hours the employee works, you need only the first two elements of a payroll deduction; you don't need to set up a payroll tax table. Skip the following section and complete the following two sections, in which you set up the liability account and the payroll deduction. Then, for each employee, calculate the total amount due for the year and divide that number by the number of pay periods in the year. When you set up the deduction for each employee in the Maintain Employees/Sales Reps window, supply that number.

To calculate union dues in any of the other three ways listed above, you need all three elements of the payroll deduction: the General Ledger account, the payroll field, and the payroll tax table to calculate the union dues amount.

As an employer, you handle union dues deductions in the same way you handle federal income tax deductions — you collect the money due from the employee and turn it over to the proper authority. So, to track the union dues collected that must be paid to the union, you need an Other Current Liabilities account on your Chart of Accounts. See Chapter 3 for help creating the account.

Setting up a payroll tax table

For most union dues calculations, we think you'll find it easiest to use payroll tax tables to calculate the amount to deduct from an employee's paycheck. Follow these steps:

1. **Choose File⇨Payroll Tax Tables⇨User-Maintained.**

   Peachtree displays the User-Maintained Payroll Tax Tables window (see Figure 19-8).

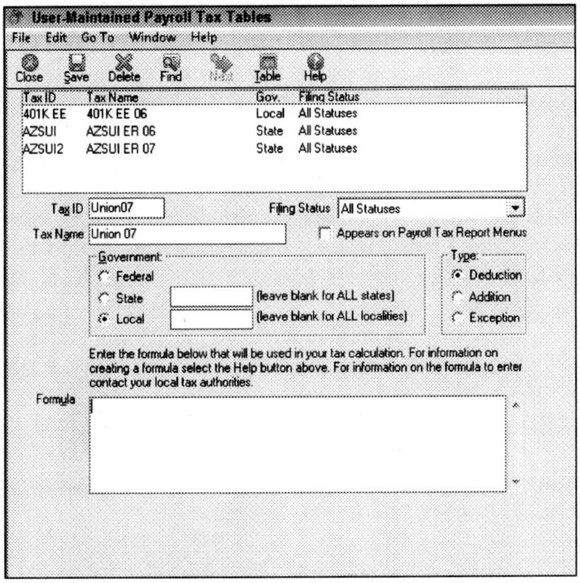

Figure 19-8:
Store
calculations
you use in
payroll that
are specific
to your
company.

2. **Type an ID for the tax table.**

   Use something like Union that helps you easily identify the purpose of the tax table.

3. **In the Tax Name text box, type a name and add to the end of the name a space and the last two digits of the year for which the tax table will be applicable.**

   For the Tax name, we typically use the same name as we type in the Tax ID text box and append the year information to it.

4. **Even though the Government section has nothing to do with union dues (no jokes, please), select the State or the Local option button there.**

5. **Enter the appropriate formula for the calculation you want Peachtree to make (see the next section).**

6. **Click the Save button to save the tax table.**

Figuring out what goes in the Formula field

The information in the Formula field will change, depending on how you need to calculate union dues. Many of the formulas that we show you use EMP_ SPECIAL1_NUMBER or EMP_SPECIAL2_NUMBER. Peachtree provides these two fields as variables that you can set for individual employees as needed. To set the values for these variables, open the Maintain Employees/Sales Reps window, select the employee, and click the Withholding Info tab. As needed, supply values in the Additional Withholding column for Special 1 and Special 2. If you're supplying a percentage, make sure you type the percentage as a percentage. For example, if the percentage is 2.65%, type **2.65**; don't use .0265, which is the rate, not the percentage.

If the formula you use requires different rates for each employee, the formula will reference EMP_SPECIAL1_NUMBER or EMP_SPECIAL2_NUMBER, and you'll need to enter each employee's rate in the employee's record. However, if the formula calls for the same rate for each employee, you should substitute that rate in the formula as a value instead of using EMP_SPECIAL1_NUMBER or EMP_SPECIAL2_NUMBER.

In the formulas that follow, we use EMP_SPECIAL1_NUMBER. If you're already using EMP_SPECIAL1_NUMBER for another purpose, substitute EMP_SPECIAL2_NUMBER.

To calculate union dues as a percentage of adjusted gross pay, use the following formula for both salaried and hourly employees:

```
ANSWER = -ADJUSTED_GROSS*EMP_SPECIAL1_NUMBER/100
```

If you need to calculate union dues based on a number of hours worked, use the following formula for hourly employees, where REGULAR, OVERTIME, and SPECIAL are the pay levels you set up in your company:

```
ANSWER = -(REGULAR+OVERTIME+SPECIAL)*EMP_SPECIAL1_NUMBER
```

If you pay your employees a salary instead of an hourly wage and need to calculate union dues based on a number of hours worked, use the following formula, where pay periods are biweekly and consist of 80 hours. If you pay some employees weekly, some biweekly, and some semimonthly, you'll need separate tax tables, one for each pay frequency. In the weekly tax table, change 80 to 40; in the semimonthly table, change 80 to 88.

```
ANSWER = -80*EMP_SPECIAL1_NUMBER/100
```

If all employees pay the same percentage, you can substitute that percentage for EMP_SPECIAL1_NUMBER/100 in the formula.

Suppose that you must deduct an amount equal to two hours of pay per month for an hourly employee. In the following formula, you enter the annualized amount you need to deduct in the Additional Withholding column of the Special 1 field on the Withholding Info tab in the Maintain Employees/Sales Reps window. Peachtree then prorates the annualized amount so that the correct amount is deducted from an employee's paycheck based on the frequency you pay. For example, if an employee earns $10 per hour, union dues would be $20 for the month or $240 for the year — and that's the number you enter in the Additional Withholding column of the Special 1 field. If you pay your employees weekly, you'd want to deduct $4.62 per paycheck. Using the

PRORATE function tells Peachtree to divide the annualized amount ($240 in our example) by the number of pay periods in the year (52 in our example) to determine the amount to deduct per pay period.

```
ANSWER = -PRORATE(EMP_SPECIAL1_NUMBER)
```

If you must deduct a flat amount based on the number of hours worked — say, 5 cents per hour — use the following formula:

```
ANSWER = -(REGULAR+OVERTIME+SPECIAL) * .05
```

REGULAR, OVERTIME, and SPECIAL are the pay levels you set up in your company.

Creating the payroll deduction for union dues

You create the payroll deduction for union dues on the EmployEE Fields tab of the Employee Defaults dialog box, using the same steps that you used to create the deduction for health insurance. Remember that the name you type appears on paycheck stubs and cannot contain spaces. Supply the liability account for union dues; and, if you created a payroll tax table to calculate union dues, place a check mark in the Calc column. The Tax Name column will then become available, and you can select the payroll tax table that you created. Remember that we called it Union. Last, be sure to click the Adjust button and select the elements of pay that Peachtree should include in ADJUSTED_GROSS when calculating union dues. At a minimum, select the Use box next to Gross.

If you didn't create a payroll tax table to calculate the union dues deduction, supply the liability account for union dues when you create the field, but don't place a check mark in the Calc column. If most employees pay the same amount for union dues, type that amount as a negative number in the Amount column, remembering to supply the amount *per pay period.* Peachtree will assign the amount you type in the Maintain Employee Defaults dialog box to *all* employees. For an employee who doesn't pay the standard amount, select the employee in the Maintain Employees/Sales Rep window and click the Employee Fields tab. Then remove the check mark from the Use Defaults column, and type the amount per pay period that you want to deduct as a negative number in the Amount column.

Showing employer contributions on paycheck stubs

Suppose that you want to display the employer's contribution on the employee's paycheck stub. No problem. In fact, although we use union dues as the example, you can display *any* employer contribution to *any* program on the employee's paycheck stub.

By default, the paycheck stub shows only the information that appears on the EmployEE tab of the Employee Defaults dialog box. But employer's contributions appear on the EmployER tab of the Employee Defaults dialog box. To make an employer contribution appear on the paycheck stub, you create a field on the EmployEE tab. To avoid affecting the employee's paycheck, make the field a memo field.

Remember that you use the memo field *in addition to* (not instead of) the EmployER field.

Employer contributions to benefit plans are handled as liabilities on the balance sheet. As such, to calculate correctly, the formula you use usually generates a negative number. If you don't mind showing the contribution as a negative value on the employee's paycheck stub, you can use the same formula for the memo field as you use for the employer's contribution. However, you might prefer to show the contribution as a positive number on check stubs so that employees don't mistakenly think you deducted the money from their paychecks. In this case, create another formula that looks just like the employer contribution formula. However, make sure that you do the following:

- ✔ Remove the negative sign from the portion of the formula that calculates the deduction.
- ✔ Set up the formula type as an Exception rather than a Deduction.

Click the Adjust button for the new memo field and make sure that you include the same fields when calculating the memo field that you included when calculating the actual employer contribution.

Adding a 401 (k) plan to an existing company

Suppose that you've been using payroll for a while and your company decides to implement a 401(k) plan. We're not going to walk you through setting up a 401(k) plan; you have the Payroll Wizard to help you do that.

The Payroll Wizard assumes that you want to assign contribution percentages individually to each employee in the Maintain Employees/Sales Reps window. If your employees' contribution rates vary greatly, you don't have much choice. Choose Maintain⇨Employees/Sales Reps and select an employee who participates in the plan. On the Withholding tab, supply the employee's contribution percentage in the 401k% field.

However, if most of your employees contribute the same percentage, you can save yourself some work (and time). Simply change the 401K EE tax table that

Peachtree creates to calculate the 401(k) contribution using the percentage that most employees contribute. That way, you need to set up specific percentages only for those employees who contribute the different rate. Let Peachtree use a default rate that matches the rate contributed by most employees. Follow these steps to modify the 401K EE tax table:

1. **Choose File⇨Payroll Tax Tables⇨User-Maintained.**

2. **Highlight the 401K EE tax table to see its formula (see Figure 19-9).**

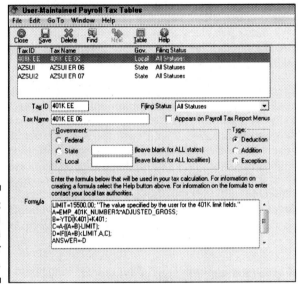

Figure 19-9:
The formula
Peachtree
creates for
a 401K field.

3. **In the Formula field, add the following three lines, placing them at the top of the tax table or immediately below the first line of the tax table that specifies the limit (the line that begins with LIMIT=):**

Be sure you *don't* type anything while the formula is highlighted.

To add lines below the first line, place the insertion point at the end of the first line and press Ctrl+J to start a new blank line. Make sure you include a semicolon at the end of each line you add.

```
E=2%;
F=EMP_401K_NUMBER%;
G=If (F=(0),E,F);
```

In the first line, type the fixed percentage used by most employees. In our example, we made the percentage 2%.

4. **Edit the line that contains the information for the A variable and replace `EMP_401K_NUMBER%` with G. After you edit the line, it should look like this:**

```
A=G*ADJUSTED_GROSS;
```

5. **Click Save.**

Next, edit *only* the records of employees who don't use the standard rate (2% in our example) and employees who don't participate in the 401(k) plan. For the employees who *don't* use the standard rate, choose Maintain⇨Employees /Sales Reps. On the Withholding tab, supply the correct rate in the Additional Withholding column of the 401k% field. For the employees who don't participate in the 401(k) plan, open the same window and click the Employee Fields tab. Then remove the check mark from the Use Defaults column and the Calculated column next to the K401 payroll field.

The modifications to the 401K EE payroll tax table that we suggest change the way Peachtree calculates the 401(k) contribution. Using our modifications, Peachtree first checks the Employee Fields tab to determine whether an employee participates in the plan. If so, Peachtree then checks the rate in the 401k% field on the Withholding Info tab of the Maintain Employees/Sales Reps window. If an employee's rate is 0, Peachtree uses the default rate specified in the formula stored in the 401K EE payroll tax table (in our example, 2%) to calculate the employee's 401(k) contribution. On the other hand, if Peachtree finds a percentage in the 401k% field in the Maintain Employees/Sales Reps window, Peachtree uses that percentage to calculate the 401(k) contribution.

Multiple state withholdings

If your business is located on the border of a state, you might employ people who live in both the state in which your company is located and in the neighboring state. In this case, your payroll is affected at two levels:

- ✔ Typically, you need to pay state unemployment insurance (SUI) for only the state in which your business is located.

- ✔ You must deduct correct state income taxes for employees based on where they reside, not where your business is located.

Look first at SUI. When you set up Payroll, Peachtree automatically creates a payroll field for state unemployment insurance for the state in which your business is located. Peachtree makes the calculation for each state based on the employee's state of residence. So, you need to edit your payroll setup to tell Peachtree to include all employees, regardless of their residence, when calculating state unemployment for your company's state. Follow these steps:

1. **Choose File⇨Payroll Tax Tables⇨User-Maintained to display the User-Maintained Payroll Tax Tables window.**

2. **Highlight the state unemployment tax table.**

   Typically, the table's name is comprised of your two-letter state abbreviation and the characters *SUI*. The state unemployment insurance tax table for Florida, for example, is FLSUI.

3. **In the State box, delete the characters that represent the two-letter abbreviation for your state.**

4. **Click the Save button to save the tax table.**

Next, you need to make sure that Peachtree uses the correct state unemployment insurance tax table. Follow these steps:

1. **Choose Maintain⇨Default Information⇨Employees.**

2. **Click the EmployER Fields tab.**

3. **Highlight your state unemployment insurance tax table.**

4. **In the Tax Name text box, select your state's payroll tax table.**

   In our example, we'd select FLSUI instead of **SUI ER.

5. **Click OK.**

Last, you need to make sure that all employees' records use the correct state.

1. **Choose Maintain⇨Employees/Sales Reps to display the Maintain Employees/Sales Reps window.**

2. **Select an employee.**

3. **On the Withholding Info tab, make sure that the state code matches the state in which the employee resides.**

Local taxes

During the initial payroll setup, you have the opportunity to set up local taxes as well as state taxes. But suppose your employees live in a variety of localities instead of just the locality in which your business is located. You need to set up additional tax tables for those other localities and assign them to the appropriate employees.

The process is similar to setting up payroll for multiple state withholdings. First, make sure you have an Other Current Liabilities account for local taxes set up in your Chart of Accounts. Then confirm that you have a Local tax payroll field set up, and assign it (if necessary) to the correct box on the W-2.

1. **Choose Maintain⇨Default Information⇨Employees to display the Employee Defaults dialog box.**

2. **Click the EmployEE Fields tab.**

3. **If you don't find a Local field, type Local on a blank line and assign the Local field to the appropriate Other Current Liabilities account.**

4. **Click OK to save the field.**

5. **Reopen the Employee Defaults dialog box by repeating Step 1.**

6. **On the General tab, click the W-2s button to display the Assign Payroll Fields for W-2s dialog box.**

7. **Select the Local payroll field you created from the Local Inc Tax list box (the last box in the dialog box).**

8. **Click OK twice to close both dialog boxes.**

Next, set up additional local tax tables by following these steps:

1. **Choose File⇨Payroll Tax Tables⇨User-Maintained.**

   Peachtree displays the User-Maintained Payroll Tax Tables window.

2. **Enter a tax ID.**

   For Marion County, for example, you might use something like Marion.

3. **In the Tax Name box, enter the tax ID and follow it with the last two digits of the current year.**

   In our example, we'd type **Marion XX**, where the Xs represents the last two digits of the current year.

4. **Set the Government type to Local. In the Local box, type a name for the locality.**

   The name can be up to 15 characters long; don't use spaces or punctuation in the name.

5. **In the State box (above the Local box), type the two-letter abbreviation for the state.**

6. **In the Formula box, type the formula for the locality.**

   Remember to place a semicolon (;) at the end of every line except the last line and press Ctrl+J to start a new line. The last line should begin with ANSWER = . A local tax formula might look something like this:

```
PERCENT = .7;
ANSWER = - PRORATE ((ANNUAL (ADJUSTED_GROSS)) * PERCENT%)
```

You'd change the percentage amount in the first line to match the percentage for your local tax.

7. **Click the Save button to save the tax table.**

8. **Repeat Steps 2–7 for each local tax you need to create and then click Close.**

Last, make sure that you assign each employee to the correct local tax. Follow these steps:

1. **Choose Maintain⇨Employees/Sales Reps.**

2. **Select an employee.**

3. **On the Withholding Info tab, check the following:**

   • The State/Locality box for the State field contains the two-letter abbreviation for the state in which the employee resides.

   • The State/Locality box for the Local field contains the name of one of the localities you created in the preceding steps.

4. **Click the Employee Fields tab.**

5. **Find the Local payroll field, remove the check mark from the Use Defaults column and place a check mark in the Calculated column.**

6. **Based on the employee's locality, select the appropriate payroll tax table you created in the preceding set of steps.**

7. **Click the Adjust button for the Local field and place check marks in the Use boxes for all fields that you want Peachtree to include when calculating Adjusted Gross Income.**

   At a minimum, place a check mark in the Use check box next to Gross. Ask your accountant about the others if you're unsure.

8. **Click Save.**

Visit this book's Web site, www.dummies.com/go/peachtreefd, for more information on Peachtree.

Part IV
The Part of Tens

The 5th Wave   By Rich Tennant

FIRED
YOU

"Nifty chart, Frank, but not entirely necessary."

In this part . . .

Move over, David Letterman. Your competition is here — *not!* Our top ten lists aren't as funny as his, but they clearly serve a practical purpose.

This part provides remedies to common Peachtree error messages and offers locations of helpful Web stuff. Okay, so we're not quitting our day jobs for prime time . . .

Chapter 20

Ten or So Common Peachtree Messages (And What You Can Do About Them)

* *

In This Chapter

▶ Surviving and mastering common errors

* *

Sometimes, computer programs just don't act the way that you expect. At any moment in time, error messages might pop up, throwing most people into a state of near panic.

This might sound a little strange, but frequently you can fix a problem if you simply exit Peachtree and restart your computer. Always try shutting down your computer before any other step. If the problem remains after restarting your computer and you're on a network, try restarting your server. If the problem still remains after that, look at this chapter or contact technical support for a resolution.

Although most error messages are easy to fix, you might need to run the Data Verification program if an error occurs because of data problems. Contact Peachtree or your Peachtree consultant *before* you attempt to run Data Verification or its more powerful counterpart, Integrity Check. You might notice that we don't even include the instructions for running Data Verification or Integrity Check anywhere in this book. We leave it out on purpose!

Here's a valuable piece of advice: Data Verification or Integrity Check must be run from Period 1. Don't run these tools unless you *really* know what you're doing and *always* make a backup before you run the program. We don't mean to scare you, but trust us on this one: We found this out the hard way. If you don't know how to run these two data repair features, contact your Peachtree consultant or Diane or Elaine at diane@thepeachtreelady.com or elaine@thepeachtreelady.com, respectively. See Chapter 17 for information on changing accounting periods.

Missing Buttons in Peachtree Windows

Although missing buttons don't equal an error message per se, sometimes this common situation occurs while working in any of the Maintain windows. We're talking about those buttons on toolbars that you don't see on your computer window. Here's the deal: Peachtree displays buttons in the Maintain windows based on the width of the window. And here's the fix: If a button seems to be missing, widen the window. A couple of the buttons we've found that sometimes are "hidden" are the Attachments button and the Outlook button.

 To widen a window, move your mouse over the right side of the window. When the pointer changes to a double-sided arrow (as shown here), drag the window boundary. You can repeat the process on the left side of the window.

 You can also maximize the window by clicking the Maximize button, which you can see in the margin here.

Period Changed to ## Due to Unposted Entries There or Cannot Change Accounting Periods Due to Unposted Entries

Our clients call us about this error message more than any other. This error usually occurs when you're using the real-time posting method and when you're trying to change your accounting period. It means that Peachtree improperly posted one or more transactions. Usually (but not always), the error occurs if you interrupt Peachtree's posting process. You can usually repair the problem by changing to a batch-posting method, posting all journals, and changing back to a real-time posting method.

To correct the error, follow these steps:

1. **Choose Maintain⇨Company Information to display the Maintain Company Information dialog box.**

2. **Click the arrow next to Posting Method to display the Posting Method dialog box.**

3. **Change the Posting Method to Batch posting and then click OK twice.**

 4. **Choose Tasks⇨System⇨Post to display the Post dialog box.**

 5. **Click OK.**

 Peachtree now posts any unposted entries.

 6. **Repeat Steps 1– 3, selecting Real-time posting in Step 3 instead of Batch posting.**

 You can now change your accounting period.

The Record You Are Trying to Access Is Currently in Use

This error, which also includes the message `Please try again when it is available`, occurs when you attempt to select, use, or modify a customer, vendor, item, employee, job, and so on when you or another user on your network has the respective Maintain window open. To access the record in question, the user who has the maintenance window open needs to close it.

Sometimes, you might get this message when the network connection gets disrupted. You can fix the problem by restarting both your server and the workstations.

No Forms to Print

Peachtree displays this message in a couple of different situations:

✔ **If you try to print forms, such as invoices or checks, and Peachtree determines that no transactions meet the requirements you specified:** For example, you tell Peachtree to print invoices, but no invoices exist without an invoice number. (Remember that Peachtree identifies invoices or checks that need to be printed based on the fact that they don't have a reference number.) Sometimes Peachtree displays the `No forms to print` message if you dated them for a future date — such as tomorrow — when you created these transactions. Unless you change the Last Date for which the invoices will print in the Options dialog box, Peachtree assumes that you want to print only the forms dated today or earlier.

✔ **If you try to reprint a customer statement after updating the customer file**

This Program Has Performed an Illegal Operation

First of all, you haven't done anything *illegal*. Rest assured that you don't have to live in fear that the Software Police are going to knock at your door and haul you away to jail (or the *hoosegow,* as Grandma called it).

Frequently, programs just decide that they won't play nice anymore, so you see this error message. There are too many reasons to list that can cause a program to crash. As a remedy, usually you can just restart the program. If that doesn't work, reboot your computer and then start the program. If *that* doesn't work, try reinstalling the program. If that *still* doesn't work, you need to contact your Peachtree consultant or Sage Software (the company that manufactures Peachtree).

GL Does Not Foot

This message occasionally appears when you attempt to print a General Ledger report. To correct the error, you need to run Peachtree's Data Verification, running both tests as the feature suggests. If that doesn't fix your problem, you need to run a specific list of Integrity Checks.

Don't run Data Verification or Integrity Check unless you *really* know what you're doing. We strongly suggest that you contact Peachtree or your Peachtree consultant *before* you run Integrity Check, and *always* make a backup before proceeding.

Could Not Find the xxx Single (Or Married) Calculation

This message appears when you're trying to generate a paycheck, and the payroll tax tables haven't been updated. We cover updating the tax tables in Chapter 17.

General Error in Module 4

This error appears with a damaged GENERAL.DAT file. The GENERAL.DAT file stores all the default settings for your company, including the fiscal periods. You can copy this file from a previous backup; however, the backup file must be from the same current fiscal year.

The GENERAL.DAT file is the only Peachtree file that you can copy from a backup. Attempting to copy any other Peachtree data file can result in serious data corruption.

Do not copy the file from another company. If you have a backup file (PTB) file, use a program such as WinZip to extract the GENERAL.DAT file. To use WinZip to extract the file, temporarily change the backup filename extension from .ptb to .zip. When you finish extracting, rename the backup filename extension to .ptb.

I/O Errors

I/O — Input/Output — errors are communication errors and mean that Peachtree might be having a problem reading or writing data to your computer's hard drive.

Frequently, this means that a problem exists with your hard drive or transmission across your network. Contact your hardware specialist to check your system. I/O errors can cause irreparable data corruption. A few files might show I/O errors that you can safely delete from your company data folder and let Peachtree re-create them. These files are EVENTLOG.DAT, ALARM.DAT, ALERT.DAT, USERPREF.DAT, and AUDITTR.DAT.

For other I/O errors, you must restore a backup, re-create your Peachtree company from scratch, or send your data out for repair. Contact your Peachtree consultant for assistance.

Unable to Determine Security Privileges

This error can occur when the company's PERMISS.DAT file becomes locked or damaged. Often, simply rebooting all computers that access Peachtree — including the server (if you have a server, of course) — remedies the problem. If the error remains after rebooting, you either have to restore a backup or send your data out for repair. Contact your Peachtree consultant for assistance.

The Account Reconciliation Screen Shows No Entries

Although this isn't an actual error message, this situation is a fairly common problem and seems to mostly occur after upgrading your company to a newer Peachtree version and sometimes after running the Year End closing procedure. You can run the Data Verification process, which forces the entries to reappear.

Don't run Data Verification unless you *really* know what you're doing. We strongly suggest that you contact your Peachtree consultant *before* you run Data Verification. If you do run it yourself, make sure you change to Accounting Period 1 and run both Data Verification tests. Review the report at the end of the Data Verification to confirm that no other underlying problems exist.

Chapter 21

Ten or So Things You Can Get From the Web

In This Chapter

▶ Getting support

▶ Communicating with companies and other users

▶ Surfing and finding helpful, interesting, and fun Web sites

*T*hrough the outstanding power of the Internet, you can find an entire world of information only a few mouse clicks away. We found numerous Web sites that are beneficial to Peachtree users. What are you waiting for? Ready, set, get clicking!

Please keep in mind that this was a tough chapter to write. So many wonderful Web sites exist, but we have room enough to list only a few.

Peachtree Software

www.peachtree.com

Well, of course, we suggest this Web site. Lots of information is accessible from the Peachtree Web site. From here, you can access support options, such as searching through the Peachtree Knowledge Center for answers to many frequently asked questions. You can click Contact Us and send suggestions and enhancements for future versions of Peachtree. (They really do listen to what the users want!)

You can also find detailed information on the many Web-based services that you can purchase from Peachtree. For example, you can find information on the Peachtree Direct Deposit service that enables you to offer your employees the benefit of paychecks directly deposited into their bank accounts.

Peachtree For Dummies, 3rd Edition, Extra Information

`www.dummies.com/go/peachtreefd`

We have so much information to share with you about Peachtree, but there just isn't enough space in the book to put it all. The kind folks at Wiley have posted a companion Web site for some of this additional information. We think that you'll find it very useful. You can find five bonus chapters there, with topics ranging from customizing Peachtree and networking Peachtree to add-on programs that coordinate with your Peachtree Accounting software. You can also read more about the accounting equation and just why and how it works. That one's not the most exciting chapter in the book, but it's a necessary one! (Besides, it tells you whom to blame.)

Just in case you didn't see the commercial announcements that we make in this book, we're giving you one more opportunity. Visit the Wiley Web site to purchase additional copies of this book and check out all the other great *For Dummies* books available (`www.dummies.com`).

The (Infernal) Internal Revenue Service

`www.irs.gov`

Visit the IRS Web site for all the forms and publications that you might need, such as the Circular E, Schedule C, or Form 1040. You can also find taxpayer help and information on electronic services, such as e-filing.

Just for fun (?!), check out the Tax Stats section, which consists of data compiled from all kinds of returns and sorted in a variety of ways. The IRS groups statistics together by various topics and downloads them in a Microsoft Excel format. And if you're actually turning to tax statistics for Internet fun, may we recommend `www.bored.com`.

PeachtreeUsers Forum

`www.peachtreeusers.com`

This site is an online community of Peachtree users and experts providing free support in the Peachtree discussion forums (message boards). You can share tips, questions, answers, and comments about Peachtree accounting software.

Small Business Administration

www.sba.gov

America's 23 million small businesses employ more than 50 percent of the private workforce, generate more than half of the nation's gross domestic product, and provide the principal source of new jobs in the U.S. economy.

The U.S. Small Business Administration (SBA) provides financial, technical, and management assistance to help Americans start, run, and grow their businesses. With a portfolio of business loans, loan guarantees, and disaster loans, the SBA is the nation's largest single financial backer of small businesses. Last year, the SBA offered management and technical assistance to more than 1 million small business owners and played a major role in the government's disaster-relief efforts by making low-interest recovery loans to both homeowners and businesses.

Checks and Forms

www.deluxeforms.com

For more than 80 years, Deluxe Forms has supplied businesses with business checks and forms that work seamlessly with Peachtree software. When ordering, reference this book and discount code R03578 to receive an additional 20 percent off your first order.

Look It Up!

www.reference.com

Stumped on a word or phrase? Don't know what it is or even how to pronounce it? Reference.com is a mostly free collection of reference tools including a dictionary, thesaurus, encyclopedia, grammar usage guide, and even a crossword solver. It features reference material from Crystal Reference, The Columbia Encyclopedia, and Wikipedia, plus Lexico's On This Day.

Is This for Real?

www.snopes.com

Day after day, we all get e-mails claiming something has happened, is happening, or can happen. The problem is that many of these "alerts" are untrue, and passing them along propagates the false rumors: for example, the rumor that drinking Mountain Dew can prevent you from having children. It's untrue. However, the rumor that Lee Marvin (actor) and Bob Keeshan, (television's Captain Kangaroo) fought together at the battle for Iwo Jima is true. Go to this Web site to check out the facts before you forward them.

Stamps.com

```
www.stamps.com
```

Stamps.com is a fee-based service that you can use to print postage from your computer.

Just for the Fun of It

```
www.funnydot.com
```

Has the computer got you down? Are you feeling major stress and need a break? Check out this site for jokes, puzzles, cartoons, games, sounds, and just plain fun. Lighten up a little!

Our Own Web Sites

Diane's Web site provides links to contact her for Peachtree support, including data repair. You can also see a list of her many other books:

```
www.thepeachtreelady.com
```

Elaine's Web site, while currently under construction, offers information about Elaine and some of her projects. (Elaine isn't terribly imaginative, which her Web address indicates, but she does have a sense of humor.) You can find her site here:

```
www.marmelenterprises.com
```

You've already seen how shameless we are when it comes to promoting what we want. What better way to promote both of our services than through our own Web sites? Can't get enough of us? Please drop by for a visit!

Index

• *D* •

Bonus Chapter 1

Customizing the Way You Work

• •

In This Chapter

▶ Defining global options

▶ Customizing task windows

▶ Working with repetitive transactions

▶ Creating an event log

▶ Finding lost transactions

• •

*I*f old Blue Eyes (that's Frank Sinatra, for all of you who are too young to remember) could do it his way, so can you. Peachtree allows customization of how the program reacts to different things you do.

In this chapter, you discover how to customize settings such as the way that numbers display when you type them in, the colors that display, and the fields that you see on your screen during data entry.

Setting Global Options

You can use the Global Options feature to set the way Peachtree functions as well as to select the color of your Peachtree windows. After all, you do want to make sure that it matches your office décor, don't you? You can set various options to control the behavior, look, and feel of the program.

To set the global options, choose Options⇨Global. The Maintain Global Options dialog box appears with the Accounting tab in the front, as shown in Figure BC1-1.

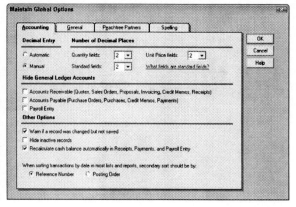

Figure BC1-1:
Personalize much of Peachtree's behavior in the Global Options dialog box.

If you have multiple users, each user can set his or her own global option preferences. See Chapter 18 for information on setting up users.

The Accounting tab

The first section on the left side of the Accounting tab — Decimal Entry — determines how Peachtree inserts decimal points and how many decimal points to use. You have a choice between allowing the Peachtree program to place a decimal point in figures and entering the decimal point yourself.

If you select the Automatic option, Peachtree inserts the decimal point before the last two digits of the number. For example, if you type **10**, Peachtree enters it as 0.10; however, if you select the Manual option for the decimal point entry, Peachtree enters 10 as 10.00.

Most people prefer to set the decimal point entry to Manual. This option affects any field that requires numbers, whether a Quantity field or a Price field.

The section on the right side of the Accounting tab determines the number of decimal places you want for particular field types. For example, if you sell your products only in whole number quantities, you might set the Quantity fields at 0 decimal places. If you charge a price like .2657 each for them, you might set the Unit Price fields to 4 decimal places. The Standard Fields box applies to fields such as Accounts Receivable amount, Average Costing, Sales weight, Total % billed. For a complete list of standard fields, click the What Fields Are Standard Fields link.

Use the middle section on the Accounting tab to optionally hide the General Ledger account number fields in certain task windows. Transactions created with the GL account number hidden automatically use the default General Ledger accounts that you have set up. (You can find out how to set default General Ledger accounts in Chapter 4.)

You can hide General Ledger accounts in the following task areas:

✔ **Accounts Receivable:** Select this option to hide GL accounts in the Quotes, Sales Orders, Sales Invoicing, and Receipts windows.

✔ **Accounts Payable:** Select this option to hide GL accounts in the Purchase Orders, Purchases/Receive Inventory, and Payments windows.

✔ **Payroll Entry:** Select this option to hide GL accounts in the Payroll Entry window.

For example, selecting the Accounts Receivable option changes the look of the Sales/Invoicing window. The Accounts Receivable account and the GL account field of each line item are hidden. When you enter a sales invoice, Peachtree uses the sales default GL account set up for the customer in Maintain Customers/Prospects. If you select an inventory item, Peachtree uses the default GL accounts set up in Maintain Inventory Items for this item.

Should you hide these accounts? Well, look at it this way. If your Chart of Accounts has one GL Sales account and one Accounts Receivable account that you use most of the time, these numbers would never change, so you might as well hide them. You can then generate your invoice faster because you don't have to press the Tab key in these fields when you create an invoice. If, however, the GL Sales account number changes depending on the product or service provided, you should leave the account numbers displayed so that you can change them as necessary.

Journal

If you choose the Hide General Ledger Accounts option, you can view and change the transaction's GL accounts by clicking the Journal button in various task windows.

Other options on the Accounting tab include

✔ **Warn If a Record Was Changed But Not Saved:** When you select this option, Peachtree displays a warning if you try to exit a new or modified record without saving it. If you deselect this option, you won't see the warning. We strongly recommend that you select this option.

✔ **Hide Inactive Records:** When you select this option, Peachtree doesn't display inactive General Ledger, customer, vendor or other records in the lookup lists.

> ✔ **Recalculate Cash Balance Automatically in Receipts, Payments, and Payroll Entry:** When you select this option, Peachtree automatically updates the Cash Balance fields in the Receipts, Payments, and Payroll Entry windows when you post or save transactions. The balance displays as of the date that appears in the task window.

The last option on this tab controls how Peachtree handles a secondary sort. In a large number of reports and in the List dialog box where you select a transaction for editing, you can sort the information by date. If two or more transactions have the same date, the option you select here determines how Peachtree sorts the matching items:

> ✔ By the transaction reference number such as the invoice or check number
>
> ✔ By the order in which you entered the transactions

The General tab

The General tab, as shown in Figure BC1-2, includes features that affect Peachtree's performance as well as the visual color schemes.

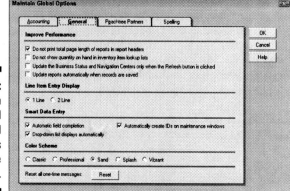

Figure BC1-2:
Options on the General tab control Peachtree's performance behavior.

The first four options affect how Peachtree performs:

> ✔ **Do Not Print Total Page Length of Reports in Report Headers:** When you deselect this option, Peachtree calculates the total number of pages in a report before printing the report. Selecting this option allows reports to print faster, skipping the initial calculation of the total number of pages prior to printing. Instead of displaying page 1 of 12 or page 2 of 12 in the report header, your reports will display page 1 or page 2.

✔ **Do Not Show Quantity on Hand in Inventory Item Lookup Lists:** Selecting this option speeds up the display of inventory item lookup lists because it skips the process of calculating each item's current quantity on hand every time you display the inventory item lookup list.

✔ **Update the Business Status and Navigation Centers Only When the Refresh Button Is Clicked:** Selecting this option improves Peachtree's performance by not refreshing the Business Status until you manually click the Refresh button on the Button Control Bar.

✔ **Update Reports Automatically When Records Are Saved:** Leaving this option unchecked helps performance whenever you have a report open in the background. Instead of recalculating each open report every time you make a change to a record, the report data updates only when you bring the open report to the foreground.

Depending on the configuration of your computer, you might or might not see a noticeable improvement when selecting these performance options.

In the Line Item Entry Display section, you can determine whether Peachtree displays one or two lines for each line item in the various task windows. For example, two-line entry displays the name and description of the account, and single-line entry allows display of more items on the window.

With the options in the Smart Data Entry section, you can enable lookup lists to display instantly and anticipate what you want to enter. These options make data entry faster in most cases. Unless you have a very slow computer, you'll probably want these features activated:

✔ **Automatic Field Completion:** Anticipates what you're typing by filling in the field with the nearest match to the characters you enter as you type them. With it, you can avoid having to type all characters.

✔ **Drop-Down List Displays Automatically:** Allows Peachtree to automatically display a list of choices when you place the insertion point in a lookup field and type at least one character. We recommend you select this option.

✔ **Automatically Create IDs on Maintenance Windows:** This option, selected by default, tells Peachtree while in the Maintain Vendor, Customers, Employees and so forth, to automatically create an ID based on data you enter in the name or description field.

In the Color Scheme section, you can select colors for Peachtree windows and dialog boxes. When you select a color scheme, this default affects all Peachtree companies you open at this computer. If you change a color scheme preference, you must exit and restart Peachtree before the color changes take effect.

These color schemes apply only to windows and dialog boxes within the Peachtree program — not to other Windows applications or the Windows desktop.

Last, you see the Reset button; as you work in Peachtree, you will see messages that you can disable. The Reset button reactivates any disabled messages so that they appear when the respective condition warrants it.

The Peachtree Partners tab

This option controls how Peachtree interacts with its partner add-in programs, such as FAS, Timeslips, or Direct Deposit. We recommend that you do not change this setting. See Bonus Chapter 4 for more information on Peachtree add-in programs.

If you use Peachtree add-in products and you use Peachtree security features, make sure you set the security access level to Full for the COM & DDE Data Access area, located in the Company Tasks area. See Chapter 18 for information on using Peachtree security.

The Spelling tab

Spelling errors can ruin the professional impression that you're trying to maintain. If your flying fingers frequently fumble (wasn't that a great alliteration?) on the keyboard, Peachtree can show you the error of your ways and often offer corrections. By default, Peachtree will check spelling in most task windows and note fields while you work, highlighting misspelled words in red as you type them. Right-click a misspelled word to see a list of suggested replacement words and then click the word you want in place of the misspelled word.

If the word is spelled correctly but Peachtree doesn't recognize it — a term specific to your industry, for example — you can add the word to the dictionary so that Peachtree recognizes it as a correctly spelled word. You manage your spelling preferences using the Spelling tab of the Maintain Global Options dialog box, as shown in Figure BC1-3.

On the Spelling tab, you can set up Peachtree to check spelling when you save or close a transaction as well as control the speed of the Spell Check feature.

Figure BC1-3:
Use this
dialog box
to control
the behavior
of the Spell
Check
feature.

You can speed up the spell-checking process if you take advantage of
Peachtree's capability to automatically correct spellings that you identify.
This feature is very useful in helping you correct typing mistakes that you
make on a regular basis or to recognize special terms you use on a regular
basis. For example, if you regularly type *teh* instead of *the,* set up an autocor-
rect action to make Peachtree automatically replace *teh* with *the* every time
you type it — without asking you about it.

Use this feature to store abbreviations for long words or phrases. For example, you can store an acronym like *ssa* and tell Peachtree to replace it with
Social Security Administration.

To add words or phrases to a custom dictionary, follow these steps:

1. **Choose Options⇨Global to open the Maintain Global Options dialog
   box; then click the Spelling tab.**

2. **Click the Custom Dictionary button.**

   Peachtree displays the Custom Dictionary dialog box, as shown in Figure
   BC1-4.

3. **In the Words text box, type the misspelling you want corrected.**

4. **In the Other Word text box, type the correct spelling.**

5. **From the Action drop-down list, select the Auto Change (Use Case of
   Checked Word) option.**

Figure BC1-4:
Use this
dialog box
to identify
misspellings
to automati-
cally replace
with the
correct
words.

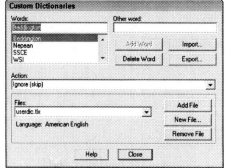

Custom Dictionaries

Words:		Other word:

Nepean
SSCE
WSI

Add Word   Import...
Delete Word   Export...

Action:
Ignore (skip)

Files:
userdic.tlx

Language: American English

Add File
New File...
Remove File

Help   Close

6. **Click the Add Word button.**

   Peachtree adds the misspelled word and its correction to the list. You
   can repeat Steps 3–6 for each misspelled word you want Peachtree to
   automatically correct.

7. **Click the Close button. Then in the Maintain Global Options dialog
   box, click OK.**

Whenever you type one of these words that you added, Peachtree replaces it
with the replacement word you provided. Note that you must type the word
that you added exactly as you added it. For example, if you add *ssa* but you
type *SSA*, Peachtree will not make the replacement.

Navigating Peachtree

We all know that some people are more analytical by nature, and others are
more artistic and graphical. Peachtree includes a feature — the Navigation
Bar — designed to satisfy the appetites of those with the creative eye. You can
find it on the left side of your screen. With seven different centers, including
the Business Status Center, you can use the Navigation Bar as an alternate
method to open transaction and maintenance windows or to run reports. You
can find out about customizing the Business Status Center in Bonus Chapter 2.

Clicking any center on the Navigation Bar displays a list of applicable and
common choices for the selected center. In Figure BC1-5, you see choices and
information related to Employees & Payroll.

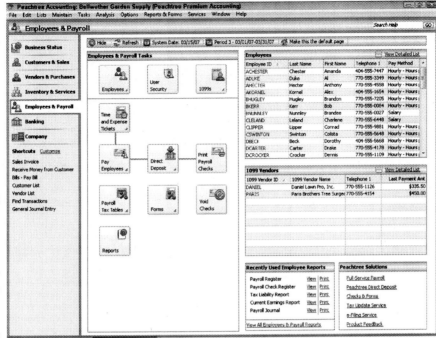

Figure BC1-5:
Use the
Navigation
Bar to
quickly
access
Peachtree
features.

You then click the choice with which you want to work. Some buttons take you directly to a specific task, while others (such as Employees) provide you with a small menu of choices. Buttons that provide a menu have a small arrow in the lower-right corner.

Customizing Shortcuts

Beneath the Navigation Bar is a series of Shortcuts (links) that take you quickly to the Peachtree screens you use in your daily business. There are seven default shortcuts, but you can customize them to better meet your personal needs by removing the ones you don't use and adding others you'd like to use. Click the Customize link to see the Customize Shortcuts dialog box, as shown in Figure BC1-6.

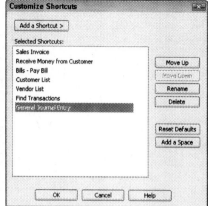

Figure BC1-6:
Add your
common
tasks and
reports to
the
Shortcuts
bar.

From the Customize Shortcuts dialog box, you can do any of the following:

✔ Select a shortcut and click the Delete button (as shown here) to remove the shortcut.

✔ Select a shortcut and click the Rename (as shown here) to give the shortcut a name more familiar to you.

✔ Select a shortcut and click the Move Up or the Move Down button (both shown here) to rearrange its order in the Shortcuts Bar.

✔ Click the Add a Shortcut button (as shown here) to display a menu of Peachtree choices, including customized reports, from which you can choose.

✔ Click the Add a Space button (as shown here) to insert a [Space] entry in the Selected Shortcuts list box. You can then move the space up to separate the shortcuts: for example, to separate the Customer shortcuts from the Vendor shortcuts.

After you make your selections, click OK. Peachtree revises the Shortcuts Bar. If you add more than ten shortcuts, you'll see a More Shortcuts link at the bottom of the bar. Click the link, and the rest of the shortcuts appear on a menu. Note that a space counts as one of the ten shortcuts that appear in the Shortcuts Bar. If you add a space within the first ten shortcuts, the Shortcuts Bar displays only nine shortcuts, and you'll see the More Shortcuts link.

Listing to the Left: Working with and Customizing List Windows

Peachtree contains lots of lists. You can see a list of almost any transaction type (such as invoices, purchases, or general journal entries) as well as lists of general records (such as customers, vendors, employees, inventory, or jobs).

Peachtree lists are extremely flexible and customizable, so you can add or delete fields; change the order by which the list is sorted; and reorganize the fields to better meet your needs. In addition, you can select records to edit, add new records, or generate tasks right from the list. For example, from the Vendor List window, you can add a new vendor, create a purchase or payment for the vendor, or view vendor-related reports.

Using list windows

Peachtree provides several ways to access lists. You can choose Lists from the main menu and then select the list you want. You can select the List option from a Navigation Center button, or you can click the List button (as shown here) from a record or task toolbar.

Any of these methods opens a list window, such as the Sales Order List window you see in Figure BC1-7.

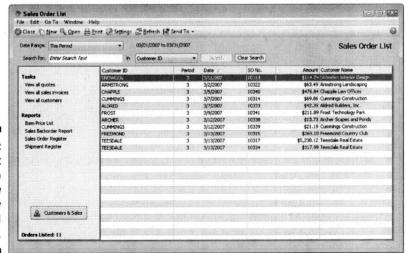

Figure BC1-7:
Open a list window to view previously saved information.

At the top of the list, you see the header information where you can select a date range. List windows that show transactions (such as customer invoices, purchase orders, or paychecks) initially show transactions for the current period. From the Date Range drop-down list, you can select a different date range or period; if you change the date range, Peachtree displays information for the new date range next time you open the window.

Date ranges are available only in the transaction list windows and not in the record maintenance lists.

In the main list section of the window are columns of data. If a column is too narrow and you can't see all the information, you can widen it. Conversely, if a column is too wide and takes up excess room, make it narrower. For either adjustment, place your mouse pointer over the small vertical bar to the right of the column heading. When the mouse pointer changes to a double arrow, drag the bar to the left or the right to resize the column.

If your List window is not large enough, you might not be able to see all the fields. Resize the window by dragging the outside window edges or maximize the window by clicking the Maximize button.

Peachtree indicates the current sort column by a small triangle in the column heading. Click any column heading to sort by that field. Click the heading again to sort by that field in descending order.

By entering information into the Search For text box, you can search your company data for the record or transaction by using criteria that you specify from the List window. For example, in the Sales Order List window in Figure BC1-7, you can search for sales orders using customer ID numbers, customer name, sales order dates, numbers, amount, or posting period.

For an alternative method for locating elusive data, see the upcoming section, "Finding Transactions."

After you select a search criterion, type some information about the transaction into the Search For box that matches the criterion you selected. The ID number and transaction dates, numbers, or totals are self explanatory; if you choose Period as your search criterion, set the Date Range field to All Transactions and enter the period number in the Search For box.

Search text is not case sensitive. Typing *Abc,* for instance, will call up values with *abc, Abc,* and *ABC* in the specified field.

Click the various buttons on the List window toolbar to create a new transaction or open an existing one. You can also use the toolbar buttons to print, e-mail, export to Excel, or even create a PDF file from your list.

Customizing a List window

Each Peachtree user, based on his or her security rights, can customize any List window, and the changes are saved exclusively for that user. In addition, if you have several companies, you can have different settings for each company. See Chapter 18 to set user security rights.

Follow these steps to customize a List window:

1. **Display the list you want to customize.**

   You can display the list through the List menu, from a Navigation Bar button, or through a Maintenance or Task window.

   ⚙ Settings

2. **Click the Settings button on the toolbar (as shown here).**

   A Settings window like the one seen in Figure BC1-8 appears. On the left is a list of fields you can use, and on the right is a list of the fields that are currently displayed.

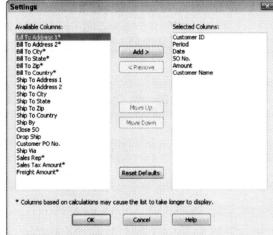

Figure BC1-8:
Select which columns you want to see in the List window.

3. **Perform any of the following actions:**

   Add >

   - *To add a field:* Click a field from the Available Columns list and then click the Add button (as shown here).

   < Remove

   - *To remove a field:* Select a field from the Selected Columns list and then click the Remove button (as shown here).

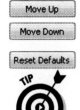

- *To change the order in which the fields appear in the List window:* Select a field in the Selected Columns section and click the Move Up or the Move Down button (both shown here).

- *To completely reset the column settings to the Peachtree defaults:* Click the Reset Defaults button (as shown here).

Fields with an asterisk next to them are calculated fields. Adding many of them to a list may slow down the performance of the list.

4. **Click OK.**

    The List displays the fields you select.

Customizing Data Entry Windows

Over the years, our clients have commented that they want to be able to enter their data quickly and go on to the next project. To aid in this goal, Peachtree allows you to modify several of the Peachtree windows to display certain portions of the window while hiding others. For example, if your business doesn't use job costing, why not hide the Job text box in the Sales/Invoicing or Purchases/Receive Inventory windows? By hiding a portion of the window, the person entering the data skips the hidden areas, which allows for faster data entry.

You can use these customized windows — known as *templates* — to enter data in the following task windows: Quotes, Proposals, Sales Orders, Sales/Invoicing, Purchase Orders, and Purchases/Receive Inventory.

For example, you can remove the Jobs and Ship To information from the Sales/Invoicing window. Here's how to customize the data entry window:

1. **Choose Tasks and then select the task window you want to customize.**

    In our example, we want the Sales/Invoicing window.

2. **Click the Layout button on the toolbar (as shown here).**

    A listing of available templates appears, with a check mark next to the template currently in use.

    You can't edit or delete predefined templates. To customize a template, you must first create a new, customized template.

3. **From the list of templates, click Customize *xxx* Template, where the *xxx* represents the task window you are using.**

In our example, the Maintain Sales/Invoicing Templates window appears. See Figure BC1-9.

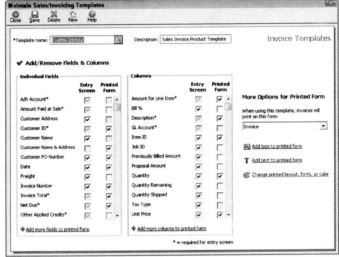

Figure BC1-9:
Customize the data entry window display.

4. **In the Template Name field, type a unique name for the template.**

   For example, you might want to use your company's name.

5. **Press the Tab key and enter a description of the template.**

   Now you can determine which fields you want to be hidden during data entry.

6. **Select the fields and columns you want on the screen and deselect the fields and columns you don't want.**

   Some fields are required and cannot be hidden. Required fields are grayed out and unavailable for change.

   You can also customize a printed form associated with this task. However, for better form design, we recommend that you customize the form as we show you in Chapter 13.

7. **When you finish modifying the template, click the Save button and then click the Close button (both as shown).**

Figure BC1-10 illustrates a Sales/Invoicing window after customizing it.

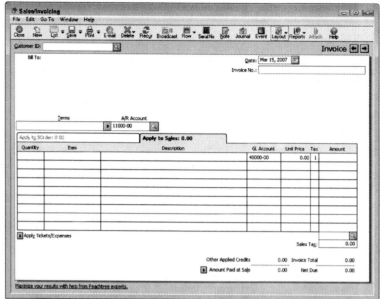

Figure BC1-10:
A customized data entry window.

Simplifying Repetitive Transactions

Memorized transactions can save you a great deal of time in repetitive data entry tasks. Because they're different from recurring transactions, you can use memorized transactions repeatedly and at whatever time interval you choose. You can enter memorized transactions for General Journal entries, Quotes, Sales Invoices, Purchase Orders, and Payments. (For some odd reason, though, you can't create memorized Purchases. We don't know why.)

With memorized transactions, you can enter the GL accounts and general information without knowing an exact amount. They are great for transactions that occur irregularly because they don't automatically post, and you can use them as needed.

Creating memorized transactions

Suppose that you sell a product line in which a customer will probably need several parts at once, instead of just one part. By creating a memorized Sales Invoice, each time one of these units is sold, you won't need to look up or enter the invoice information. As an example, in the sample company, we sell birdhouses. When a customer orders a birdhouse and a pole, we give the customer some birdseed at no charge. To create a memorized transaction to store the invoice information, follow these steps:

1. **Choose Maintain⇨Memorized Transactions.**

   A submenu of available memorized transactions types appears.

2. **Select the type of transaction: in this example, Sales Invoices.**

   The Maintain Memorized Sales Invoices window appears.

3. **Create an ID and description that defines the transaction.**

   IDs can be up to 20 alphanumeric characters, and the description can be up to 30 characters in length.

4. **Set the customer ID:**

   - *If you're designing this memorized invoice for a specific customer:* enter the customer ID in the Customer ID text box.

   - *If you're designing this invoice for any customer:* Leave the Customer ID text box blank so that you can use it for any of your customers.

5. **Enter the transaction information.**

   See Figure BC1-11 for an example. Note that this transaction doesn't have an invoice number or date because not all transaction fields are maintained in memorized transactions. The date and invoice number fields display when you actually use the memorized transaction.

Figure BC1-11:
Memorize transaction for future use.

Quantity	Item	Description	GL Account	Unit Price	Tax	Amount	Job
1.00	AVRY-10120	Redwood 12-Room Bird House. Attracts P	40000-AV	89.99	1	89.99	
1.00	AVRY-10110	Three-Section pole that will place the bird	40000-AV	49.99	1	49.99	
1.00	AVRY-10140	Thistle Bird Seed Mix 6 lb. Bag	40000-AV	0.00	1		
				0.00	1		

6. **Click the Save button (as shown here).**

Using memorized transactions

You can use a memorized transaction at any time. To see how to use the invoice we create in the preceding section, follow these steps:

1. **Choose Task⇨Sales/Invoicing (or whatever type of transaction you want to use) to display a task window.**

2. **Click the arrow to the right of the List button and click the Select button (both shown here).**

   The Select Memorized Transaction dialog box appears, displaying all the memorized transactions relative to the current window.

3. **Click the transaction you want to use and then click OK.**

Voilà! The invoice information appears on-screen. You need to enter only the header information, such as customer name, invoice number, date, and so forth. You can edit the transaction lines as needed. We told you this could save you time!

You can find out how to enter invoices in Chapter 7.

You can also use existing transactions as memorized transactions for later use. After entering the transaction, click the arrow to the right of the Save button and choose the Memorize button (both shown here). Enter an ID and description for the transaction.

Action Items: May I Have Your Attention, Please?

Because being busy is part of daily life, overlooking a circumstance you intended to monitor does happen. Peachtree includes Action Items that assist you in tracking events and situations that are most important to your business. In the Action Items window, you can create events to keep track of certain occurrences or to remind you when a particular situation occurs.

A strange turn of events

Are you a sticky-note fanatic? Is your desk littered with lots of little notes with no clear place to put them, yet you know they are important? If these notes pertain to customers, vendors, or employees, you might want to take a look at the Peachtree Event feature.

Turning off the automatic events

We all know that too much of a good thing is not so good. So it is with the event log. By default, Peachtree keeps a log file of every type of transaction you make for customers, vendors, and employees. No, we're not talking about the journals where the actual transactions are stored. Instead, we're talking about a second place to store a list of transactions. Although the log file is a nice-enough feature, Peachtree's default event log settings tend to clutter a very useful screen with redundant data.

We recommend that you turn off the event log automatic features and create events only when you want them.

To turn off the automatic events, follow these steps:

1. **Choose Tasks⇨Action Items.**

   The Action Items and Event Log Options window opens.

2. **Click the Options button (as shown here).**

3. **Click the Transactions tab and remove all the check marks from the Create Event column. (See Figure BC1-12.)**

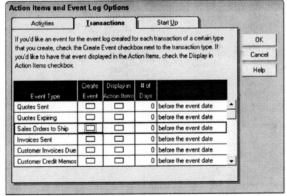

Figure BC1-12:
Keep track of happenings by using Events.

4. **Click OK and then click the Close button (as shown here).**

   Peachtree no longer automatically creates transactions in the Event Log file.

Creating your own events

Suppose that you contacted a delinquent customer and would like to make a note of the conversation, or perhaps an employee received a favorable comment from a customer or a reprimand for being late. Maybe your favorite vendor sales representative has promised you a special discount on your next order. For notes like these, you can effectively use Peachtree's event log. Throw those sticky notes away! (Well, okay, if you don't want to throw them away, stick them on the cat.)

You can create events from the Maintain Customers, Vendor, or Employees windows; from most task windows involving customers, vendors, or employees; or even from the Action Items window (also available under the Tasks menu).

For this example, we create an event note tracking a telephone call we received about one of our employees:

1. **Choose Maintain⇨Employees/Sales Reps to display the Maintain Employees & Sales Reps window.**

   Optionally, open the Maintain Customer/Prospects or Maintain Vendor windows to enter events pertaining to customers or vendors.

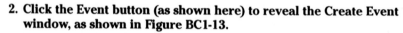

2. **Click the Event button (as shown here) to reveal the Create Event window, as shown in Figure BC1-13.**

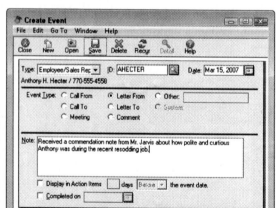

Figure BC1-13:
Record notes in the Create Event window.

Click the Open button to modify an existing event.

3. **Choose the employee ID from the ID lookup list.**

4. **(Optional) Change the date of the event.**

   You can type the event date or select a date from the calendar icon.

5. **Select the option that best describes the note you want to make in the Event Type section.**

   If you select the Other option, you can write your own description for the type of event.

6. **Type a note describing the event (for example, a telephone conversation) in the Note text box.**

   You can enter up to 255 characters in the Note text box. To start a new paragraph in the Note text box, press Ctrl+Enter.

   Click the Open button to modify an existing event.

7. **Click the Save button (as shown here) and then close the Event window.**

Looking at the event log

You can view the event log through the Maintain Customers, Vendors, or Employees windows. You can see or print all the events pertaining to a customer, vendor, or employee by following these steps:

1. **Choose Maintain⇨Employees & Sales Reps (or Customer/Prospects or Vendors).**

   The Maintain Employees & Sales Reps (or Customer/Prospects or Vendors) window appears.

2. **Enter the employee ID in the Employee ID text box or choose it from the lookup list.**

3. **Click the Log button, and Peachtree displays the log file.**

To print the event log, click the Print button (as shown here).

Making a to-do list

One of the more useful Action Items features is creating a to-do list. Keeping track of the things you need to do with the Action Items feature is like having your own little Personal Information Manager (PIM) stored right in Peachtree.

Follow these steps to use the Action Items feature:

1. **Choose Tasks⇨Action Items to display the Action Items window.**

2. **Click the To Do tab.**

   Use the To Do tab to set up a list of tasks that you need to complete. These tasks are not associated with a vendor, customer, or employee.

3. **Enter a date for the first To Do item.**

   Peachtree assumes that you want to accomplish this task as of the current date.

4. **Click the Notes section of the first line and type your first task. See Figure BC1-14.**

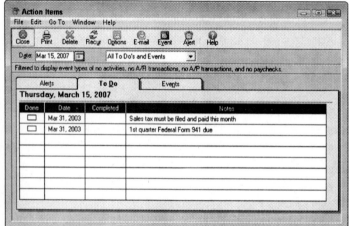

Figure BC1-14:
Help
yourself
become
organized
with the To
Do list.

After you complete a task, select the Done check box at the beginning of the line. To hide completed items, click the arrow next to the All To Do's and Events drop-down list (at the top of the window) and then choose Uncompleted Events. Peachtree then hides the completed events.

Although you see only eight lines for to-do items, when you reach the last line and press the Tab key in the Notes text box, Peachtree creates a new line and adds a scroll bar.

Other useful buttons are the Delete button to delete a selected to-do task and the Print button to print a copy of your to-do list. (Both buttons are shown in the margin.)

When you close the window, Peachtree automatically saves the to-do list for you.

Setting alerts

Alerts are conditions that you want to be aware of as they happen so that you can take further action. Alerts might warn you of low inventory, a customer credit card about to expire, or an employee working too much overtime.

When the conditions for an alert are met, Peachtree can display it on an alert list or send someone an e-mail about the condition. You can create alerts for employees, vendors, customers, inventory items, and General Ledger accounts that meet certain criteria. Follow these steps to create an alert:

1. **Choose Tasks⇨Action Items to display the Action Items window.**

2. **To create a new alert condition, click the Alert button (as shown here).**

   The Set Company Alerts dialog box appears, as shown in Figure BC1-15.

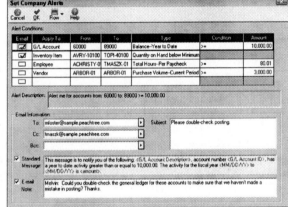

Figure BC1-15: E-mail a standard alert message, a customized message, or both.

3. **Click the next available blank line in the list.**

4. **Select the E-mail check box if you want to send an e-mail message notifying someone of the alert condition.**

   You enter the e-mail recipient information in the bottom section of the window. Alternatively, click the arrow next to a recipient box to display a list of all customer, vendor, and employee e-mail addresses stored within Peachtree.

   To generate e-mail messages from within Peachtree, you must use a MAPI-compliant, default e-mail application such as Outlook or Outlook Express. If your default e-mail system is AOL, you can't send e-mail alerts from Peachtree because AOL is not a fully MAPI-compliant e-mail application.

5. **Select whether the alert condition applies to a customer, vendor, employee, inventory item, or GL account, as well as which customer, vendor, employee, or GL accounts you want to include.**

   Peachtree does not allow you to leave fields blank or amounts at zero.

6. **Select the information type you want the alert condition to monitor.**

   The available options depend on whether you are monitoring a customer, a vendor, an inventory item, or a GL account.

7. **Select the condition you want to monitor and enter an amount appropriate to the type of information you have chosen.**

   The choices you see vary, depending on the type of alert selected.

8. **Click OK.**

Peachtree doesn't automatically send the alert messages. Choose Tasks, Action Items, and then click the E-mail button to generate the e-mail alerts in batch mode.

Click the Alerts tab in the Action Items window to see a list of current alerts.

Finding Transactions

Sherlock Holmes, where are you? Looking for specific transactions can be time consuming and feel like detective work. In many cases, the Customer and Vendor ledger reports give a lot of information, but what about employees? What if you're looking for inventory information that could be affecting a customer or a vendor, such as which customers purchased product XYZ this year? Fortunately, Peachtree includes a Find Transactions feature that makes your sleuthing work much easier.

You can activate the Find Transaction feature at any time or from any window in Peachtree. To search for transactions, follow these steps:

1. **Choose Edit⇨Find Transactions or press Ctrl+F.**

   The Find Transactions window opens, showing a number of conditions by which to search.

2. **Enter the criteria for which you want to search.**

   You can use any option by itself or in combination with another option. If you combine two options, Peachtree searches for a transaction that matches both criteria, so using more than one option limits the number of transactions Peachtree finds. Here are the conditions you can use to search:

   • *Date:* Find transactions based on To and From dates.

   • *Transaction Type:* Find transactions based on the type of transaction such as Invoice, Purchase, or Inventory Adjustment.

- *Reference Number:* Find transactions based on the transaction reference number. You entered this number when you created the transactions. For payments, the reference number usually refers to the check number.

- *Customer, Vendor, or Employee ID:* Find transactions for a specific or range of customers, vendors, or employees.

- *Job ID:* Find transactions related to a specified job.

- *Item ID:* Find transactions related to a specified inventory item.

- *Transaction Amount:* Find transactions equal to, greater than, less than, or within a specified dollar range.

- *Account ID:* Find transactions that affect specified GL accounts.

Figure BC1-16 shows an example. We want to see any transaction this year involving our garden hoses, which are our inventory item IDs of EQWT-15110 through EQWT-15120. We let the Find Transactions feature do the detective work for us.

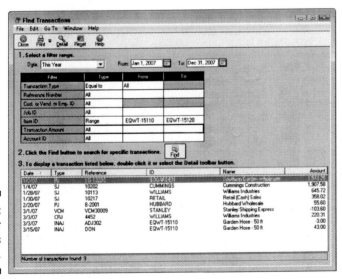

Figure BC1-16:
Search for transactions here.

3. **Click the Find button (as shown here).**

   Peachtree searches all journals for any transactions referring to the field(s) data you specify. The results display at the bottom of the Find Transactions window.

The window lists each transaction with the date, type, reference, ID, name, and amount. The Type field indicates the source of the transaction. Table BC1-1 shows the possible transaction types as well as the name of their respective journals and the source of the reference.

Table BC1-1	Transaction Types and Sources	
Type	*Name*	*Source*
ASBY	Assemblies Adjustment Journal	Build/Unbuild Assemblies
CDJ	Cash Disbursement Journal	Payments
CM	Credit Memo	Customer Credit Memos
CRJ	Cash Receipts Journal	Receipts
ET	Expense Ticket	Time/Expense
GENJ	General Journal	General Journal Entry
INAJ	Inventory Adjustments Journal	Inventory Adjustments
PJ	Purchase Journal	Purchase/Receive Inventory
PO	Purchase Order Journal	Purchase Orders
PRJ	Payroll Journal	Payroll
QT	Quote	Quotes
SJ	Sales Journal	Sales/Invoicing
SO	Sales Order Journal	Sales Order
TT	Time Ticket	Time/Expense
VCM	Vendor Credit Memo	Vendor Credit Memos

Click any column heading to sort the transactions in descending order by the selected column. Click the column heading again to sort the transactions in ascending order.

Double-click any transaction line to view or edit the actual transaction. Click the Reset button to clear the criteria and start a new search.

Click the Print button (as shown here) to print a report.

After you finish reviewing the transactions, click the Close button (as shown here) to close the Find Transactions window.

Peachtree also includes a Find Transaction report. Choose Reports & Forms⇨Company and then double-click the Find Transactions Report. The default report shows all transactions (assemblies, credit memos, general journal entries, invoices and so forth) for the current date. Click the Options button to filter the report. See Chapter 14 for information on filtering reports.

Bonus Chapter 2

Managing Your Business's Money

*A*ccounting for the money is only half the battle. Managing the money is the rest. In addition to helping you account for your money, Peachtree contains some tools that help you manage your money — and this chapter is your guide to exactly that.

Meet the Financial Manager

The Peachtree Financial Manager can give you a quick view of your financial picture. It displays an overview of key ratios and key balances that can help you check the pulse of your business without analyzing reports.

Business Summary view

Choose Analysis⇨Financial Manager to see the window shown in Figure BC2-1. By default, Peachtree displays the Business Summary view, which contains four panes of financial information presented as percentages.

 If you prefer, you can see click the S.Sheet button to view the numbers in the row/column format presented by spreadsheets. You can also set the As Of date to any date as far back as the first open period.

Figure BC2-1:
The
Business
Summary
view
focuses
primarily on
key ratios
in your
business.

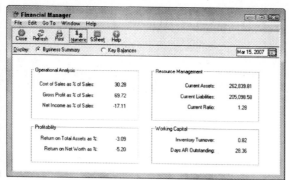

Financial analysts and bankers calculate dozens of ratios to help them understand the financial picture of a company. Peachtree provides some of the more basic ones in the Business Summary view, using information you can find on your income statement and balance sheet.

The numbers you see in the four panes of the Business Summary are percentages, but we describe ratios here. You must multiply the result of each of the following calculations by 100 to adjust for percentages. (Remember that high school math? Ugh!)

Ratios by themselves are meaningless; you need to compare the ratios with either historical data for your company or to other companies in your industry. You might want to take a look at Leo Troy's *Almanac of Business and Industrial Financial Ratios* (published by CCH, Inc.). You can purchase the book from several vendors, including www.amazon.com.

Operational Analysis

To calculate the Cost of Sales as a Percentage of Sales, Peachtree uses your income statement and divides Total Cost of Sales by Total Revenues. The higher the ratio, the more it costs you to make your sales — thus reducing your gross profit.

To calculate Gross Profit as a Percentage of Sales, again, Peachtree uses your income statement and divides Gross Profit by Total Revenues. This ratio plus the previous ratio will total 100 percent, so you can expect that a lower ratio indicates that your cost of sales is high.

To calculate Net Income as a Percentage of Sales, Peachtree again uses your income statement and divides Net Income by Total Revenues. This ratio takes into consideration both your cost of sales and your operating expenses. A higher ratio means that you've kept your expenses down.

Profitability

To calculate Return on Total Assets as a percentage, Peachtree uses both your Income Statement and your Balance Sheet, dividing Net Income on your Income Statement by Total Assets on your Balance Sheet. If the resulting ratio is high, either you have a high profit margin, or you turn over your assets quickly.

To calculate Return on Net Worth as a percentage, Peachtree again uses both your Income Statement and your Balance Sheet and divides Net Income by Total Equity (or Capital). The higher the ratio, the better, because it indicates that you're making more money on the money you invested.

Resource Management

In the Resource Management section, Peachtree lists your Current Assets and Current Liabilities (both found on your Balance Sheet) and then calculates the Current Ratio by dividing Current Assets by Current Liabilities. The Current Ratio gives you a measure of your ability to cover your debts with your assets in case of an emergency. A number less than 1 indicates that your assets would not cover your liabilities.

Working Capital

To calculate Inventory Turnover, Peachtree uses both the Income Statement and the Balance Sheet and divides Total Cost of Sales by Inventory. This ratio helps you measure how long items remain in inventory before you sell them. A higher number indicates that you keep items in inventory longer.

The Days A/R Outstanding entry represents the average length of time (in days) that your receivables remain outstanding. To calculate Days A/R Outstanding, Peachtree first divides Total Sales by the number of days in the period — call the result *Sales Per Day*. Then Peachtree divides Average Accounts Receivable for the period by Sales Per Day to determine the average number of days receivables remain outstanding.

Key Balances view

The Key Balances view of the Financial Manager window (see Figure BC2-2) provides key balances for certain balance sheet accounts and, in the Operations section, a summarized version of your Income Statement. Select the Key Balances radio button to switch to this view.

Figure BC2-2:
View key
balances on
both your
Income
Statement
and your
Balance
Sheet at a
glance.

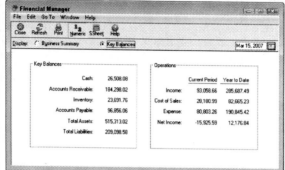

While viewing Key Balances, you can click the S.Sheet button to have
Peachtree display corresponding monthly values.

Understanding the Cash Manager

"I *really* need to know how much cash I'm going to have at the end of the
month." Have you heard yourself say that? Let the Peachtree Cash Manager
do the math for you.

The Cash Manager window, as shown in Figure BC2-3, shows you the company's expected cash balance for a particular date, taking into consideration
sales you are due to collect (outstanding receivables), payments you are due
to make (outstanding payables), payroll you are due to meet, and any cash
adjustments. To open this window, choose Analysis⇨Cash Manager.

If you use batch posting, you need to post before using the information in
this window to get an accurate picture of your cash position.

If pictures speak to you more than numbers, select the Graph radio button to
view the information in the Cash Manager window in graphic format (see
Figure BC2-4).

You can switch to Spreadsheet view by clicking the S.Sheet button, but we're
going to work in the Numeric view shown in Figure BC2-3. Display this view
by clicking the Numeric toolbar button (as shown here) and then selecting
the Numeric display radio button.

Graph button

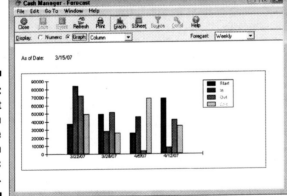

Figure BC2-3: Predict your cash balance on a particular date.

		Due By:	Due By:	Due By:	Due By:
As of Date:	3/15/07	3/22/07	3/29/07	4/5/07	4/12/07
	Starting Cash:	36,975.11	49,202.75	26,024.79	68,425.36
Add:					
	Sales To Collect:	84,217.84	28,092.23	46,054.52	8,254.87
	Cash Adjustments (+):	0.00	0.00	0.00	0.00
	Total Available:	121,192.95	77,294.98	72,079.31	76,680.23
Less:					
	Payments To Make:	69,319.95	16,985.00	983.70	7,665.96
	Payroll To Pay:	2,670.25	34,285.19	2,670.25	34,285.19
	Cash Adjustments (-):	0.00	0.00	0.00	0.00
	Ending Cash:	49,202.75	26,024.79	68,425.36	34,729.08

Cash adjustments

Figure BC2-4: Check out your cash balance prediction in graphic format.

To calculate the first Starting Cash balance shown on the screen, Peachtree sums the balances in all accounts you defined as cash accounts in your Chart of Accounts. All subsequent starting cash balances equal the ending cash balance from the prior period. You can change the forecast frequency from its default of Weekly to Biweekly or Monthly from the Forecast drop-down list.

Suppose that you're hoping to close a large deal, and you'd like to see what the cash picture will look like if you're successful. Or suppose that you might buy a truck during the time period, and you'd like to include the effects of the down payment in Cash Manager. You can include these what-if scenarios in the Cash Adjustments lines. To add cash to the picture, double-click any number on the Cash Adjustments (+) line. To subtract cash from the picture, double-click any number on the Cash Adjustments (–) line. Peachtree displays the Spreadsheet view for the appropriate adjustments line. Record the adjustment in the appropriate column (the column headings are dates) and click the Numeric button to redisplay the view shown in Figure BC2-3. If you click Save, you can review the adjustments at a later time when you return to the Cash Manager window.

To subtract cash, record the adjustment using the Cash Adjustments (–) line and enter a positive — not a negative — number.

Using the Payment Manager

The Payment Manager can help you select and pay bills. When you open the Payment Manager window by choosing Analysis⇨Payment Manager, you see the window shown in Figure BC2-5.

Even if your business operates on a cash basis, you'll see bars that represent unpaid bills in this window.

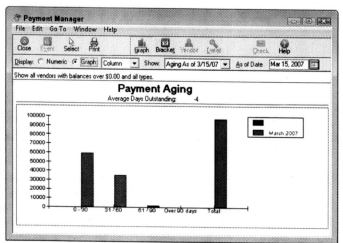

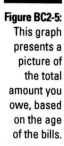

Figure BC2-5: This graph presents a picture of the total amount you owe, based on the age of the bills.

You can view the information numerically by selecting the Numeric view option, but we're going to continue working in the Graph view.

The information that Peachtree presents is aged like the balances you see on the Aged Payables report. Peachtree typically sets the As Of date field to today's date, but you can change it, too. You can use a date in the Show list to compare last month with this month or this month last year with this month this year date. Initially, the date in the Show field matches the As Of date.

Suppose that you want to see the details that make up the 31-60 bar. Double-click the bar, and a window appears like the one shown in Figure BC2-6.

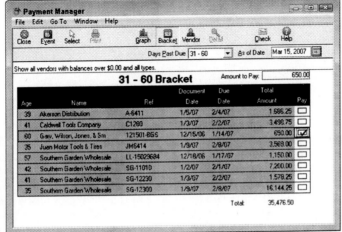

Figure BC2-6: Use this window to select bills to pay.

Place a check mark next to bills that you want to pay and then click the Check button at the top of the window. Peachtree allows you to select a form and print checks for the selected bills.

Using the Collection Manager

Managing accounts receivable can be critical to the survival of your business. If you don't collect money that your customers owe you in a timely fashion, you might not have enough money to buy the things you need to continue your business. A cash flow crunch could squeeze you out of business.

From the Collection Manager window, as shown in Figure BC2-7, you can monitor your receivables and even create collection letters to send to your customers. Choose Analysis⇨Collection Manager to open this window.

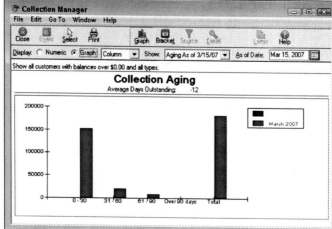

Figure BC2-7:
Use the
Collection
Manager to
help you
manage
accounts
receivable.

The Collection Manager works a lot like the Payment Manager. You can view the information numerically and change the dates you're viewing. And, if you double-click a bar on the chart, you can view details of the invoices that are past due for that period.

In the Collection Manager window, you can select invoices for which you want to send collection letters. Click the Letter button on the toolbar at the top of the window, and then select a letter format. You can view and change the text for each letter format, which range from gentle reminders to firm requests for payment, from the Reports & Forms window. Click Reports & Forms, point at Forms, and click Customer Labels and Letters. Select the letter you want to view and click the Customize button.

Peachtree treats collection letters as forms; therefore, you can modify the various collection letters the same way you modify other forms. You can find the collection letters by opening the Select a Report or Form window for Accounts Receivable and looking for a folder called Collection Letters. Also note that the form letters used in the Collection Manager are *not* the same ones used by the Mail Merge function. Unfortunately, there's no slick way to create a collection letter through the Mail Merge function for customers selected in the Collection Manager.

See Chapter 13 for more information on customizing forms and Mail Merge.

Looking at the Business Status Center

If you are using Peachtree Complete or higher, when you first opened your company in Peachtree, you probably noticed the Business Status Center — the first page of Peachtree's Navigation Centers (see Figure BC2-8). You can think of the Business Status Center as an information center for your company. By default, Peachtree displays (in the Aged Receivables section) a breakdown of your receivables and lets you view your customer list and your Aged Receivables report. You also can record a customer payment from the Business Status Center.

You can change the default page from the Business Status Center to any of the other centers — for example, Customers & Sales Center or Employees & Payroll Center — by clicking the tab for that center and then clicking the Make This The Default Page button that appears above the information in that center.

In the Vendors to Pay area, you also see a list of vendors to pay and the amounts owed and dates due. You also can view your vendor list or pay bills from the Business Status Center.

At the bottom of the page, you can use the Find a Report section to help you select a report to print.

You can customize the Shortcuts area just below the tabs of the Navigation Centers. See Bonus Chapter 1 for details.

You can customize the Business Status Center to display a variety of information. For example, you can monitor information such as the current period net income and year-to-date balances in certain accounts. We like to watch bank accounts, Accounts Payable, and Accounts Receivable.

We include our suspense account in this group to make sure that its balance is always zero. We use a suspense account to handle unusual transactions such as adding labor burden to a job, and we always want the account's balance to be zero.

Customize This Page button

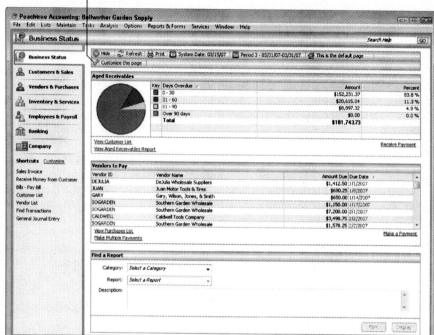

Figure BC2-8:
The
Business
Status
Center
provides an
overview of
vital areas
on your
company.

Displaying information such as Account Balances or Top Customers might take longer than displaying other types of information. The amount of time Peachtree needs to display information depends on the amount of information you store in your Peachtree company.

You also can display your top customers over the past 12 months and your year-to-date revenue information. And, depending on the information you choose to display, you can print certain reports directly from this page.

Peachtree security settings control how much information appears to each user, based on the user's security settings. For example, if a user doesn't have security privileges for payroll information, that user doesn't see the Employees & Payroll Center. For more information on setting security in Peachtree, see Chapter 18.

To customize the page, follow these steps:

1. Click the Customize This Page button.

Peachtree displays the Customize Business Status dialog box (see Figure BC2-9).

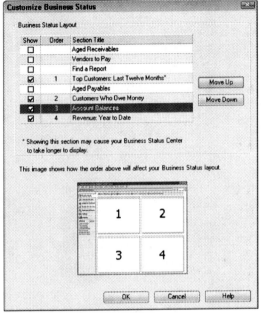

Figure BC2-9:
Use this dialog box to select information to display on the Business Status Center.

2. **Select check boxes in the Show column to select sections to display.**

   Checks appear beside each section you select, and the Preview area shows how Peachtree will lay out the Business Status Center.

3. **To change the order of appearance, select a section and click either the Move Up or the Move Down button.**

4. **Click OK.**

   Peachtree displays your new Business Status Center (see Figure BC2-10).

If you choose to display account balances, you can click the Customize link in that section to select the accounts you want to view. Peachtree displays the Customize Account Balances dialog box (see Figure BC2-11). Select the check box for each account you want to display. Toward the bottom of the box, you can choose whether to display accounts that have a $0 balance. You also can choose whether you want to display current period balances or year-to-date balances as well as display the same accounts in the Banking Center.

Notice that you can print certain reports associated with each kind of information. For example, if you display the Top Customers section, Peachtree provides a link to display the Customer Sales History report.

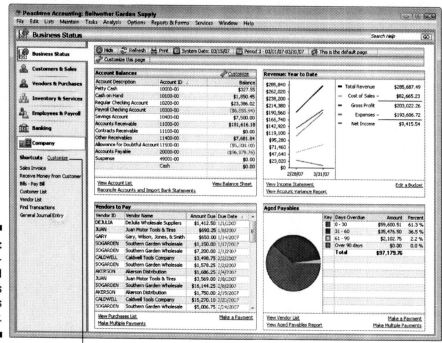

Figure BC2-10: A customized Business Status Center.

Customize link

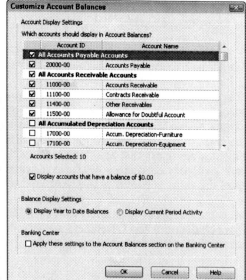

Figure BC2-11: Use this dialog box to select the accounts you want to display on the Business Status Center.

Bonus Chapter 3

Peachtree and Networking

. . . .

. . . .

*I*f you're not a geeky type of person who fools around with networking, skip this chapter. Go to lunch, take a nap, hug a tree, whatever. However, if you're the one responsible for keeping Peachtree running across your net-work, read on. You might find something in this chapter that you can use.

Peachtree Complete Accounting and above are the only multi-user products. You can't use Peachtree Pro Accounting or Peachtree First Accounting in a network environment. Also, to function in a network environment, you must purchase the multi-user license version of the product or purchase a single user copy for each PC on which you want to install Peachtree. Otherwise, two users can't access the data files at the same time.

What Type of Network Can Be Used?

The most typical types of networks in use today are peer-to-peer networks and client/server networks:

✔ A *peer-to-peer* network environment allows each connected computer to act as a server or a workstation or both. Each computer can share its hard drive, printers, and other devices with all other computers in the network. This makes each computer on the network equal to the other computers — a *peer*.

✔ A *client/server* network environment has one computer — the server — acting as a central unit with several workstations connected to it. The server is where you store the data shared by the workstations.

Peachtree will not operate properly on a Novell network.

This chapter provides general guidelines for installing Peachtree on a network. You can also obtain guidelines providing specific system requirements for Peachtree to run successfully on various network types. Go to the Peachtree Web site at www.peachtree.com/support and search the Peachtree Knowledge Base for networking.

Where Do Files Reside?

Peachtree divides all its files into two main sets:

- ✔ **Program files:** Program files do not need to be shared. They need to reside on each individual machine.

- ✔ **Data files:** Data files must be shared in a networked environment. Data files include help files, the status.dat file, the options.dat file, the global taxtable file, and form files as well as all company folders that include the data files when you create your Peachtree company.

In a client/server network, data files are stored on the server. In a peer-to-peer network — which doesn't have a traditional server — the administrator's machine is usually designated as the main computer. Ideally, this computer is the fastest and has the largest amount of available memory and hard drive space.

Installing Peachtree on a Network

Peachtree must be loaded on a computer using administrator rights. Individual users don't need administrator rights to use Peachtree after it's loaded on their computers. However, they do need rights to modify the data on the server where the Peachtree data is located. Additionally, they need read/write access to the C:\Program Files\Common Files\Peach folder and to C:\Winnt or C:\Windows. They also need rights to the Registry for Peachtree.

This is important! You MUST install Peachtree on the system where the data files will be stored (the server) first. Key files are copied to the server during the installation process. After you install Peachtree on the server, then you can install on the rest of the workstations.

Mapping the drive

During Peachtree installation, you'll be asked for a data path. So, before you install Peachtree on the workstations, you must map a drive letter to the server. (We like to use the letter *P* for our mapped drive. *P* for *Peachtree* — get it?) The data location you select must be a shared folder. Because peer-to-peer networks allow you to share the entire hard drive or only a particular folder, before you load Peachtree, you should know whether you're sharing the entire drive or just the Peachtree folder. If you're planning to share only to a particular folder, here are a few strategies to keep in mind:

- ✔ If you're planning to map Peachtree workstations to a specific folder, such as making `P:` point directly to the `\Program Files\Peachtree\` folder, your data path would read

  ```
  P:\Company\
  ```

- ✔ If you are mapping the entire Program Files folder as `P:`, your data path would read

  ```
  P:\Peachtree\Company\
  ```

- ✔ If you map the entire hard drive as `P:`, the data path would read

  ```
  P:\Program Files\Peachtree\Company\
  ```

- ✔ If you're performing the Peachtree installation on the server, the program path and data path should be the same. However, when installing on the workstation, the program path should be on a local hard drive (`C:\Program Files\Peachtree\`), and the data path should point to the Company folder on the server computer: for example

  ```
  P:\Program Files\Peachtree\Company
  ```

Installing the program

When you insert the Peachtree CD into the drive, the Autorun screen should appear, welcoming you to Peachtree and offering you three choices:

- ✔ Install Peachtree Accounting
- ✔ Install Server Components Only
- ✔ Remove or Modify Peachtree Accounting

If installing on the server, you can choose either of the first two options. When installing on the workstations, however, you must choose the first option. During the workstation installation process, follow the on-screen prompts and pay close attention to the screen that asks for the data path. On the workstations, the data path should point to the mapped drive — to the Company folder.

Do not point the data path directly to YOUR company folder. Point the data path to the folder actually named Company.

During the install, Peachtree will advise you if it needs to add additional programs, such as Microsoft .NET. It's a pretty smart installation program; let it install what it needs.

Because installing Peachtree writes to the Windows Registry, you should restart your system after installation but before you use the application.

If you're installing to the server, be sure to warn any users who might be using other applications on the server that you're going to restart the system.

Just a Few Final Notes

We told you this was really geeky stuff! Here are a few little ditties you might want to know if you need to make changes to your Peachtree settings.

Data folders

For each company you create in Peachtree, Peachtree creates a folder in which to store the company information. The folder name comes from the company name. Generally, Peachtree takes the first three letters of the first word of the company name, the first three letters of the second word of the company name, and the first two letters of the third word of the company name. If your company name contains one or two words, Peachtree uses only those words but a total of eight letters if possible. Confused? Here are some examples:

- ✔ If your company name is All Business Service, Peachtree creates a folder named ALLBUSSE.

- ✔ If your company name is Marmel Enterprises, LLC, Peachtree creates a folder named MARENTLL.

- ✔ If your company name is Bo the Handyman, Peachtree creates a folder named BOTHEHAN.

✔ If your company name is Magic Fingers, Peachtree creates a folder named MAGFINGE.

✔ If your company name is Wanderbusters, Peachtree creates a folder named WANDERBU.

You get the idea.

The Forms folder

During installation, Peachtree automatically creates a Forms folder and places it under the Company folder. This is at the same level as your company data folder. All Peachtree standard forms as well as forms that you customize are located in the Forms folder.

Peachtree uses an .frm extension for its forms. The first several letters indicate the form type, and the form name follows in a numerical format. For example, INV01430.frm is an invoice form, PRC0130.frm is a payroll check form. Peachtree standard forms all have a value greater than 1000, and customized forms have a value less than 1000. If you see a form named APC00001.frm, that means that it's a customized accounts payable check. You can read about customizing forms in Chapter 13.

Do not move the Forms folder to a different location unless you are changing the data path. See the upcoming section, "Changing the data path."

Changing from single user to multi-user

If you first installed Peachtree as a standalone program, but now you need to network it, we suggest that you uninstall Peachtree and then reinstall the program. Different settings are used when installing as a single user versus as a multi-user. You can uninstall Peachtree either through the Windows Control Panel or by inserting the Peachtree installation CD and choosing the Remove or Modify Peachtree Accounting option.

Changing the data path

In Peachtree 2007 and later, if you need to change the data path location, you must uninstall Peachtree and reinstall it. You can uninstall Peachtree either through the Windows Control Panel or by inserting the Peachtree installation CD and choosing the Remove or Modify Peachtree Accounting option.

Special hardware and software issues

This section contains suggestions — not requirements — for networking. However, we have found that Peachtree responds much better if you follow these guidelines:

- **Same Operating System:** Peachtree works best if all workstations use the same version of Windows. If you're using Windows Vista, for example, make sure that everyone is using Windows Vista. Peachtree might operate if you use different operating systems, but the risk for problems increases.

- **Latest Windows update:** Make sure that all workstations are using the latest update of their Windows version. To check for updates, visit www.windowsupdate.com from each computer.

- **Same network card brand:** Make sure that all workstations have the same brand of network card. We've seen a number of instances where replacing the network cards so that all workstations use the same brand substantially improved Peachtree performance. We don't really know why it works better, but it does.

- **Enough memory:** Make sure the workstations have enough memory. If you're on a network, chances are your Peachtree data files will be larger than a single user simply because you have more people entering data. More memory means much better performance.

System Requirements

For Peachtree Premium, the recommended system requirements (per Peachtree) are as follows:

- 1 GHz Intel Pentium III (or equivalent) for single user and 1.8 GHz Intel Pentium 4 (or equivalent) for multiple concurrent users
- 512MB of RAM for single user and 1GB for multiple concurrent users
- Windows 2000 SP3, XP SP2, or Vista
- 1GB of disk space for installation
- Internet Explorer 6.0 or higher required (provided on CD; requires an additional 70MB of disk space)

- ✔ Microsoft .NET Framework CLR 1.1 (provided on CD; requires an additional 150MB of disk space)
- ✔ At least high-color (16-bit) SVGA video; supports 800 x 600 resolution with small fonts
- ✔ Optimized for 1024 x 768
- ✔ 2x CD-ROM
- ✔ All online features/services require Internet access with at least a 56 Kbps modem

Integration/compatibility requirements

- ✔ Excel, Outlook, and Word integration requires Microsoft Excel, Outlook, and Word 2000, 2002, 2003, or 2007.
- ✔ Printers need to be supported by Microsoft Windows 2000/XP/Vista.
- ✔ In-product demos require Macromedia Flash Player.
- ✔ Additional 55MB available hard drive space is required to install Guided Tour.
- ✔ Adobe Reader 7.0 is required and provided on CD (requires an additional 90MB available hard drive space to install).

Multi-user mode

Multi-user mode is optimized for Windows 2000 Server or Windows Server 2003 client-server networks, and Windows 2000/XP/Vista peer-to-peer networks.

Terminal Services

Windows 2000 or 2003 Server along with Remote Desktop Connection or Remote Desktop Web Connection client is required to run in a Windows Terminal Services environment. Only Peachtree Premium and above versions support Terminal Services.

Add-On Products for Peachtree

* *

In This Chapter

▶ Attitude POSitive

▶ Sage Software

▶ DataSoft

▶ Invertech

▶ Multiware, Inc.

▶ Wizard Business Solutions

* *

By itself, Peachtree might just meet your needs. However, several vendors provide solutions that enhance Peachtree's functionality. In this chapter, we give you a brief overview of some of these products — and information on contacting the vendors for more information.

Attitude POSitive

www.attitudepositive.com

Attitude POSitive sells *AccuPOS Retail Point of Sale,* which is a point-of-sale system that links to Peachtree Complete Accounting or higher. You can visit the company Web site or call toll free at 877-888-0880.

Sage Software (The Owners of Peachtree)

www.peachtree.com

In the box in which your Peachtree software arrives, you'll find one add-on product: ACT! Link for Peachtree. If you purchase Peachtree Premium, you'll find one additional add-on product: Crystal Reports. Sage Software, which owns Peachtree, also makes available a variety of other add-on products. In the following paragraphs, we give you a brief description of each of these add-on products. You can find more detailed information at the Peachtree Web site.

ACT! Link for Peachtree

ACT! is a contact management system that handles all the tasks and information related to developing and maintaining business relationships. ACT! links to Peachtree so that you synchronize customer and vendor information between ACT! and Peachtree.

Both Peachtree and ACT! are products of Sage Software.

Timeslips Accounting Link

Timeslips is a time-and-billing software package that provides great flexibility to consultants, lawyers, accountants, architects, and others who bill for their time by allowing them to track time spent, prepare a client bill, record payments from clients, and track outstanding receivables. The Timeslips Corporation sells two add-on products that link Timeslips to Peachtree.

Timeslips Accounting Link (TAL) translates your Timeslips activity into debits and credits that update Peachtree's General Ledger, enabling you to use Peachtree to track the expense and payroll side of your business and still view a complete picture of your financial situation.

TAL Pro enables a two-way transfer between Peachtree and Timeslips; in addition to sending revenue information from Timeslips to Peachtree, you can send expense information (checks you write that need to be billed to clients as reimbursable expenses) from Peachtree to Timeslips.

Both Peachtree and Timeslips are products of Sage Software.

Crystal Reports

Crystal Reports is a custom report writer that you can use to create reports that don't come with Peachtree. The Crystal Reports program comes with Premium and above and can be purchased to work with Peachtree Complete and Peachtree Pro. Crystal Reports does not work with First Accounting.

Peachtree Payment Solutions

With the *Peachtree Payment Solutions* service, you can accept and authorize credit card transactions from inside Peachtree using your existing business bank account so that you can expand payment options for your customers without any hardware additions.

Peachtree Bill Pay Service

You can sign up for this service and pay your bills electronically. After you sign up, you're ready to go, with no additional products to install. Just use the existing windows in Peachtree and your existing bank account. This service is available for all versions of Peachtree except Peachtree First Accounting.

Peachtree Online Backup

In partnership with Iron Mountain, *Peachtree Online Backup* enables you to protect your company data by storing a backup of your data securely offsite on a remote server. You use Peachtree to schedule the backup to occur anytime that's convenient for you.

WebsiteCreator Pro

Using the *WebsiteCreator Pro* add-on, you can build a Web site for your business with customizable pages and an online catalog, including inventory items that you can upload from your Peachtree Accounting software.

WebsiteTrader

Using the *WebsiteTrader* add-on, you can sell your products and services online and transfer Web orders into Peachtree. This service is available with all versions of Peachtree except Peachtree First Accounting.

Peachtree Payroll Service

If you're looking for an outside payroll service, check out the *Peachtree Payroll Service*, which handles all payroll functions for you and, of course, integrates with Peachtree. After each payroll processed by the Peachtree

Payroll Service, you synchronize your data to update your General Ledger and job information with payroll information. This service is available with all versions of Peachtree except Peachtree First Accounting.

Peachtree Direct Deposit

With the *Peachtree Direct Deposit* service, you can automatically deposit your employees' paychecks into up to four different bank accounts. And it's okay if only some employees participate; you can still prepare paychecks for those who don't. This service is available for all versions of Peachtree except Peachtree First Accounting; however, you must also subscribe to a Peachtree payroll solution.

ePeachtree Internet Accounting

A Web-based accounting solution with tools like check writing, invoicing, sales orders, inventory, and business reporting, *ePeachtree* lets you do your accounting whenever you want and wherever you are as long as you have an Internet connection.

Peachtree Web Accounting

With the *Peachtree Web Accounting* service, you or anyone whom you authorize (like your accountant) can remotely access your Peachtree data from home or while traveling and perform daily tasks such as entering transactions and running reports. This service is available with all versions of Peachtree except Peachtree First Accounting.

Peachtree Fixed Asset System

If your company owns assets with a useful life of more than one year, you own *fixed assets*. From an accounting perspective, you treat a fixed asset differently from another type of asset because you depreciate it over its estimated useful life to spread out the cost of the asset instead of recognizing its entire cost in the year that you buy the asset. If you have lots of fixed assets, tracking their value and associated depreciation can be problematic. Consider trying *Peachtree FAS*, which ships with Peachtree Complete and higher.

Peachtree Fixed Assets Tax Update

For Peachtree Pro and higher, *Peachtree Fixed Assets Tax Update* service provides updates to the federal tax depreciation calculations and reporting forms supported in the software, including updates for changes to all supported MACRS and ACRS depreciation methods, the annual Section 179 deduction limit, yearly changes to passenger automobile depreciable limits, and modifications to the federal form 4562 worksheet.

DataSoft

www.dscorp.com

DataSoft carries an impressive line of reporting tools linked to Peachtree data. These specialized reports help you better manage your inventory, pay sales commissions, and analyze job profitability. The DataSoft product line also includes a series of utilities that can clean up old Peachtree data files. Contact DataSoft online or call toll free at 800-662-0188.

Invertech

www.invertech-corp.com

Invertech designed its *Peach Pro Suite* with a direct link between Peachtree and their main products. These add-on products include Inventory Control and Material Scheduling; Manufacturing Resource Planning and Job Costing; Sales Commission Management; Physical Inventory, and Communication with Microsoft Outlook that transfers customer, vendor, and employee information. You can contact the folks at Invertech at 513-942-6333, extension 202, or visit them online.

Multiware, Inc.

www.multiwareinc.com

Multiware, Inc. provides *PawCom*, an Access end application, and other add-on tools that extend the functionality of Peachtree and provide a programming environment for developing custom forms and reports and for integrating Peachtree with your own application. For more information on their tools, contact Multiware, Inc., at 530-756-3291.

Wizard Business Solutions

www.wizard-net.com

Wizard Business Solutions specializes in producing add-on products that expand the capabilities of Peachtree. These products vary widely in range, including a barcode tool, a time clock tool, a direct deposit tool, and a variety of payroll-oriented solutions to produce magnetic media payroll reports. You can contact Wizard Business Solutions at 800-322-4650 or visit online for complete information.

Peachtree Third-Party Add-On Solutions

www.peachtree.com

The Peachtree Web site lists software designed and developed by third-party vendors. These solutions have undergone a product review by Sage Software developers and can enhance your use of Peachtree.

PrintBoss

www.wellspringsoftware.com

PrintBoss, from Wellspring Software, enables you to securely print checks onto blank check stock. Visit the Web site for more information.

The Accounting Equation — Whom to Blame and How It Works

. . . .

In This Chapter

▶ The history of the accounting equation

▶ Understanding the accounting equation

. . . .

*W*e're going to start with a little history. After all, debits and credits didn't just magically appear. And, with the history lesson, at least you'll know whom to hate for inventing debits and credits. (We've always found that directing anger correctly is more productive than being angry in general.)

The History of the Accounting Equation

You can trace double-entry bookkeeping back to Luca Pacioli's book, *Summa de Arithmetica, Geometria, Proportioni et Proportionalita* (*Everything about Arithmetic, Geometry, and Proportion*). Pacioli was a Franciscan friar in Venice, Italy, and wrote the *Summa* in 1494. One part of his book described a method of keeping accounts so that a trader could get, without delay, information about his assets and liabilities. Pacioli's interrelating system of accounts was based on two fundamental principles that are still the foundation of accounting today:

✔ **The accounting equation (also called an *accounting model*)**

Assets = Liabilities + Owner's equity

- *Assets* are things of value, such as cash, receivables, inventory, equipment, deposits, and investments that your company owns. These things of value help you operate your business.

- *Liabilities* are the debts owed by the company, such as accounts payable, loans, taxes, and interest.

- *Owner's equity* (also called equity, capital, and paid-in capital) is the owner's interest in the company.

✔ **Debits = credits**

Understanding the Accounting Equation

To understand how the accounting equation works, we'll start a fictitious cash-based business with $1,000 of our own money, giving the company one asset of cash. To represent our investment into the business, we record the $1,000 as equity, as you can see from Line 1 in the following table of fictitious accounting transactions.

Line	Assets	=	Liabilities	+	Owner's Equity
1	$1,000	=			$1,000
2	$3,000	=	$3,000		
	$4,000	=	$3,000	+	$1,000
3	$2,000	=			$2,000
4	($1,200)	=			($1,200)
	$4,800	=	$3,000	+	$1,800

To run our business, we purchase a delivery truck by borrowing $3,000 from the bank (it's a cheap truck), which we record as Line 2 in the table. Combining this entry with the original investment, we have $4,000 of assets (the initial cash and the truck), $3,000 of liabilities (the bank loan for the truck), and $1,000 of equity. Note that the accounting equation balances. That is, assets equal liabilities plus owner's equity. The table is looking suspiciously like a Balance Sheet — and now you can understand why it's called a *Balance* Sheet.

Every business has income from sales (or it won't stay in business very long) and expenses. Pacioli realized this, too. We're sure you would agree that what you earn belongs to you. At least, you should get to keep most of it. We handle income and expenses in the accounting equation by expanding the equation to include them in owner's equity:

Equity = Original investment + Income − Expenses

In our example, the original investment was $1,000. Suppose that we made $2,000 of cash sales and pay for $1,200 of expenses. What would happen to our accounting model? Line 3 in the table shows how $2,000 of cash sales increases our assets (cash) and the income portion of owner's equity. Line 4 shows that $1,200 of cash expenses decreases our assets (cash) and the expense portion of owner's equity.

Income minus expenses is *net income* — and the business pays taxes on this amount. And, when you close the year, Peachtree posts net income after taxes to the equity section of the Balance Sheet. You can gain numerous insights about your business by studying your Balance Sheet and Income Statement. Wish we had space to show you, but . . . if we could write a book on Peachtree in Wiley's Bible series, we'd have plenty of room. So, contact Wiley and help us lobby for a Peachtree Bible.

Now consider Pacioli's second principle of accounting: Debits = Credits. Pacioli needed some mechanical device to make sure that the accounting equation was always in balance. He developed the following four rules, which we find most helpful when preparing journal entries:

✔ *Debits* increase Asset accounts and decrease Liability and Equity accounts.

✔ *Credits* do the opposite; they decrease Asset accounts and increase Liability and Equity accounts.

Expense and Income accounts behave like Equity accounts, so

✔ *Debits* increase Expense accounts and decrease Income accounts.

✔ *Credits* (surprise!) do the opposite; they decrease Expense accounts and increase Income accounts.

Return to our example to see how these work. In Line 1 of the table, we started our business by investing $1,000. We increased our assets and increased our equities. According to Rules 1 and 2, we debited assets and credited equity.

Line 2 shows how we handled the purchase of our truck. Because both an asset (purchase of truck) and a liability (borrowed money) increased, we debited assets and credited liabilities (again, Rules 1 and 2).

In our last transactions (Lines 3 and 4 of the table) we earned $2,000 of income and paid $1,200 of expenses. Note the following:

✔ The income increased our cash asset by $2,000 and also increased our income by the same amount. Therefore, Rules 1 and 4 say we should debit (increase) the cash asset and credit (increase) income.

✔ Expense transactions have the opposite effect; therefore, Rules 2 and 3 say we should credit (decrease) the cash asset and debit (increase) expenses.

These debit/credit rules are necessary to make sure we always keep the accounting model in balance.

Printed in the United States of America
ED-05-08-12